Louis XV's Navy, 1748–1762:
A Study of Organization and Administration

Louis XV's Navy presents a sharply detailed picture of an institution caught between its Colbertian legacy of organization and role and contemporary challenges arising from overseas development and imperial rivalry. James Pritchard analyses the changes that occurred in naval organization and administration in the years between the end of the War of Austrian Succession and the conclusion of the Seven Years' War. During this time the French navy was reorganized, rebuilt, and fought a major war in which it was annihilated and its officer corps militarily humiliated. Yet this period also established the conditions that made it possible for the navy to become the major arm of French foreign policy for the only time in French history.

Pritchard's chief concern is to explain why Bourbon France, the richest and most powerful state in Europe in the middle of the eighteenth century, failed to exercise its power at sea. Through a close examination of naval organization – the secretaries of state for the navy, central bureaux, shipbuilding, ordnance production and material acquisition, and finances – he shows the navy as both an institution embedded in society and an instrument of government. The tensions arising from the contradiction between an institution composed of individuals who sought to advance their own and group interests and an instrument that existed to fulfil government ends were enhanced by an administration of men rather than norms. Pritchard traces many of the shortcomings of naval administration to the intensely personal bonds and idiosyncratic behaviour of the individuals who ran it.

Many of Pritchard's conclusions run counter to the generally accepted accounts of problems in the French navy during this period and to the usual view of Choiseul as the saviour of French maritime power. This is the first complete study of this period of French naval administration, paralleling Baugh's work on the British navy.

James Pritchard is a member of the Department of History at Queen's University.

Louis XV's Navy 1748–1762

A Study of Organization and Administration

JAMES PRITCHARD

McGill-Queen's University Press
Kingston and Montreal

©McGill-Queen's University Press 1987
ISBN 0-7735-0570-9

Legal deposit second quarter 1987
Bibliothèque nationale du Québec

Printed in Canada

This book has been published with the help of a grant from
the Social Science Federation of Canada, using funds
provided by the Social Sciences and Humanities Research
Council of Canada.

Printed on acid-free paper

Canadian Cataloguing in Publication Data

Pritchard, James S., 1939–
    Louis XV's navy, 1748–1762
    Includes bibliographical references and index.
    ISBN 0-7735-0570-9
    1. France. Marine – History – 18th century.
    I. Title.
    DC52.P75 1987   359'.00944   C87-093566-6

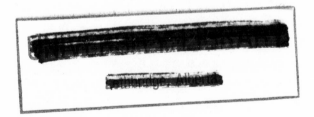

Cover illustration: Photo courtesy of the Musée
de la Marine; the original is in the Archives
nationales, Paris.

To the memory of my Father

Contents

Tables

Figures

Preface

This book developed from an interest in French colonial administration during the Old Regime. Initial research into the career of a colonial administrator quickly showed the serious limitations of the biographical approach to administrative history. Colonial administration needs to be placed in the larger context of naval administration in particular and government administration in general. Further research confirmed this initial assessment. French naval administrative history is relatively unknown, either ignored or treated monolithically by most of those historians who have bothered to treat it at all. Such general statements as exist provide plenty of room for disagreement and seldom relieve puzzlement; the chief causes of naval failure in the middle of the eighteenth century might be the disorder of the administration, deplorable conduct of operations, unpreparedness, want of money, or a combination of any two of these or other generalizations. How and why these explanatory elements affected the navy are usually left to the reader. A great deal of recent historical writing has been devoted to Bourbon government administration, but little attention has been focused on the spending departments or the middle portion of Louis xv's reign, though general agreement exists on the significance of the period as a prelude to the revolution.[1] Little is known about naval personnel, matériel, or finances or about the relations between these features of naval administration and naval operations. Yet the interrelatedness of these elements considerably affected the successes and failures of the French navy during the mid-century wars for empire.

The aim of this study is to describe and analyse the response of naval organization to the challenges it faced by focusing upon three essential elements: the navy as an institution composed of individuals in several formal and informal subgroups, the relations between individuals and groups in the navy and their links with the larger society and economy of which they were a part, and naval finances. Smaller than the army, the

French navy was nevertheless highly organized, widespread, and prolific in expenditure. Both official and unofficial developments affecting naval organization and matériel acquisition are emphasized in this study, which argues that the financial element governed all the rest.

For more than twenty years historians have been reassessing the administrative history of the Bourbon monarchy. Monographs of high quality pour from French, English, and American presses, overthrowing past interpretations, clarifying issues, and opening new directions for historical investigation. Innovative methodologies and new sources have illumined the social complexity and administrative ambiguities of government organization.[2] This work is indebted to many of these recent studies that have dissipated so much heat and shed so much light. Naval administration has not escaped revisionist treatment. Historians have permanently altered earlier historiographical traditions, placing new emphasis on the human, material, financial, and political aspects of naval history.[3] Nevertheless, new treatments generally cover a limited dimension over a broad period of time or remain confined to the seventeenth century. Few shed much light on the most crucial event in the history of the first French empire, the Seven Years' War. The present study is intended to contribute to the new historiography and a revaluation of the French role in the war.

Here I must acknowledge an intellectual debt and request an indulgence. First, to Professor Daniel A. Baugh, whose study *British Naval Administration in the Age of Walpole* (Princeton, NJ 1965) remains a model of administrative naval history. His work was a constant companion during research and writing, providing both inspiration and challenge. I hope this book complements his by giving the view from the other side. Second, I am conscious of the danger of writing an everything-you-wanted-to-know-but-were-afraid-to-ask kind of book and have guarded against excessive detail. If at times I descend to less than Olympian heights, the text reveals the importance of getting the story right.

The terminal dates were chosen with care; a longer time frame might satisfy some readers but sacrifice depth to breadth, analysis to narrative. Historiographical and personal reasons led to selection of the fourteen years between 1748 and 1762 as the period of study. In the first place, only two studies of the period utilize French sources.[4] Both presuppose the existence of a naval organization, are prejudiced against naval administrators and uncritical of the officer corps, and deal inadequately with problems of matériel and finances, frequently getting the story wrong. Few recent studies of a more general political nature exist for the period.[5] Finally, the maritime aspects of the Great War for Empire have been studied from British, American, and Canadian viewpoints, but rarely using

French sources.[6] The years from 1748 to 1762 also possess intrinsic interest and a certain coherence in French history, commencing and concluding with a cessation of hostilities between France and Great Britain. The navy was caught between past and present. While its traditions, role, and organization were inherited legacies, current challenges shaped its administrative procedures, internal difficulties, and operational objectives. New concepts of empire based upon naval and military power challenged old commercial attitudes towards colonies experiencing the impact of renewed overseas aggression and rapidly expanding maritime trade. In 1748 and 1749, the navy concluded one war and began preparing for the next; the galley corps was united to the sailing navy, the secretary of state for the navy during the past quarter of a century was dismissed; and naval finances were profoundly altered. In subsequent years the French rebuilt their navy, fought a maritime war, lost their North American empire, and experienced government bankruptcy. The navy plunged to the nadir of its fortunes. At the same time, activity within naval administration foreshadowed much that came afterward.

The period divides in two; the first seven years witnessed organizational change, naval reconstruction, and planning. Construction relates directly to strategic intentions and, like operational planning, reflects them. How the navy executed reconstruction, recruitment, and training and acquired stores, arms, and financing during those years reveals much about the crisis in naval organization and administration. During the next eight years the navy experienced the most disastrous maritime war in French history.[7] The period ended with the destruction of the navy as a fighting force, but also with the establishment of several preconditions that subsequently enabled the navy to become the major arm of French foreign policy for the first and only time in French history.[8]

Purists may not excuse an inconsistency in the text. I have retained technical terms and titles occurring in isolation in French only when translation would confuse. Scrivener is thus used for *écrivain*, treasurer and treasurers-general for *trésorier* and *trésoriers-généraux*. "Intendant of naval forces," however, means little to English readers. Moreover, terms such as *secrétaire du roi*, *commissaire de la marine*, and *premier commis* help to capture the atmosphere of the period and avoid misunderstanding bound to occur if readers were confronted with "king's secretary," "naval commissary," and "first clerk." Naval ranks also remain in French; *gardes de la marine* were not midshipmen nor did "squadron leaders" fly airplanes in the eighteenth century. The *grand maître des eaux et forêts* runs no danger, as might his equivalent in English, of being thought the chieftain of a clan of woodland fairies. On the other hand, since government documents usually lack distinction or originality of style, quotations from them appear in translation.

I have incurred many debts which I gratefully acknowledge. My deepest obligations are to Paul W. Bamford, J.F. Bosher, William J. Eccles, and T.J.A. Le Goff. Their warm interest, generosity, and encouragement together with their critical assessments and editorial comment contributed in major ways to this study. I also owe special thanks to naval archivists at different locations in France. At Paris, M. Henrat, *conservateur* of the naval archives deposited in the Archives nationales, provided much assistance and cheerfully overcame delays. M. Audouy, *conservateur en chef*, and M. Busson, *conservateur* of the historical library, both of the Service historique de la marine at the Château de Vincennes, were always helpful. At Rochefort, Toulon, and Brest, Messieurs Marc Fardet and Henri Castel, and a charming lady whose name I have lost, went beyond reasonable expectations to provide full, rapid assistance. I thank, too, Professor Marc Perrichet for sharing his knowledge of French naval administration and for many small kindnesses. Archivists and librarians at the Archives nationales and Bibliothèque nationale also deserve my thanks. Several colleagues read portions and early versions of the manuscript, offering valuable criticism that influenced its final form. Among them were Robert Malcolmson, Donald Schurman, Geoffrey Smith, and George Rawlyk.

I gratefully acknowledge the financial assistance of the Canada Council, since 1978 the Social Sciences and Humanities Research Council of Canada, which supported me with Summer Research Grants in 1977 and 1979 and a Leave Fellowship in 1981–2. Queen's University granted me a sabbatical leave, allowing me to devote myself to finishing the manuscript; the university's Advisory Research Committee, the History Department, and the School of Graduate Studies and Research also provided funds to complete the project. My profoundest hope is that this book justifies their support.

I am also indebted to Ross Hough of the Cartographic Division, Geography Department, Queen's University, who prepared the map and graph. I thank Enid Scott who typed several early draft chapters and, especially, Karen Donnelly who cheerfully transformed my hen-scratching into readable typescript and prepared a final draft remarkably free of typographical errors. Lastly, I want to acknowledge my deep personal debt to my wife, Suzanne, and our children. Their contribution was indirect, but their love and support forms an integral part of this book.

Louis XV's Navy, 1748–1762

CHAPTER ONE

Louis XV and His Naval Secretaries of State

Between 1748 and 1762 seven secretaries of state for the navy attempted to prepare for and fight a war for which the navy was not ready. The continuing devolution of power during the period, the brevity of the secretaries' tenure of office, their personal conduct, the lack of strong support from Louis xv, and the system of government made the task almost impossible. Regardless of the strength or weakness of character and political influence of individual secretaries of state the French absolute monarchy had reached a point where existing institutions and interest groups severely limited the development and execution of the central will.

The office of secretary of state for the navy was not an important one in the French government of the Old Regime. The difference between ministers and secretaries of state, the conciliar form of absolute government and the weak connections between departments and royal councils left the decision-making part of government uninformed about its own affairs and administration and wide open to outside influence. Ministers of state were members of the most senior of the royal councils, the Council of State. In theory the king decided all matters: ministers were without portfolio. Secretaries of state, on the other hand, were heads of government departments; they were automatically members of, and most active in, the Council of Dispatches. Although it met weekly, sometimes even more frequently, and its importance grew during Louis xv's reign, it dealt chiefly with domestic questions. The secretary of state for the navy, for example, reported on colonial rather than naval matters while his colleagues dealt with affairs in the metropolitan provinces.[1] For twenty-seven months after April 1749 and again from June to October 1758, the naval secretary of state was not a minister, and had no entry to the Council of State where discussion of foreign policy and war strategy occurred.[2] Secretaries of state for the navy were responsible to the king for the entire administration of the navy, yet remained chiefly liable for executing rather than formulating naval policy.

This was quite in keeping with the traditions of French absolutism. The institutions of the monarchy remained quite stable during the eighteenth century, but their roles and relative importance continued to evolve. The declining frequency of council meetings, especially concerning financial matters, and the growing importance of personal encounters between secretaries of state and the king marked the decade of the 1750s. The influence of naval secretaries of state depended to a greater degree than before on the personal relations that each man cultivated with Louis xv.

After the mid-1740s when the king's personality played a determining role in the government, the history of the secretaries of state became one of increasing Byzantine intrigue and bizarre situations. Contemporaries left a multitude of diaries, memoirs, and letters written in a pithy style, loaded with delicious tidbits that glitter like sparks from the axes being ground. Style and quotability have been the major criteria for selection by historians who, though quick to deny any validity to "great man" theories of history, seem ready to evoke a "bad man" theory or perhaps just a "bad mistress" theory.[3] Madame de Pompadour's influence is still over-emphasized and Louis xv's behaviour frequently misunderstood or absolved. Ministers and secretaries of state are often seen as knaves, fools, or worse; their actions are portrayed in the absence of any discussion of the political circumstances and social structures which limited their activities and left control of the administration in a shambles.[4] Twenty-three ministers and secretaries of state occupied the four major government departments of foreign affairs, war, navy, and finances between 1748 and 1762. Lack of continuity and confusion over priorities, rather than the personal weakness or indecision of its members, characterized the central government and its decision-making processes.

Circumstance rather than will governed relations between Louis and his naval secretaries of state, so that only the salient characteristics of the king's behaviour need be recalled.[5] Shyness which approached neurasthenia in its domination of the king's conduct was the outstanding feature of Louis xv's personality. Orphaned at the age of two, unacquainted with childhood and family intimacy throughout his life, the king had acquired in his isolated youth a horror of crowds and strange faces that made him reluctant to give up ministers who were familiar with his ways. The excessive respect he felt for his pious wife meant that the king's mistresses were challenged to provide the warm, comfortable, intimate environment that he craved. Yet the success achieved by Madame de Pompadour left the king with a profound sense of sin, tormented by religious remorse for the pain that his life caused his children whom he adored. That he soon ceased to live in sexual intimacy with Madame de Pompadour did not alter this aspect of Louis' character for he continued to have intercourse with other women. During his long reign the king never succeeded in breaking out of the isolation that his personality, upbringing, and position had created. As he died, so he had lived – alone.

Louis xv's natural indecision was long encouraged by his teacher, Cardinal Fleury, whose death left him ill-equipped to rule alone. Reliance on the old cardinal strengthened the king's shyness, weakened his self-regard and made him fearful of expressing his will or rejecting advice of which he did not approve.[6] But he was not simply the mouthpiece of his councils. When senior ministers of state advised him to declare war on England in the fall of 1754, the king ignored their advice and continued to search for peaceful resolution of the conflict.[7] Intelligent, prescient, and moderate in judgment, he was reluctant to assert himself. Desiring to do good, he was haunted by doubts about his own abilities. Modesty that would have been a virtue in his great-grandfather became a vice. Always able to see a second point of view, he often believed his own to be wrong. Timidity, propriety, and benevolence led to a paralysis of will.[8]

Yet Louis did not fear work. His well-known and often criticized self-indulgence testified to boundless physical energy rather than lethargy.[9] Claims that the king scarcely saw his senior advisers are not true. Michel Antoine has convincingly demonstrated that throughout his adult life Louis regularly presided over his main councils: the Council of State every Sunday and Wednesday, and the Council of Dispatches on Saturday. The Royal councils of finances and commerce met with decreasing frequency on alternate Tuesdays, but extraordinary sessions of the two major councils more than made up the difference in demands on the king's time. Each met for at least two hours; longer sessions were not infrequent. Each day of the week also contained set hours to receive the chancellor, keeper of the seals, four secretaries of state, controller-general of finances, and the holder of the portfolio of benefices, as well as to give impromptu audiences.[10] The king worked regularly at his metier; naval archives are filled with evidence of the hours he spent going over the smallest details of only one department.

But the king did not rule. His councils lacked cohesion; his ministers and secretaries of state acquired no sense of the collective identity that comes of working as equals below the monarch. Each was independent from the others, yet each sought allies. Members of the councils failed to use their time to the best advantage, often became caught up in details, and left important matters of state to lesser officials.[11] Each had his own relationship to the king and sought to develop it as best he could. Under Louis xv the secretaries of state reached the apogee of their administrative power, but few possessed a general view of the interest of the state. The old duc de Noailles feared that after the navy was reestablished, "there would be neither the prudence nor a wise policy to allow it to be perceived."[12]

During the increasingly agitated times after May 1749, when the controller-general of finances persuaded the king to impose permanently the *vingtième* on the revenues of the privileged classes, the already disturbed political equilibrium in France became upset. Goverment came to function by faction and intrigue. Faction may be an essential component of absolute government; as a political mechanism in some cases it is the only feasible alternative to having the ruler take sides, and it permits him to obtain several points of view. But success requires a forceful and decisive monarch to control the dynamics of such a process. Nevertheless, it would be a mistake to assume that a strong, self-willed monarch could impose his authority and coordinate the wheels of government. French finances were largely beyond the monarch's control or ability to change, yet growing in their central importance as government extended its functions. While Louis xv provided little leadership for his ministers and secretaries of state, the financial system severely limited any man's ability to correct defects in the organization of the government.

Changes in the personnel of the royal councils came about by death, ill-health, or unforeseen circumstances. Factional struggles among the king's ministers and secretaries of state became a crucial element of French absolute government. On the other hand, "the court politics by which royal ministers rose and fell were largely private, even secret, and revealed to the educated public through gossip," which, it might be added, views government not in terms of national purpose but of the relationship to one another of the key personalities in the administration.[13] In the final analysis, we often remain uncertain how once powerful men fell from grace and were replaced.

In 1743 the three secretaries of state successfully governed through a sort of commission or cabinet council with the king directing and coordinating their activities. But thereafter the defects of Louis xv's character increasingly affected the government of France. The unhealthy atmosphere of intrigue at Versailles and the vacillating character of the king soon imposed limitations. Secretaries of state began to change with a rapidity never before – or for that matter ever again – witnessed, and with devastating effect on policy-formulation, decison-making, and control of the central administration. In December 1745 Louis sacrificed the controller-general of finances to the rising star of the Pâris brothers. Thirteen months later he dismissed the minister of foreign affairs, René-Louis de Voyer, marquis d'Argenson, who had incurred the wrath of Maurice de Saxe and offended Spain by his diplomatic activity.[14] The navy's turn came in April 1749 when the king dismissed the comte de Maurepas and exiled him to Bourges. Viewed in conjunction with the two previous dismissals, the causes are to be found in the minister's failings, the growing influence of new factions at court, in particular the marriage of "la noblesse financière" to the court and robe nobilities, and the lamentable condition of naval finances.

Maurepas' dismissal caught several by surprise, but knowledgeable observers attributed it to the minister's behaviour in council.[15] On 16 March 1749 Maurepas and the war minister quarrelled in the council over a large reduction in funds allotted to the war department and a major increase in the navy's ordinary funds; the argument deeply offended the king.[16] Maurepas' falling out with his colleague and one-time friend and fears about his ability to deal effectively with the navy's debt on the eve of launching a major naval rebuilding program also cost him the support of the controller-general. Preoccupied with Pâris-Duvernay's plan to impose the *vingtième*, Machault had neither time for, nor interest in, Maurepas' difficulties. He may have agreed that Maurepas was incapable of restoring the navy.[17] A week later blame for France's worsening diplomatic position in the Baltic fell on Maurepas and on 24 April his growing isolation in the council reached its logical conclusion in Louis xv's brief note requesting his resignation. These developments, reflecting the growing influence of financiers on the government and the king's horror of quarrels, contributed more strongly to Maurepas' disgrace than his penchant for composing bawdy songs.

Louis appointed Antoine-Louis Rouillé, comte de Jouy, secretary of state for the navy. Although elderly, subject to ill-health, and reluctant to assume the burden of the portfolio, he enjoyed the support of Pâris de Montmartel.[18] His long career in government administration qualified him for the task at hand. Considered to possess limited abilities, Rouillé nevertheless worked inordinately hard to master the details of naval administration; he exerted close control over his subordinates and a tight rein on their activities that had not been seen in naval administration for years.

Rouillé relied heavily on the advice of the newly appointed naval intendants at Brest and Rochefort, Gilles Hocquart and Sébastien Lenormant de Mézy, and a junior flag officer, Roland-Michel Barrin, marquis de La Galissonière, who was named to the Anglo-French commission created to settle boundary claims in North America and placed in charge of the Hydrographic Office in Paris in order to give him freedom to advise the new secretary of state.[19] The three had been Maurepas' confidants but the most remarkable aspect of their careers was their identification with colonial rather than naval administration. A fourth adviser, Bernard-René Pallu, who played an important but shadowy role, had singular qualifications; in addition to being a royal provincial intendant, he was Rouillé's brother-in-law of seventeen years' standing, and lived in the same household with the secretary of state.[20] Relying on the advice of these four men, Rouillé appeared to circumvent or at least develop alternative support to the growing influence of the department's central bureaux.

Rouillé's contribution to the navy is often explained merely as the continuation of his predecessor's plans, but Maurepas' policies had proved unrealistic, certainly uncoordinated, and had forced the new secretary of state to reconsider and modify them.[21] Moreover, the devolution of administrative control in the department had progressed to such an extent that decision-making had become confused and reactive. Low morale, insubordination, and independent behaviour were apparent at every level of the *corps d'épée* and the *corps de plume*. Rouillé's refusal to delegate authority and close supervision of details made it easier to reimpose the secretary of state's control over the general administration of the department. His tenure of office was a valuable period when administrative control was largely reestablished and the navy rebuilt. Failure to achieve complete success indicated the pervasiveness and seriousness of the problem as much as evidence of Rouillé's lack of a strong will.

Rouillé's replacement by Jean-Baptiste de Machault illustrates the limited power of the royal will to alter the composition of the Council of State where there had been no changes since August 1751. Three years later Louis xv's indecision had allowed strong factions to appear. On 24 July 1754 the marquis de Saint-Contest died unexpectedly at Versailles. His death created no crisis, merely the need to find a replacement, but it triggered several changes in the Council of State. Rouillé's move to Foreign Affairs quickly became common knowledge but not the name of his successor at the Navy. The court gave some credence to rumours that Lenormant de Mézy and Pallu were being considered; Etienne de Silouette's name was also bruited, but on 30 July Louis appointed Machault.[22]

Considerable conjecture surrounds this "cabinet shuffle" and its signifi-cance for the navy, but the king's own explanation reveals nothing beyond his desire to offend no one or introduce any disturbance into his council. Louis appointed Rouillé to Foreign Affairs on the ground that this minister "is fully informed on matters and of our way of thinking; thus," he added, "he will bring fewer alterations than any other who might think differently." Machault's appointment to the navy was made at his own request: "The Keeper of the Seals who for a long time has wanted to leave finances, has asked me to transfer him to the navy."[23] The king's personal desire for peace and quiet in council and accommodation of his hard-working servant appeared paramount. Président Hénault's later view that "The ministers were changing then like the decorations at the opera," well captures the effect of changes make to suit personal interests and the lack of continuity in administration.[24]

Historians generally agree on the ability of the new secretary of state for the navy.[25] Machault freed himself from the torrent of paper that poured daily into the bureaux of his immense department. No papers but a small notebook were seen on his writing-desk. Renewed each month, it contained only three reports, on the navy's funds, total stores, and the situation of the fleet.[26] An energetic man of broad views, cold, taciturn, and rigid, he had a reputation for honesty and for being Louis xv's favourite minister.[27] He was more aware than anyone else of the kingdom's financial difficulties and the danger of war. As leader of a faction, possessing a personality forceful enough to push pronounced views in the council, he might have benefited the navy, but his behaviour after his appointment and the state of domestic politics suggest that Machault did not carry his one-time reforming zeal into naval affairs.

Machault vigorously supported New France after hostilities broke out in North America but maintained an ambiguous attitude towards colonies. Though not an outright anticolonialist like many aristocrats and intellectuals, he nonetheless considered Dupleix's imperialist adventuring in India as foolishness of the most dangerous order and favoured his recall. Deeply aware of France's seriously overextended resources in the defence of the colonial empire, he refused to acquire additional obligations. But he had no doubts about defending existing French possessions. In the West Indies, he instructed Maximin de Bompar to seize Saint Lucia on the first news of a rupture with Great Britain, and in North America, ordered Governor-general Rigaud de Vaudreuil-Cavagnal to respond militarily to any English "incursions ... on the unsettled lands of Canada."[28] But if Machault understood the weakness of the French colonies and remained willing to defend them, his consideration of France's position in Europe worked against the defence of empire. Ten years in domestic politics had not prepared him for foreign affairs in which Louis xv was playing a personal, secret role. Machault was also the only anti-Prussian member of the council, and later strongly supported the Franco-Austrian alliance that made it impossible to find sufficient resources to mount a successful maritime and colonial defence during the Seven Years' War. In the spring of 1755 a lucid statement of French war aims predicted Britain's declared intention to destroy the French empire, but proposed to compensate for France's naval weakness by securing military successes in Europe, seizing the Netherlands, and preparing for a descent on England.[29]

Machault's attitude never changed. Following the loss of two warships in the summer of 1755, he and the other ministers appeared confused. Continentalists suddenly advocated a sea war, while Machault was strangely reluctant to seize the moment.[30] In September, a month after the British cabinet had unleashed the navy against French maritime commerce, Machault thought British warships limited to inspecting merchantmen.[31] During 1756 his position in the council steadily declined before the continentalists who reasserted their original views.[32]

The war led to demands for new taxes, disturbing the already delicate relations between the government and the Paris parlement; Machault, still keeper of the seals, became more deeply enmeshed in domestic politics.[33] Frederick the Great's invasion of Saxony on 29 August occasioned a major debate in the council over the priorities to be established between continental and maritime strategies.[34] Comte d'Argenson's successful arguments in favour of the continent greatly strengthened his position at court among the nobility. By the end of the year Machault also became part of the problem of the parlement. Following his disastrous policy in December, when he attempted to coerce the magistrates, he became a liability to be sacrificed by the peace-loving king.[35]

The navy had been on a war-footing during most of the two and a half years that Machault served as minister and secretary of state; a major expedition had been readied for Canada in the winter of 1754–5, and another during the next winter for Minorca. Minimal naval support went out to the colonies in 1756, but with increased funds a large, complicated plan to support the West Indies and North America was being implemented at the time of Machault's disgrace. Although he was clearly energetic and resourceful, Machault's inability to divorce himself from domestic politics and the factional intrigues that brought him to power proved his greatest failing. His removal seriously hampered the effectiveness of a badly divided naval service in coping with the quickened pace of sea-borne operations and the accompanying financial obligations. Its difficulties were compounded by the limp character of his successor.

Just why Louis appointed 38-year-old François-Marie Peyrenc de Moras to the naval portfolio is unclear. His position as controller-general during the past ten months may have influenced the appointment but he entered the Council of State only two days before receiving his new office. On the one hand, the new appointment may have reflected an effort to meet the department's extraordinary expenses which the treasurers-general had left unpaid for the previous two years.[36] On the other hand, the king may have simply desired a familiar face in the council after the recent attempt to kill him. The attack had destroyed what little initiative the king possessed and the government fell on evil days.

When Controller-general Moras became secretary of state for the navy, the same man held these two offices for the first time since Pontchartrain the elder, in the 1690s.[37] But Moras was not the equal of Louis xiv's minister in administrative talent, forcefulness of personality, or political wisdom. Moras immediately turned to Rouillé's brother-in-law, Bernard Pallu, whom he appointed intendant of the classes and entrusted with the daily administration of the fisheries, coast guard, and maritime fortifications as well as naval conscription.[38] Moras also relied on the marquis de Massiac, *lieutenant-général des armées navales*, for advice concerning the appointment of naval commanders.[39] After six months the double offices became too great a burden and on 25 August Moras relinquished finances to Jean de Boullongne in order to deal full-time with the navy.

Moras' failure to promote officers of the sword exacerbated the spirit of insubordination in both officer corps.[40] A second, increasingly serious problem arose from the capture of Minorca: what to do with the Mediterranean fleet in the face of devastated colonial commerce in the Caribbean. Any answer involved the question of neutral passports, which his predecessor had failed to solve; Moras' solution improved the situation, but left him open to charges of favouritism and corruption.[41] Moras' greatest difficulties, however, were financial.

As controller-general he authorized expenditures far beyond the ability of the treasurers-general of the navy to pay.[42] The arsenals equipped the large fleet dispatched to North America, but by the year's end no plans could be made for 1758.[43] Although the navy was in the best material condition since the previous century, it was so far in arrears in payments of all sorts that it could no longer continue normal operations. Short-term financial demands dominated the concerns of the department. Strict separation of military and administrative duties and responsibilities in naval organization reinforced this development. While naval officers had not the slightest idea of the problem's dimensions, naval administrators could conceive of nothing more serious. By the end of 1757 the controller-general of finances rather than the naval secretary of state formulated naval policy.

Though not a bad administrator, Moras lacked the strength of character, experience and breadth of view required to deal with the multiple problems that daily grew more burdensome. His tenure was marked by failure to achieve positive results at sea, and the reverses of 1758 and 1759 were retroactively attributed to his administration. Preoccupied with the navy's debt during the early months of 1758, Moras successfully entreated Louis to relieve him of his burden, and gratefully retired at the end of May, leaving the unrequited navy to struggle on under a new secretary of state.[44]

Recruitment of secretaries of state evolved rapidly during the 1750s. The court nobility and clergy had furnished ministers of state since the Regency, and the ministerial route to power and influence was never again closed to courtiers. The long struggle with the parlement and Damien's attempt on the king's life encouraged this development. For the first time in more than a century a courtier was named to the Royal Council on 2 January 1757, when Abbé de Bernis entered the Council of State. His appointment as secretary of state for foreign affairs on 28 June marked a significant change in the evolution of French absolutism.[45] Nine months later the duc de Belle-Isle's appointment as minister and secretary of state for war confirmed the new reality. All of the precedents had been recently established when, on 31 May 1758, Claude-Louis d'Espinal, marquis de Massiac, became the first naval officer to serve as secretary of state for the navy.

A relatively rare type of naval officer, the son of a military engineer and

protégé of two *premiers commis* in the naval department, Massiac was a
courtier.[46] He obtained flag rank (*chef d'escadre*) in 1751, and a year later
was appointed commandant of Toulon. After being called to the court in
1754, he returned to Toulon in the spring of 1756 to preside over
preparations for the Minorca expedition; promotion to *lieutenant-général*
followed in October.[47] Massiac remained at Toulon, corresponding closely
with Moras, until in November 1757 he returned to the court where he
advised the minister on naval appointments.[48]

His appointment was scarcely surprising in view of his long sojourns at
court and his connections, but the lack of more qualified naval officers was
painfully apparent. Age excluded one *vice-amiral* and pride the other.
Recently made marshal of France and destined to command the Atlantic
fleet, Hubert de Brienne, comte de Conflans, thought the charge of
secretary of state beneath his dignity.[49] Three senior *lieutenants-généraux*
were also unavailable; comte de Maulevrier-Langeron, the eldest, was a
relic of the galley corps. Comte Dubois de la Motte had been pensioned off
with the honours and appointments of a *vice-amiral* at the time of
Conflans' elevation to marshal; and the comte de Vaudreuil was politically
impossible.[50] Three *lieutenants-généraux* junior to Massiac had no greater
ability and lacked his fortune and influence.[51]

The appointment of an *homme de métier* was a victory for the officer
corps in one sense; it climaxed three months of effort, commencing with
the elevation of Conflans, to appease naval officers whose spirit of
insubordination had almost reached the stage of open revolt. It also
reflected the continuing recruitment of the sword nobility into government. With the exception of Massiac's successor, the robe nobility never
again possessed the departments of navy, war or foreign affairs during the
sixteen years remaining in Louis xv's reign.[52]

Recent events also established precedents for Sébastien Lenormant de
Mézy's appointment as deputy minister. The new secretaries of state
neither knew nor desired to know how their departments functioned. Louis
appointed an assistant to Bernis at Foreign Affairs and a lieutenant-general
to administer the daily business of the war department in order to overcome
Belle-Isle's scruples. The admission of two *maîtres de requêtes* into the
Council of Dispatches in October 1757 to aid in its daily work showed that
the Royal Council itself required professional administrators.[53] As with the
two previous appointments, Massiac was given a professional assistant to
manage the torrent of paper that poured across his desk.

Premiers commis of the department's central bureaux were not taken
into account for they belonged to a secretary of state's personal entourage,
not the naval corps of administrative officers. Bernard Pallu had died two
months before Moras' resignation, and rather than name a successor Louis
approved the combining of the two senior posts in the administration and

appointed Lenormant de Mézy *intendant-général de la marine et des colonies.*[54] *Intendant des armées navales* since the beginning of 1755, Lenormant had worked as a trouble-shooter for Machault and Moras; Massiac himself requested that Lenormant be empowered "to authorize and sign all orders and dispatches," acknowledging that such authority was unparalleled in the navy's history.[55] Lenormant de Mézy held the entire management of the department in his hands.

The animosity of the new intendant-general's enemies, his own prejudices, and the imminent financial collapse of the government overshadowed his abilities. Although he possessed "a staunch, acknowledged probity," his enemies saw only "an ill-natured clerk, short-sighted and full of arrogance."[56] Jealous of Lenormant's rise to prominence, *premiers commis* refused to work under his direction and did their best to embarrass him.[57] Contemporaries also blamed the personalities and shared prejudices of the new secretary and his deputy rather than organizational flaws or administrative weaknesses; Massiac, they said, was too ignorant of the court and Lenormant too plain-spoken and headstrong.[58] But neither man's position was strong enough to withstand the effect of the shocks to French public opinion during the summer of 1758, and the sudden singling out of the navy for investigation and reform by members of the Council of State spelled the end of their careers.

The fall of Louisbourg on 26 June, British descents on the Channel coast – St Malo on 5 June, Cherbourg on 7 August, and St Cast on 11 September – the capture of Senegal, and even the attack on Aix Roads in the previous April were all laid at the door of the new secretary of state and his deputy.[59] Additional circumstances further isolated the navy from the rest of the government. Two former ministers, Rouillé and Moras, retired from the Council of State in June, and men with no interest in the maritime war filled the vacancies.[60] Massaic never entered the council; the navy's interests ceased to be debated before the king in council. The utter financial dilapidation of the state appeared imminent. Abbé de Bernis sought to reorganize the government by investigating its financial administration; he became the moving force behind a committee of ministers formed to inquire into the spending departments of government. At its first meeting, committee members reduced the Royal Household accounts by 6 million livres, but so great was the uproar that the committee turned elsewhere.[61] Without a naval minister present, Marshal de Belle-Isle was unopposed in his insistence that the navy be examined before the War Department.[62] By September the navy had been singled out as a sink of iniquity in need of immediate cleansing.[63] On 18 October the king appointed a royal commission to examine and validate the debts which further undermined public credit and confidence in the navy.[64] Unsupported in the king's councils, facing public opprobrium and growing hostility from naval suppliers, Massiac and his deputy were dismissed at the end of the month and the former was succeeded by Nicolas-René Berryer. The suggestion that a distinguished sailor, the Chevalier de Mirabeau, might have replaced Massiac reflects only the desire of naval officers of a later age that an able member of the corps might have headed the department.[65]

The choice of Berryer, who received the naval portfolio on 1 November, was in keeping with Louis xv's preference for familiar faces in the Royal Council. Berryer was also more familiar with the daily workings and problems of the councils than any other outsider, having worked in the Council of Dispatches since October 1757 and recently entered the Royal Council of Finances and the Council of State.[66] His selection as secretary of state for the navy reflected an eighteenth-century propensity to account for failings in government administration in terms of personal corruption and malfeasance; ten years as *lieutenant-général* of the police of Paris had qualified him for the task of getting a grip on the department's debt. He has been unfairly judged the worst naval minister of the Old Regime.[67] While disaster after disaster befell the navy and the empire, he single-mindedly pursued his policy of cleansing the Augean stables that he perceived in the department. He gave little attention to the strategic direction of the war at sea or even to the needs of the fleet. But he was not in a position to do so. The Council of State had approved the 1759 plan of naval operations before he assumed his charge.[68] Bompar's failure to relieve Guadeloupe in March 1759, Admiral Laclue's defeat off Lagos the following August, and Conflans' failure in Quiberon Bay in November left Berryer without a fleet and raised doubts about the ability of the navy's officers. The arrival of news that the comte d'Aché had retreated from Pondicherry to Ile de France confirmed these suspicions. For two years Berryer was a naval minister without a fleet.

Moreover, naval debts did not go away. Indeed, in October 1759 the government faced financial collapse. The terrible load of debt inherited from his two predecessors forced Berryer to suspend payment of colonial bills and pare naval expenses to the bone. Without an effective navy or financial means to reestablish one Berryer turned his policeman's talents on the department. Ruthlessly cutting and pruning personnel and material, punishing malversation and incompetence wherever he found it, Berryer checked the department's drift and established the watchwords for the navy's future direction: reform, rebuild, and revenge. In so doing, however, he created tremendous resentment in the service.[69] But unlike his three predecessors who were dismissed, Berryer retired owing to poor health – he had less than a year to live – and when Louis appointed him keeper of the seals, he publicly acknowledged his regard for his old minister.

Etienne-François de Choiseul, comte de Stainville (recently become duc de Choiseul), replaced Berryer. He had succeeded Bernis at Foreign Affairs when Berryer replaced Massiac at the Navy. Both men enjoyed the support of Madame de Pompadour but Choiseul came to dominate her and quickly rose to preeminence in the Royal Council, which had been drifting without the king's attention since the assassination attempt. With the signing of the Third Versailles Treaty in March 1759 Choiseul assumed strategic direction of the war. Berryer became his willing assistant; in July Choiseul rather than Berryer presented a plan for an armed descent on England, and in November 1760 Berryer drew up a plan for worldwide naval operations for the coming year, but Choiseul presented it to the council.[70] Choiseul succeeded Belle-Isle as secretary of state for war in February 1761 and in mid-October accepted the naval portfolio. Louis passed titular control of Foreign Affairs to the future duc de Praslin, and for the last year of hostilities Choiseul headed the three government departments concerned with peace and war.

Soldier, diplomat, and peer of France, Choiseul was the antithesis of the secretary of state envisioned by Louis xiv. When he arrived at Foreign Affairs late in 1758, he knew nothing of administration and organization, but displayed a grasp of political reality long missing from the council. Moreover, Louis xv grew to like him for the rapidity with which he worked and the clarity of his mind.[71] Although a partisan of the Franco-Austrian alliance, Choiseul saw the folly of lavishing French treasure on a union from which France had so little to gain and much to lose. By the Third Treaty of Versailles he negotiated a reduction in French subsidies to Vienna, confined military operations to western Germany, stimulated northern diplomacy in an effort to upset the British, and, in a desperate attempt to redress British preponderance at sea, turned towards the Spaniards to bring their navy into the war on the French side.[72] Despite his policy of disengagement, Choiseul remained a continentalist, accepting the dictum that colonial losses could be recouped by victories in Europe. Faced with failure to bring Spain into the war, he staked everything on a victorious descent on England itself.[73] With the plans of 1759 awash in the waters off Lagos and in Quiberon Bay, Choiseul spent the next two years negotiating the *pacte de famille* which was signed on 15 August 1761.[74] In October he instructed the Comte de Blénac to relieve the Antilles and take part in a combined Franco-Spanish attack on Jamaica; less than two months later a Spanish declaration of war against England rewarded his efforts.

For a brief nine months Choiseul entertained hopes that continued hostilities at sea would bear fruit.[75] The new minister acted: first, to restore the navy's credit with suppliers and provisioners, and second, to mount a major expedition to defend the remaining French islands in the West Indies. The first attempt achieved partial success but Blénac's failure to relieve Martinique in February 1762 had a crushing effect. Choiseul turned to pin-prick raids, all that the navy remained capable of mounting. The Spaniards proved a liability rather than an asset and Choiseul was driven to the peace table in November 1762, when a cessation of hostilities was signed at Paris.

Lack of time and the seriousness of the problems permitted Choiseul only to recognize the need to reorganize the naval service. Major changes awaited the future, but Berryer and Choiseul established the route to be taken. An aroused public offered funds to rebuild the devastated fleet, and under Choiseul's guidance the navy gained more prestige than ever before. During the next twenty years it became the major instrument of French foreign policy. In order for this to happen, however, the navy had first to descend to the nadir of its fortunes.

Louis xv governed through his councils but his role was more nominal than executive. Lacking influence in the Council of State, the navy frequently became a power unto itself. The view once expressed by the marquis d'Argenson that secretaries of state for war and the navy need not be ministers reflected a widely held attitude that questions of logistics and administration had no bearing on policy and men concerned with such matters lacked sufficient breadth of view to consider major questions of grand strategy.[76] The separation of the naval department from the policy-making Council of State is a significant feature of French naval history. Naval policy was linked to the growth of French maritime and colonial commerce but during the second quarter of the eighteenth century they appeared to develop independently of each other. On the one hand, the navy was neglected, and on the other, colonial maritime commerce grew as never before; both developed without relation to foreign policy. No evidence suggests that growth of colonial commerce materially altered French strategic concerns on the continent. Neither overseas trade nor colonial possessions were the backbone of French national strength, which lay in the indigenous resources of land and population. The separate development of naval and foreign policy accounts largely for French failure to develop a comprehensive naval strategy and justified D'Argenson's commonly held view. Whether a comprehensive naval strategy can precede awareness of a relation between naval and foreign policy, especially in a government committed to dynastic politics and dominated by the army, is doubtful, but the failure to develop a naval strategy is clear. The naval department's tenuous connections with the Royal Council, based on personal relations between men, some of whom had never seen a warship let alone known what one could accomplish, appeared designed to prevent a strategy from ever emerging in the policy-making bodies of the crown.

During the fourteen years between the cessation of hostilities in the War of the Austrian Succession and the cease-fire that concluded the Seven Years' War, the secretaries of state for the navy, with one or two exceptions, were undistinguished. Lacour-Gayet correctly characterized the period as one of "fleeting ministries"; more men held office during these years than had presided over naval administration for the previous eighty.[77] Periods of tenure were often so brief as to leave some in ignorance of what the department was doing or hoped to do. Yet, if none were strong men, most were conscientious; Tramond is unduly harsh in describing their sole inspiration as "the desire to maintain themselves in power, while flattering national conceit."[78] Like most men in high office, Louis xv's secretaries of state for the navy made many enemies whose partisan calumnies and insinuations have received considerable credence. As was the case with most of their contemporaries with an eye to the main chance, altruism was not a strong point in their character, but they did try to carry out their tasks. Nevertheless, they confronted an environment they had not created. Necessity also drove them to take positions and make decisions without time for reflection. Matters of urgency competed with long-range considerations, often gaining attention at the latter's expense. While the political ability and personal conduct of the secretaries of state were not above reproach, few perceived the machine-like qualities of naval institutions. Few saw the navy as a complex, multifaceted organization possessing a hierarchy of competing interests in which internal tensions and external circumstances limited the development of strategic thinking and operational planning. Naval organization and administration existed in a social, economic, and political environment containing other institutions whose dynamic relations constantly worked to limit or obstruct the emergence of, among other things, professional competence. Condemning personal behaviour, critics fail to consider that political and financial conjunctures, social and organizational structures, and administrative processes imposed limitations on individuals.

Although in theory France was governed by the royal councils, the principle that decisions were made by the king-in-council was largely fictitious. There were no positions in this constitutional structure for *de facto* roles played by courtiers, the king's mistress, or court bankers. Abbé de Bernis made foreign policy when Rouillé had long been secretary of state for foreign affairs. The duc de Belle-Isle had far greater influence on military policy than the secretary of state, the marquis de Paulmy. Choiseul largely superseded Berryer long before he assumed control of the department, and of course, Rouillé had not always been, and Massiac never was, a member of the Council of State. While secretaries of state also ignored the councils, they were sometimes ignored by their own departments. A classic government dilemma had arisen in France. Naval secretaries of state relied to a large degree on the work of their central bureaux. They depended on those whose work they oversaw for much of the information necessary to regulate the activities of the department.

Hence they usually ratified policy "suggestions" sent by those being supervised. To what degree secretaries of state influenced the formulation of naval policy depended not only on their personal relations with Louis xv but on equally important connections with their officials in the central secretariat. The influence of the bureaux often outweighed that of the councils and sometimes of the secretaries of state. For it was there that questions were thoroughly investigated and dealt with before the secretary of state placed them privately or in council before the king. There, too, reports from naval intendants and *commissaires-ordonnateurs* to the secretary of state were received, read, and appreciated and outgoing replies drafted. Obviously a crucial factor in executing royal commands was the secretary of state's degree of control over his bureaux. His knowledge of their procedures, the degree of attention he gave to the incoming correspondence, whether he read it at all or only the summaries provided by clerks in the bureaux, and whether he supervised and read the replies are significant questions in any consideration of the devolution of power in the navy. In order to discover part of the answer we must leave the secretaries of state and their court intrigues and descend to another level of naval organization to explore the world of the central secretariat.

CHAPTER TWO

The Central Bureaux

Past legacies and changing challenges rather than a rational search for efficient procedures shaped the navy's central administration. A naval department did not exist for more than a century after the first secretaries of state were named in 1547.[1] Under Louis XIII, Cardinal Richelieu gathered naval administration to himself, but secretaries of state for foreign affairs and war continued to deal with financial questions affecting the Atlantic and Mediterranean fleets.[2] Unification of naval administration began only under Jean-Baptiste Colbert, who established the department in 1669. At that time the organizational pendulum swung from dispersion to concentration, a reflection of Colbert's personal influence and authority rather than any new rationalist ideal in government. The new department was charged with supervising commerce, consulates, and colonies, as well as maintaining relations with the galley corps and the Admiralty in addition to the navy proper. The secretary of state personally supervised the central administration, running the department with the assistance of three clerks, only one of whom is known by name.[3] In 1673 Colbert deputized his son, the marquis de Seignelay, to supervise the naval secretariat; a decade later, when he succeeded his father as secretary of state, about ten clerks comprised the central naval administration.[4] Provision for examining naval accounts appeared in 1687, and a bureau of commerce was added shortly before Seignelay's death.[5] Seignelay also created an archives which obtained permanent location in 1699.[6] In brief, Seignelay strove to consolidate the institutional and legislative components of the framework erected by his father. The Naval Ordinance of 1689 which brought both together was his greatest monument.[7] Significantly, however, it contains nothing about the central administration. Government at the centre remained intensely personal; scriveners and clerks continued to be part of the secretary of state's personal retinue, carrying out their tasks under his close supervision.

Expansion of naval administration really began with the advent of the Phélypeaux, father and son, in 1691. Departmental organization, divided between traditional geographical jurisdictions of Ponant and Levant, contained curious admixtures of responsibilities. The Ponant bureau dealt with Canada and the Senegal and Guinea companies while the Bureau of the Levant supervised the West Indian Islands, North African relations, and consular offices in the eastern Mediterranean.[8] This functional confusion probably owed its origin to Colbert's and the elder Pontchartrain's simultaneous possession of the charges of secretary of state for the navy and controller-general of finances. Separation of the two offices after 1699 and the death and retirement of the first clerks taken into naval administration led to partial abandonment of the territorial in favour of the functional principle. Bureaux for disabled seamen and consulates appeared in 1709, but the creation in the same year of a separate office for Le Havre and Dunkirk – the naval Channel ports – removing them from the bureau of the Ponant, was a sign that the geographical principle remained alive. This arrangement lasted for only a few years, and bureaux of colonies and naval conscription appeared in 1711.[9]

On the face of the evidence one might agree that events between 1698 and 1715 were crucial to the development of French bureaucratic government and profoundly affected naval administration.[10] But they were not. Functional division of responsibilities, one of several criteria used to identify a bureaucratic form of government, was more apparent than real. Seignelay had been ably assisted in the ports by an *intendant-général des armées navales*, and in 1692 his successor established the position of *intendant des classes* to supervise naval conscription. The strong personal influence of these two officials over the central administration, however, led to ambiguity in relations between senior officials in the field and those at the central secretariat. The common image of a large and unwieldy royal bureaucracy almost entirely composed of men who bought their offices and acquired the right to bequeath them to their heirs does not accurately portray naval administration. While central naval administration appeared to expand and reorganize in accordance with modern bureaucratic notions of functionalism, the navy itself was ruined, experiencing the greatest moral and material crisis in its history.[11] Early examples of modern organization left no imprint. Moreover, they had been largely cosmetic. Pontchartrain created the colonial bureau in order to find an honorable position close to the court for his cousin, Antoine-Denis Raudot, whose subsequent appointment as intendant of the classes joined colonies to naval conscription, destroying any apparent functional organization and transforming the post into a sinecure which Raudot held until his death more than twenty years later.[12]

Under the Regency, the navy was left largely to its own devices. The bureau of funds regained its former responsibility for disabled seamen. A hydrographic office split off from the archives in 1720, but chiefly to accommodate a naval courtier, Charles-Hercule d'Albert de Luynes; the bureau waited thirty years for a sufficiently interested head to provide it with any activities.[13] The succession in 1723 of Jean-Frédéric Phélypeaux, comte de Maurepas, to his father's old charge of secretary of state for the navy brought no new development. Maurepas relied on experienced *premiers commis* or bureau chiefs to guide his actions.[14] The previous century's administrative legacy of government by men rather than norms continued to influence the evolution of the navy's central bureaux. The number of *premiers commis* expanded from three in 1715 to five in 1729. The geographical designations of the two major bureaux disappeared following their merger in 1738 in a single office of port administration. The same year a single office also united the bureaux of commerce and consulates.[15] Despite unification of bureaux, however, by 1743 the number of *premiers commis* had grown to six.[16] Expansion continued under Rouillé and his successors. By 1753 the central bureaux employed eight *premiers commis*, a director of the hydrographic bureau plus the minister's personal secretary, together with sixty-five clerks and scriveners.[17] Numbers declined during the Seven Years' War but increased afterwards until by 1775 the central administration comprised twelve bureaux, ten *premiers commis* and 105 writers and clerks.[18]

Except for the archives and the hydrographic office the navy's central bureaux possessed no permanent address. In 1748 the four policy bureaux – police, colonies, classes, and commerce – and the secretary of state's own cabinet were located at Versailles where clerks and scriveners occupied two houses in the rue des Bons-Enfants.[19] *Premiers commis* and one or two subordinates from each bureau followed the annual movements of the court, from Versailles to Compiègne in summer, to Fontainebleau in autumn.[20] Travel constantly disrupted work, and most personnel remained at Versailles away from their chiefs' supervision. Working in unsatisfactory conditions, clerks simply tried to preserve their papers amid the confusion of a temporary resting-place.[21] A pavilion located in the garden of the Augustinians (*Les Petits Pères*), near the Place des Victoires, jointly housed the archives and the hydrographic office – *bureau des papiers de la marine* and *dépôt des cartes, plans et journaux* – but impermanence and isolation characterized the third Paris office, the *bureau de l'examen des comptes* or accounts office. The special nature of the bureau's duties and responsibilities may have forced its staff to keep close to the places of business of the treasurers-general of the navy. Choiseul brought the policy bureaux together temporarily in 1763, housing them on the second and third floors of the newly built foreign affairs department archives at Versailles, but absolutist government remained remarkably makeshift.[22]

The number of personnel in the central bureaux remained astonishingly small. In 1750, for example, the bureaux employed fifty-one clerks and scriveners in addition to *premiers commis*. Three and nine years later, sixty-five and eighty-eight clerks, respectively, worked in the central administration.[23] The staff grew chiefly under Rouillé. The slight increase in numbers under Machault and of stability under Moras and Massiac hides the growth in personnel from outside the corps of the pen, men paid secretly or out of non-naval funds. But after 1759 the total number of personnel in the administration declined. Only sixty clerks remained on strength during the second half of 1761 and further reductions occurred in the following year.[24] Between 1748 and 1762, when the navy underwent rapid expansion, experienced great demands on its material and human resources, and fought and lost a long war, fewer than one hundred men maintained the department's central administration. Although large size is not synonymous with bureaucratic organization, such small size generally precludes it. Small numbers and lack of permanent location for its offices characterized French naval administration, and, as we shall see, they may also reflect two fundamental weaknesses.

Eight bureaux constituted the central secretariat in 1748. The first was the *bureau de police des ports*, entrusted with enormous responsibilities: shipbuilding, commissioning and laying up warships, naval ordnance and provisioning the arsenals. Coastal fortifications had been added in 1744, but under Rouillé became attached to the bureau of the classes where they remained until removed to the War Office in 1759.[25] Joseph Pellerin, the younger, who headed the bureau, owed his influence chiefly to the awesome talents of his father and predecessor. The elder Pellerin's experience and breadth of view was such that he, rather than the *intendant des armées navales* or senior admirals, as in Louis xiv's reign, had advised the secretary of state on the fleet's readiness and on the potential disposition of squadrons. Pellerin the elder continued to advise the department until his death in 1783, but he retired in 1745 after ensuring his son's succession to his place.

The personal nature of bonds within the administration, however, ensured that Joseph, the younger, did not automatically succeed to his father's prestige and influence. Maurepas' disgrace rudely shattered whatever expectations he might have had, for Rouillé relied on outsiders for advice and executive assistance. Pellerin's role appeared confined to his own bureau until after Machault followed Rouillé in office. Upon Moras' accession, however, Pellerin's influence once again declined until Berryer came to power late in 1758. During the interval Sébastien Lenormant de Mézy rose rapidly to the top of the administration. Significantly, Pellerin welcomed Berryer's appointment, writing to the intendant of Toulon that "it is certain that things have changed, and we ought to hope with certitude that the navy finally is going to take on a greater firmness than it has ever had; at least in what concerns the good order of its administration."[26] Lenormant de Mézy's former position as *intendant des armées navales* remained vacant for a year and a half, but in April 1760 Pellerin finally obtained the appointment, an event which carried symbolic as well as political significance and marked the return of the old guard to control the central administration.

In 1750 Pellerin's bureau employed eight clerks and an *élève*.[27] The number increased by one, three years later, but the bureau lost several responsibilities and supervisory clerks after Machault's accession to office. Details concerning troops, convicts, passports, prizes, and prisoners of war were handled by a separate bureau under nominal supervision of the minister's son, who also obtained the income from the charge of intendant of the classes.[28] Kept separate for a brief period after Machault's disgrace, these matters were absorbed into a new bureau of naval personnel in 1758. As a consequence, Pellerin's bureau employed fewer staff during the early years of the Seven Years' War than at the beginning of the decade.[29] The naval disasters of 1759 greatly lessened the importance of the *bureau de police*, but its personnel nearly doubled to fifteen a year later, reflecting Pellerin's increased influence under Berryer. In the middle of 1761 Laurent Truguet, who had once served Pellerin as *second commis*, succeeded to the bureau's direction.

Truguet's position as *premier commis* of the naval archives since 1754 illustrates, as perhaps no other comparable career does, the crucial importance of the personalities of the secretaries of state, their needs and the bonds they forged with bureau chiefs. The archives held all of the royal edicts, ordinances, decrees, authorizations and regulations concerning the service, and was therefore a valuable repository for new secretaries of state seeking a grasp of naval policy. Rouillé, for example, ordered an archives clerk to work in his own office to compile an eleven-volume collection of ordinances issued since 1689.[30] François-Maurice Laffilard, director of the archives since 1740, employed a staff of six or seven clerks preparing reports on all manner of naval subjects for the minister, most notably on personnel. In 1752 Rouillé also set the former intendant of the galley corps to work in a separate office to prepare a history of French naval policy since Colbert.[31] Truguet's appointment, following Laffilard's death in July 1754, indicates how important the bureau had become. Its importance increased under Rouillé's successors, but after Berryer cancelled the history project in 1759 and gave renewed weight to Pellerin's bureau, Truguet prepared to leave. He regained his influence, however, after the war concluded, becoming Choiseul's closest adviser on reform and restoration.[32] Under his successor the archives once more faded into relative obscurity.

The bureau of funds had been the second most important office in the administration as recently as 1747, when the influential *premier commis* of twenty years, Louis Gourdan, departed for honorary retirement as *intendant des armées navales*. Major changes in the bureau's organization during the next three years left it with a more rational definition of responsibilities, yet less influence. Before the War of the Austrian Succession, the *premier commis* concerned himself chiefly with financial matters relating to officers' stipends and pensions, which absorbed the bulk of the navy's ordinary funds; hence his great influence.[33] In 1747, however, Maurepas removed all matters concerning officers of the sword to the care of his own secretary, leaving the new *premier commis*, Michel Bégon, to deal more directly with current financial questions.[34] By 1753 the bureau contained the same number of staff as Pellerin's. Bégon left the bureau in November 1756 to assume the post of intendant of Dunkirk and thereafter the office declined in importance; financial chaos simply made it irrelevant. In an effort to check independent activity in naval accounting, coordinate all activities concerning the government's financial difficulties and restore public confidence, Choiseul placed the bureau of funds together with the bureau of accounts under the direction of an outsider, Joseph-François Foullon, *intendant de guerre* and assistant to Lieutenant-General de Cremailles on financial matters at the War Department.[35]

The *bureau de l'examen des comptes* attempted to audit the department's expenditures before reporting to the *Chambre des Comptes*, enabling the court to receive the treasurers-general's accounts with some degree of understanding.[36] The bureau had always been important to naval administration but its role as a service rather than policy office, concern for past expenditures, location apart from the other Paris bureaux and from Versailles, and special relationship with the treasurers-general of the navy left it isolated. The bureau's work concerned the past, pursuing the financial loose ends of long-forgotten episodes. Soon after becoming secretary of state Rouillé learned that the last complete account approved by the Chamber of Accounts was for 1743. In 1751 Charles-Joseph Nitard, Rouillé's former secretary, replaced M. Girard as *premier commis*.[37] The appointment suggests that the secretary of state gave new importance to the work of the bureau, but in 1760 the bureau was still struggling with naval expenditures for 1748 and 1749. Its placement under Foullon's direction marked an important change, though the two bureaux remained in the central secretariat of the navy.

A legacy from the days of Colbert's close supervision of French commercial policy, the presence of the bureau of commerce in the department had little to do with the rest of naval administration; by the mid-eighteenth century its function was chiefly diplomatic. United with the former bureau of consulates since 1738, the bureau's numbers declined from seven clerks in 1750 to five after 1759. Effective 1 January 1762, Choiseul transferred the bureau, its operating costs, and staff to the Department of Foreign Affairs.[38]

Choiseul, however, was not the sole initiator of change in the navy's central administration. More important alterations had occurred under his predecessors. A *bureau des officiers* owed its origin to Maurepas' decision in 1747 to remove matters concerning officers of the sword from the bureau of funds to his own cabinet. There his secretary, Charles-Alexandre Salley, directed the work of two clerks until the spring of 1749. Shortly after assuming office Rouillé withdrew responsibility for officers of the pen from the bureau of funds and by 1753 had established a separate bureau of officers under his former private secretary and now *premier commis*, Jean-Marie Gaudin.[39] Gaudin followed his master to Foreign Affairs in 1754, and the bureau's fate under Machault and Moras remains uncertain; its duties and responsibilities probably continued under the management of personal secretariats. But in 1758 André-Julien Rodier was appointed *premier commis* and placed in charge of a new *bureau des officiers d'épée, et de plume, des troupes et des chiourmes*. Rodier obtained responsibility for naval conscription four years later and thus by the end of the Seven Years' War a personnel bureau had emerged in the department.[40]

The administration of naval seamen was also reorganized during the 1750s. During the previous decade the bureau had disintegrated. It was nominally under the direction of the *intendant des classes*, a once influential officer who now enjoyed a sinecure. The incumbent, Antoine de Ferriol, comte de Pont-de-Veyle, a close friend of Maurepas, enjoyed a stipend of between 16 and 17,000 livres, "but only on condition that he did not fulfil his duties." Three clerks in the bureau reported directly to the minister on questions concerning conscription, fisheries, and litigation between the navy and Admiralty. Rouillé moved immediately to improve this appalling state of affairs. Leaving Pont-de-Veyle to enjoy his emoluments for nearly a year, Rouillé installed his brother-in-law, Bernard Pallu, as *premier commis* of the bureau of the classes and established its duties by January 1750.[41] The bureau's responsibilities expanded to include maritime fortifications, the coast guard, and fisheries. Its staff grew from seven clerks in 1750 to twelve three years later when it was the largest of the central offices and reflected Pallu's growing influence. The bureau attempted to collect all information concerning ship movements in France and provide an accurate record of all ships and seafarers in the kingdom. Its chief duties, however, were to verify crew rolls, prepare annual reports on navigation and commerce, and examine requests for advances and conduct money for called-up seamen obliged to travel to the arsenals and for payment of their wages after their ships reached home. The bureau also registered the fitting out and laying up of all ships in France, kept a list of newly built vessels commencing navigation, and maintained registers of newly classed seamen as well as of *arrêts, édits, declarations, règlements,* and *ordonnances* concerning seafaring. Finally, through Pallu's bureau flowed all correspondence to and from the many officers of the classes employed in the maritime departments of the kingdom.[42]

Rouillé's reforms, built on those of his brother-in-law, could not last in view of the personal nature of administrative bonds, where *premiers commis* were more important than their bureaux. In 1755 Machault got rid of Pallu, arranging for him to be sent on an embassy to Venice, and transferred his appointments to his son.[43] Less than two years later Peyrenc de Moras arranged for Pallu's return, appointed him to the unheard of post of *intendant-général des classes, pêches, gardes côtes et fortifications maritimes,* and authorized him to correspond "en ministre" with naval intendants in the arsenals concerning these subjects.[44] Pallu's appointment again failed to last. Following his death in April 1758, the bureau of the classes remained in the hands of a *second commis* for two years; in January 1759, it was partially dismembered. A *premier commis* was named but the staff had shrunk considerably.[45] After 1762 the bureau lost its separate existence and was integrated into André Rodier's responsibilities.

The presence of only three clerks under the direction of Arnauld de La Porte in 1753 belied the colonial bureau's crucial importance to the navy's financial well-being during the 1750s and the considerable influence of its *premier commis.* La Porte's rise in naval administration, beginning in 1731, had been meteoric; marriage to the elder Pellerin's daughter in 1736 had assured his future. For the next twenty years La Porte forged an empire of loyal assistants, distributed favours, and protected friends from outside interference. Sheltered by his brother-in-law, he built a nearly impenetrable barrier between his bureau and the secretary of state. He so impressed Maurepas as to obtain his brother's promotion to *commissaire-général de la marine* and Rouillé named him intendant of St Domingue. Later on La Porte so influenced Machault as to subvert an investigation into the conduct of the intendant of Canada, François Bigot.[46] In 1755 he started his eighteen-year-old son and namesake on his ascent to the highest grades of naval administration. Nothing less than uncontrolled financial chaos in the colonies ultimately led to his downfall.[47] Nevertheless, it further illustrations were needed that men not bureaux were the key to understanding naval administration, Arnauld de la Porte's career provides a vivid example.

The colonial bureau, like the bureau of the classes, subsequently remained without direction for nearly two years. Jean-Augustin Accaron's appointment is curious. After spending six years as a clerk in the bureau of commerce, he suddenly obtained naval rank as a principal scrivener, promotion to *commissaire de la marine,* and appointment to the court, all in the space of six months in 1755.[48] He clearly possessed influence but he did not survive the loss of Guadeloupe, Canada, and Martinique, and retired in 1764.[49]

The *dépôt des cartes, plans et journaux*, or Hydrographic Office, had accomplished little since its establishment in 1720. It was unique among the navy's central offices in being directed by a naval officer, whose interest, influence, and enthusiasm were prerequisites to success. Between 1734 and 1750 the office had been under the direction of Antoine Du Chesne, marquis d'Albert, a naval courtier. His successor, the marquis de La Galissonière, was quite the opposite: an active, serving officer who received his flag as reward for the past two and a half years spent as interim governor of Canada. Knowing the navigational dangers of Canadian waters, possessing strong views on the role of the French North American colonies in the coming struggle with Great Britain, intelligent, energetic, possessed of scientific curiosity, and enjoying a special relationship with the new secretary of state, La Galissonière rejuvenated the Hydrographic Office. Almost immediately he organized three important scientific expeditions. The first, carried out in 1750 and 1751, quickly led to publication of the first accurate surveys of the coast of Nova Scotia based on astronomical observations. The second resulted in new astronomical determinations of longitudes and charts of the French coast, the Iberian peninsula, and the island of Madeira, while the third, conducted in cooperation with the Royal Academy of Sciences, sent Abbé Nicolas-Louis de la Caille to the Cape of Good Hope and Indian Ocean to compile a star catalogue of the southern hemisphere.[50] In Paris, the department also began to publish marine charts.[51] The office acquired the surviving plates of the old *Neptune françois (sic)*, published in 1693, and Rouillé ordered a new, revised edition which appeared in 1753.[52] The department also obtained its own small observatory at Paris a year later in the Hôtel de Cluny; and Rouillé attached Joseph-Nicolas Delisle to the office as "astronomer of the navy" and purchased his vast collection of astronomical and geographical data.[53] Finally, in 1756 the department inspired publication of *Hydrographie française*.[54] Based on naval surveys and sailing directions collected and collated over three and a half decades, the publication represented a major advance in European marine cartography, placing the first truly scientifically constructed charts in the hands of French naval officers.

La Galissonière's successors, Antoine-Alexis Perier de Salvet and Maximin de Bompar, were both active flag officers but Perier's selection as director in 1756 made the position once again a sinecure. Perier was ill – he died in 1757 – and his appointment appeared an honorable retirement. Neither man possessed any interest in the work of the Hydrographic Office. The appointment in November 1761 of François-Bernard, comte de Narbonne-Pelet, as director having only the rank of lieutenant returned the office to the custody of a naval courtier.[55] What influences lay behind the appointment remain unknown. It seems clear, however, that the recent changes illustrate the crucial influence that directors held over the office's activities and the way in which they personally affected its importance. Naval administration remained very much the product of men rather than norms, particularly in the case of Barrin de la Galissonière, who was the force behind the scientific growth that flourished in the early 1750s.

Into the bureaux flowed correspondence from three major arsenals, several lesser establishments, perhaps twenty consular offices in Europe and the Near East, and several colonial administrations in North America and the West Indies. Fewer than 100 men received thousands of letters, reports, and memoranda, all of which were noted, minuted, dealt with, and filed. Each year, in turn, they sent out thousands of replies and instructions. The organization and procedures of the central bureaux appear to present important features of the growing stage of modern bureaucratic government: a hierarchy of officials, a chain of command, trainees, specialized bureaux and employees, periodic payment of salaries, reliance upon expertise, knowledge of forms, preservation of documents in a central archives, and, finally, administration based on written records. These are all Weberian criteria for testing the maturity of bureaucratic governments in the age of absolutism.[56]

In the mid-eighteenth century, however, the navy's central bureaux exhibited only a superficial resemblance to Weber's ideal bureaucracy. Certainly they comprised part of an organization designed to accomplish large-scale administrative tasks, but few mechanisms in place allowed the systematic coordination of work. The bureaux themselves are partial evidence that fixed, regular duties were in effect, that considerable specialization had already occurred. But other key traits of bureaucratic organization were scarcely present at all. Any hierarchy of authority was more apparent than real. The influence of *premiers commis* remained entirely personal and depended on secretaries of state rather than on the bureaux; a shift in their influence affected the entire bureau under their control. A system of evenly adopted rules and regulations did not apply; the naval ordinance makes no mention of the bureaux. Other bureaucratic features were entirely absent. Employment was not based on technical qualifications nor can official conduct concerning administrative decisions be described as impersonal. Bureaucracy is associated with close, detailed supervision of work, regular procedures, systematic application of general laws and regulations, and modern notions of public service; none of these had appeared in the administration of French absolute monarchy.[57]

Central naval administration, with few employees, separate bureaux, and impermanent locations was not even a nascent bureaucratic organization. Although bearing some bureaucratic features, they were not those that characterize the latter – great size, isolation from society, absence of sensitivity, and machine-like qualities of complex articulation. On the contrary, the social system embraced naval administration naturally and constantly interfered with it.[58] Naval administration suffered from confusion, division of authority, absence of coordination, and breakdown of understanding despite the good will of generally talented personnel. Clive Church identifies more general features of Louis xv's administration that hampered the development of bureaucracy: the conciliar screen that complicated the position of the departments, the underdevelopment of administrative law and of personnel management, flaws in the salary system, poor organization of duties, and interference of local and regional bodies that left ministerial staffs in ambiguous positions.[59] The social preeminence of venal office-holders which affected the standing and operations of ministry staffs did not influence naval organization itself, but remained close by in the office of treasurers-general of the navy, the department of the controller-general of finances, the courts, and among some naval personnel and the royal provincial intendants with whom departmental staff constantly dealt. Moreover, employment in the central bureaux did not preclude venal office-holding; for instance, a scrivener employed in the bureau of general port administration possessed two venal charges, *valet de garde robe ordinaire du roy* and *concierge du salon de Marly.*[60] Taken together these features account for the general inability of contemporaries to see form and structure within monarchical administration or to characterize flaws and breakdown in organizational terms. Eighteenth-century men overemphasized character and circumstance and the divisive effect of personality in accounting for defects in naval administration; few questioned the degree to which conflict was institutionalized in the clashes that occurred. Removal of men from office, political trials, and advancement of personal and group interests became common devices to check inefficiency and error. The impulse toward reform most often came from an ideal vision of the pristine state of earlier arrangements rather than from present challenges.

Support for the above view also follows from a consideration of the evolution of the *premiers commis*. The term requires some explanation. Not only is the position difficult to define, but it had altered significantly during the previous seventy years and continued to evolve during the remainder of the eighteenth century. Prior to the 1680s close personal bonds existed between the secretaries of state and their clerical assistants. Lineage and loyalty predominated; relations between patron and client prevailed in recruitment of a minister's entourage. A small number of men staffed the bureaux whose activities could be supervised by the minister within his larger circle. *Premiers commis* were chosen normally from among close relatives and several became secretaries of state and ministers. A decline in the number of *premiers commis* selected from close relatives during the last half of Louis xiv's reign signified an important change. During the eighteenth century no *premier commis* became a secretary of state.

Several factors account for the change. First, sons often succeeded fathers as secretaries of state. The navy is a prime example; there, two families, Colbert and Phélypeaux, led the department for eighty years. Second, the growing power of royal provincial intendants also established a new path to secretarial rank. Third, the increased power exercised by ministers and their numerous alliances with court nobility reinforced the gradual separation of *premiers commis* from high office, a development that grew significantly after 1750 when court nobility actually began to occupy the office of secretary of state. Finally, the ever-extending responsibilities of departments increased the separation by creating a need for greater numbers of *premiers commis*. In addition to seven *premiers commis* at the navy in 1762, the War Office employed thirteen, Foreign Affairs seven, and the controller-general's department thirty-two.[61] Well before mid-century these changes had sufficiently weakened the old bonds between master and servant so as to require liaison between secretaries of state and their *premiers commis*. Private secretaries and cabinets introduced into departmental administration filled the need, but these persons and offices acted as filters as well as links. Moreover, personal secretaries became influential in their own right. Several one-time secretaries of Maurepas and Rouillé became *premiers commis* in the department, illustrating that the old bonds were by no means dead. Recruitment of *premiers commis* and personal secretaries continued to be based on a minister's initiative and responsibility, a personal choice in which the king did not meddle.[62]

Nevertheless, *premiers commis* continued to enjoy great influence because they commanded rare expertise. While their more eminent superiors acted on the stage of public life, they remained discreetly in the background. Their special knowledge of procedures to translate decisions into reality allowed them to hold the key to much power and to play important political as well as administrative roles.[63] Their influence, however, remained personally attached to a secretary of state's character and to circumstances rather than to the duties of their bureaux. When ministers like Moras or Massiac were not up to their tasks, for whatever reasons, *premiers commis* acted and took decisions in their place. When others, like Machault, Berryer or Choiseul were on top of their responsibilities and delegated their authority, *premiers commis* remained subordinate to their wills and earned further trust.[64] On the other hand, when one like Rouillé preferred to attend to business himself or relied on advisers from beyond the bureaux, or when a *premier commis*, like Jean-Augustin

TABLE 1

Premiers Commis of the Navy's Central Bureaux, 1748–1762

Bureau	Name	Dates of Appointment		
Police	Joseph Pellerin, *fils*	Jan.	1745–June	1761
	Laurent Truguet		1761–Dec.	1770
Funds	Michael Bégon vii		1747–Nov.	1756
	Chevalier	Nov.	1756–Aug.	1761
	Jean Cartault	Sept.	1761–Nov.	1761
	de Geneté	Nov.	1761–June	1763
Colonies	Arnauld de la Porte		1738–Jan.	1758
	Jean-Augustin Accaron	Oct.	1759–Oct.	1764
Commerce	Charles-Cardin Le Guay		–Mar.	1750
	Le Guay, *fils*	Jan.	1750–Mar.	1773
Classes	Bernard-René Pallu		1750–May	1758
	La Rivière (acting)		1758–	1760
	Louis-François Le Tourneur		1760–May	1762
Officers	Charles-Alexandre Salley	Feb.	1747–Apr.	1749
	Jean-Marie Gaudin		–Mar.	1755
	André-Julien Rodier		1758–Nov.	1774
Archives	François-Maurice Laffilard	Jan.	1740–July	1754
	Laurent Truguet	Aug.	1754–	1760
	Jean-Charles Horque de Hamecourt		1760–	1785
Accounts	Girard		1742–	1751
	Charles-Joseph Nitard	Oct.	1751–June	1763

Note: Naval officers directing the Hydrographic Bureau are not included.

Accaron, possessed little character, the latter's role became more adminis-trative, a task of keeping his bureau in good order.[65] Mutual respect and friendship, together with the legacy of the past, also enhanced the role of *premiers commis* who sometimes were men of exceptional talent. Finally, stability, the chief characteristic of their positions, reinforced their influence in a government of factions, especially in the naval department where the office of secretary of state remained unimportant in the Royal Council and was occupied by seven men in the short space of fourteen years.

The same forces separating *premiers commis* from the route to ministerial power increased their separation from their subordinates.[66]

TABLE 2

Stipends of Naval *Premiers Commis* in Selected Years, 1748–1761

Bureau	Stipends (in livres)				
	1748	*1753*	*1759*	*1761 (Apr.)*	*1761 (Dec.)*
Police	15,300	13,600	15,200	12,800	11,200
Funds	11,200	12,400	13,900	13,900	11,500
Colonies	8,100	16,500	12,500	11,400	8,100
Commerce	13,000	13,100	17,400	17,400	12,000
Classes	–	15,200	nil	14,400	11,000
Officers	–	8,400	19,000	15,400	10,200
Archives	5,800	9,800	10,600	10,600	4,000
Accounts	10,200	8,400	10,000	12,090	7,600
Total	63,600	98,400	98,600	107,990	75,600

Source: Marine C^2, 116–17.

Under Maurepas several *premiers commis* turned their bureaux into fiefs, for it was there each year that the thousands of pieces of correspondence were summarized, annotated, criticized, and brought to the secretary of state's attention, and where replies were drafted for his signature. Owing to the prevailing attitude that naval administration ought not to affect questions of royal policy, naval *premiers commis* did not work with the king, but they were not far away, living and working in the heady atmosphere of the court. Nevertheless, the short distance between the department and the Royal Council allowed *premiers commis* to surround their bureaux with walls that only their own knowledge of facts could penetrate. They were little kings. Holding normally the rank of *commissaire de la marine*, a *premier commis'* proximity to the court far outweighed the credit of more senior administrative ranks in the arsenals. To this influence, which acknowledged their merit and connections, Louis xv added a generosity of material blessings that grew until new ideas and a growing need to limit expenditures imposed restrictions.[67]

Annual emoluments paid to six *premiers commis* in 1748 and 1749 amounted to more than twice the total paid to all subordinate personnel.[68] In 1753 the stipends of ten heads of bureaux consumed nearly half the entire cost of operating the bureaux. These increased substantially until the end of 1761 when the duc de Choiseul introduced major reductions. Individual amounts, however, were attached to persons rather than their bureaux. The personal status and prestige of *premiers commis* undermined any development of administrative hierarchy based upon formal or abstract positions, the importance of individual bureaux in the organization, or duties performed within each. Only a full-scale study of the entire personnel of the navy – of the kind undertaken by Marc Perrichet – will reveal the extent of the roles played by patronage and pedigree in naval affairs, but the presence of nepotism in the central bureaux is unquestionable.[69] Two incumbent *premiers commis*, Pellerin and Le Guay, succeeded their fathers in the direction of their bureaux, and two more, Chevalier and La Porte, obtained the coveted grade of *petit commissaire* and junior positions in their own bureaux for their sons. A fifth, Laffillard, employed his brother-in-law as one of two clerks at the archives, and a sixth, Rodier, placed his son as Moras' private secretary.[70] It is not clear whether clerks in the bureaux were paid directly, or whether their emoluments were advanced to *premiers commis* who disposed of these sums at will or granted favours in the place of salaries, thereby lining their own pockets and ensuring the loyalty of their underlings. Bureaux in the controller-general's department contained individuals serving a master who was more important than the bureau as a whole; and there seems to be no reason why similarly dependent relations did not exist in the navy department.[71] To the degree that senior clerks later possessed rank in the corps of the pen – *commissaire* and *commis de classes*, *écrivain ordinaire*, and *élève écrivain* – payment of their wages may have been regularized. But the majority were simple *commis*, holding no warrants or commissions, and subject to the pay practices of *premiers commis*. Thus, while some regularity can be observed in the administration's pay system, it was hardly characteristic.

The quarter-century under Maurepas had witnessed the growing influence of *premiers commis* and the emasculation of the once great authority of the two senior intendants at court. Both developments were challenged during the 1750s. A third development, the isolation of naval intendants by the central bureaux, which contributed to the loss of control and command during Maurepas' long tenure, also met resistance during the decade. Naval intendants grew old in their posts under Maurepas. The intendants of Brest and Rochefort both died in 1749, each having spent more than half a century in the service; the intendants of Toulon and Le Havre were septuagenarians. At mid-century these men paid little attention to the arsenals in their care; clerks from the central bureaux corresponded directly with junior personnel, breaking the hierarchical connection between king and intendant on which the system depended. Evidence of impersonal, functional mechanisms for governance might be claimed had this behaviour been approved, as part of a rational reorganization of naval administration, but no collective control or responsibility existed or was developing. Naval intendants remained individually and personally responsible to the king for their administration of naval arsenals. By mid-century, however, they had lost a good deal of control to the central bureaux.

Bernard Pallu's introduction as *premier commis* of the rejuvenated bureau of the classes and the marquis de la Galissonière's appointment as director of the hydrographic bureau were attempts to shake up the central administration and resist the first two developments. But the rise and fall of Sébastien Lenormant de Mézy during the 1750s was the most significant illustration of the struggle between the forces of centralization at Versailles and the intendants in the arsenals. Rouillé's confirmation and later employment of Lenormant de Mézy as intendant of Rochefort and confidential adviser indicated his desire to get closer to men with broad experience in operational and executive sectors of naval administration and to avoid becoming a prisoner of the bureaux. Although Lenormant had served for thirty years, he had never been employed in France – let alone at court – when in May 1750 he assumed his duties as intendant of Rochefort; his previous service had been in the colonies. For the next four years he spared neither himself nor his subordinates in the effort to reestablish "rule, good order and economy" in the arsenal, but during this time he spent two lengthy periods, four months in 1751 and eleven months in 1753, at court advising Rouillé. The death of the *intendant des armées navales*, Louis Gourdan, on 22 December 1753, provided an opportunity to advance Lenormant and restore influence to this once important position. Two other candidates, Trousset d'Héricourt and De Clieu d'Erchigny, had been intendant of the galley corps and intendant of Le Havre respectively. Trousset had no naval experience and De Clieu was an octogenarian. Their candidacies reflected the prevailing attitude that the position was a sinecure, ensuring "a decent, comfortable retirement" (*un repose honête [sic] et commode*).[72] Lenormant's appointment, dated 3 January 1754, clearly represented a change in the nature of the office.[73] Lenormant did not take up his new appointment before Rouillé left the department, but Machault wasted no time bringing him to court, employing him immediately as a trouble-shooter and later as preceptor for his son. Together with several high-ranking naval officers and the marquis de Vallière, *doyen* of French artillerists, he sat on an *ad hoc* committee investigating naval ordnance production.[74] By the spring of 1755 Lenormant was rumoured to have actual charge of the department.[75] The marquis d'Argenson's claim is no doubt exaggerated, but Lenormant's presence clearly disturbed the *premiers commis*. Indeed, they may have sabotaged his relations with the minister for Lenormant had no love for *premiers commis*, once referring to "the errors into which they fall, the false principles that they adopt daily, the continual contradiction in decisions, false dispositions and dangerous pliancy in giving heed to new systems from which no one can unravel the truth."[76]

Bernard Pallu, now armed with the prerogatives of his office as *intendant des classes*, joined Lenormant during Peyrenc de Moras' sixteen months in office; senior intendancies appeared restored to a degree of influence that had been seen only under Louis xiv. But the power of these offices, removed from the ambitions of, and threatening to, *premiers commis*, was not to last. Following Pallu's death in April 1758 and Moras' resignation a month later, Lenormant de Mézy assumed the vacant position and was named *intendant-général de la marine et des colonies*; he became deputy minister or permanent undersecretary of state for the navy under the marquis de Massiac, completely supplanting Joseph Pellerin the younger. But usurping the position and interests of the *premier commis* in a ministry headed by a naval officer without the usual entourage of clerical assistants foredoomed Lenormant's five months in office. Neither Lenormant nor his chief could withstand the opprobrium directed at the navy during the summer and fall of 1758, and both men retired in November.

Following Lenormant's departure the old pattern reemerged. Naval intendants once again were viewed as the chief cause of poor administration in the navy.[77] Berryer made few changes in the central administration except to consolidate payments to *premiers commis*.[78] More significantly, all the disturbing elements introduced by Rouillé disappeared. Several important changes in the organization and status of central personnel occurred under the duc de Choiseul. Naval officers of the pen were prevented from serving in the bureaux; personnel of the central bureaux were to be known only as *commis* and *premier commis*. At the same time, Choiseul transferred the bureau of commerce to the Foreign Affairs Department and consolidated the bureaux of funds and accounts together with the archives under Joseph Foullon at the War Department in order to control naval spending.[79] In contrast to previous changes in organization, however, this attempt to check the power of naval *premiers commis* originated with the person directing all three departments of government concerned with the war and involved the transference of bureaux to other ministries rather than the introduction of personnel from outside the bureaux.

By mid-eighteenth century the devolution of power into the hands of several *premiers commis* whose influence eroded the authority of the secretary of state had become the chief characteristic of the central naval administration. The resultant confusion led to a displacement of responsibility within the organization as succeeding secretaries of state attempted to reduce the influence of bureau chiefs during the next decade. Rouillé's attempts to bypass *premiers commis* had a very limited effect. Rapid replacement of his successors reinforced the influence of *premiers commis* who provided continuity in the administration. Just as there were no positions in the constitutional structure of French absolutism for the king's mistresses or court bankers, there were no longer positions in naval administration for a minister's brother-in-law or son, certainly not if the ministers themselves failed to hold on to office. Nor was there place for an *adjoint* or deputy minister unconnected by personal loyalty to the secretary of state. Constant reorganization of details within the bureaux accomplished little beyond confirming the relatively strong influence of permanent officials.

The central bureaux gave an air of permanence and stability to naval administration, but its coherence and competence may be questioned. No central purchasing administration existed in any bureau and financial administration was extremely limited. The two, once prestigious, senior posts in the central administration remained functionally useless despite efforts by Bernard Pallu and Lenormant de Mézy to build significance into their positions. *Premiers commis* occupied well-entrenched positions reinforced by widespread bonds of kinship stretching from one bureau to another, to the arsenals and colonies, and to other departments of government, not a bad thing in itself but raising significant obstacles to improved performance. The practice of recruiting a secretary of state's closest assistants from among family and friends reinforced the traditional separation of land and sea personnel in the navy. No provision existed to introduce talented men from the sea service into the central administration – the Hydrographic office being the sole exception. *Premiers commis* were not indolent but they possessed no sea experience; it is moot whether some had even seen the sea let alone ventured aboard a warship. For their part, naval officers remained generally uninterested in carrying out administrative duties, were largely ignorant of procedures, and feared derogation if ever summoned to administration. Members of the central administration knew a great deal but remained strangely unaware of the seriousness of many naval problems. Administrative routine was both cause and consequence of a lack of critical spirit, mental laziness and excessive respect for established practices. Like secretaries of state, *premiers commis* and clerks carried out their duties without questioning their own behaviour, reassured by their competence, attachment to the crown, and real concern for the public weal, and by a feeling of certitude derived from following the revered path traced by Colbert and the style of government hallowed by the glory of Louis xiv.[80]

CHAPTER THREE

Officers of the Pen

By mid-century the corps of the pen had suffered half a century of neglect and manipulation. Ministerial control was relaxed, discipline had deteriorated, many senior officers had surrendered their authority in the arsenals, and officers of the pen defined for themselves what it meant to be the king's confidential agent. Critics accused officers of the pen of incapacity to carry out tasks entrusted to them, lack of knowledge of their duties and responsibilities and generally poor relations with naval provisioners.[1] The corps of the pen also suffered from ossification. Closed in upon itself, incapable of introducing new blood, poorly trained, wrapped in administrative routine, officers of the pen were ill equipped to meet the demands that arose during the years of renewal and expansion after 1748.

Events preceding the Seven Years' War and during the war revealed the corps' inadequacies and provided incentives for its renewal. The so-called reforms of the duc de Choiseul were well under way before he assumed the office of secretary of state for the navy. Yet naval administrative reforms failed during the next quarter of a century because officers of the pen had been wrongly singled out as the chief, indeed, sometimes the sole cause of the navy's failure during the war – the inadequacies of men having been confused with failings in organization.

French naval administration was the creation of Jean-Baptiste Colbert. Unique problems arising from the creation of a naval officer corps out of the military, landed nobility led him to turn elsewhere to organize the new navy. The corps of the pen ensued. It drew many attached to Colbert by family and service, and its numbers grew rapidly.[2] Colbert desired young men with sea experience from good families; the freedom from venality of the new corps suggests that he sought to draw widely for recruits, and may have recognized the need to overcome a reluctance to enter naval administration which was new and had little in common with the occupations of other corps of *officiers* in the kingdom.[3] Free admission existed during most of the eighteenth century but the corps itself became the chief source of its own recruits. This narrow base of recruitment blurred the former distinction between revocable *commissaires* as agents of Bourbon centralization and *officiers* who possessed property-rights in their charges, and the growth of group independence among officers of the pen accompanied this evolution.[4] Both developments seriously affected the navy's well-being, for naval administrators were isolated from other governing elites. In contrast to the appointment of royal provincial intendants, who enjoyed a common early training in law, most often at Paris, preparation for senior naval appointment occurred entirely within the navy itself, in colonies and arsenals far from the centre of royal power.[5]

The corps of the pen remained the instrument through which the crown exercised executive power in all naval matters except the strictly military. Although the navy possessed two officer corps, no substantive distinction existed between civilian and military in eighteenth-century France. Officers of the pen did not bear arms but several were members of the *noblesse de robe*, and not all *noblesse d'épée* were officers who lived by the sword. The corps of the pen was part of the military society that ruled the country.[6] The hierarchy of precedence within the corps of the pen, equivalence of grades with the corps of the sword, and honours rendered at funerals of commissioned officers all reflected the military features of the *corps de plume*.[7] Although the pen gave way to the sword at each equivalent grade, its personnel maintained precedence over junior officers of the sword.

Officers of the pen were not administrators in the modern sense; the convergence of judicial, political, and financial authority in single persons requires brief elaboration. In general "la police" constituted the totality of measures taken by an absolute government to ensure public order and prosperity.[8] Officers of the pen pursued these aims in the navy's arsenals, in colonies, or wherever their duties took them. But "la police" also constituted a branch of justice that together with reason and will provided the traditional basis of monarchical authority. This convergence of power is foreign to notions of administration characteristic of modern social systems that multiply and separate institutional roles and depend upon specialists possessing a well-defined expertise.[9] Officers of the pen were professional administrators in the sense that the corps of the pen offered a formal pattern of training, appointment as scrivener conferred certification as a prerequisite to assuming administrative duties and further advancement, and membership in the corps provided a regular, full-time, paid career. Unlike modern professsionals, the officers were not recruited on the basis of demonstrable competence. But the major distinction between eighteenth- and twentieth-century professional administrators lies in the powers of the former not possessed by the latter.

Naval intendants and *commissaires-généraux* were judges in their own jurisdictions; their authority was founded on clauses in the Naval Ordinance of 1689 (Book 12, title 1, clause 1), their royal commissions as intendants or *ordonnateurs*, and instructions that established them as sole judge of all misdemeanours committed in the arsenals, naval storehouses, and workshops, wherever they might be, by sailors, workers, soldiers, and others.[10] In minor cases intendants judged alone, definitively, and without appeal. In cases demanding corporal punishment, they alone decided to demand a court martial or to convoke the civil magistracy. In more serious cases they possessed full power to sentence offenders to death.[11] Finally, naval intendants possessed the power to arrest anyone anywhere in their jurisdiction suspected of committing an offence in the arsenal.[12] The patriarchal nature of the intendants' authority over those under their command, extending to wives and children, is even more foreign to modern notions of administration. The intendant at Rochefort once confined the wife of the arsenal's surgeon-dentist to a convent because her scandalous public conduct made it impossible for her husband to live with her and the arsenal needed his talents.[13] Senior naval officers of the pen were military men but not soldiers, and professionals but not merely administrators.

Administration was not yet synonymous with "la police." In the middle of the eighteenth century it referred only to logistics or the organization of naval supplies and thus to only one of several important roles entrusted to the corps of the pen. On the eve of the French Revolution, Gabriel de Bory provided an ideal definition of naval administration: "The administration of a Navy can be reduced to the four following heads. First it is the purchase and receipt of raw materials. Second is the manufacture of these raw materials ... Third is the care of materials, either raw or manufactured. Fourth is the sailing of the commissioned vessel, that is to say, furnished with all military stores. The first three were committed to the care of a corps call the Pen, and the fourth to the Military."[14] In Bory's view, naval administration could be fairly clearly defined, but he was no friend of the *corps de plume* and naval organization had been somewhat clarified by 1789.

In 1754 Sebastien Lenormant de Mézy gave a more accurate description of relations between the two corps in the performance of their duties:

There are two distinct corps in the navy, the one of military officers destined for all operations of war and the other of the officers of the pen charged with the preparation, conversion, reception and consumption of all munitions, arms, implements necessary for the service, for the construction, armament and fitting out of vessels, raising seamen and generally all that relates to justice, police and finances of the navy in the arsenals ... One cannot encroach on the duties of those who are charged with them without altering the sinews of administration. Indeed, these same officers of the pen have the right to inspect the conduct of the others, as the former have equally the right to oversee the operations of the latter in certain circumstances.[15]

Lenormant's statement reveals no well-defined demarcation of duties and responsibilities between officers of the pen and sword. Bory's first three branches of administration were not confined to the sole care of the pen nor was the fourth branch confined alone to the care of the sword. Officers of the sword participated actively in the receipt and inspection of raw materials, especially masts, at the arsenals, the construction of warships, and the manufacture of naval ordnance. Officers of the pen exercised their own authority afloat, controlling the issue of provisions and stores, regulation of sick seamen, and preparation and maintenance of muster-rolls, shipboard inventories, and crews' pay registers. Finally, they were empowered to communicate directly with the secretary of state concerning the conduct of commanding officers.

The independence of the pen from the sword was clearly established, yet the Naval Ordinance of 1689 was a product of history more than reason. Here was the nub of many difficulties, for the Naval Ordinance incorporated notions of judicial administrative authority from the past while the royal government was currently moving towards greater executive administrative authority. Its terms were imprecise, overlapping and often contradictory concerning the duties and responsibilities of officers of the two corps. Whereas late in the eighteenth century, Bory, an officer of the sword, saw distinct branches of administration confined to the separate care of different officers, Lenormant de Mézy, one of the pen's most vigorous defenders, claimed the right of the pen to inspect the conduct of the sword, admitting the right of the latter to oversee the operations of the pen only "in certain circumstances." Naval organization and administration strongly institutionalized conflict between officers of the two corps.

An *arrêt* of 1 May 1716 established the corps of the pen with an authorized strength of 216 men, including 58 in the galley service. Officers of the classes responsible for administering naval conscription were in the corps but not of it. In 1728, in response to complaints, Louis xv established the commissioned grade of *commissaire aux classes* to rank immediately after *commissaire de la marine*, but recruits were from among clerks of the classes rather than the corps of the pen.[16] Membership in the corps increased slowly under Maurepas, to nearly two-thirds beyond the establishment, and rapidly under his successors. Demands for increased personnel to staff the reinvigorated details in the arsenals accompanied the navy's rebuilding program.[17] In 1751 Rouillé increased the authorized number of *commissaires* to 70 and doubled the number of scriveners to 240. Normally fewer than eight men annually entered the corps at mid-century. But in 1751 and 1752 one hundred new entrants added considerably to its size. A few years later the strain of war created demands for more scriveners following the posting of increased numbers into warships for sea service. Complaints from Toulon, whence men were taken to staff the new establishment at Minorca, stimulated Peyrenc de Moras to readjust the establishment in July 1757.[18] He fixed the number of scriveners and principal scriveners at 250 and 70, respectively, and proposed to set the establishment of officers of the classes at 76.[19] During his last eleven months in office the minister also admitted 140 new entrants to the corps, placed 72 on *haute paye*, and advanced 76 in grade.[20] No wonder that officers of the sword were resentful; the corps of the pen had more than doubled its original establishment. On 1 November 1758 the entire naval administration including 409 officers of the pen numbered 524.[21] Thereafter, defeat at sea, decline in the arsenals, and Berryer's economizing measures led to a reduction in numbers. Fewer than twenty men entered the corps during the next four years.[22]

On 23 March 1762 the duc de Choiseul suppressed and consolidated grades and reserved the right to authorize the establishments of each arsenal. The new corps of the pen contained only 157 officers from the new grade of *écrivain de la marine* to *commissaire-général* and 64 officers of the classes.[23] Desiring greater administrative efficiency and meeting the needs of political expediency, Choiseul also reduced the power of the pen and introduced officers of the sword into naval administration. His ordinance was the first effort to undo Colbert's and Seignelay's administrative organization. But, like all future attempts at reorganization and reform, it failed. The hundreds of clauses of the 1689 Naval Ordinance captured the essence of royal absolutism in a way that eighteenth-century government reformers could not. Their reforms, which increasingly separated and compartmentalized executive authority, always included the monarchy in which all power and authority converged. The idea of the natural inequality of man was essential to the subordination of the pen to the sword, but inasmuch as the pen represented monarchical authority, any proposal for its subordination remained unacceptable.

Naval arsenals also employed large numbers of copyists, known as *commis aux écritures* or *commis extraordinaires*, who were appointed by intendants to meet unforeseen demands. Lack of control led to abuses and proliferation; there were thirty-five such cases by November 1758. Berryer condemned the practice and regularized clerical appointments, which thereafter received the secretary of state's approval.[24] Officers of the pen insisted on the need to distinguish clerks (*commis*) from scriveners (*écrivains*); the former needed only good penmanship, some knowledge of arithmetic, and assiduous, regular conduct to keep the multitude of registers in the bureaux in good order, whereas the latter were constituted by royal warrants to manage the king's interests, and their social condition allowed them to advance in the corps of the pen.[25] Nevertheless, copyists proved to be essential; by October 1761 the navy's arsenals employed 120.[26] Subordinate to scriveners, their position was a means of entry into the corps. Of lowly origins, owing their advancement to intendants, *commis aux écritures* may have been the only recruits to the corps of the pen who had to demonstrate administrative competence to gain entry.[27] However, membership in the corps remained confined to those in the grades from *écrivain ordinaire* to *commissaire-général* claiming equivalent rank with the sword.

Intendants normally were of the corps of the pen but not in it; royal appointees, they held office according to the king's will. Normally five naval intendants were located at Toulon, Marseilles, Rochefort, Brest, and Le Havre, and three colonial intendants at Martinique, St Domingue, and Canada. A temporary reduction in numbers occurred after the incumbent at Marseilles was reduced to the authority of *ordonnateur* in 1750, but six years later Dunkirk obtained an intendant, returning the total number to eight.[28]

In 1748 almost all the naval intendants were old men. At seventy-nine, Jacques Bigot de la Motte at Brest was probably the oldest; Louis-Balthasar de Ricouart, comte de Herouville, at Rochefort and François-Noël Levasseur de Villeblanche at Toulon were not much younger, having entered the navy one and two years after Bigot, in 1693 and 1694 respectively. Mathieu de Clieu d'Erchigny had only recently been appointed to Le Havre, but in 1748 he was seventy-three years old. The single exception was Benigne-Jérome du Trousset d'Héricourt at Marseilles, who at fifty-two was still in his prime. As intendant-general of the galleys, however, he became redundant the next year, and never gained anything but superficial employment in the naval archives at Paris.[29] Age is no impediment to executive authority and carries the benefit of experience. But these septuagenarians had been subjected to decades of neglect, the disastrous effect of which on naval organization was clear for all to see as the War of the Austrian Succession drew to a close. The intendants were unlikely to check disorder in the arsenals nor were they the ones to organize the naval rebuilding program already envisioned by Maurepas. Fortunately or otherwise, Ricouart, who had been absent from Rochefort for long periods, died on 1 April 1749, and Bigot de la Motte retired a month later. Maurepas had already decided that service in the colonies was a necessary prerequisite for new naval intendants in France and these vacancies permitted appointment of two younger men to the key Atlantic arsenals.[30]

Gilles Hocquart, intendant of New France since 1731, and Sébastien Lenormant de Mézy, *commissaire-général* and former *ordonnateur* of Louisbourg, Cap François, and Louisiana, were fifty-five and forty-seven years old respectively, when appointed to Brest and Rochefort in 1749.[31] In 1754 the elderly D'Erchigny retired at Le Havre, and was replaced by Jean-Louis Ranché who had been intendant of Martinique from 1746 to 1750. Machault and Moras did not adhere strictly to the recent policy requiring colonial experience for naval intendants in France. In November 1756 Machault appointed Michel Bégon to Dunkirk. Although he had never served in the colonies, at thirty-nine he was the youngest man to become a naval intendant in recent times. Lack of colonial experience, however, may have delayed appointment of Lenormant's successor at Rochefort. Charles-Claude Ruis-Embito de la Chesnardière remained a *commissaire général-ordonnateur* for nearly three years before Moras appointed him intendant in June 1757. Villeblanche stayed at Toulon until 1757 when he finally retired after sixty-three years in the navy. His successor, Barthélemy-Louis Charron, the younger, appointed in June, was a much younger man, only forty- five years old, but like Ruis he had never served in the colonies. Charron died three years later and Berryer promptly named 48-year-old Charles-Marin Hurson, intendant of Martinique from 1750 to 1754, to succeed him.[32]

A complete change in the navy's senior administration occurred during the decade after 1748. The new naval intendants were younger men, often with colonial experience, and the last appointee had no direct antecedents in the corps of the pen. Lenormant de Mézy was the son of a *commissaire de la marine*, but other appointees were sons or nephews of naval intendants, *commissaires-généraux* or *premiers commis*. Hurson, on the other hand, was the son of a councillor of the parlement of Paris and had been a councillor himself since 1733.[33] His appointment might have reflected no more than Berryer's admiration for a reform-minded individual. But two similar appointments to colonial intendancies during the 1750s suggest that naval secretaries of state were making a deliberate attempt to alter the social and professional bases of naval administration.

In 1748 Maurepas appointed François Bigot to New France. Although he had progressed through the corps of the pen Bigot had no recent family connection with it. The intendants of the Greater and Lesser Antilles, Simon Maillart and Louis Ranché, were strongly attached to the corps; but in 1750 Rouillé appointed Hurson intendant of Martinique. His successor, Antoine Lefebvre de Givry, was the son of a *commissaire-général* and *premier commis* of the old Naval Council of the Regency, but the next intendant, Pierre-Paul Lemercier de la Rivière, appointed in December 1757, was the son of an intendant of finances at Tours, and like Hurson, a councillor of the parlement of Paris.[34] Sons of the corps continued to serve as intendants at St Domingue, but their successor Jean-Etienne Bernard de Clugny de Nuis, appointed at the beginning of 1760, had no relations in the corps; his father was a councillor of the parlement of Dijon.[35]

The appointments of Hurson, Lemercier de la Rivière, and Clugny de Nuis may have been an indictment of the competence of senior officers in the corps of the pen. But they also represent a major movement towards its reform and its closer integration into the government of France. Lemercier de la Rivière had worked in the central bureaux of the government at Versailles and as a conciliator between court and parlement had attracted the attention of Madame de Pompadour and Abbé de Bernis.[36] Hurson and Clugny had also been close to the central levers of government before their appointments. Indeed, colonial intendants never again appeared from the navy's corps of the pen, but from the *noblesse de robe*, which had long been moving sucessfully into the army, court and government.[37]

The changes between 1748 and 1762 severed the personal ties with Louis xiv's navy and the seventeenth century. Men as much as two generations younger than their immediate predecessors, some with no connection to the old corps of the pen, moved into senior naval administrative posts. Their presence reflected the corps' inadequacies and foreshadowed Choiseul's attempts to reform it. But institutions prove more resistant to change than individuals. Appointing naval intendants from outside the corps of the pen was relatively easy, but the corps itself resisted piecemeal tampering, in part because expediency governed its mid-century expansion.

The senior officers of the corps were the *commissaires-généraux*.[38] Their numbers had declined under Maurepas until there were only fourteen after the union of the galley corps to the navy in 1748.[39] As chiefs of the corps of the pen, *commissaires-généraux* had under their orders all officers of the pen employed in the arsenals. They possessed most of the intendant's powers including those of justice and *ordonnancement* in the latter's absence. In the intendant's presence *commissaires-généraux* had charge of one of the major details in the arsenal in addition to their coordinating duties. In ports lacking naval intendants, Marseilles, Bordeaux, Port Louis, St Malo, Calais, and Dunkirk, *commissaires-généraux* were designated *ordonnateurs*, possessing all of the attributes and powers of intendants. They directed naval services in the region and supervised officers charged with maintaining the system of naval conscription. A few *commissaires-généraux* also served at court as *premiers commis* while others discharged their duties in the colonies.[40] At Rochefort, one worked only for the colonial service while at Madrid another represented the department with the title of commercial and naval agent.[41]

By mid-eighteenth century the majority of *commissaires-généraux* were brothers, sons, or nephews of men who had possessed the same rank. But the influence of the central secretariat through its close proximity to the secretary of state frequently affected advancement of this grade. Several *commissaires-généraux* whose parents and relations had not held the rank had been related to *premiers commis*, while two men with lowly antecedents or none at all in the corps had first served as private secretaries to Maurepas; two more were sons of *commissaires de la marine* and the antecedents of five men remain unknown.[42]

Promotion to the corps' most senior grade bypassed junior officers of the pen lacking appropriate family connections and ministerial influence. Not surprisingly, many ignored their duties or performed them perfunctorily with little interest in the navy or its problems, personal fulfilment and advancement being found elsewhere than in a professional career. A profound gap existed between the professional norms and institutional practice of naval administration. Unlike the political philosopher, the enlightened political administrator could not be found outside the institution in the independent functioning of the intellectual community. Acceptance of a professional role, as La Rivière found, also meant acceptance of institutional norms whereby power was unevenly distributed, frequently overlapping, and advancement uncertain.

Commissaires de la marine held the key rank in the corps of the pen. Enjoying a status equivalent to *capitaine de vaisseau*, these seventy or so officers constituted the armature on which naval administration was based. Like their seniors they possessed judicial and administrative powers, permitting them to carry out "la police" as it related to the navy, and like them, too, they held appointment by royal commission. *Commissaires* in each arsenal were individually entrusted with the administration of major details and could be sent "en mission" to the forests, forges, or wherever the navy's business needed to be pursued.

Access to this grade was more open than in the case of senior ones. Although the favour of intendants was decisive in the majority of promotions, the court also influenced advancement.[43] Nevertheless, nearly four-fifths of the *commissaires* in 1749 possessed very close family connections with the navy. Of forty-seven of fifty-nine *commissaires* whose antecedents were found, twenty-nine were sons, nephews, or grandsons of men who had served in the corps of the pen, three more were related to officers of the sword, two to officers of the Admiral of France, two to naval shipbuilders, and one to a clerk of a former naval victualler.[44]

Petits commissaires were selected from young men recommended by their birth or family services. A *règlement* of the Naval Council of May 1716 established four appointments, giving each appointee a royal warrant (*brevet*) and an annual stipend of 1,000 livres. Intended to raise the status and increase the attractiveness of the corps by encouraging youths of good social standing in the ports to join, the position made it possible to enter directly into line for promotion to senior administrative grades without having to proceed through subordinate ranks.[45] The grade quickly became a self-perpetuating mechanism for senior families of the corps. Trousset d'Hèricourt, Hocquart, Ruis-Embito, Clairambault, and Bégon all began their careers as *petits commissaires*; all had fathers who reached senior rank under Louis xiv.[46]

Under Maurepas, this tool for family advancement was gradually removed from the influence of the corps. The minister may even have wished for its disappearance, making only three appointments during the 1740s.[47] Under his inexperienced successors, intendants and *commissaires-généraux* contended with *permiers commis* and others for appointment of their nominees.[48] Rouillé resisted their appeals but a brief revival occurred during the Seven Years' War. According to Gilles Hocquart, the grade was needed to attract persons distinguished not only by birth, "equal or almost to those of the military," but by a good education and a certain ease of manner, so as to be able to fill the first positions in the corps with dignity. The grades of scrivener and principal scrivener had insufficient prominence to attract fathers of well-born families to solicit them for their children. In contrast, the functions of *petits commissaires* were honourable from the beginning.[49] Hocquart obtained an appointment for his nephew as did Villeblanche; *commissaires-généraux* got four for their sons, but Peyrenc de Moras also gave at least three to relations of *premiers commis*, and one to the nephew of the architect Gabriel who designed his townhouse in Paris.[50]

Gardes magasins or storekeepers were an anomaly in the eighteenth-century corps. Senior to all scriveners in rank, salary and responsibility, they never obtained promotion to *commissaire de la marine*. *Gardes magasins* no longer reported to the intendant and were supervised by a *commissaire*.[51] Located at Bayonne, Brest, Dunkirk, Le Havre, Marseilles, Port Louis, Rochefort, and Toulon, storekeepers were responsible for all rigging, stores, and munitions received, manufactured, and issued to warships in the arsenals. In daily contact with naval provisioners and responsible for issuing the crucial "certificats de réception," they enjoyed great influence. As a result of the substantial opportunities for self-enrichment, combined with the lack of opportunity for advancement, the position became chiefly hereditary. In 1749, of five storekeepers whose antecedents are known, four were sons of former storekeepers.[52]

General, principal, and ordinary scriveners were the work-horses of the "corps de plume." They made up more than three-quarters of the corps' membership. Possession of royal warrants rather than commissions distinguished them from their seniors. Like them, however, more than half had direct antecedents in the "corps de plume." Only the major arsenals employed *écrivains-généraux*, whose principal duty lay in supervising ordinary scriveners in divers details, workshops, construction projects, and general stores. They also policed the arsenal, inspecting watchmen and gatekeepers. The grade appeared to have been a consolation for elderly scriveners without hope of advancement to commissioned rank. Following the death of the octogenarian general scrivener at Marseilles, Berryer suppressed the position.[53]

The key grade was *écrivain principal*, which originally designated those holding nonsupervisory roles among their peers, such as apportioning work loads. The grade was intended to reduce disputes among scriveners and to train men marked for promotion. But as details in the arsenals multiplied and immediate supervision by *commissaires* became problematic, principal scriveners ceased to be first among equals. They assumed an authority over scriveners which increased tension and often led to insubordination. Recent declarations that principal and ordinary scriveners carried out similar duties proved ineffective. By mid-century many principal scriveners ignored their subordinate duties in the arsenals and claimed the prerogatives of junior *commissaires*.[54]

The grade was a mark of favour rather than merit. A list of twenty-three nominees for the grade in 1749 carried more names from the court than senior officers of the pen.[55] So crucial was the appointment and so fierce the competition that the number of ordinary scriveners in the corps sometimes fell, resulting in administrative chaos in the arsenals. Berryer recommended abolition of the grade in 1759 in order to reimpose order among junior ranks of the pen, but this failed to occur before 1762 when a royal ordinance of 23 March designated all general, principal and ordinary scriveners as *écrivains de la marine* and reduced their number by half.

In response to the inexperience and outright incompetence of many scriveners, provision for orderly recruitment and training of young men appeared in 1716 with the appointment of *élèves-écrivains* or scriveners-in-training. Appointment was by letter from the secretary of state, and these trainees were not really members of the corps of the pen. Aged about sixteen years, *élèves* worked under the direction of a *commissaire* and received formal instruction in mathematics from the same teacher who instructed *gardes de la marine*. If after two years they satisfied the intendant, he so advised the secretary of state who sent the candidate a warrant as *écrivain ordinaire*.[56] The establishment of *elèves-ecrivains* failed to accomplish its intended end. Most *élèves* at mid-century were already at colleges at Paris or Versailles and sufficiently well educated not to remain *in statu pupiliari* in the corps. At least there were no reports as in 1680 that many *écrivains* were incapable of writing correctly; nor did eighteenth-century secretaries of state require, like Seignelay, that *écrivains* submit examples of their penmanship.[57]

Patronage subverted any system of recruitment, training and advancement based on formal qualifications. As many scriveners entered the corps on the basis of recommendations from the court as entered from the ranks of the *élèves*.[58] During the three and a half years prior to June 1757, when Moras suppressed the appointment, the court submitted 169 requests.[59]

Moreover, intendants were not interested in wide recruitment; they paid as much attention to the social origins of new recruits as did any corps of patrimonial *officiers*. Pleading for permission to increase temporarily the number of scriveners at Toulon, Intendant Villeblanche assured the minister that the proposed "sujets extraordinaires" could not and would not be accepted into the corps. "I will take care to dismiss them," he wrote, "it being not at all suitable to admit them afterwards into the corps of the pen where it is customary to receive only the children of the corps or young *gens de famille*."[60] According to Villeblanche, good relations between the pen and the sword depended on this exclusiveness.[61] Concern for the purity and well-being of the corps led intendants to take great care over scriveners' marriages, ensuring that prospective brides were sufficiently wealthy or well-born to add to its lustre. Letters asking permission on behalf of junior officers of the pen to marry, or explaining why they could not, fill arsenal correspondence. If young men were clamorous and unruly intendants quickly dispatched them off to sea to cool their ardour.

The positions of *petit commissaire* and *élève-écrivain* failed to attract the kind of people that Colbert had sought to organize the navy: young men of good families from the seaports with seagoing experience. Maurepas virtually halted appointments of the former and in 1757 Peyrenc de Moras ceased to appoint the latter, but he did not address the problem of the corps' renewal. The duc de Choiseul officially suppressed both appointments in March 1762, and by introducing the grade of *élève-commissaire* three years later, he effectively shut the door on drawing recruits from the seaports.

Despite overall increases in personnel during the 1750s, only negligible shifts occurred in the proportion of the corps assigned to each area. Slightly less than two-thirds of the corps laboured in the three major arsenals, one-fifth served elsewhere in France, and the remainder were fairly evenly divided between the central bureaux and the colonies.[62] The corps' expansion during the 1750s was in response to real needs in the arsenals rather than a sign of the pen's growing power over the sword. The increase from twenty-six to forty-two officers of the pen in the central bureaux, however, shows the degree to which clerks of the ministry were gaining access to the pen.

The naval organization established by Colbert and Seignelay gave the pen the largest powers ashore. Rouillé once advised that intendants and commandants, "each in his own part, ought to be the eyes of the minister."[63] But the development of unity between members of separate, equal corps of officers in the navy remained no more than a pious hope. Inasmuch as Louis xv administered his navy as part of his personal domain, all executive power in the arsenals lay in the hands of the intendant representing the king's authority. The intendant alone defended the king's interest against all, including officers of the sword. Years of warfare and action during the seventeenth century encouraged officers of the sword to content themselves with their reduced role ashore; moreover, the independence of the pen from the sword was not officially entrenched until 1692. But their constant struggle against the extended powers of officers of the pen filled the greater part of the next century.

In the eyes of the sword, the pen comprised a few gentlemen, *bon bourgeois*, and sons of artisans: a veritable nest of Saint-Simon's "vile bourgeois" that ought to be subordinate to the sword. Accompanying this social prejudice was the apparently logical claim that the continual opposition to each other of the two corps would form a monster whose parts would languish and which would destroy itself. Officers of the sword pressed strongly the view that only naval officers who went to sea should be charged with the inspection of material, munitions, stores, and provisions.[64] Unfortunately, little evidence exists to show that naval officers were interested in, or capable of, executing the duties of the pen.

Lacking the social prestige of the sword, officers of the pen relied upon the independence of their corps and their own expert knowledge to withstand the sword's onslaught. Seriously undermined during the final years of Louis XIV's reign and the Regency, the corps' independence from the sword was officially confirmed by Maurepas in 1734, by a ruling that when serving ashore officers of the pen were subordinate only to the intendant. Nine years later he confirmed that scriveners were not subordinate to naval officers. Official statements, however, could not overcome the frequent hostility of the sword.[65]

Personal insults frequently occurred at the highest level. When Lenormant de Mézy arrived to take up his new appointment as intendant of Rochefort he received no honours at all from officers of the sword. A shocked observer fresh from Canada reported that "there is not an *enseigne* who does not believe himself above the intendant."[66] On the occasion of Hocquart's marriage at Brest, the commandant refused any honours to his wife. Later, when he was intendant at Brest, Ruis-Embito was afraid to circulate through the arsenal, being unarmed and fearing insults from junior naval officers.[67] Quarrels, altercations, and duels commonly broke out between *gardes de la marine* or *enseignes de vaisseaux* and junior officers of the pen, but insults at intermediate levels were more subtle. When mustering *gardes de la marine* at Rochefort for inspection by the *commissaire* charged with their review it was customary for officers not to wear their swords.[68] Soldiers in the arsenal were inspected monthly by a *commissaire* who kept the muster rolls.[69] At Toulon, *Commissaire-général* Michel viewed their commander's behaviour towards this officer as an example of "the scorn that the military has striven for some years to inspire in all circumstances against officers of the pen ."[70] The rancour generated in the heart of the marquis de Massiac, the commandant at Toulon, against Jean-Baptiste Michel de Caseneuve had serious consequences, for the latter did not succeed Villeblanche as intendant, being transferred instead to Rochefort without promotion after the commandant became secretary of state.

Naval artillery officers in the arsenals came under the authority of the intendant, who alone possessed the right to order inspections of naval ordnance, controlled production and received their reports. The discomfort and displeasure of these officers at their subordinate position led to "conduct full of incidents of anxiety and insubordination," and contributed to delays in producing sufficient numbers of guns for the fleet.[71] Commandants often supported artillery officers, ordering them to produce reports on the quality, number and designation of guns in the forges and arsenals owing to intendants' refusals to impart this information. Other inspections gave rise to similar difficulties, commandants seeking information and intendants and their officers refusing to divulge it on the ground that officers of the sword neither had need to know nor authorization to receive it.[72]

The bitter resentment of social inferiors engaged in essential but unrewarding tasks underlay the lack of cooperation of officers of the pen. In their eyes their loyal service and zealous probity was never sufficiently acknowledged. After a multitude of honours and favours had been showered on officers who took part in the Minorca campaign, Villeblanche bitterly rebuked Machault for giving recognition to the military who rendered only momentary service while the men under his command who worked year in and year out were forgotten.[73] Hocquart was no different at Brest, complaining bitterly over the lack of rewards for his nominees and its bad effect on his staff: "I have the discomfort of seeing them without encouragement in circumstances where the difficulty of labour and costliness of living seem to combine to sicken them."[74]

Ministers could not resolve the animosity between members of the two corps for rigid adherence to the articles of the 1689 Naval Ordinance often left officers of the pen technically correct in their quarrels with the other corps. The ordinance entangled duties and jurisdictions of the two corps in a multitude of imprecise, overlapping, and contradictory ways. The sensitive issue of command afloat and the position of officers of the pen aboard warships clearly reveals the dilemma. Appealing to Book 1, title 11, clause 18 of the ordinance, naval scriveners claimed not to need a captain's permission to go ashore, contending that they merely had to tell him that they were doing so. Captains, on the other hand, appealed to Book 4, title 4, clause 30, which forbade anyone going ashore without their permission. Captains delighted in harassing junior officers of the pen when ships were being fitted out and scriveners moved constantly back and forth from ship to shore and from ship to ship. While the largest squadron in years was being readied at Brest in the spring of 1755, the practice grew to such an extent that the minister finally administered a stern rebuke to its commander to order his captains to cease harassment.[75] On the other hand, scriveners were often provocative. When the commander of a galley squadron ordered copies of the crew, convict and passenger rolls from his captains, the scrivener on board one galley refused, going so far as to shake his finger at his captain while crying that he was not a copyist.[76] In June 1757 a royal ordinance attempted to resolve this delicate issue of the right of independent movement of scriveners by ordering them in future to seek permission from commanding officers before leaving their ships and denying the latter the right of refusal without reasons. The king reserved to himself the right to deal with scriveners who asked unnecessarily and officers who refused.[77] The ordinance failed, for it acknowledged the independence of the pen from the sword and exacerbated conflict with the latter, whose members saw themselves within a hair's breadth of winning the struggle.

But if tension between the corps was institutionalized in the Naval Ordinance, new social forces were appearing during the 1750s. Efforts by Rouillé and Machault to check the pretensions of the sword and reimpose unity of command in the arsenals account for the fierceness of the quarrels during the years leading up to the Seven Years' War and during the war itself. If the conflicts between the pen and the sword were minimal under Maurepas, it was because the minister did little to curb the sword's striving for independence ashore or to check the decline of the intendants' power in the arsenals.[78] Discipline and centralization of authority had collapsed during the War of the Austrian Succession.[79] Rouillé recognized the deleterious effect of this development and quickly affirmed his desire to restore unity of command in the arsenals. "Please inform *messieurs*, the officers in your department," he instructed the intendant of Toulon "that they will receive no reply and I will not give any consideration to requests that they make directly to me or that come to me by any other way than through you."[80] A member of the *noblesse administratif* himself, Rouillé backed the pen to regain control of the navy's general administration. According to Lenormant de Mézy, Rochefort's two previous intendants had been plagued by encroachments of the sword. "They abandoned, so to speak, the reins of the service that were confided to them; and to have peace, they renounced their prerogatives from which followed a general laxity in both corps."[81] Encroachments of the sword fatigued some, disheartened others and undermined enthusiasm and good will for the service. In the absence of support from the court, compliance replaced discouragement as the surest means to achieve harmony and preserve some personal consideration from officers of the sword. But from compliance it was a short step to the state of discredit and ignorance that characterized the corps of the pen at mid-century. After 1750, however, officers of the pen increasingly resisted the sword. Lacking the property interests of venal office-holders, they placed great emphasis on their corporate interests which can be defined as those preserving their independence from officers of the sword. This was possible because officers of the sword had a far stronger self-interest that militated against a unified corporate thrust by the sword against the pen. Ironically, the appointment of three intendants and promotions to *commissaire-général* from outside the corps suggest that the greatest threat to the corporate interests of officers of the pen had subtly shifted from the sword to the *noblesse de robe* and the court just when officers of the pen sought to succeed against their old rivals.

The two objectives, control over disputes between officers of the two corps and restoration of unity of command in the arsenals, were mutually exclusive in the volatile tinderbox of French domestic politics. Only the utter annihilation of the navy enabled reform to surface at the end of the Seven Years' War. To extinguish rivalry and control the administration required the overthrow of the 1689 Naval Ordinance. In the eyes of royal administrators, who viewed the ordinance in its pristine state as a pillar of monarchical absolutism, this was clearly impossible. But unlike Berryer and his predecessors, who were members of the monarchy's administrative elite, the duc de Choiseul was ripe to hear the pleas of naval officers to overthrow the pen. A soldier, statesman, and peer of France, disgusted with the weapon that turned in his hand, he willingly subordinated intendants to commandants in the ports and permitted the sword to invade the commissariat. The royal ordinance of 23 March 1762 not only reformed the corps of the pen and reduced its numbers, it was the first step leading to its subordination to the sword.[82] But the incompetence of naval officers of the sword and the minister's need to rely on *premiers commis* in the central bureaux saved the pen. A second reforming ordinance issued three years later abolished the official appellation of "corps de plume" and reorganized its members as *officiers d'administration*. But by substituting their own draft of the ordinance for one prepared by a naval officer and surrendering intendants' powers over naval officers ashore, the corps of the pen preserved the substance of its independence.[83] After Choiseul's departure, the pendulum of favour swung back to the pen where special expertise and knowledge of forms were more in keeping with the challenge of modernization than the reactionary reformism of officers of the sword. Efforts to reform naval organization continued to the end of the Old Regime, favouring first one then the other corps, but never reconciling administrative and military duties or determining the relationship between them.

Nevertheless, conflict within the navy may have contributed to the department's ability to change to meet current challenges. Despite the evidence of animosity, tension and quarrelling that fills pages of correspondence between the arsenals and the court, a great deal was accomplished. The arsenals were revived, materials received and manufactured, ships built and fitted out, and crews levied. Moreover, the greatest obstacles to administrative success were neither the personnel of the pen nor the Naval Ordinance of 1689 which gave them so much power ashore, but long-term financial constraints and heavy short-term demands. If, in view of the small scale of naval organization, the margin between order and chaos was narrow, it required only a short bridge to span the gap.[84]

Only a few hundred men organized and prepared the navy to meet the government's demands, levying thousands of sailors to man the king's ships and thousands more to labour in his arsenals. The small scale of naval organization checked chaos in two ways. First, the multiple converging roles of senior naval administrators, political, judicial and financial, limited the degree to which the periphery could move from the centre. The centralized bureaucratic control condemned by historians like Tocqueville was beyond the reach of mid-eighteenth-century government officials. But neither was the goal too far away. The navy, after all, was a new institution organized after Louis xiv came to power. Few local elites possessing legally entrenched property rights existed to contend with the royal authority. There was only the natural tendency of agents of the monarchy who lived and worked among local elites to reach accommodations with them. The deficiency lay in the serious failure to recruit officers of the pen from the commercial class in the seaports which may be presumed to have been familiar with the sea. Second, family relations and broader associations arising from marriage played positive roles in the small-scale naval organization, reducing rivalries between members of opposed social groups, and generating unorganized efforts to accomplish the navy's aims. Naval administrators were specialists only to the degree that they employed their expert knowledge in a society that depended on social elites to exercise royal authority. Independent behaviour was natural among officers of the pen. The navy existed to accomplish goals separate from those of members of the organization. The interests of the organization were not incompatible with, but neither were they identical to, the individual interests of those whose task it was to achieve the navy's goals. Promotion, wealth, social advancement, political power, and prestige were all legitimate goals of individuals, but the navy did not exist to foster any of them. Groups were formed within the navy to pursue their own interests. These group formations, however, were both social and organizational. The most conspicuous social group-formations were the two officer corps, but subordinate social groups also existed, and these cut across formal organizations within the navy, reducing tensions between the arsenals, between the central bureaux and the arsenals, and between the two corps of officers.

The corps of the pen was the greatest source of its own recruits, but entrants also came from the corps of the sword. Brothers of Ruis-Embito and Hocquart were *capitaines des vaisseaux*, Michel Bégon's first cousin was *Chef d'escadre* Barrin de la Galissonière, Bigot de la Motte's son was among the navy's most intelligent and active officers of the sword. Family connections also extended far beyond the navy into finances, army, magistracy, and the court. Hocquart, for example, had two more brothers who were treasurer-general of artillery and engineering and farmer-general respectively.[85] Louis Charron the younger succeeded his father as *chevalier d'honneur* in the *Cour des monnaies* before becoming a naval *commissaire-général*, and Lenormant de Mézy was distantly related by marriage to Madame de Pompadour.[86] Only extensive research into the social origins and alliances of the entire naval personnel of the pen and the sword will reveal the extent of cross-corps relations, but there is no doubt that it was extensive.[87] Family ties and associations, extending beyond the navy in pursuit of self-interest, militated against prejudices that character-ized each corps, reduced tensions between them, and were the means of achieving response to change.

Finally, conflict from outside the navy in the form of the Seven Years' War itself fostered demands and generated possibilities for reform of naval organization. One might well ask whether interpersonal and intergroup conflict within the navy encouraged flexibility and responsiveness to such demands for change. Equilibrium, harmony, and stability in organizations may not be the conditions in which change is most likely to occur in response to outside stimuli. Lack of equilibrium, disharmony, and instability, so pronounced in eighteenth-century French naval organiza-tion, may not be deficiencies as has been almost universally claimed. Conflict arising from uneven distribution of power and rewards in the navy may have contributed significantly to change.[88]

During the 1750s the design and construction of warships came into full flower, naval ordnance production went through a technological revolu-tion, and arsenals, neglected for decades, revived and expanded. These developments must be weighed in any assessment of officers of the pen. Universally condemned by their contemporaries of the sword and most historians ever since, officers of the pen and the organization through which they exercised power during the 1750s have been made scapegoats for French naval failures during the century. In order to consider this judgment, however, we must go on to examine more closely their compeers of the sword.

CHAPTER FOUR

Officers of the Sword

Naval officers comprised only a small cadre in the large French military establishment. But their minor position contrasted sharply with the navy's relation to France's commercial well-being, the large sums of money expended on it, and its strategic importance. These anomalies grew out of the economic development of the French colonies, the growth of maritime trade during the second quarter of the eighteenth century, and the absence of any comprehensive naval strategy in France. Maritime commercial and colonial growth appeared to develop independently of foreign policy, and without the development of a comprehensive naval strategy, it was not at all clear that any relation existed between naval and foreign policy. As a result, naval policy lagged behind new realities, remaining subject to the traditional continentalist orientations of French statesmen. The navy largely reacted to events that it did not influence.

The naval response to the challenge of empire during the 1740s proved weak and the next decade saw the challenge renewed more strongly. Initially, French reaction was vigorous, but during the Seven Years' War the officer corps was professionally and militarily humiliated. Public odium rose to unheard-of heights and the government soon became of the same mind. By the end of 1761 the naval secretary of state shunned the officer corps and aimed at its reform. That the French navy failed to develop an adequate response to new challenges in wartime was largely a product of the attitudes, values, and behaviour of the officer corps.

In the absence of any royal interest in naval power, naval officers possessed no central focus of loyalty. Past traditions focused upon operations in the Mediterranean and the English Channel. Ideas of squadron warfare competed with the realities of privateering and the traditions of galley combat. Perhaps the greatest weakness of the eighteenth-century French navy was not a shortage of courageous and

TABLE 3

Size of the Officer Corps and *Gardes de la Marine*, 1749–1763

Grade	Numbers						
	1749	1751	1755	1757	1759	1761	1763
Vice-amiral	–	1	2	2	2	2	2
Lt.-général des armées navales	5	4	5	6	6	5	5
Chef d'escadre	21	15	13	16	18	17	16
Capitaine de Vaisseau	130	125	148	200	208	181	134
Lieutenant de Vaisseau	203	195	230	321	323	300	313
Capitaine de brûlot	6	5	5	7	10	7	?
Enseigne de Vaisseau	366	353	361	395	406	356	359
Lieutenant de Frégate	14	13	14	16	27	25	?
Capitaine de Flûte	4	4	3	3	5	4	?
Total (officers)	749	715	781	966	1005	897	829?
Gardes du Pavillon		59			46		
Gardes de la Marine		169			521		
Total (gardes)		228			567		

Sources: Marine G, 38; 121, ff. 203–13; 127, f. 161; 128, f. 22; 244; and BN, Mss. frs., nos. 14, 286–7.

devoted officers, but the inability of these men to explain to statesmen what the navy could and could not do.

French naval officers were not numerous; in 1748 few were available for duty at sea. Despite some growth during the 1740s, the corps remained smaller than at the end of Louis xiv's reign, and its spirit was demoralized.[1] In 1751 the corps comprised 715 officers of all grades (table 3). Numbers grew by less than 10 per cent during the next four years, but the corps' strength increased by 24 per cent in the two years following the opening of hostilities. Thereafter growth was very slow; from 1759 onwards the number of officers declined. The causes lay in the deaths of many old officers and the navy's poor performance, which led to a deliberate reduction in an effort to begin the reform of the corps. The scarcity of promotions after 1757 and the forced retirement of more than one hundred officers also led many young men to leave the service before the war concluded.[2]

The lack of strong direction and influence on the part of the most senior naval officers, as well as the absence of anyone who was known and respected throughout the naval service, further weakened the corps. In a society where military service and values permeated the institutions of the nobility, poor social and professional leadership made it difficult for junior officers to establish a separate identity from the army or to find cohesion among themselves. Naval esprit de corps remained characterized by exclusiveness, factionalism, and insubordination rather than by loyalty to the service.[3]

No tradition of a unified naval service existed in France. Cardinal Richelieu attempted unification of the kingdom's maritime forces by suppressing the charge of admiral, assuming the title of Admiral of Brittany, forcing the governor of Provence to cease calling himself Admiral of the Levant, and purchasing the generalcy of the galleys.[4] But Richelieu's efforts failed and further attempts awaited Colbert who was not entirely successful. Colbert revived the office of Admiral of France, but checked its influence and removed a potential focus for unity by reserving the charge for the king's natural sons. Jean-Louis-Marie de Bourbon, duc de Penthièvre, who obtained the charge in 1737 at the age of twelve, failed to develop an interest in the navy, and the office of Admiral of France reverted to its former character of having several valuable financial perquisites but no executive duties and little influence. The General of the Galleys had once been an influencial charge, but it too became a sinecure confided to the natural sons of the Bourbon family. The last incumbent, Jean-Philippe, chevalier d'Orléans, had been appointed in 1708 at the age of five. He also became Grand Prior of France of the Military Hospitaller Order of Saint John of Jerusalem and wielded considerable influence among his fellow Knights of Malta in the navy. His fight to keep the independent galley corps as an integral part of French naval power weakened the drive for unity.[5] Only after the chevalier's unexpected demise in June 1748 was the galley corps integrated into the sailing navy; only then could the officer corps be said to have been unified, although not united.

Most galley officers retired; but twenty-eight, including three flag officers, transferred to the sailing navy.[6] The influence of the galley corps persisted through these officers, many of whom were also Knights of Malta and among the most aristocratic officers in the navy.[7] France's oldest naval traditions were associated with the Knights of Malta, over half of whom were French. In 1755, fifty knights served in the navy and four years later there were seventy-three.[8] The navy's relation to the order was so close that young officers and *gardes de la marine* who were aspiring knights could absent themselves from duty for two years to make their first *caravane* in the famous Galleys of the Religion at Malta. By the mid-eighteenth century, however, the principal task of the order's vessels was to voyage in the Western Mediterranean to collect the revenues of different commanderies. On Malta novice knights lived a dissolute life; nothing remained of the religious aspects of their careers. Although their tours merely gave knights opportunities for duelling, gaming, and scandals, the navy continued to pay their appointments and even for the time spent voyaging to and from the island.[9] Knights of the order had to make four *caravanes* before the age of fifty to be eligible to possess commanderies, which disrupted their subsequent service to the king. Thus, in the absence of direction from the king or senior naval officers of the crown, the government's close relation to the Order of Saint John drove a further wedge into the potential unity of the officer corps, dividing its members and providing a competing focus for loyalty.

General officers of the corps, too, failed to provide alternative examples for emulation. Three grades of general officers stood at the head of the officer corps: *vice-amiral, lieutenant-général des armées navales,* and *chef d'escadre.*

Vice-amiral had no military equivalent, for it was senior to army *lieutenant-général* yet inferior to marshal of France. Despite its elevation and prestige, holders of the rank generally had little influence. For more than three years prior to 1750 the navy did not even have its most senior grade filled. *Vice-amiraux* had been drawn from great noble houses but Rouillé ignored the tradition of selecting men from great families and obtained agreement to the appointment of Vincent de Salaberry de Benneville, and Claude-Elisée de Court de la Bruyère, aged eighty-six and eighty-three respectively. The age and infirmities of these men and their successors lessened the navy's influence at court, for they came and went with great rapidity; nine more officers who advanced to the grade by 1762 were on average seventy-seven years old.

Lieutenants-généraux des armées navales were the senior naval officers afloat. Designated for independent command afloat, *lieutenants-généraux* had little influence on naval planning. Their professional conduct, however, was all-important concerning the success of naval operations. The junior grade of general officer, *chef d'escadre,* sometimes exercised independent command.[10] Port commandants were normally chosen from *chefs d'escadre,* but when given command afloat, these officers were generally failures. None carried out a successful mission during the Seven Years' War. A fourth senior grade, *maréchal de France,* was rarely conferred on naval officers. *Vice-amiral* Conflans, who obtained his baton on 18 March 1758, was the sixth and last naval marshal of the Old Regime.

Promotion of general grade officers by seniority regularized the service, but also reflected their lack of influence. It was unusual for considerations of interest and favour not to influence senior promotions. To insist upon seniority as the basis for promotion challenged an absolute monarch's prerogative to reward distinguished service and grant favours or else reflected upon the importance of the position in question. Seniority was not a basis for influence. The notion of personal merit was also foreign to the officer corps. Promotion due to personal merit is a middle-class concept that ignores aristocratic values of pedigree and privilege. Seniority rather than favour can be blamed for the poor quality of the navy's general officers.

By mid-century the navy's general officers had grown old in the service. Four-fifths had joined the navy during the previous reign; several as long ago as the 1680s. In 1749 the average age of general officers was sixty-nine.[11] The typical general officer had entered the navy in his early teens, spent twenty-nine years as a junior officer, sixteen more as *capitaine de vaisseau,* and was promoted *chef d'escadre* in his fifty-ninth year. Afterwards he held general grade until his death at the age of seventy-two.[12]

Age need not be a critical factor, but the last half-century of inactivity had exacted its toll. Lethargy, caution, and inexperience were the chief professional characteristics of the navy's general officers during the Seven Years' War. They had lived through several decades of government neglect. Most were middle-aged before they achieved their first command and this had usually occurred only after 1744. Many conducted themselves bravely, but few had ever commanded large formations, nor was there opportunity to obtain experience during the years of peace.

The most regular executive responsibilities of general officers were exercised by port commandants who were assigned to each arsenal in 1745.[13] The new charges were not sinecures, for commandants were responsible for ordering officers to embark on ships and for assigning them elsewhere in the department or to other maritime departments.[14] Commandants also received missives from the secretary of state who stated his complaints about officers' conduct and forwarded others from parents, wives, and creditors. Commandants were quick, however, to defend officers from the minister's wrath, excuse those who were absent without leave, and intercede on behalf of those ruined by drink and cards or who were in trouble with civil authorities. The arrogant, immature behaviour of young officers and *gardes de la marine* often left commandants defending assault, rape, and even murder while bemoaning the wickedness and bad will of victims who called civil authorities to their aid. The independent behaviour of these aristocrats, often quick to draw the sword and reluctant to obey others on the basis of seniority or rank, severely limited the freedom of action of commandants, who customarily gained the respect and esteem of their officers to the degree that they could defend them and advance their careers.[15] Their letter-books became filled with requests on behalf of captains and junior officers for favours, pensions, gratuities, honours, and for permision to marry or to leave the service.

Aside from an officer's own conduct, the influence of families also constrained naval discipline. Marriage requests had to be taken seriously, creditors handled delicately, and demands for three-month and one-year leaves treated with tact and diplomacy when balanced against the needs of the service. Intendants who jealously guarded their prerogative to give orders to officers in their jurisdiction also checked the authority of commandants. As *chefs d'escadre* most commandants were outranked in naval precedence by intendants. But despite these limitations commandants were indispensable for imposing subordination among officers, and were important precursors of a unified corps.

The navy divided its *officiers particuliers* into *capitaines des vaisseaux* and *officiers subalternes*, chiefly *lieutenants des vaisseaux* and *enseignes des vaisseaux*. Only captains possessed royal commissions; the rest held their ranks by brevet. Promotion to all grades was by favour and distinguished service, as well as seniority, but never, as in the British navy, by post or employment. Captain's rank was not attached to command of a ship of twenty guns or more as in Great Britain. Indeed, at mid-century French ships of the line normally carried two *capitaines des vaisseaux*, the *capitaine commandant* and *commandant en second*, whose status aboard was below that of the senior lieutenant or first officer; second captains were aboard to gain experience before obtaining their own commands.[16]

Of 128 *capitaines des vaisseaux* in 1749, sixty-two had been promoted before 1744 and sixty-six afterwards.[17] They had served an average of thirty-four years as subaltern officers, five years longer than current general grade officers.[18] Almost all had held commands by 1749 and many saw action during the War of the Austrian Succession. But as a group the captains were old and many were infirm. Forty-four had not been to sea in the previous five years and ten years later more than one-third of the total number had died.[19] Some were killed in action, but most succumbed to sickness or old age. Hoary old sea-dogs (*loups der mer*) some might be, but fifty years of decline and neglect had obscured the living connection with the battle tradition of Louis xiv's young navy and produced a great many over-aged junior officers, too long passed over for promotion. The cautious advancement of their own careers during the first half of the century inhibited vigorous action as *capitaines des vaiseaux* during the great mid-century maritime and colonial struggle. New captains appeared, to be sure, but the captains of 1749 and the general officers set the tone of the entire corps during the war.

About twenty-five captains held shore appointments. In theory the remaining captains were available for sea appointments, but with many quite elderly, others inexperienced in command, and the fleet approaching sixty ships of the line, each requiring two *capitaines des vaisseaux*, there was no excess of captains. Indeed, it is a great myth that the officer corps suffered from an excess of numbers, especially in wartime, for the French navy lacked any reserve of officers. This was also true of *les officiers subalternes*. It is sometimes reported that in 1756 about seven hundred of 914 officers in the navy had no other duties than to mount eight or nine 24-hour guards each year, but the statement is clearly untrue.[20]

A large proportion of junior officers, perhaps one-third of the corps, served in the *compagnies franches de la marine*, and additional duties occupied 113 more junior officers. The remainder were theoretically available for sea duty but the shortage of naval officers remained. The expedition fitting out for North America in 1755 required an estimated 360 officers. At Brest, where the scarcity was most severe, twenty-five *lieutenants* and thirty-five *enseignes* were summoned from Toulon and Rochefort.[21] The burst of promotions between 1755 and 1757 reflected the greatly expanded need for junior officers. By 1759 three-quarters of all *lieutenants* and *enseignes* had reached their grade during the first three years of hostilities.[22]

The navy also possessed four intermediate grades: *capitaine de frégate, capitaine de brûlot, lieutenant de frégate,* and *capitaine de flûte.* Although never widespread in the corps these grades had once been held by current senior officers. But by the middle of the eighteenth century *capitaine de frégate* had disappeared entirely and the other grades had fallen into contempt.[23] Nobles no matter how inexperienced refused to obey commoners no matter how talented.[24]

Only twenty-two intermediate grade officers remained in the navy in 1755, the same number as four years before. But the lack of a reserve officer corps, the navigational inexperience of many junior officers, and the growing demands of wartime service, especially for skilled sailors to serve in the hard pressed corvettes and frigates engaged in unrewarding but essential escort duties, protecting supply and munitions convoys to Brest and Rochefort, led to the idea of admitting commoners to the navy with intermediate grades.[25] These were the *officiers bleus*, so-called to contrast them with the *officiers rouges* of the grand corps.[26] By 1759 the number of intermediate grade officers had nearly doubled to forty-two.[27] The increase in number aroused a storm of protest from the corps out of all proportion to the number of new officers. If such entries continued, warned a commander of a company of *gardes*, parents would withdraw their sons from the service.[28] Though in no mood to relieve naval officers' bruised feelings, Berryer was forced to consider the corps' intransigent attitude.[29] Choiseul thought otherwise and sought to increase the number of intermediate grade officers as a major step in reforming the officer corps. After the war he reestablished the grade of *capitaine de frégate*, promoted fifty officers to the rank, and opened the more junior intermediate grades to merchant captains of proven dash.[30] But Choiseul's attempt to recreate the corps on a new footing was doomed to failure; he alone could not overcome the social and political influence of the nobility, nor is it clear that he wished to.[31]

About 5 per cent of the navy's officers served in the artillery branch. But the legacy of confusion and resentment over advancement of these officers and the anomalies in respect to their grades and those of other officers before 1750 added to intraservice tension caused by the presence of commoners in the corps. On the other hand, the presence of twelve former artillery officers, nearly 10 per cent of the total, in the 1749 captains' list testified to the talent and hard-working practices of this small group.

The artillery had first attracted commoners who could not expect to enter the *gardes*, but by the middle of the eighteenth century this was no longer true. Nevertheless the artillery remained a valuable route to high command. Senior *gardes* without fortune or favour, who might wait many years before becoming officers and whose classmates were already *enseignes*, found refuge in the service. The artillery also attracted the ambitious and talented, as well as men simply bored in the neglected, peacetime navy who perceived a challenge in mastering the difficult art of the guns: men who hoped to attract attention by their special skill and continuous service.

In addition to the questionable origins of some artillery officers and the intermediate nature of their grades, the control of their movements in the arsenals by intendants proved another obstacle to integrating the artillery branch into the grand corps. This subordination of professionals to administrators galled the officers, who frequently attempted to assert their independence, but in the eyes of their compeers they were less than full members of the corps.[32] The branch had been reformed in 1741 in an effort to reduce distinctions between naval officers and improve morale among artillery officers, but the changes met with only partial success.[33] By 1748 morale was at a new low and the drive to achieve parity with the rest of the officer corps was strong. Two years later Rouillé reformed the artillery branch again.[34] Rouillé favoured artillery officers, for most were talented and hard working, but he failed to see, now that parity with sea officers was achieved, that a separate service was no longer needed in a navy long familiar with battles at sea. Some officers in the grand corps resented the altered position of artillery officers and the branch became viewed as a fraudulent means to achieve rapid promotion.[35] Late in 1761 the duc de Choiseul recognized that a separate artillery service was no longer needed and got rid of a divisive element in the officer corps by uniting it to the reorganized Regiment of Royal Artillery.[36]

Port officers made up the fourth and final element of the officer corps. In 1759 there were forty-four port officers.[37] Once a route for commoners to enter the navy, this branch of the service, too, had become more exclusive as sons followed their fathers' footsteps. Although *enseignes, lieutenants,* and *capitaines de port* were carried on officer lists with equivalence to similar grades in the grand corps, they were not considered members in the eyes of some because they were responsible to the intendant for their duties and did not sit on courts martial.[38] Attitudes towards port officers conflicted, for their importance in the arsenals was so great that contempt for their origins and their status under the intendant could not obscure the merits of their service.[39]

So unhappy was the organization of the officer corps that it failed to promote either unity in or loyalty to the service. The various grades and appointments only promoted divisions. Although lip service was paid to entry into the officer corps from the merchant marine through intermediate grades, the navy clearly held few attractions for merchant officers or the sons of wealthy ship outfitters and merchants in the seaports. By denying ambitious commoners an opportunity to purchase rank and status the absence of venality actually contributed to the navy's unattractiveness and reinforced its caste-like nature. But although the navy remained the preserve of the nobility, social exclusiveness did not promote unity.

Entry into the eighteenth-century officer corps was through the three companies of *gardes de la marine* established at Brest, Rochefort, and Toulon and the company of *gardes du pavillon-amiral* stationed in two detachments at Brest and Toulon. Although no difference in rank existed, an important distinction among *gardes* had been created. While commoners had been rare in the seventeenth century, the long interval of peace between 1713 and 1740 and reduction in the size of the officer corps made the mid-eighteenth-century corps more exclusive than before.

The Naval Ordinance of 1689 omitted to fix the age of admission, but candidates generally reached the arsenals in their fifteenth year.[40] At least a few twelve-year-olds, however, entered the *gardes* at the beginning of the Seven Years' War, which may have led Berryer to restrict admission to those between sixteen and twenty.[41]

Prior to 1750 a *garde*'s seniority in the navy dated from the moment his letter of appointment (*certificat*) was registered in the arsenal to which he was posted rather than from its date of issue. This gave an important advantage to those living close to the arsenal over those who lived weeks of travel away from their assigned ports. In an effort to be more equitable Rouillé ordered commandants to allow *gardes* six weeks to report before registering their letters. But so closed had the navy become that Rouillé was forced to establish two classes of *gardes*: "les enfants du corps" and the rest. Sons, grandsons, and nephews on the paternal side were to have precedence over other *gardes* who entered at the same time. Thus, in addition to distinctions between *gardes du pavillon* and *gardes*, a reinforced obstacle of birth was substituted for one of distance.[42]

The 1689 ordinance also stipulated that parents provide new *gardes* with at least 400 livres annually in order that they might live in a manner befitting the officer corps. Their annual appointments of 216 livres were clearly inadequate, for *gardes* were expected to feed and lodge themselves in private chambers in the port. Careful parents assigned such funds to a trusted friend or to the treasurer of the navy in the port, who doled them out parsimoniously to the adolescent, but others armed their sons directly with incomes approaching those of a *capitaine de vaisseau*.[43] From the beginning of their naval careers, then, birth and wealth created distinctions among *gardes* which no amount of naval esprit could overcome. Individual *gardes* pursued their own careers according to their personal endowments and idiosyncratic behaviour.

The court nobility was never well represented in the navy, which provided fewer attractions and less prestige than the army. In 1755 when the navy's general officers numbered twenty, the army contained an astonishing total of 786 officers possessing general grades.[44] The royal navy was less than three generations old while the origins of the senior service were lost in the mists of time. Moreover, the army was the last bastion of the old aristocracy and if great families were present in the navy at all, it was younger sons who were found there. Although the navy possessed a few members of great families, Louis xv's lack of personal interest in the navy denied high social position to naval officers at court. While in theory the king controlled access to the officer corps, in practice the corps controlled its own membership.

By mid-century the prime source of officers was the navy itself. At least twenty of fifty-four general officers who served between 1748 and 1762 had direct naval antecedents, and a similar situation existed among *officiers particuliers* and *gardes de la marine*. Of 361 *enseignes des vaisseaux* in 1755, 112 (31 per cent) had direct paternal antecedents, including fathers, grandfathers, and uncles. Despite claims to the contrary, the *corps de plume* had few representatives at this rank, which suggests in another way the growing exclusiveness of the corps.[45] Moreover, in a society dedicated to family continuity as much as to social advancement, naval officers from the pen were invariably younger sons.[46] Louis xv set the seal on recruitment from the pen in 1750 with official instructions that sons, grandsons, and nephews of intendants, *commissaires-généraux*, and *commissaires de la marine* were to enjoy all of the privileges of "enfants du corps" when admitted to the *gardes*.[47] By mid-century, however, the largest number of *gardes* with naval antecedents came from the sword.

The navy chiefly attracted the provincial nobility. Toulon was practically the preserve of the nobility of Provence and Languedoc which had been oriented towards the Mediterranean world of the galleys for centuries, while Brittany supplied the largest share of officers for the sailing navy.[48] Few officers came from Burgundy or central and eastern France and surprisingly few from Normandy. With perhaps more than 50 per cent of all officers from the southeast and Brittany, the areas most remote from Versailles, regional origins increased the divisions created by social origin and varied status within the service. Geographical separation of the officer corps by port reinforced this provincialism.[49] Provençal officers made great efforts to remain at Toulon and struggled to return there when posted away under Rouillé's and Machault's policy of encouraging the circulation of officers throughout the ports.[50] The cultural differences between contrasting historical legacies of Mediterranian and Atlantic officers reinforced the geographical separation to create two distinct officer corps.

With so many divisions and tensions in the officer corps it would be unfair to blame the education of naval officers for deficiencies that are traceable to other sources. Nevertheless, naval education left much to be desired. The degree of professional and scientific knowledge varied greatly among officers. The curious argument of some naval historians that paucity of training in naval warfare was compensated by a strong orientation towards scientific inquiry that produced a militarily passive but brilliant, scholarly officer corps does not stand up to scrutiny.[51] The scientific accomplishments of the few were exceptions to the general indifference and ignorance of the many. By mid-century commanding officers had even abandoned the custom of depositing their navigation journals in the arsenals on their return from sea and the practice of charting unknown shores and harbour entrances had grown rare.[52]

The earliest system of education for naval officers was introduced in response to the navy's considerable growth under Colbert, the wretched quality of navigation, and the demand for professionalism in a land-oriented, aristocratic officer corps unfamiliar with the sea.[53] Maurepas appeared dissatisfied with the quality of *gardes'* education during the 1740s, and when the professor of hydrography at Toulon, Father Jean-Jacques Duchâtelard, published his *Cahiers de géometrie* in 1748, three hundred copies were purchased for instructional use.[54] The same year Duchâtelard published his much larger *Recueil de traités de mathématiques à l'usagae des gardes de la marine* in two volumes and the navy immediately purchased two hundred copies for distribution to Brest and Rochefort and presented a gratuity of 1,800 livres to its author.[55] Duchâtelard's work served as the basic professional text in naval education for the next fourteen years. *Gardes* also received practical instruction in design and navigation from the master painter and senior pilot (*pilot de vice-amiral*) in each arsenal.

The educational arrangements ought to have provided the navy with a well-educated officer corps. Instruction was obviously elementary, considering the youth and varied experience of the *gardes*, but mathematics formed the core of the curriculum. Mental discipline might have been imposed and scientific curiosity developed, but in general neither condition obtained. Practical difficulties frequently intervened. Opposition between types of instruction can be traced to the 1689 Naval Ordinance, where one hour a week was set aside for mathematics and two hours daily were devoted to dancing, fencing, and exercise with the pike. The twofold character of *gardes'* education, ashore and afloat, reinforced the other difficulties. Education required continuity while practical navigation depended upon the availability of ships, time, and the demands of the service. Senior officers generally opposed educational demands at sea. War interrupted training afloat and peacetime often ended it. *Gardes* sometimes did not return to sea for years. Entry into the *gardes* and their organization provided a further difficulty. Entry was without examination, and lack of uniform standards of education and age of admission made it almost impossible to teach anything beyond the simplest concepts. Moreover, the practice of dating seniority from entry into the *gardes* rather than from date of promotion to *enseigne de vaisseau* ran counter to a rational system of education. Aristocratic *gardes* were not amenable to discipline administered by civilian teachers; and the presence of *gardes du pavillon* and *enfants du corps* established important distinctions among students.

No one thought highly of naval schools. One critic claimed that "many of these gentlemen leave school scarcely more educated than when they enter"; another claimed that officers scarcely knew how to write their names.[56] Others blamed the crushing defeats of the war on the poor quality of education. But this was unfair and far from the mark.[57] The form of naval education could be justified as producing clear-thinking officers, but its twofold purpose was directed elsewhere. First, it was designed to recruit officers from a land-oriented, military aristocracy into the navy rather than educate those it had; and second, as was the case in the army, it aimed to seal off the navy from the civilian world of dangerous ideas and provide its own modern basis of aristocratic culture.[58]

Lack of social and cultural homogeneity, internal divisions and external rivalries, poor education and professional training characterized the naval officer corps. The eighty or so years of its modern existence had not provided sufficent common experience to create a unified body. Geographical separation and competing traditions hindered emergence of a single naval tradition, while lack of prestige and diverse social and regional origins promoted disharmony. Far from a band of brothers being created, the existence of different groups with clashing interests and relations marked by animosity and envy resulted in a vicious factionalism. A shocked and horrified Berryer summed up the corps when he wrote that "in the navy they all hate one another."[59] Social position and family connections might be thought to count for less in a young service that demanded considerable technical skill, but a hierarchy of birth clashed continually with one of naval rank. Favour and influence challenged seniority and merit in a naval officer's advancement from his entry into the *gardes de la marine* to his final promotion. This was especially so by mid-century when all efforts were directed to turn gentlemen into sailors and no attempt was made in the opposite direction. In a corps so completely divided against itself the struggle for influence and favour was incessant.

Requests for command, honours, leaves of absence, and special consideration and petitions for promotion and preferment bombarded naval secretaries of state and commandants, who sometimes tried to resist but normally granted the favours requested. Commandants' recommendations were crucial for no officer could leave his assigned port without their permission. Appointment to command was made at court but often on commandants' recommendations: the assignment of the remaining officers to warships was left largely in their hands.[60] Ship captains also had influence; they customarily selected their junior officers, and by right they could name one *lieutenant* and one *enseigne* to their ships.[61] Captains also requested promotions for relatives or for themselves, and as receipt of favour acknowledged the petitioner's influence, they did not restrict themselves to family or class.

Despite assertions to the contrary, French naval officers were not well paid by comparison with their British counterparts.[62] But French officers were paid quarterly if residing in their assigned department whereas British officers required posting to a ship to receive their full salary on a *per diem* basis. Half-pay was not intended, as in Great Britain, to maintain a reserve of active officers, but was a stipend paid to officers or their heirs in lieu of a pension for wounds received in the service. More to the point, French naval officers were poorly paid in contrast to their equivalents in the French army. Whereas army officers' salaries had increased several times during the eighteenth century, those of naval officers had not varied from the amounts laid down in the 1689 naval ordinance.[63]

Numerous practices of varying degrees of shoddiness, such as carrying salt as ballast for later sale in the colonies, shipping their own merchandise "en pacotille," lading freight on their own account or for colonists rather than the king, and selling fresh meat and provisions to their crews allowed captains to increase their incomes illegally. Regulations against engaging in commerce were ignored.[64] In 1758 officers at Rochefort even refused to carry royal stores destined for Louisbourg; they claimed the right to balance supplies of water and victuals with ballast. But everyone knew, wrote the angry intendant, that they carried goods on their own account and if the practice did not stop the king would have to charter more merchantmen.[65] It is safe to say that long before the middle of the century commerce had become an important part of a naval officer's way of life. But the commercial practices of many officers must be weighed against the failure to pay many of them during wartime. By mid-1758 officers at Brest were a year behind in receipt of their salaries, and by April 1760 those at Toulon were owed the last six months of 1758, the first nine months of 1759, and the first three months of 1760.[66] Lack of regular payments contributed strongly to the insubordination, intraservice rivalry, and personal antagonism that so marked the officer corps during the Seven Years' War.

Les grâces – promotion, decorations, gratuities, supplements, and pensions – were the chief objects of the officer corps. Insufficient rewards during the War of the Austrian Succession had been a major cause of the corps' demoralization in 1748.[67] On the other hand, the secretary of state's ability to resist the inundation of requests for *les grâces* was intimately related to the whole question of discipline and officers' excesses.

The most sought-after naval decoration was the Knight's Cross of the Military Order of St Louis. Rouillé made genuine efforts to raise morale in the officer corps. He obtained entry into the Order of St Louis for thirty-six officers in 1750 and the same number two years later. During the interval he also promoted 185 officers and halted the abuse of awarding the Knight's Cross to officers on the eve of their retirement.[68] Although peacetime provided few opportunities to dispense rewards, the state of morale required the secretary of state's acquiescence. Wartime, when any action or even inaction was followed by a flood of petitions and requests, further reduced resistance. Gratuities as high as 3,000 livres were paid to captains of Du Bois de la Motte's squadron in 1755 simply for completing their mission.[69] The rewards to officers in La Galissonière's squadron were enormous.[70] The strengthening of ministerial resistance to pressure and the tightening of discipline appeared only late in the war.[71] Allowing commandants to name the majority of ships' officers may have improved discipline in the naval departments, but the central bureaux appeared to lose control over the corps. Louis XV's order to absent officers to return to duty once moved Peyrenc de Moras to ask commandants to inform the absentees because Versailles had no idea who or how many were absent.[72]

The government was reluctant to move against insubordination or bad conduct; disciplining aristocrats was always difficult. The commandant of Toulon claimed to be helpless before the obstinacy even of one as junior as an *enseigne* who had been absent without leave for a year, was unable to meet his creditors, and "maintained a conduct unsuitable to his birth and to a naval officer."[73] Captains had trouble making their officers carry out watch-keeping duties at sea.[74] Officers who failed to obey their official instructions had to be dealt with, but they suffered little.[75] The intendant of Rochefort bitterly denounced naval officers as men who "do nothing themselves, think only of themselves, work for themselves and possess honour and courage only for themselves."[76]

Machault favoured the sword over the pen, which resulted in hundreds of promotions between 1754 and 1757.[77] But while he enjoyed peace and the respect of naval officers, his actions probably undid what little his predecessor had accomplished to unify command. Moreover, his behaviour made it impossible for the young, relatively inexperienced Peyrenc de Moras to assert any influence over the corps. Massiac's period in office was too brief for him to be blamed for the lack of promotions, and few officers had grounds for claiming favours under Berryer. When several protested his decision to lay up several ships in the Vilaine River after Quiberon Bay and pay off their crews, the minister erupted, dismissing some from the service and imprisoning Captain Villars de la Brosse for two years.[78] Naval officers only hugged their resentment more closely. *Officiers bleus*, merchants who refused to allow naval officers to command frigates that they had privately armed, and a few outstanding members of their own corps whose devotion to duty was rewarded became targets of their animosity.

Berryer was disgusted with the officer corps and lack of confidence in its abilities and conduct mounted under his successor. Choiseul thought that "the sole remedy was the complete suppression of the corps of the sword and its recreation on a different footing."[79] Choiseul's view of the corps is best seen, however, in his sea appointments for the remainder of the war. In the spring of 1762, after the dilatory *chef d'escadre*, comte de Blénac, waited two months before leaving Brest and failed to reach Martinique in time to deliver his reinforcements, Choiseul shunned the navy's general officers and turned to junior officers of proven dash. In May he gave command of a division of five ships to the chevalier de Ternay with orders to attack Newfoundland, and in September he appointed Port Captain Louis-Joseph Beaussier de L'Isle acting *chef d'escadre* and commander of an expedition to Rio de Janeiro. Command of troops in the force was given to an army *lieutenant-général*, the 32-year-old comte d'Estaing, who was named *chef d'escadre* on 1 October.[80] Less than a year later Choiseul appointed Louis-Antoine de Bougainville, former aide to the marquis de Montcalm in Canada, *capitaine de vaisseau*.[81] The minister also followed his predecessor in punishing insubordination. He court-martialled and imprisoned a captain and a first officer who had resigned their commissions in the midst of the comte d'Aché's campaign.[82]

In the middle of the eighteenth century the officer corps was pinned between its past legacies and traditions and its present challenges and future aspirations. Senior officers and captains in general performed badly. No other conclusion can be reached about a military organization and its institutions that fail the supreme test for which they exist. But the fifties also witnessed deeper awareness than in the past of the faults of both the navy and the officer corps. The Seven Years' War also gave junior officers much needed experience, separated them from the legacy of Louis xiv's navy, and prepared the way for many of Choiseul's reforms, many of which began during the war itself. Nearly all *enseignes des vaisseaux* promoted in 1756 and 1757 spent only eighteen to twenty months as *gardes*. Taking part in only one or two campaigns, they scarcely had time to deepen the theoretical and practical knowledge of their profession. By the end of 1761, however, senior *gardes* had four to six years' seniority, had fought in two to four actions and major battles, and had acquired a wealth of experience from which the navy benefited during the next quarter of a century.[83]

Several prerequisites for professionalization of the officer corps were present in the mid-century navy, notably a system of recruitment, training, and advancement and hierarchical order. But these were weakly established, insufficient in themselves, and inadequate when applied. The companies of *gardes* need not be criticized for trying to make sailors out of aristocrats; there is nothing logically impossible about the task. But in a society erected on military values with a strong orientation towards the army, the navy attracted too few influential noble families. Lack of venality served no useful purpose and may have been detrimental, attracting poor nobles whose provincial origins almost guaranteed reactionary responses to new problems of imperial naval warfare. A system of advancement was in place but the rules changed according to the individual concerned. Seniority might be considered along with manifest ability and distinguished conduct, but the basis of promotion was never clear because of the pervasiveness of pedigree and patronage. Moreover, general officers themselves were the models for the insubordination that was endemic in the corps.

The inability of the navy to provide a basis for unity through sufficient common experience at sea is the final important consideration, for this might have provided the essential prerequisite that failed to develop, loyalty to the service, from which efficiency and impartiality could later come. The navy did not provide sinecures. It was a hazardous occupation requiring technical skill and energy, but owing to the failure of loyalty to the service to develop, attachment to class and region remained too intense. By the mid-eighteenth century the naval officer corps was little more than a part-time, seasonal career for provincial nobles who had never developed a collective identity and who defined for themselves what it meant to serve the king.

CHAPTER FIVE

The Manning Problem

Manning the ships of the royal navy in the middle of the eighteenth century remained as serious a problem as eighty years before on the eve of French naval expansion. Naval authorities still closed ports and resorted to impressment in order to find men for the king's ships in wartime. Incomplete crews remained the most common cause of delayed ship departures during the Seven Years' War. Traditional explanations for this dismal state of affairs emphasize the insufficient number of trained seamen in France, structural and operational weaknesses in administering conscription, and competing demands for manpower. But while these factors affected the manning problem at different times and with varying degrees of seriousness, they do not provide an adequate explanation of the problem or even go to the heart of the matter. It is questionable whether the failure to meet the navy's wartime needs arose from an insufficient number of trained seamen in France. Moreover, problems in administration of the system of naval conscription and competing demands for manpower disguise more serious checks on recruitment that came from capture by the enemy and the ravages of disease. But above all, the manning problem arose from the crown's state of financial malnutrition which left the navy unable to pay its crews and drove seamen to resist the levies, desert in large numbers, and flee the country.

No European maritime power was assured of adequate numbers of trained sailors for its navy in wartime, but the French government's system of naval conscription came as near to a solution as any.[1] By the articles of Book 8 of the great Naval Ordinance of 1689, the registration of all able-bodied seamen (*matelots*) and petty-officers (*officiers mariniers*) between eighteen and sixty years of age became compulsory and the notion of class of service was introduced. In return for a lifetime of obligation, registered or "classed" seamen received several modest legal and fiscal privileges: exemptions from billeting troops, guardianship and wardship, night watch, tax collection and suspension of civil proceedings for debt against them.[2] The notion of regularity of service did not extend to wartime when the navy required from one-third to one-half of the nation's sailors, and it became unworkable in peacetime when the government could not afford to keep sailors on half-pay with only a vague expectation that they might be called up. As a result, the navy could not establish its own general reserve of seamen; maritime commerce bore the entire burden of creating the navy's necessary manpower.

Soon after becoming secretary of state for the navy Maurepas tried to reimpose order in the classes.[3] He permitted seamen not required for the king's service in the year of their call-up to seek employment in merchantmen. Thereafter, the individual tour of duty replaced class of service and became the guiding principle of conscription. Two consequences followed from this change. First, *la demi-solde* or half-pay, which Colbert had designed to retain fit seamen ashore for the navy, was finally acknowledged to be a program of compensation for aged and infirm sailors.[4] Second, the individual tour of duty placed a greatly increased burden upon the probity of those who administered the system of the classes. In order to supervise their conduct Maurepas established a *Bureau du contrôle-général des classes* at Versailles where copies of district registers were deposited and kept constantly up to date.

Lower numbers of trained seamen during the 1720s than before may reveal not so much a significant decline in the maritime population as a tightening of administrative procedures through regular inspections and increased centralized control. Slight manpower demands during the 1730s lulled the government into believing that changes in the system of the classes had reimposed control over recruiting officers and solved the problem of numbers.[5] On the eve of the War of the Austrian Succession between 30,000 and 40,000 petty officers and able-bodied seamen were available for service.[6] Although the navy was smaller during this war than under Louis xiv, the old difficulties returned as the navy's demands multiplied.[7] Furthermore, wartime losses, estimated at 10,000, represented between one-quarter and one-third of the total number available. A common complaint by 1748 referred to the absence of any trained sailors at all. Nevertheless, naval authorities thought the losses could be recovered in two or three years.

Some also hoped to return to the original system of the classes, but restoration of Colbert's design required reestablishment of half-pay to ensure a general naval reserve, which the navy could not afford.[8] By 1750 the secretary of state had resigned himself to accepting recruitment based on individuals from each class serving by turn, and advised officers of the classes to retain only the required numbers of the most junior and senior men of each class and release the remainder to serve in the merchant marine.[9] The system of the classes existed in name only. It was merely a means to register seamen.

As recruiting officers expected, recovery appeared quickly. The merchant marine employed more than 13,000 *matelots* annually, independent of three or four thousand serving the coastal trade and the India Company, in the years between 1749 and 1754.[10] On the eve of renewed hostilities, naval officials estimated that 52,466 trained men were available for naval service.[11] Two years later, in May 1757, they reported 55,905 trained men in the classes even though 3,000 men had died in the king's ships or on commercial and privateering ventures during the interval.[12] A third figure prepared in 1758 or 1759 gives 60,137 petty officers and able-bodied seamen in the classes.[13] By the end of the decade, then, when the navy was starved for manpower, the number of trained seamen appeared greater than in any previous year in recent French history.

The figures for the 1750s cannot be easily dismissed. They come from the Bureau of the Classes rather than reports to the king and formed the basis of the navy's own discussions of manpower. Moreover, the final figure is taken from a detailed district-by-district census, perhaps the only one of its type to survive from the Old Regime. Although the figures may be inflated, the potential manpower available to the navy appeared at least as large as in the late seventeenth century.

Table 4 summarizes the data in the 1758–9 census, and reveals several important characteristics of the French seafaring population. The uneven distribution of sailors in France is the most important feature. Little more than one-sixth (17.3 per cent) of all trained men lived in Languedoc and Provence while the remainder resided in the Atlantic and Channel regions; this is true even after novices and boys have been included. In addition, fewer than half the total number of sailors in the Midi were petty officers and able-bodied seamen. No other region in France had such a low proportion of registered men fit for naval service.[14] Yet after 1750 the government kept one-third of the fleet in the Mediterranean. Although no shortage of potential seamen for the navy existed nationally, France's southern sailors clearly bore a heavier burden, increased by the circumstances of the war, which provided few obstacles to maritime commerce and encouraged privateering in the Mediterranean.

A second important feature is that only 55 per cent of all registered sailors were petty officers and able-bodied seamen available for naval service. Captains, owners, and masters were exempt from naval service so long as they continued to go to sea.[15] Volunteers were usually the sons of *armateurs*, shipowners, and seaport merchants, and recruiting officers rarely inscribed them in the registers of the classes. The small number of registered volunteers caused some discontent among sailors, but failure to distinguish sufficiently between volunteers and other crew members or

TABLE 4
"Classed" Seamen in France, c. 1758–1759

Classes	Toulon No.	%	Rochefort No.	%	Brest No.	%	Havre & Dunkerque No.	%	Total No.	%
Petty officers & seamen	10,426	49.8	17,128	56.4	18,532	52.4	14,051	63.7	60,137	55.3
Captains, owners, & masters	1,685	8.0	1,357	4.5	773	2.2	915	4.2	4,730	4.4
Volunteers	817	3.9	9	0.0	362	1.0	227	1.0	1,415	1.3
Novices & boys	2,750	13.1	3,609	11.9	5,899	16.7	2,034	9.2	14,292	13.1
Workers	1,344	6.4	4,102	13.5	5,446	15.4	1,854	8.4	12,746	11.7
Seamen (hors service)	3,916	18.7	4,182	13.8	4,327	12.2	2,963	13.4	15,388	14.2
Total	20,938	100.0	30,387	100.0	35,339	100.0	22,044	100.0	108,708	100.0
% of total in each dept.	19.3		28.0		32.5		20.3		100.0	

Source: Marine, C⁴, 156, ["Mémoire concernant les classes"] (133 fols.)

protect them from the contempt of junior officers and *gardes de la marine* left many reluctant to serve the king. Few were ever found in warships.[16] Workers included rope-makers, pulley-makers, wood-carvers, joiners, ironworkers, who laboured in the dockyards, while carpenters, caulkers, and sail-makers served at sea and were treated as petty officers and able-bodied seamen. The category *hors service* denotes petty officers and seamen who were fifty-five to sixty years of age or became infirm or crippled; some received naval half-pay, but most remained employed in merchantmen. By the spring of 1759, however, a great number of classed petty officers and able-bodied seamen belonged more properly in the category *hors service,* for while not crippled or infirm, they were normally too old for naval service.[17]

Novices included lads between the ages of sixteen and twenty-five years employed in the freshwater fishery or who navigated in river mouths. Others had never been to sea and were attracted from the interior by opportunities for employment. After two voyages they had to choose whether they intended to go to sea again, in which case they were registered as able-bodied seamen.[18] An ordinance of 1745 increased the ratio of novices from one-tenth to one-fifth of the total number of men required in merchant crews but merchants avoided the obligation when and where possible. Novices were classed as seamen when in the navy. In the spring of 1759 one-third of the crew of *Le Glorieux*, 74-guns, comprised novices who had never been to sea.[19] In December a royal ordinance allowed all novices in the country to present themselves at the arsenals and guaranteed them all the privileges, pay, and rations of able-bodied seamen in the king's service. Additional encouragement guaranteed novices the right to leave the service and exemption from the classes after the war.[20]

Mousses or cabin boys were younger, and came generally from the seafaring population. The 1689 ordinance obliged merchantmen to carry one boy for every ten crew members and warships to embark six boys per hundred crewmen. At the age of eighteen boys were considered to be *matelots* and inscribed in the registers of the district where they lived. This regulation left the navy disadvantaged with respect to boys and fostered attempts to recruit inexperienced novices, for the latter could be classed as *matelots* within two years of going to sea. Recent practices prevented many boys from being classed as seamen. At La Rochelle and Marseilles merchant captains preferred orphans to children of seafarers to the detriment of the navy, for they were more likely to renounce the sea on reaching the age of registration.[21] Artisans and other landsmen in some areas solicited favours from officers of the classes and placed their children in the merchant marine to the prejudice of sailors' children. Having their children at sea relieved parents of the cost of their upbringing for several years before they became of age to be apprenticed. In 1751, in an effort to halt the practice, recruiting officers received instructions to note the father's condition in the case of each boy in the registers and confine the category to the sons of sailors.[22] Other proposals to increase the number of trained men, ranging from sending 3,000 orphans annually from the general hospitals into the navy to marrying orphan girls to sailors to inhibit desertion, accomplished little.[23] The attempt to improve the registration of boys, however, may have contributed more seamen to the classes by the middle of the decade, for boys served in the navy in greater numbers than before. In January 1755 boys made up about 8 per cent of the total requirement for the extraordinary armament required for Canada.[24] By 1760 Berryer proposed to include boys up to 10 per cent of the total of all new levies in the department of Rochefort.[25] But while the increased number of petty officers and seamen in the classes during the 1750s may have been partly due to including young boys, inexperienced youths, and old sailors previously not classed as fit for naval service, the expansion of the system of the classes to include formerly unclassed men provided yet another means to increase the number of trained sailors.[26]

At first provincial intendants appeared to cooperate. In May 1756 subdelegates of the intendant of Auch were registering boatmen and raftsmen on the Adour and Adouze rivers, and he hoped that *consuls* and *jurats* at places on several smaller rivers would register even fishermen; he himself promised to turn his own attention to the town of Grenade which had become a refuge for "unclassed" sailors. Only demands on the population for militia service checked the zealous intendant at Montauban. The rigorous efforts of the *commissaire-général* at Bordeaux, Henri de Rostan, to expand registration, however, soon cooled the intendants' ardour. By the year's end Chaumont de la Galazière feared the cessation of river navigation in his *généralité* if local exemptions did not remain in force. By 1758 ministry officials charged him with failing to assist recruiting officers, and ordered him not to listen to the complaints of those who had been classed. Intendant Megret d'Etigny behaved similarly, defending his subdelegate's opposition to an officer of the classes who had tried to conscript raftsmen on the small rivers above Toulouse, and demanding exemptions after interrupted ferry service on the Garonne cut connections between Auch and Bordeaux and Montauban (i.e., Paris); employees and even the sons of passengers had been conscripted.[27]

The harshness of officers of the classes and the concern of provincial intendants to preserve social stability and economic well-being pulled in opposite directions. Failure of conscription officers to advise intendants of their actions aroused the latter to fury. The *commissaire des classes* at Montauban threw the entire area into an uproar in 1760 when he began to register men along the Agout and Ladon Rivers, and proposed to extend the classes to villages and hamlets on non-navigable rivers in the mountains in the dioceses of Albi, Castres, and Lavour. Such pretensions proved intolerable.[28] Owners of ferries and skiffs deserted the rivers; local residents were up in arms, threatening agriculture and even the militia. Berryer's failure to admonish or protect the officer only led to demoralization and confusion. Indeed, towards the war's end Ruis-Embito at Rochefort admitted partial failure of the navy's policy. Extending the classes up the Lot River, he wrote, was "against nature," and his own powers as a naval intendant proved limited when confronted by a thoroughly aroused provincial intendant.[29] While allowing for the probability that hard-pressed officers of the classes inflated figures in order to please their superior officers, the animosity generated between the navy and local notables, provincial intendants, and populace was scarcely worth the extra men obtained. How many were gathered into the classes is beside the point.

The system of the classes divided France's five maritime intendancies into nineteen departments containing about sixty districts. A *commissaire-général* or *commissaire de la marine* directed each department. An officer of the classes, a *commis de classes*, or in the case of a large important district a *commissaire de classes* in turn directed each district. In the department of Toulon, for example, four *commissaires des classes* sat at Marseilles, Antibes, Arles, and Agde, each of them entrusted with two to four dependencies, the famous *quartiers* or districts. In major parishes of a district, *commissaires* might also install a syndic chosen from among sailors too old or infirm for service.[30]

The number of officers of the classes varied little throughout the period from the ninety-three employed in 1749.[31] Clearly a large, insensitive bureaucracy was not a problem, nor were there too few officers. There were, instead, too many poorly paid junior officers of the classes whose status was too low in view of their importance to the navy and vis-à-vis the local notables with whom they often had to deal. *Commissaires des classes* remained subordinate to *commissaires de la marine* and shut out from advancement in the corps of the pen. *Commis* or clerks of the classes also remained inferior to naval scriveners, and their respective emoluments reinforced the disparity in status.[32] At least one-half of the *commis des classes* held their grade only by royal order rather than brevet and many were not carried on naval appointment lists. Instead, they received annual gratuities often less than 100 livres.[33] The position of a junior officer of the classes was so unattractive that many *quartiers* had to be consolidated during the 1750s and the number of syndics increased.[34] This administrative weakness was corrected only in March 1762 by the duc de Choiseul, who reduced the total number of officers of the classes to sixty-four, maintained the same number of *commissaires de classes*, increased the number of departments to twenty-five, but abolished all distinctions between principal and ordinary clerks of the classes and naval scriveners. Henceforth, all these junior officers were to be known as *écrivains de la marine*, a move that considerably elevated the lowly status of junior recruiting officers.[35]

Weakness in control and command of the administrative process of naval conscription increased the deleterious effect of low status and poor pay. The office of intendant of the classes had become entirely honorific during the 1740s and Bernard Pallu's position remained unofficial from 1750 to 1757. Pallu was an outsider unable to protect recruiting officers at court from the group interests of the central secretariat and in the arsenals from officers of the pen. On the other hand, there was little or no opportunity for a well-intentioned intendant of the classes and three or four clerks presiding over the duplicate registers at court to supervise the activities of recruiting officers, who were not expected to live off their naval emoluments. Clerks in the districts frequently fell under the protection of local notables and held other minor offices. Low stipends, local patronage, and additional emoluments increased their independence from the navy. Clerks at Versailles often listened uncritically to complaints emanating from the districts, which further contributed to the independence of officers of the classes.[36] Periodic reviews of the entire system proved ineffectual. Inspectors showed little sympathy for officers of the classes and their reports were unavailing, consisting of long lists of complaints and few recommendations to alleviate the problems of recruiting officers.[37]

Local bureaux of the classes in the arsenals, charged with the direction of seamen and maintenance of a general register, further undermined central control of the classes. The absence of official crew establishments before 1761 left intendants and *commissaires* charged with the classes subject to pressure from flag-officers. Because crew states varied during peacetime and wartime and according to length of campaign, which determined whether ships had to carry all their provisions from departure or could replenish themselves, destination, which affected wastage from disease and desertion, and mission, which dictated whether a ship was on patrol, convoy escort, or *en flute*, it made sense to establish manpower requirements individually. But such *ad hoc* demands arrived late and interfered with long-range planning and orderly call-up. Senior officers naturally wanted as many men as possible, while the demands of social prestige and status encouraged commanding officers to demand as many men as had previously manned ships of similar rates regardless of campaign, destination or mission.

The *commissaire de la marine* charged with the classes apportioned manpower demands among the districts. The officer of the classes in each area called up the required number of men. On their arrival at an arsenal seamen presented themselves at the fitting-out bureau and were inscribed in a ship's muster-book. From that moment each man had to be followed in the registers. If he fell ill, died, or deserted, he had to be replaced. Failure to maintain the registers led to double and triple demands on the recruiting officers and overmanning of ships.[38] In mid-September 1756 the intendant of Toulon claimed to have recruited crews for La Galissonière's squadron three times since its return from sea in mid-July; it had been refitted and ready to sail since late August, but sailors had been deserting daily. The final review in November revealed that more than 800 sailors had gone.[39] A year later, after receiving 434 more men than were required by the crew states, warships at Toulon remained unable to sail owing to incomplete crews.[40] Some means might have been found to supervise recruiting officers from the arsenals, but the multiplicity of tasks in the bureaux, increased demand for officers of the pen to serve at sea, and interference from naval officers and Versailles militated against improvement. Instead, additional pressure was experienced by the recruiting officers in the districts.

Peacetime demands weighed lightly on officers of the classes. They encouraged foreigners to navigate on French vessels, verified embarkation of the required numbers of novices and boys as stipulated by the ordinances, tried to prevent masters, pilots, and commanders from abusing their exemption from service, and kept an eye on the men employed in the fishery. Although they exercised police powers over all classed seamen in their jurisdiction, sailors turned to them for protection from the greed and injustice of local merchants, the exactions of local authorities who often ignored their petty privileges, and those who exploited their need for loans. Officers of the classes were the natural defenders of sailors ashore.[41]

Pressures greatly increased in wartime, however, and their relationship with sailors deteriorated. Naval authorities at court failed to provide sufficient advance notice of manpower requirements, which prevented even the most upright officer from exercising any discretion. Constant pressure from court and arsenal led officers to extend ruthlessly their jurisdiction and act harshly towards the men and families under their authority. An officer's success depended largely upon his own character and integrity. How well he knew the sailors of his district, their homes, and hiding places was a critical factor, as, too, was his ability to stand up to local notables. Some understood the manner of governing sailors, but others caved in under the multiple pressures and let their registers fall into disorder.[42] Accused by their superiors, provincial intendants, and local notables of acting in bad faith, and by sailors of behaving as sovereigns, and seen by both as stirring themselves only to procure money and influence, the officer of the classes became an object of loathing.[43] Some took bribes, but all were overworked, poorly supported, and underpaid; even the best were hard put to carry out their duties. But before Choiseul's reform in 1762, the navy made no effort to relieve the social and political pressures that tested the probity of these officers. During the Seven Years' War, as perhaps never before, failure to pay seamen their wages made the position of recruiting officers intolerable and unfairly turned them into scapegoats for the organizational and administrative failings of the system.

Competing demands for manpower were quite insufficient to account for the navy's lack of seamen. Fifty-five per cent of the registered seamen in southern France at the beginning of 1756 were already in the navy or the merchant marine, and the remainder were in the districts or employed in coastal traffic when the navy levied the crews of La Galissonière's squadron.[44] The new levy was greater than the manpower immediately available, but La Galissonière's ships were fully manned in record time. Nearly 800 men were declared surplus and employed in the arsenal or on lesser warships on the eve of the admiral's departure.[45] Two years after hostilities had broken out at sea, in May 1757, less than 40 per cent of France's petty officers and able-bodied seamen served in the king's ships. But of the 12,338 (22 per cent) in the districts or in coastal traffic approximately 2,000 had been levied for warships at Rochefort and almost as many had been ordered from Provence and Languedoc to Toulon. This increased the proportion in the navy that year to approximately 46 per cent. Those left in the districts consisted chiefly of men recently discharged from the king's ships and infected with scurvy and other endemic diseases.[46] Fewer than 1 per cent of the total were listed as deserters.

The same data shows, however, that the India Company seriously interfered with the system of the classes; it diverted the equivalent of one-fifth of the petty officers and able-bodied seamen in the king's service into its employ. Owing to this requirement the navy did not draw men from the district of Port Louis, which included Lorient; 1,540 men from that district alone served in the company's ships. The remainder came from other districts in Brittany. The navy also did not draw sailors from Belle Isle, where they enlisted in the island's guard.[47] As a consequence, little more than one-third (36.8 per cent) of Brittany's classed men actually served in the navy.

Privateering was not the major cause of the navy's manpower shortage, as has been traditionally maintained.[48] Privateering diverted ships from trade but not an unusually large proportion of trained sailors. Special studies of several seaports during the Seven Years' War show a very rapid decline in commercial traffic.[49] The war provoked enormous increases in transportation costs in the Atlantic ports as wages and insurance rates rose. Merchants could not employ higher freight rates to compensate without considering the commodities involved, for prices, especially of colonial reexports to Europe, were set by international conditions and less likely to rise. This reduced profitability led merchants to withdraw for the duration.[50]

As a consequence a majority of the 12,028 men in merchantmen and privateers in May 1757 were probably in the latter owing to the decline of commerce.

The very real attractions of privateering and the ambivalence of naval ministers should not be overstated, because the majority of crewmen were not classed seamen. Privateering was attractive at Bayonne and Saint Jean de Luz where 6,093 men manned forty-four privateers by January 1757.[51] Many, however, were unclassed Basques, and early successes drew men from Iberian ports throughout the western Mediterranean. Privateering was never widely practised at Bordeaux, Lorient, and Vannes, and not at all at La Rochelle during the war. *Armateurs* in the largest port claimed that their sailors maintained a "decided distance" from such bellicose activity, and La Rochelle's two privateers were captured within two months of the war's beginning.[52] Farther north in the English Channel privateering continued to exert its age-old attraction. The governor of Normandy advised *armateurs* to fit out ships for *la course* as early as August 1755.[53] At Dunkirk privateers were regularly fitted out during the war, but all the evidence indicates that their crews were composed almost entirely of foreign sailors: Italians, Spanish, Portuguese, Brabanters, Swedes, and Danes, many of whom had deserted from the British navy.[54] Very few classed seamen served in Dunkirk privateers. The proximity of Bayonne to Spain suggests that the same condition prevailed there as well.

The loss of French manpower owing to capture by the British may have been the most serious drain on the navy's resources. Indeed, the chance of capture and death in English prisons probably equalled the risk of death through action and disease in French sailors' own warships.[55] Of 64,373 French prisoners received by the British Admiralty's Commissioners for Sick and Hurt Seamen between 14 October 1755 and 11 November 1762, 8,499 or 13 per cent died in Great Britain.[56] The actual number of trained French seamen taken prisoner may never be known owing to the poorly documented role of the British colonies and the British failure to distinguish between "classed" seamen and the remainder. Many of the Admiralty's prisoners were Basques, Flemings, Italians, and other foreigners, as well as boys, masters, and unfortunate passengers. Nevertheless, by May 1757, 4,703 "classed" petty officers and able-bodied seamen were among the 14,406 prisoners in the charge of the Sick and Hurt Commissioners.[57] This number represented 8.4 per cent of all such classed men in France and more than one-fifth of the total number of seamen in the navy. The number of trained men among prisoners certainly grew after the naval disasters at Cartegena and Louisbourg early the following year. By the end of 1758, when Marshal de Belle-Isle privately acknowledged that the British had 20,000 prisoners to France's 3,000, as much as one-half of the total may have comprised classed seamen.[58] Recognition that the growing number of prisoners had become a serious problem occurred at the same time. In December the intendant of Toulon identified loss through capture by the enemy together with sailors' wages as major causes of delay in fitting out ships.[59]

Few prisoner exchanges and exchange cartels occurred after 1757 when most British prisoners had been repatriated.[60] The annual number of French prisoners received by the Sick and Hurt Commissioners declined during the last four years of the war but those in their care grew steadily from nearly 20,000 in 1758 to more than 26,000 in 1762, a number borne out by the 25,793 prisoners still in British hands on the signing of the Treaty of Paris.[61] This heretofore little-known factor may have played a crucial role in preventing the navy from manning its ships with trained men.

Living conditions in the king's ships were so appallingly bad that even at two centuries' remove accounts of the effects of poor diet, lack of hygiene, and disease retain their sinister quality. Nevertheless, though disease was a potent killer, the poor health of sailors was not a prime cause of the lack of sufficient manpower for the navy. No estimate of losses during the Seven Years' War comparable to the loss of one-quarter of the men employed during the previous war has been found. But the rate of attrition was probably higher owing to the longer duration of the war, the large numbers of sailors' deaths in English prisons, and a typhus epidemic that struck Brest during the winter of 1757–8. Even so, casualties in the French navy never approached those of the enemy who, between Christmas 1754 and Christmas 1757, lost 135 men killed in action or perished of wounds while 7,665 men drowned or died of disease.[62]

The navy appears to have assumed a 10 per cent loss rate when ordering wartime levies, but this may reflect the wretched living conditions ashore as much as at sea. Sailors often arrived at the arsenals in poor health, and during their stay, which could last three or four months, little was done to improve their condition. Seamen were often so debilitated and poorly fed before their departure as to be in no condition to withstand the strain on their health imposed by service at sea. In the spring of 1758, for example, all the levies from the districts of Toulouse, Marmande, Montauban, La Teste, and elsewhere in the Department of Bordeaux arrived at Rochefort riddled with scabies. Many had to be dismissed and most of the remainder were hospitalized.[63] Traditionally sailors sold most of their clothing en route to the arsenals and frequently arrived in a beggarly state. Once at the arsenals they were too often fed on sea-biscuit and salt meat taken off returning warships, and, as there were no barracks designed for them, they lodged in town where they fell prey to tavern owners, loan sharks, and whores. A special situation prevailed at Rochefort where malaria was endemic in the low-lying area surrounding the port.

Seamen's diet probably improved at sea. It was more than adequate in bulk, indeed, French seamen consumed more calories *per diem* than the general populace.[64] But though high in caloric content their diet was both deficient and unbalanced. In addition to the well-known Vitamin C deficiency characteristic of all shipboard diets of the time, French sailors lacked sufficient quantities of other vitamins and protein for which no abundance of carbohydrates, fats, or sugars could compensate. Equally important, the diet failed to provide resistance to their disease-ridden environment.

Badly ventilated, filthy, humid, and congested warships incubated diseases that quickly hatched and spread virulently among already weakened sailors. Fevers, dysentry, pulmonary infections, scurvy, and typhus (so common as to be called ship-fever) were endemic. Sailors generally neglected personal and collective hygiene, lacked a change of clothing, and customarily shared hammocks which increased the risk of contagion.

Once implanted, infectious disease raced through a ship's company sparing no one. Ships became floating hells that defy description. The frigate *La Sirenne* returned to Brest in May 1748 after losing half the ship's company to an unknown contagious disease.[65] Pulmonary infections carried off many crew members in the comte de Macnémara's squadron in the spring of 1755 owing to a lack of clothing among the seamen.[66] Four days before the Battle of Minorca officers in La Galissonière's squadron reported 41 dead and 233 sick while 38 men were killed and 175 wounded during the battle itself.[67] Failure to enforce cleanliness on board *Le Léopard* led to the loss of the captain, first officer, an ensign, surgeon, chaplain, sixty of the crew, together with thirty soldiers being carried to Canada.[68] Such disasters usually remained confined to a single ship, but an outbreak of typhus in Dubois de la Motte's squadron in 1757 significantly affected the navy's manning difficulties for the remainder of the war.

The origin of the contagion remains obscure. Whereas contemporaries located the infection in ships from Rochefort that dropped off sailors suffering from malaria at Brest before sailing across the Atlantic, medical historians strongly opt for an origin in one or several of the ships at sea.[69] At Louisbourg, the destination of La Motte's force, the first men to show signs of typhus were still suffering from malaria. When the squadron departed on 30 October, it left 400 men behind and embarked about 1,000 convalescents. On its arrival at Brest on 22 November nearly 4,000 sailors were sick. About 1,350 of the 1,600 who died at Brest before the end of the year were sailors; in addition, 480 convicts succumbed in the arsenal.[70] By the end of February 1758 from 10 to 12,000 were hospitalized in Brest alone, and men fleeing the hospitals quickly spread the disease through Brittany. As early as December, Quimper, Lorient, Morlaix, and Vannes were infected. Within five weeks more than 10,000 sailors had died or been dismissed to convalesce.[71] With the exception of bacillary dysentry that struck twenty-two years later, the typhus epidemic of 1757–8 was the most devastating event to visit eighteenth-century Brittany.[72] At Rochefort, where six ships from the expedition arrived in December, the result was nearly as severe though fewer numbers were affected. During December, January, and February 500 sailors died and the contagion continued to spread. Rochefort's hospital mortuary register shows 1,073 deaths in 1758 or more than one-fifth of the total number of dead for fifteen years between 1748 and 1762; this was three times the annual mean.[73]

The impact on manning was immediate. At the end of January naval authorities reported no sailors at Brest; they halted all privateers arriving in the port and extended the classes up rivers as far away as the Seine with renewed vigour.[74] By April novices comprised almost all the men in the levies, and authorities predicted that a frigate would have to be laid up to find the men for Le Raisonable, 64-guns; the arsenal even lacked sufficient seamen to rig ships being fitted out.[75] The threat of mutiny seriously increased during the summer as men from older levies could not be released. In May it was claimed that the province of Brittany would be entirely denuded of trained manpower following the departure of frigates currently being armed.[76] Six months later, "the lack of crews [was] the greatest obstacle that the intendant had to surmount"; only 180 petty officers and able-bodied seamen appeared of 1,000 called up in the most recent levy.[77] Indeed, the Breton levies never recovered.

In May 1759 the Brest squadron lacked 3,507 petty officers and able seamen and a general review at Lorient showed a shortage of 443 men.[78] A year later Ruis-Embito at Rochefort reported that "it is an established fact that the classes of this department [which included the entire southwest] are drained." So few sailors were available that shipyard workers completed the crew of L'Intrepide, 74-guns.[79] In 1761 naval authorities finally acknowledged that as no levy could be made in Brittany and in view of the Midi sailors' hostility to Rochefort, new levies for the latter port would have to come partly from Le Havre and Dunkirk.[80] In the spring of 1762 men arriving at Brest had neither sufficient strength nor age; many were newly returned from the East Indies (i.e., recuperating from scurvy and other shipboard diseases). Few were even sailors. The chevalier de Ternay's vessels were readied only by taking 300 petty officers and able-bodied seamen from Le Glorieux and Le Sphinx which had just reached Brest after escaping from the Vilaine River.[81]

After all that has been said about the problems and abuses arising from operating the system of the classes, including lack of surplus numbers, competing attractions of commerce and privateering, manpower demands of the India Company, and losses due to capture by the enemy, and after the risks to life and limb have been identified and assessed, there remains for consideration one factor, lack of funds, which was the most critical in rendering the manning problem insoluble. For it was lack of pay that led sailors to flee the coastal regions and even the country rather than enter the king's service.

The thousands of seamen of 1757 melted away owing to failure to pay their wages. The case of Toulon is the most instructive because the terrible typhus epidemic during the winter of 1757–8 did not infect the Mediterranean seafaring population. At the beginning of 1759 the marquis de La Clue's twelve ships required almost 5,000 seamen. But in contrast to three years before, the intendant at Toulon counted on drawing only 2,000 men from Provence and Languedoc. Another 1,000 might be drawn from Italy, where many French sailors had fled; several hundred more could be saved by cheese-paring, reducing ships' complements, and increasing the proportion of soldiers in the crews; one thousand or so might also be found by closing Marseilles and levying merchant crews including captains and even ships' clerks; but the remaining seven or eight hundred seamen would have to come from Toulouse and Bordeaux.[82] The clearest illustration that payment of wages was of critical importance in dealing with the manpower problem, however, was the prompt formation of crews of the comte de Rochemore's squadron a year later. The squadron's expenses were paid in full by Marseilles' Chamber of Commerce.[83]

French sailors ordinarily received two months' wages on first muster, but it had become necessary to pay five months' wages in advance by the end of the War of the Austrian Succession in order to obtain any crews at all.[84] Advance payments declined on the return to peace but in 1750 intendants still paid sailors a three months' advance and this appears to have become normal. After the outbreak of hostilities, the minister also promised a bounty of 12 livres to those who promptly answered his appeal for men. He also ordered that their entire pay was to date from the day of joining their ship rather than from its departure from harbour.[85] But these measures had a limited effect. Bounties paid to foreign sailors were expensive and met with little success. Most of the four or five hundred men recruited from Genoa in 1756 had never been to sea; many were, "lame, infirm, vagabonds, thieves and scoundrels"; and more than two-thirds were returned to Italy.[86]

The first signs of difficulty appeared in the spring of 1756. Sailors were reported fleeing to the countryside; by June none could be found around Toulon. A large levy from Guienne also failed to reach the arsenal. Irregular patrols of known haunts produced no seamen. Sailors in service were restive, and repeated punishments of *la cale* (keel-hauling) failed to return them to duty. By October sailors were deserting in large numbers even though they mustered daily, ships anchored well offshore in the

Grand Roads, and armed sentries mounted fore and aft shot men swimming in the water.[87] A year later authorities feared that the rigour of the law could not be used against 1,200 "libertins" in Toulon and suspended a levy of sailors.[88]

In the rigid, legalistic view of officers of the pen, failure to pay seamen made it all but impossible to punish desertion and insubordination. Unpaid men could only be called absentees; punishments for desertion could not be applied. Discipline relaxed as the war progressed. Desertion was officially punished by life sentence to the galleys, but apprehended deserters at Rochefort were sentenced only to undertake additional campaigns at lower rates of pay.[89] At the end of 1757 a royal amnesty granted relief to all petty officers and able-bodied seamen who had deserted, but its renewal five years later suggests that it had little effect.[90] At Brest punishments became so moderate by the spring of 1759 that petty officers and seamen ran few risks through desertion.[91] Most sailors quite willingly risked eight days' imprisonment for hiding from call-up, or three months' embarkation without pay for failing to report for duty after being called, or even three years in the galleys for desertion. This last punishment considerably moderated the former life sentence, which was now reserved for those fleeing the country altogether. Moreover, the punishments were largely a dead letter. Judgments pronounced on absentees were negated if any deserter surrendered within three months of the sentence. Instead, he was punished for failure to report for duty.[92] Such was the effect of failure to meet the wages of the king's sailors.

The chief reason for this behaviour was the sailors' fear for their families. Repeating earlier proposals, in 1756 *Commissaire-général* Charron recommended that two sous *per diem* be distributed to each member of a sailor's family while he was in service in order to lead families to encourage sailors to enter the navy.[93] But after becoming intendant of Toulon, he became more realistic. So too did Berryer. In his very first letter to the intendant of Brest the minister insisted that all discharged sailors must be paid in full. Shortly afterward he rebuked Rochefort's intendant, advising him to stop playing games and pay off all discharged men, not just those from 1755 and 1756. Charron at Toulon hastened to support the minister.[94] But without funds the minister's injunctions remained in the realm of good intentions.

Brutalization and victimization also discouraged seamen from entering the navy. Local authorities often ignored sailors' modest privileges and exemptions guaranteed by the Naval Ordinance of 1689. Sailors petitioned against the demands of provincial intendants and local landowners for *corvées*, against municipal officers who demanded their services as watchmen and tax collectors, and against "the anxieties" inflicted upon their wives, but even with an intendant's strong support few petitions led to redress.[95] Even in coastal regions sailors usually constituted a minority of the population and were easy to victimize. In the maritime parishes of *pays d'élections* sailors were frequently named to collect the *taille*. This task normally occupied them for two years which forced them to remain ashore or pay someone to carry out the task to the detriment of both maritime commerce and the navy. Petty violations of sailors' privileges succeeded because it was often necessary to go all the way to the Royal Council to defend those privileges. A sailor named as a tax-collector at Rouen required and *arrêt* of the council to free him, even though his nomination had been illegal.[96] Municipal authorities at Cherbourg billeted troops in the homes of women whose husbands even then were serving in the king's ships, despite the fact that all sailors registered in the classes, not just those currently in the navy, were exempt from such impositions. The intendant of Caen proposed to moderate this illegal practice, but only by restricting billets to homes where husbands were at sea in merchantmen. The intendant at La Rochelle three times refused to cease billeting troops on sailors' families.[97] Fears for the safety and welfare of their families increased the misery resulting from lack of pay.

As desertions mounted most administrative officers demanded harsher treatment for sailors. "The seafaring people of this country," wrote one, "being naturally dissolute, insubordinate, and always treated with too much gentleness, ... I see that only repeated and harsher punishments than the galleys may return them industrious to the port."[98] Intendant Charron knew better; "circumstances," he wrote, "have not allowed us to treat them well enough to keep and attach them to the king's service."[99] In 1758, Admiral Duquesne failed to obtain obedience from his crews even after executing four or five men. They claimed to prefer to die rather than serve without pay. An internal memorandum, written in February, accurately summed up the problem: "The levies of sailors for new outfits are made with difficulty, not so much because of the scarcity of men, although it is real, than because of defaulting in payments for laying up that are due. They hide to avoid service in the king's ships, and those who are found ask with justice, which is unsatisfied, that they be paid what is owed them so that their families are able to live in their absence."[100]

According to Hocquart, lack of money was the principal cause of all his difficulties, which were increasing daily; waywardness, mutiny, and relaxation of punishment all followed from lack of money.[101] Charron pointed out that the full rigour of naval discipline could be applied only to sailors in receipt of regular pay.[102] Proposals to increase the number of trained seamen in France appeared throughout the 1750s, but few before 1760 emphasized the need to protect sailors' families from the illegal exactions of landsmen or the need to pay their wages promptly.[103] By then it was a question of closing the gate after the horses had fled.

The simple fact was that unless sailors were paid ships would not sail.

Bompar's squadron, fitting out at Brest in the autumn of 1758, needed 300,000 livres for the crews.[104] But by this time about 17 million livres in pay and wages were owing to the entire personnel of the navy: officers, workers, and sailors alike. More than 5 million were due to sailors discharged from the service.[105] More than 1.25 million livres remained owing to sailors at Toulon in September 1758.[106] A year later the provision of back pay was a necessary condition to obtain the seven or eight thousand sailors required for the planned invasion of England, and the same condition obtained in the spring of 1762 at Toulon in the wake of unsuccessful attempts to fill the levies.[107] The treasurer-general of the navy sent only 269,000 livres in *rescriptions* of 400,000 livres required to pay off crews of seven ships arrived at Toulon from Cadiz in 1760.[108] At Brest, at the same time, more than 1.5 million livres remained to be paid on the decommissioned ships from 1755 to 1758.[109] This sum was still unpaid nineteen months later when Hocquart received 4 million livres to discharge the fiscal obligations of 1760 and 1761; however, he was explicitly instructed not to employ a sou on earlier fiscal years.[110] The crews of 1759 received the same treatment. Sailors from Normandy were still owed 862,000 livres in unpaid wages a year after their ships were laid up.[111] In August 1761 Rochefort crews, laid up in 1757, had yet to receive three-quarters of the nearly 350,000 livres owed to them.[112] Choiseul was no more effective than his predecessors in solving the manning problem because, like them, he could not pay the crews. Moreover, he had little intention of doing so. He preferred to ignore the king's debts to his sailors and emphasized, instead, the malversations of other servants of the crown.

Although sufficient numbers of trained petty officers and able-bodied seamen existed in mid-eighteenth century France to man the warships, the royal government had clearly reached a point beyond which it could not go to draw these men into the navy. Competing demands for manpower did not divert many trained men; only the India Company drew significant numbers. More serious limitations arose from major flaws in the organization of recruiting officers and administrative processes that undermined control and command of their activities. The circumstances of the war, capture by the enemy, and attrition due to disease, also hampered the system of the classes. But it was the navy's limited financial resources that rendered the flaws irreparable and the circumstances overwhelming. Indeed, in the light of the failure to pay seamen their wages from the earliest days of the war, it is perhaps most astonishing of all that warships continued to sail for as long as they did.

CHAPTER SIX

The Arsenals

French naval arsenals were among the largest industrial establishments in eighteenth-century Europe. The smallest employed nearly as many men as the largest British shore establishment.[1] But though shipbuilding was among the first crafts to be turned into an industry, employing enormous capital and a huge labour force, naval arsenals were not factories. Production remained a traditional handicraft affair and attempts to divide labour and rationalize tasks continually encountered this fundamental characteristic.[2] The arsenals display a complexity in their organization and operation that no other royal service reveals to the same degree, but they had a simple, well-defined objective, the warship. This and several other features justify discussing them together. Widely separated from each other, French arsenals were wedded by necessity to self-sufficiency. Distance prevented movement toward specialization of tasks such as Daniel Baugh observed in English shipyards.[3] Consequently, though each possessed special characteristics and faced different challenges, systems of organization, administration, and labour, as well as problems related to delivery, storage, and employment of stores, were common to all. Chronic underfunding was another common feature. The arsenals are therefore best studied together.

MAJOR NAVAL ESTABLISHMENTS

Brest. The navy's largest anchorage lay at Brest at the western extremity of Brittany, a poor province, neither productive nor populous, where land communications were quite inferior. The Breton peninsula possessed no navigable rivers or canals, and the arsenal lay hundreds of miles from the mouths of the Loire and Seine rivers. But the large number of sailors available in this most maritime of French provinces and the great natural roadstead extending over fifty square miles behind the Crozon peninsula partially outweighed these disadvantages. Brest's strategic location to windward of British naval dockyards, its proximity to major trade routes between Europe and the rest of the world, and its easy defensibility also account for the arsenal's presence. Warships could quickly depart unobserved to America or southwards when easterly gales blew, while the prevailing westerlies often kept enemies eastward in the English Channel.

Brest had been starved of funds during the half-century preceding the War of the Austrian Succession. The war's end found the arsenal with most of the ships remaining in the fleet, but without the means to maintain them. Nor had Brest yet recovered from two disastrous fires that occurred in December 1742 and January 1744.[4] In September 1749 one million livres' weight of hemp was still required to complete the rigging of ships in harbour and the arsenal continued to lack masts, spars, and gun-carriages. Not a single cannon had been delivered in fifteen months.[5]

During the next six years Gilles Hocquart instituted a new regime, pulling down old, condemned buildings together with all unauthorized sheds and lean-tos and introducing new security measures against theft and fire.[6] Labour continually had to be shifted from new buildings and new ships to maintain and repair old ones during the early years, but Brest gradually resumed its old image.[7] New forges appeared, the harbour was dredged, and improved bake ovens were erected on the provisions wharf. A prison and compound to house recently arrived convicts appeared, and newly laid pipes carried increased volumes of fresh water into the arsenal.

Toulon. Physically separated from the busy commercial world of Marseilles, Toulon's spacious roadstead was close enough for the navy to levy merchant seamen and benefit from the support of wealthy merchants anxious to obtain protection for their ventures at sea. Its proximity to the mouth of the Rhone River permitted easy access to a rich hinterland for timber, naval stores, and provisions. But though Toulon fulfilled France's major strategic purpose in the Mediterranean, the ease with which French naval forces were contained there remained a major drawback. The capture of Minorca in 1756 removed the possibility of a permanent blockade of Toulon, but did little to improve France's position in regard to America or increase the importance of the Mediterranean theatre of operations during the Seven Years' War.[8]

Like Brest, Toulon had been rebuilt by Vauban in the 1690s. The port stagnated following the Treaty of Utrecht and suffered a hammer blow during the visitation of the plague in 1720 when its population fell by a half. Recovery was very slow; by 1750 Toulon numbered about 17,000 and may have reached about 22,000 during the Seven Years' War.[9] Only four small warships and two frigates were built between 1726 and 1740. The absence of further disasters and the few demands on its resources, however, preserved its potential. Between 1740 and 1748 thirteen ships of the line and three frigates were laid down and during the next fourteen years seventeen of the line and seven frigates were built. Plans to build a drydock, provisions warehouse, and the arsenal's own hospital were never implemented, but Vauban had built well.[10] The arsenal was capable of producing whatever the smaller navy of Louis xv demanded.[11]

Rochefort. Rochefort, located on the lower reaches of a sluggish river some thirteen miles from the sea, seems a strange place to build a naval arsenal. But the spacious Basque Roads between the islands of Ré and Oléron and the island of Aix off its mouth explains Rochefort's continued usefulness. Indeed, Basque Roads was an integral part of the arsenal, for only there could ships of the line take on ordnance and water after moving down the Charente to the sea. Well situated for assembling convoys of merchantmen for the West Indies and New France, the roads encouraged development of Rochefort's special role in provisioning the extensive and growing forces of the king in America. Nantes and Bordeaux, France's largest commercial ports, reinforced Rochefort's strategic significance midway between the Loire and the head of the Gironde Estuary, as did several fertile provinces and the furnaces and foundries of nearby Angoumois and Périgord which manufactured the bulk of the navy's ordnance. The Charente itself made transportation to and from the hinterland quite easy, and Bordeaux and Nantes drew from the Garonne, Dordogne, and Loire what the Charente could not furnish. Endemic maladies reigning over the marshy salt flats around Rochefort provided the port's chief disadvantage.

On the other hand, Rochefort was a far cry from the splendid model arsenal begun by Colbert more than three-quarters of a century before.[12] In the eyes of its newly appointed intendant Rochefort resembled little more than a chaotic farmyard. Stagnant, malaria-laden water had accumulated throughout the arsenal; cobblestones lay buried under layers of rotting wood chips; piles of rotten timber and scraps obstructed easy passage; and good timber lay indiscriminately in the park. Mud buried cannon, ball, and shot; tools lay scattered everywhere. Innumerable shanties facilitated thefts and served as hiding-places to dispense strong drink to idle workers.[13] According to the controller-general of finances, fraud and contraband occurred more frequently at Rochefort than at any other port in the kingdom.[14] Storehouses served as public shops where anyone took whatever he required. Timber hangers had long been used to stable oxen employed in the port; two feet of manure lay piled round about. Rochefort merchants anchored their ships in the port, unloaded their cargoes at the royal wharves, and Lenormant de Mézy even found a merchantman being rebuilt in the graving dock. The masting ponds had fallen into ruin: sluices were neglected, ponds silted up, masts partly submerged in mud, some entirely dry and others bent, all mingled together without arrangement. Complacency had been pushed to the point of allowing gardens and farmyards inside the arsenal where workers tended fowl, pigs, and cows.[15]

As elsewhere, the new broom swept vigorously, cleaning, repairing walls and work sites, and building new workshops. But while Rochefort's technical capacity quickly improved, serious threats to health continued. Lack of funds prevented completion of a new hospital.[16] Shortage of good drinking water almost destroyed the port during the Seven Years' War. Wooden conduits that had been carrying water from Tonnay-Charente since the seventeenth century required constant repairs and the inhabitants were often forced to take water from contaminated wells or the Charente itself.[17] Despite great efforts, involving much expense and labour improvements, the results failed to meet expectations.[18]

SECONDARY NAVAL ESTABLISHMENTS

Several lesser establishments were spread across France, some of limited usefulness, but others of no use at all. Despite the zeal of Berryer and the force of Choiseul, only death reduced the grasp of some naval officials on place. But the reduction of several small departments between the end of 1759 and 1762 was among the earliest reforms of naval administration.

Le Havre. Le Havre was poorly thought of. Although the only port available to the navy on the English Channel, it had fallen into ruin by the middle of the eighteenth century. Le Havre served chiefly as an entrepôt for naval provisions, especially hemp and timber.[19] The naval establishment consisted of a general storehouse and offices for the classes and timber and employed twenty-six naval personnel.[20] The intendant carried on a considerable business with naval provisioners, managed the costly transshipment of timber and stores to Brest and Rochefort, and prior to the Seven Years' War supervised construction of frigates. In the spring of 1759 he also organized construction of 150 *bateaux plats.*[21]

Berryer's enthusiasm for economy struck the port in December 1759.[22] Three months later all foremen in the workshops were ordered dismissed and the cooperage abolished.[23] The financial crisis, the end of the "invasion" of England, and the effectiveness of enemy cruisers off the coast in halting timber shipments to Brest had reduced the navy's business at Le Havre to nil. In July 1760 Berryer ordered Intendant de Ranché to halt all work and employ only caretakers in the basin.[24] The duc de Choiseul retired the intendant at the beginning of 1762 and reduced Le Havre to the direction of a *commissaire.*[25] The long delay in reducing its status reflected the influence of the last two incumbents. Mathieu de Clieu Derchigny was so old as to be impossible to remove before his death in July 1754, and

Jean-Louis de Ranché, who had occupied the curious post of "Intendant at Court" since returning from Martinique, could not be given a lesser post. Nor, as Joseph Pellerin's brother-in-law, could he be easily retired.

Dunkirk. Dunkirk's value to France swiftly declined following demolition of the port's fortifications as required by the Treaty of Utrecht. An *ordonnateur* replaced the intendant in 1739 and by mid-century naval correspondence chiefly concerned the reception of gunpowder from Saint Omer and its shipment to Brest.[26] The French began to refortify the port in August 1755, and a year later the Chamber of Commerce received orders to clean up the harbour to allow entry to 50-gun frigates.[27] In November 1756 Michel Bégon, former *premier commis* of the bureau of funds, occupied the reestablished naval intendancy.

Bégon actively encouraged construction of the port's defences and promoted fitting out naval frigates as privateers.[28] Apparently he also organized an intelligence service, receiving correspondence from secret agents and paying them, procured and translated English newspapers for dispatch to the secretary of state, and concerned himself with the care and exchange of English prisoners.[29] His duties quickened in the spring of 1759 after receiving orders to build fifty *bateaux plats*.[30] But following Choiseul's appointment to the naval ministry, Bégon retired and the department was suppressed.[31]

Port Louis. The small naval staff at Port Louis remained a vestige of the seventeenth century. Situated at the mouth of the estuary of the Scorff and Blavet Rivers across from Lorient and the dockyard of the India Company, the department preserved its independence but was in decline. *Commissaire-général* Charles-Alexis de Clairambault had been entrusted with its management since 1744. His slight responsibilities were confined to supervising the system of the classes in southern Brittany and maintaining liaison with the India Company, whose crews were conscripted from the district. Berryer forced Clairambault into retirement in 1759 and placed the establishment under a *commissaire* supervised from Brest.[32]

Nantes, Bordeaux, St Malo, Marseilles, and Port Mahon. The presence of naval staffs at Nantes, Bordeaux, and St Malo arose from the need to maintain close liaison with merchants and naval provisioners residing in these wealthy commercial ports. Each was directed by a *commissaire-général*: Louis-Elie Millain at Nantes, Henri de Rostan at Bordeaux, and Jean-Joseph Guillot at St Malo. Large supplies of timber were shipped down the Loire, chiefly to the Island of Indret, two leagues below Nantes, whence Millain arranged for its transfer to Brest and Rochefort. This was a rather simple task in peacetime since the timber moved in the navy's own storeships, but after war broke out transportation became increasingly difficult, until by 1759 most movement had ceased altogether. At Bordeaux, Rostan saw that Bayonne timber as well as foodstuffs, naval stores, and sailors from southwestern France kept flowing to Rochefort. Liaison with the agent of the victualler-general who supplied wine, flour, and other foodstuffs to the navy from this fertile region was a major duty.

Although technically under the jurisdiction of the intendants of Brest and Rochefort, Millain and Rostan jealously guarded their independence. Rostan spent the last thirty-five of his fifty-six years of naval service at Bordeaux, allegedly paying only lip service to the navy's requirements, being more concerned with commerce and privateering, and deciding according to his own priorities whether to supply aid to Rochefort.[33] He proved impossible to remove or reprove. Following his death in January 1761, Berryer quickly suppressed the office together with its subsidiary department at Bayonne and reunited both under the direct authority of Rochefort's intendant.[34] Millain proved to be just as difficult; though ordered to report to Brest on the expenses of his office, he failed to obey.[35] Guillot at St Malo, on the other hand, appeared to do little or nothing at all. During the first six months of 1756 he authorized a mere 3,356 livres in payments.[36]

Marseilles functioned for three years after the suppression of the galley corps while its former intendant, Bénigne-Jérôme du Trousset d'Héricourt, supervised the transfer of galley oarsmen and liquidated the navy's business there. The strong merchant community and large seafaring population required continual liaison, and as the navy continued to provide frigates and other lesser vessels for commercial escorts, Héricourt was succeeded by *Commissaire-général* Charron the younger, his second-in-command since 1749.[37] After the conquest of Minorca, Marseilles supplied the thousands of troops on the island more easily than Toulon. The growing financial support of the city's Chamber of Commerce also encouraged the continued presence of naval administrators. But Berryer was receptive to complaints from Toulon's intendant that this arrangement placed extra work loads on his staff, and in December 1759 Marseilles met the same fate as Le Havre and Port Louis. Berryer ordered all officers and employees to return to Toulon and leased the arsenal to private interests.[38] Port Mahon, Minorca, acquired a small naval staff under the direction of *Commissaire-général* Félix-Antoine Dasque. Late in 1760, however, Berryer also abolished this department and the officers returned to Toulon.[39] Later the duc de Choiseul reopened Marseilles to build galleys and maintain storehouses, a hospital, and a prison.[40] Six galleys with a major portion of the convicts were transferred from Toulon.[41]

Elsewhere. Several administrative officers, usually possessing the power of *ordonnancement*, served independently as liaison officers in smaller commercial ports at Calais, Vannes, and La Rochelle, and as timber commissioners in the interior of the kingdom. The timber officer for the critically important region of the Pyrennes resided generally at Bordeaux, while the commissioner for Burgundy-Franche Comté and Lorraine normally resided at Auxonne where he safeguarded naval timber in the forests from the demands of local industries and purchased and transported timber and hemp for Toulon; their work on the navy's behalf was negligible.[42] By mid-century the administration of Burgundy-Franche Comté had become the preserve of two related families in the corps of the pen, and only death loosened their grip on place. The demise in 1759 of Louis-Charles Maillart de la Motte, controller of Burgundy, encouraged Berryer to suppress the department and force Maillart's brother-in-law, *Commissaire-général* François Potier, *ordonnateur* of Franche-Comté, into retirement.[43]

French colonies overseas in America were an integral part of the naval department; the admiration of each resembled an arsenal's. As in France, intendants directed and supervised the activities of controllers, scriveners, and storekeepers. Officers of the pen moved easily from colonial to naval administration and back again. Curiously, for all that, France did not possess a useful naval base overseas. A naval shipyard was established at Quebec in 1739 and several warships were launched.[44] A large careening wharf, the nucleus of any dockyard, was built at Louisbourg, but lacked the gear to function properly. But in the West Indies, where ships quickly became fouled, nothing at all was done to provide services to refit, repair, and replenish French warships.[45]

During the years from 1748 to 1762, activities in the arsenals fell into two phases. Until 1754 efforts to build the fleet predominated. New ship construction pressed ahead and refits were held to a minimum. Beginning in 1753, however, the navy began to reapportion its resources away from day wages – the crucial indicator of arsenal activity – and to mark time. Machault ordered no new ship construction during his first year in office, being content to complete the last ships ordered by his predecessor. After hostilities broke out in 1755 attention necessarily shifted from construction to refitting ships for sea. Thereafter the navy's straitened financial circumstances continually prevented any serious return to shipbuilding in order to replace warships being lost. By the time enthusiasm for the navy began to grow after 1760 the arsenals were so run down as to unable to respond until after the war.

INTENDANTS AND ARSENAL OFFICERS

Too much has been made of the enormous authority possessed by naval intendants and their primacy in the arsenals over officers of the sword. The notion that naval intendants were absolute masters of their domains is quite misleading. Contradictions between administration and control arose from the 1689 Naval Ordinance itself, while developments within and outside the navy during the first half of the eighteenth century eroded much of the intendants' power. Officers of the sword, the commandant, port major, senior artillery officer, and naval captains persistently attacked intendants' jurisdictions in several areas. Commandants insisted on possessing powers of petty appointment and inserted naval officers wherever possible into the procedures for receiving and inspecting naval stores.[46] Port majors constantly disputed intendants' authority over soldiers employed in the arsenals.[47] *Commissaires-généraux d'artillerie* attempted to supervise and direct production of all implements employed with the guns, interfered in ordnance workshops, and undermined the pen's authority over workers.[48] Commanding officers sought to inspect materials put into their ships during refits.[49]

The growing influence of *premiers commis* and their bureaux at court also undermined intendants, while the rise of royal provincial intendants and renascent corps of *officiers* like the *maîtres des eaux et forêts* imposed new limitations on intendants' jurisdiction outside the arsenals. Moreover, naval underfunding, which became chronic during the first half of the eighteenth century, forced intendants into close collaboration with the treasurers of the navy over whom they had no authority. While rationality lay behind the creation of French naval administration, the role of financial expediency must not be underestimated. Short-term fiscal demands rather than budgetary forecasting and management dominated the daily activities of intendants. Feeling overworked and unappreciated, Ruis-Embito once complained that he had become merely "the first worker of the arsenal."[50]

The years between the end of the War of the Austrian Succession and the end of the Seven Years' War were significant precisely because efforts to reverse the foregoing trends invariably increased opportunities for conflict. After decades of acquiescence in the erosion of their authority and prerogatives, intendants began vigorously to reassert their jurisdiction. But they were not reformers; intendants were profoundly conservative. They sought to remove excrescences and return to the pristine path once trod by the Colberts. Any real changes in naval administration were imposed from the top by the last two ministers of the period, Berryer and Choiseul. Meanwhile, intendants struggled to build and repair ships and service the fleet.

The whole order, distribution of work, and management of an arsenal's operations bore essentially on the warship in its passage from conception to construction and from repair to fitting out and laying up. Arsenals contained all of the materials, workers, and sailors to fulfil these several purposes. The direction and supervision of workers required an organization and the purchase of materials. The latter required a treasurer's chest, and for this reason the arsenal contained officers who reported on what had been spent. Finally, expenditures had to be verified and validated, which required a system of accounting and a host of procedures and signatures to establish economy, prevent arbitrariness, and subject the work of one to the inspection of several. This key administrative principle lay at the heart of many difficulties, for in some minds inspection came to mean direction. The requirements of the Naval Ordinance kept the two functions of administration and control in perpetual conflict.[51]

The intendant of each arsenal supervised the operations of from eight to ten departments or details. In theory each one was headed by an experienced *commissaire de la marine* who directed the activities of several scriveners and copyists. But the reality was otherwise. In 1751 at Rochefort, Lenormant claimed to need ten *commissaires* but had only three.[52] Seven years later Ruis-Embito had only four; little wonder that he strongly protested a proposal to send one off on sea duty.[53] The lack of *commissaires* was serious. Important details became entrusted to principal scriveners, who were insufficiently experienced, often aped their superiors, and refused to carry out the daily accounting duties essential to smooth operations in the arsenal. Such behaviour inspired resentment among their peers who generally refused to do any daily labour in their details, and left registers in the hands of copyists who knew not a word of the language employed in naval administration.[54]

Administration assumed the presence of highly motivated officers of the pen in the king's service, equipped with the requisite arithmetic and accounting skills to keep the system functioning. Constant complaints of negligence and incompetence suggest that want of these skills seriously limited efficiency. Missing timber at Rochefort was attributed to poor accounting as much as to theft.[55] Hocquart took nearly a year to complete a census of timber on hand at Brest because monthly reports had not been made for several years.[56] During the early 1750s intendants and the minister constantly complained of the ignorance of, and lack of training provided for, junior officers of the pen. Rouillé found the evidence crossing his desk deeply disturbing and demanded punishments to encourage the others. "If it is necessary to foster emulation by the advancement of good men," he wrote, "it is also very important to make examples of severity that may constrain those who are disposed to slacken off."[57]

The *Magasin-général*, or General Stores, represented an arsenal's supply service. Administration consisted of receiving, storing, and delivering materials and managing the payment of workers employed there and in the dependent workshops. The storekeeper, or *garde-magasin*, was a bookkeeper working under a senior *commissaire* who also directed the activities of several scriveners and copyists in keeping the registers.[58] The *commissaire* charged with the detail supervised the storekeeper, authorized and verified his daily balances, and presided over the entry and exit of stores which he reported monthly to the intendant. The controller of the arsenal also assigned a scrivener or clerk to witness the daily opening and closing of the General Stores and maintain a second set of registers.

The arsenals consumed four principal items: timber, iron, hemp, and sail-cloth, which provided work for nearly a score of workshops. An intendant's chief advisory responsibility lay in forecasting these needs in a semi-annual statement sent to the court. Unless the secretary of state contracted for major items himself, the intendant also held responsibility for acquiring the materials. In theory the terms of any agreement required ministerial approval before going into effect, but the need to get ships to sea and exigencies of time rendered such regulations illusory. Even if acting in the best interest of the service, intendants' independence left the central bureaux and the minister in the dark concerning encumbrances on current expenditures. Berryer once expressed outrage on receiving in December copies of completed contracts signed at Rochefort in April, May, and June, and ordered Ruis to get himself to Versailles to explain.[59]

According to the Naval Ordinance, intendants were to ensure that sufficient stores were on hand to build a ship in eight months from its date of order (Book 12, title 1, clause 11), but this requirement was so far from realization that at the end of the War of the Austrian Succession some ships had been on the stocks for four years. At the end of the next war some ships had been under construction for up to five years. An arsenal received stores in only one way. In the case of timber, intendants ordered an inspection of all items by the *commissaire* of the construction detail, port officers, and shipwrights from ships being built. If rejected, timber remained on the supplier's account, but when it was acknowledged to be of good quality the *commissaire* of the detail issued a "bon" (for "bon à recevoir") and General Stores received the supply. The storekeeper became accountable by marking the receipt, registering it, and delivering a "certificat de fourniture" to the supplier. Material only left the General Stores to be used, or worked before use. Scriveners attached to each warship under construction, repair, or fitting out were responsible for acquiring materials for their ship. In the case of the timber, a scrivener from the Construction office requested the necessary pieces on behalf of the *constructeur* or master shipwright. On receipt of the request the *commissaire* of General Stores had the material delivered and the storekeeper carried the item to the expenditure side of his register. The scrivener from Construction entered the item as a credit in his register and became accountable for all timber on the stocks. After a ship was completed the account was returned to General Stores. These scriveners were also responsible for work as well as materials.

In the ropeyard, for example, a scrivener kept registers of all hemp received and delivered to the master ropemaker and maintained registers of rope, tow, and dust produced during manufacture. Every Saturday evening he weighed the yarn in the presence of the *commissaire* charged with the General Stores and the controller or his designate. He received rope orders from the *commissaire*, and after its manufacture weighed it before the storekeeper and the *commissaire* before supervising tarring operations.[60] Well-trained junior officers of the pen needed attention to detail, a sense of responsibility, and knowledge of manufacturing.

In similar fashion officers of the pen staffed and managed the details of Repairs and Refits, Timber, Fitting-out, Troops, Hospitals, Provisions, Funds, and, at Rochefort, Colonies. A final detail, actually the first, was the office of control, usually directed by the senior *commissaire* in the arsenal. As in any organization the actual physical task of carrying out its objectives fell to the persons at the lowest level of the administrative hierarchy. The chaos of the 1740s appears to have been chiefly the result of failing to maintain registers, while any improvements in the next decade arose from reimposing control and keeping them up to date.

Construction, Repairs and Refits, and Timber details encompassed the major activity of the arsenals. Technical management was left to *constructeurs*, but supervision of their activities remained with officers of the pen. Intendants ideally chose a *commissaire* for his fidelity, knowledge of principles of shipbuilding, and ability to detect poor workmanship and misuse of materials. *Commissaires* recommended master carpenters for advancement and a balance was achieved between the former's ability to advance shipwrights' interests and the latter's willingness to obtain productive labour from workers. Administration consisted chiefly of keeping track of materials, preventing waste, and supervising employment registers and pay rolls. Keeping books rather than managing men was the main business of naval administration.

A separate *commissaire* normally managed the timber detail but so great was the threat of mismanagement that usually a scrivener from the controller's office maintained a second set of registers.[61] Toulon also maintained a workers' bureau under the direction of a *commissaire* whose chief task lay in relieving his counterpart in the Construction bureau from endless difficulties arising from workers' behaviour, pay, and debts. This officer also presided every fortnight over payment of workers and possessed a general police role in regard to their movements in the arsenal.[62]

The port captain or harbour master was closely connected to the Construction and Repairs offices and was a key arsenal officer. Charged with the preservation and care of all ships in the arsenals, port captains also commanded the shipkeepers in the port. They controlled all ship movements into and out of harbour, mooring, and unmooring; their certificates were needed for any movements within the arsenals, docking, careening, and shifting berths. Port captains also presided over launchings, and directed masting, rigging, ballasting, and stowing ships readying for sea. They directed the movement of all barges, rafts, and boats; and they or one of their subordinates were responsible for sounding the harbours and keeping them clear. Expert qualities in shiphandling, vigilance, and constant devotion to duty, uncommon attributes in naval officers, were primary requirements in port captains. Additional demands also set them apart from other naval officers. The port captain followed his intendant's orders and reported to him concerning the conservation, maintenance, equipping, and provisioning of ships. Only when ships were ready for sea did he accept the commandant's orders to lead them into the roadstead.

Port captains had to cooperate with the *commissaires* in charge of the Construction and Repairs bureaux, for it was the latter who released the hundreds of workers for all the above tasks and supplied materials for internal operations on the water; they prepared reports on ship's tackle and running gear jointly.[63] Port captains also held an advisory role concerning construction, repairs, and refits, which often led to serious conflict. During the late 1740s Rochefort had been the scene of several damaging disputes between the port captain and shipwrights who claimed independence from him.[64] At Toulon the port captain encroached on the duties of others, but the intendant attributed his behaviour to zeal rather than bad will.[65] Port captains also inspected the work of shipwrights and caulkers, a responsibility exercised jointly with *commissaires* of the appropriate details and the controller, but the role of all three officers was advisory and they were not permitted to direct the work. The only recourse in the event of disputes was to inform the intendant who then acted as arbiter.

More serious problems arose when commanding officers of ships fitting out claimed the right to scrutinize materials going into their ships or when commandants sent naval officers to inspect timber and masts entering the arsenal. Fatigued by dealings with naval officers and obstacles placed in their way, port captains often gave way to obtain peace, which undermined the intendant's authority and led to further confusion.[66]

The navy did not possess a central victualling office, but contracted the provisioning of the fleet and the care of sick and wounded sailors to private groups and religious institutions. Berryer proposed to alter the latter arrangement by establishing a *régie*, which he thought could slash costs by more than 50 per cent, aggregating payments to doctors, surgeons, nurses, and domestics and eliminating current payments for linen, drugs, medication, and rations.[67] But nothing came of the proposal and the existing costly arrangement continued. Work in Hospital and Provisioning details was chiefly clerical and at Brest and Rochefort one *commissaire* managed both. At Toulon, the Hospital office was combined with a special chaingang detail in view of sickness among the large number of convicts in the port. The Provisions office received victuals from the victualler-general of the navy, apportioned them to ships fitting out, and accounted for their consumption after returning from sea.[68] Lenormant de Mézy complained that this was a particularly difficult detail owing to "the abuses that can be committed to the supplies, and dangerous favours that the provisioners know how to procure in the bureaux at court and even in the ports, demanding ... on the part of the *commissaire* the most scrupulous attention and greatest firmness."[69]

Rochefort possessed a Colonial Office which recorded receipts and expenses for all munitions and stores destined for the colonies, dispatched ships, and requested and divided funds assigned to expenses.[70] As much as one-fifth of the intendant's annual correspondence during the early fifties was stamped "colonies," which provides some indication of how burdensome this detail had become and of the degree of specialization in the port.

The Bureau of Funds was not what its name suggests, for naval administrators did not handle funds. But this bureau prepared the crucial *décharges en forme*, or formal releases, that enabled the navy's creditors to receive payments from the treasurers-general of the navy. Funds offices were always difficult to staff with sufficiently knowledgeable personnel. In 1750 and again four years later, the intendant at Rochefort could not find a suitable candidate to take charge.[71] Lenormant criticized the corps of the pen itself regarding the matter: "the lack of attention to attaching individuals to it [Funds] and stimulating the emulation of those who would have been able to serve usefully has alienated, so to speak, everyone from this detail, in which the work to be done involves a certain dryness."[72] For his part, Lenormant thought the detail sufficiently important to establish its office in the intendancy where he could keep an eye on its activities. Hocquart did the same at Brest, but after the introduction in 1760 of new model statements for reporting to the minister, Brest and Toulon established separate bureaux to deal with all correspondence on expenses and payments.[73] Even so, Brest continued in greater disarray than elsewhere; Berryer's marginalia concerning accounting procedures in the port were especially caustic.[74] In the chronically underfunded navy, smooth operation of the Funds Office proved difficult if not well nigh impossible, yet it was crucial to the success of the navy's operation.

The arsenal's controller was the king's attorney-general charged with the preservation of his interests.[75] In Lenormant's words, he was also "the registrar and public part of the port."[76] Unfortunately, the principle of unified authority in the arsenal did not provide controllers with sufficient independence from the intendant. The clauses of title 4 of Book 12 of the Naval Ordinance suggested that controllers were independent, but did not deny that they were subordinate to intendants or that the latter were absolute heads of the administration.[77] Moreover, the controller's junior position within the corps of the pen and his reliance upon intendants for promotion and reward ensured his subordination. Although he could correspond directly with the naval minister, the duality of his duties increased the ambiguity of his role, for the controller was both an administrator and an accountant. The controller or his designates verified the operation of all details. His office contained all the commands, regulations, and letters containing ministerial orders, as well as duplicate registers of all receipts and expenses. All contracts and tenders were signed in the controller's presence. His charge was to maintain the established procedures of naval administration. The position demanded a *commissaire* who, beyond the qualities indispensable to his rank, was exact and well informed concerning all the ordinances and the quality and price of naval stores and munitions. He also had to be clear in his writing, orderly in his files, and, moreover, must have passed through all the details in the arsenal. He was invariably the senior *commissaire* in the arsenal and could anticipate promotion to *commissaire-général*. Indeed, service as controller was almost a prerequisite for further advancement in the corps of the pen.

The major task of all bureaux in an arsenal was to direct accounting documents to the treasurer, who was not, however, a naval officer or subject to the intendant's executive authority. To some degree the intendant established priorities for the use of funds and reported on the management of the treasurer's chests; but the latter was an employee of the treasurers-general of the navy, primarily a businessman in his own right. Three additional limits also checked intendants' financial powers. First, they could not exceed the total annual funds assigned to their arsenal or transfer funds from their designated purpose. Second, controllers had to be called in on all important financial operations, and third, as the sole person empowered to authorize payments on the king's behalf, intendants could not touch the funds themselves. Under the crushing pressure of underfunding, however, these limitations fell by the wayside. Controllers became collaborators in rather than checks on intendants' financial activities. Intendants frequently exceeded spending limits and reassigned funds to meet immediate demands. They sometimes borrowed on their own signatures and collaborated actively with treasurers to retain extraordinary revenues in the arsenals. To the degree that treasurers were businessmen, borrowing and lending money on their anticipated revenues, intendants by their close collaboration in obtaining funds became businessmen too. J. F. Bosher had uncovered evidence of hundreds of thousands of livres generated annually at Rochefort by the activities of intendant and treasurer acting together.[78]

Whether the multiplicity and diversity of expenditures made accounting an interesting activity or merely a difficult one depended upon one's point of view, but all accounting operations could be reduced to two, to verify expense and to validate payment. Intendants directed operations in the arsenal and controllers, port officers, *commissaires*, and scriveners implemented them. Management consisted of ordering, executing, and consuming. Each type of service occupied a place in the construction, repair, fitting out, and laying up of warships. Together with accounting, these operations formed the whole essence of naval administration from which all details of the service flowed.

Intendants kept the pulse of the arsenals by means of regular conferences with their staffs. These meetings accustomed those entrusted with some detail to report to the intendant, and informed him of work in progress and the state of the storehouses and workshops, as well as the employment of workers. They also enabled intendants to make their dispositions and give orders for the following days. Lenormant de Mézy preferred to hold daily conferences each evening after workers departed. *Commissaires-généraux*, port officers, *commissaires*, controller, principal scriveners in charge of details, treasurer, storekeeper, master shipwrights, and even engineers were all regular participants; other officers of the pen were free to attend. There the intendant clarified difficulties arising from misunderstood or poorly conveyed orders, resolved clashes between different bureaux and the workshops, assessed errors, allotted blame, and accorded praise. The conferences treated everything respecting the receipt and preparation of stores, provisions and munitions, shipbuilding, repairs, careenings and launchings, commissioning and laying up warships, levying and paying crews and workers, and everything concerning troops, hospitals, funds, fortifications, police and justice, in short, everything relative to intendants' administration.[79]

Although the close accounting procedures appeared impressive, they were not. Even assuming fulfilment of existing regulations, serious problems remained in the arsenal's administrative processes. Consider again the example of timber entering the arsenal; once received by the storekeeper into General Stores, timber entered the timber park and became subject to abuse. Needing to report only timber in and timber out, storekeepers cared not at all if it became damaged or spoiled while in storage; they blamed custodians whom they did not supervise.[80] Ironworkers similarly escaped close supervision because naval administration was so closely tied to accounting. Ironworkers behaved almost independently in the arsenals, chiefly because they worked *par économie*, on a time rather than a job basis. Workers burned excessive quantities of charcoal, stealing it whenever possible. Wastage was high and work was often redone, at the crown's expense of course. Workers frequently cut up long bar iron when shorter pieces would have sufficed, and stole the unused portions.

Old iron salvaged from demolitions and rebuildings was often abandoned to the first person to find it. Moreover, ironworkers spent far too much time furnishing offices and officers' lodgings; indeed, so well established was the custom that officers of both corps failed to take the trouble to hide the practice.[81] Obsession with accounting sometimes ignored common sense, with the result that so many possessed a vested interest in disorder that, in the opinion of some, abuses could only be halted by "firmly sustained force [*autorité*]."[82]

The question naturally arises to what extent administration in the arsenals filled a need. But it is important to distinguish between policy and administration, between the determination of what is to be done and the art of getting things done, which is concerned with processes and methods to ensure action. French naval intendants were not members of any collective administrative or policy-making body of the navy, nor were they supervised by any body with collective responsibility. Each was directly responsible for his actions through the secretary of state for the navy to the king.[83] In theory intendants consulted with the secretary of state, and each made periodic journeys to the court and advised on matters of policy. In practice, however, consultation depended upon the personal rather than formal relationship that each man developed with the different secretaries of state. Every fortnight intendants sent to the court a statement of all work done in the arsenal, but the multiplicity of details in their correspondence and the size of the labour force under their authority hid the lack of initiative in their actions. Intendants obeyed the king's orders.

Although intendants were of crucial importance to the operational efficiency of the arsenals, the prolonged absences of Lenormant de Mézy during the early 1750s and of Hocquart from Brest during the Seven Years' War, the illnesses of Villeblanche and his successor at Toulon, and the lengthy intervals between replacements suggest that the role was essentially a supervisory one. Intendants at Le Havre and Dunkirk and *commissaires-généraux* outside the arsenals appear to have been little more than placemen, but chiefly because they had little to supervise. The task of directing, advising, and chastising their juniors required active intendants. The extreme age, infirmities, and isolation from the court of naval intendants during the 1740s had been a primary cause of the chaos that reigned in the three major arsenals. But intendants did not require their enormous legislative and judicial powers, for their real authority came from their ability to protect juniors, advance them to favoured appointments within the arsenals, and recommend them for promotion and reward.

Although sometimes required to act before consulting the secretaries of state, intendants appear to have been unused to taking initiatives. Naval correspondence is filled with trivia. Like busy orderly sergeants, intendants constantly pressed details on the minister, perhaps chiefly in order to show the latter how busy and overworked they were. After the disastrous summer of 1759 Berryer and later Choiseul often expressed annoyance. Commenting on the "désordre" discovered during a general inventory of Toulon's General Stores, Berryer refused to allow *Commissaire-général* Dasque to write off unaccounted consumption. "On the contrary," he admonished, "I think that this deficit is neither pardonable nor even excusable by the circumstances of the scarcity of scriveners and extra-ordinary movements in the port"; Dasque was to investigate the conduct of scriveners and porters.[84] In the summer of 1760 Berryer's marginalia complained of long-winded letters from intendants justifying the need to keep their staffs. Ruis-Embito appeared particularly pedantic and punctilious. "He has only to be less trivial, less detailed, less hesitant ... and all will be accomplished as I desire," Berryer wrote.[85] On another letter, he minuted that "all his reason, reasonings and excuses are only scribbling [*barbouillage*] done in the ordinary way."[86] Choiseul criticized Hocquart for proliferation and for requesting decisions and authorizations for trivial actions; "it is sufficient," he wrote to the intendant, "to declare yourself and leave them [these matters] to your disposition."[87] In an angry letter to the commandant of Brest, Choiseul concluded, "I sent word to M. Hocquart that I do not want advice but your decision."[88] Clearly naval intendants were uncomfortable executives and comparatively happy accountants.

The question of whether administrative staffs were too large or too small, or whether they hindered or advanced the arsenals' objectives is impossible to answer. No criteria of efficiency existed. Critics of the pen pointed to the rapid increase in the size of the corps and its paper-chasing since the death of Louis xiv, whereas intendants constantly blamed disorder on insufficient numbers. After the onset of war there appeared to be some justice in the latter complaints. In 1755 Ruis-Embito ceased to send monthly summaries of work done, pleading insufficient personnel to prepare the reports.[89] A year later Villeblanche complained that receipts for stores, munitions, and finished work could not be sent because "the lack of persons and multiplicity of operations" in the controller's bureau, "where new personnel cannot be introduced," prevented their verification.[90] The practice of choosing the best scriveners for sea appointments and special duties outside the arsenal added to the burden imposed by the scarcity of *commissaires*. Villeblanche complained that the bureaux were so undermanned that all book-keeping was in arrears.[91] Hocquart, too, claimed that his staff at Brest was "overwhelmed by book-keeping in the bureaux."[92] A poor climate affected Rochefort where sickness sometimes incapacitated half the scriveners in the port.[93] Old age and infirmity afflicted Toulon where more than a fifth of the principal scriveners and a tenth of the ordinary scriveners were septuagenarians or octogenarians.[94]

Delays in reporting became frequent as wartime tasks proliferated.[95] At Brest, formal releases were issued up to fifteen months after stores had been delivered and *récépissés* were often eighteen months late.[96]

Inadequate training of junior officers of the pen appears to have been a major failing of naval administration. Lenormant de Mézy blamed lack of trained personnel in addition to the sudden increase in work loads in response to Rouillé's complaints concerning arithmetical errors and delays in sending invoices from Rochefort's colonial bureau to the court.[97] Ruis-Embito criticized the prevailing attitude of denigrating talent. Years before, he had tried to establish on-the-job training for student-scriveners but attitudes within the service frustrated his attempts. In 1760 he complained that current training still failed to fill the needs of the administration, adding, "it is the same in almost all circumstances in the navy that everywhere still require the talents, knowledge and activity of useful men."[98]

Berryer had no doubt that excessive numbers of administrative personnel and duplication of work accounted for inefficiency in the arsenals and he therefore cut clerical personnel as well as workers. But Ruis-Embito complained that he could not carry out the tasks demanded. Admitting that scriveners were often mediocre, he remarked that good ones were crushed by overwork and rarely paid in proportion.[99] Berryer paid no heed to such protests and pruned the administrations at all three arsenals to about 200 officers of the pen and 104 copyists by October 1761.[100] Six months later his successor slashed the staffs further, leaving Rochefort with only thirty scriveners even though up to eighteen might be required for sea duty. The intendant was left virtually with none but copyists to manage the clerical duties in the arsenal.[101]

The visibility of officers of the pen after 1759 made cutbacks good politics, especially to appease the sword's hostility. But the move resulted in few economies. With registers falling behind and a weak tradition of local executive action, the old problems returned. Berryer abolished administrative practices that often owed their origins to negligence and the passage of time.[102] But though well intentioned, his actions ignored the starved condition of naval finances and the fact that large staffs would be required in order to separate control and direction in the arsenals. The duc de Choiseul was no more perceptive. His ordinance regulating the size of the corps of the pen made it difficult for that body to perform its tasks efficiently. The size of the arsenals may have worked against achieving greater efficiency. As the pace of activity increased during wartime, administrative tasks proliferated and paperwork overwhelmed staffs. Despite ministerial complaints and hostility on the part of the sword nobility, however, the fact remains that a few hundred men supervised and directed the activities of thousands of workers and sailors and kept the arsenals running remarkably well. As the search for funds came to dominate intendants' waking hours, the continued functioning of the arsenals provided the best demonstration of the fundamental soundness of their organization and administration.

CHAPTER SEVEN

Arsenal Workers

Craftsmen, day-labourers, and convicts comprised the labour force in naval arsenals. Mastercraftsmen and foremen, called *entretenus*, probably amounted to fewer than 6 or 7 per cent of the free labour force. The majority, day-labourers, or *journaliers*, included a wide variety of skilled, semiskilled, and unskilled workers who were paid normally every fortnight on a straight-time basis. Convicts were generally not paid at all. Introduced into naval arsenals in 1749, the latter performed what contemporaries euphemistically termed "la fatigue." But as financial constraints bit ever deeper into the navy's activities, convict labour exercised an ever larger, more important role. As sailors and workers deserted owing to the nonpayment of their wages, more and more convicts became employed at new tasks. The presence of thousands of convicts at Brest and Toulon provides the major reason why these arsenals continued to function after 1760 when attrition was rapidly increasing among workers.

Following the suppression of the galley corps in September 1748, nearly 4,000 oarsmen remained at Marseilles,[1] and during the next two or three years were distributed to Toulon and Brest. Rochefort did not recieve convicts before 1767. By October 1750 about 2,400 convicts had been sent to Toulon.[2] Monthly musters varied little thereafter. From December 1751 to April 1759 the Toulon *chiourme*, or convict-gang, contained an average of 2,364 men.[3] Similar data is missing for the next two and a half years but newly condemned prisoners continued to arrive, and the above number probably remained approximate until the end of 1761.[4] The majority of convicts were afterwards transferred to Marseilles, leaving Toulon with only 600 prisoners and the two galleys that housed them.[5]

One thousand oarsmen suffering from typhus and dysentery were transferred to Brest in April 1749 but only 196 were fit to work.[6] Newly condemned prisoners sent directly to the arsenal augmented their number, but several chain-gangs were required to bring the *chiourme* to the proposed 1,500 men. The size of Brest's chain-gang during the next decade remains unknown. But Hocquart was so pleased with the new arrivals that he urged the minister to send extra chain-gangs, and by the end of 1755 claimed to be able to house 3,000 convicts.[7] Numbers never reached his wishes but as many as 1,730 convicts may have been at Brest by July 1757.[8] Fourteen months later there were nearly 2,000, yet during the interval 1,010 had been attacked by the typhus epidemic.[9] The *chiourme* probably continued to grow, for too many newly condemned prisoners reached Brest during the Seven Years' War merely to replace the ordinary turnover.[10]

Six hundred, or 15 per cent of 4,000, was thought a sufficient number to balance the annual decrease from death or release during the last days of the galley corps and the arsenals required no greater number. In the past, four chain-gangs of prisoners had wound their way across France as regularly as the seasons; after 1748 Brest received the first Paris and the Guienne chains, while the second Paris chain, integrated with the smallest one from the Midi, was destined for Toulon.[11] Such was Brest's demand for convicts, however, that both Paris chains were directed there in 1756, 1758, and 1759.[12]

Condemned prisoners faced worse rigors on the march than in the arsenals. Of 338 sent to Toulon in 1753, 109 were sick on arrival and 60 more fell ill immediately afterward. Eighty-nine men in the chain that reached Brest in 1761 had typhus or putrid fever.[13] Once prisoners were taken on strength, intendants tried to improve their lot. The sight of the first chain-gang to reach Brest deeply moved Hocquart; he was outraged on learning of Marseilles's tradition of building convict rations around bad bread.[14] At his urging, the rigors of the Paris chain were reduced by transporting the prisoners by boat down the Loire from Orléans to Nantes.[15] Soon after their transfer to the arsenals convicts apparently received improved rations of thirty ounces of bread and four ounces of peas, and for those on fatigue one-third of a pint of wine formerly given only to galley oarsmen at sea.[16]

Chained in couples and under their keepers' supervision, convicts did heavy labour, scraping ships' hulls during careening, unloading, weighing, and carrying coal, iron bars, anchors and cannon, shifting ballast, inspecting mooring chains and cables, and rigging ships. A shortage of keepers initially kept them from other employment, for regulations required one guard for every five couples.[17] Convicts at Brest were also employed to dredge the harbour after the regular contractor agreed to pay the cost of feeding them.[18] Released convicts sometimes continued to work in the arsenals as freemen, but the replacement of free labour by convicts during the Seven Years' War was a more important development.[19] By July 1757 Hocquart was employing "some hundreds" of convicts widely distributed throughout the arsenal on jobs formerly performed by sailors.[20]

Later on Toulon authorities introduced convicts into the forges until only ten freemen remained as ironmasters. Stopping the rations of convict-smiths and substituting pay of 12 *sous* daily led to considerable savings. [21]

The number of free workers employed at any one time in the naval arsenals remains unknown. As many as 9,500 may have been at work during the early 1750s. In June 1755, after Brest had completed fitting out two squadrons and was building ten ships and frigates, the naval minister complained that more than 4,000 workers, not including convicts, were too many. [22] But the labour force continued to grow. Three years later, after typhus had carried off thousands of sailors, workers, and convicts, the arsenal still counted 5,446 workers, including 900 employed among the coastal batteries of Brittany. [23] Thereafter financial constraints forced layoffs at an accelerating rate. Hocquart discharged 500 foreign workers in October 1758 and planned to release 150 caulkers at the end of the month. [24] But Berryer criticized the intendant for increasing the number of sailmakers and coopers without dismissing equivalent numbers among carpenters in order to diminish the daily wage bill. [25] Even though Hocquart dismissed 314 workers in the first week of June 1759, Berryer continued to complain, expressing satisfaction only in the following January. Dismissals continued; Hocquart released fifty workers in September and planned to discharge eighty to one hundred more from the workshops. [26] By the end of 1760 the shortage of funds had become so serious that essential workers could only be kept by closing the arsenal for two days a week. [27]

As many as 1,900 workers may have been employed at Rochefort, which contained no convicts. But well before the Seven Years' War, Lenormant de Mézy had discharged "a considerable number of workers," retaining only enough to complete construction work and shift the emphasis to serving the fleet. [28] Endemic malaria in the arsenal led to seasonal attempts to vary the size of the labour force, with layoffs commencing in midsummer and heavy recruiting in late winter and spring. [29] But this "humanitarianism" disguised the need for economy. Late in 1759 Berryer ordered reductions throughout the navy, and authorized layoffs went into effect at Rochefort on 1 April 1760. [30] A week later Ruis reported that 297 families had become dependent upon the charity of the parish curé. [31] Reductions continued during the year. By June little more than one-third of the spinners employed five or six years earlier worked in the ropeyard. [32] The caulkers' brigade of 136 men contained only half the number required to preserve the ships in port as summer heat opened their seams. [33] Elsewhere in the arsenal 150 skilled workers, carpenters, drillers, smiths, nailers, and spinners were formed into a heavy labour brigade in order to reduce their wages while attempting to keep them together in the arsenal. [34] Between January and December 1760 average monthly wages fell 42 per cent, from 23,633 livres to 13,685 livres, and Berryer demanded that the monthly total not exceed 14,000 livres during 1761. [35]

Fever prevented even this reduced labour force from working effectively. When the monthly number of sick in the hospitals at Rochefort mounted to 500 or 600 men, the actual number entering and leaving was between 2,000 and 2,500 men, a condition that prevailed during the summers of 1757, 1758, and 1759.[36] The slightly reduced totals in the monthly hospital musters for August and September 1760 reflect the reduced numbers in the arsenal rather than improved conditions.[37]

Rochefort's workers obtained some slight relief in May 1761 when 200 carpenters and caulkers, 50 sailmakers, and 30 coopers were taken on to fit out a squadron of six warships, a frigate and seven "prames," but Ruis lost no time in discharging men as soon as possible.[38] Berryer was delighted to learn of the dismissal of 957 workers during the month of June; in July, Ruis dismissed 148 workers from the timber brigade, set its authorized number at one hundred, and ordered it to meet all of the arsenal's needs.[39] Workshops quickly returned to their earlier dormant condition. By October Rochefort workers counted on finding only incidental labour there.[40]

Toulon's labour force was probably not much larger than Rochefort's during the early 1750s, but wartime demands for service to the Mediterranean fleet may have led to greater growth between 1755 and 1758. The arsenal required 500 carpenters for the preparation of La Galissonière's squadron in the spring of 1756.[41] But a decline set in soon afterwards. At the end of June 1758 *Commissaire-général* Michel began to dismiss all foreign workers and sailors employed in the arsenal, claiming a monthly savings of 10,000 livres. More than one hundred workers were dismissed from the ropeyard in October. [42] By then the new intendant, Charron, claimed to be saving a further 4,000 livres a month through dismissals of men employed on the rolls through protection or patronage. His chief complaint was that being unable to pay nearly eight months' back wages he could not dismiss more of them. Dismissals continued, however, and by the following April Charron reported savings of more than 500 livres a day.[43] The pace of work slowed considerably. Whereas in 1756 and 1757 Toulon's port captain had employed 995 men, including 150 *entretenus*, 495 day workers, 50 apprentice gunners, and 300 convicts, by March 1759 his labour force numbered only 669 men. The proportion of convicts rose from 30 to 66 per cent. Gunners were no longer employed in the port at all; "a great part [of the men] are very old," he wrote, and convicts fell ill in such numbers that five or six hundred were always in hospital. Only by scrounging 200 soldiers to man the capstans could he bring two ships into the careening wharves in one day.[44]

These developments affected intendants' attitudes. Charron's concern shifted from economizing to the arsenal's well-being; he became increasingly reluctant to dismiss workers. Wartime interruption of trade left men without alternative employment, while the navy needed to keep good workers together. To meet these concerns, he proposed general reductions in wage rates for all workers and dismissal only of the most junior.[45] But despite his intentions, heavy-handed dismissals continued. During the two years after Berryer's order to increase attrition among arsenal workers, more than 1,500 workers left the arsenal. By the last quarter of 1760, day wages paid for construction work, workshops, and repairs, the three largest categories of expenditure, had declined to less than half the amount paid during the previous final quarter. By the beginning of 1761 Toulon employed only 412 caulkers and drillers and 264 carpenters.[46]

As at Rochefort, Toulon authorities tried to retain a critical mass of skilled employees. According to the new intendant, all single workers had already left France. Half of the workers discharged since 1759 were gone and the other half, he wrote, were dying of hunger. Far better, he declared, to give half a loaf to twenty than a full one to ten.[47] To rescue the situation he proposed to close the arsenal two days a week. In February 1761 Toulon closed its gates one day a week, on Saturday; one ship remaining on the stocks was abandoned, while the intendant continued to urge a second day's closing to conserve the arsenal's workforce.[48] A year later his fears were realized. Placards announcing construction of three new warships went unanswered. Despite assurances of exact payment at new higher fixed prices rather than on a time basis, so few workers trickled into the arsenal during the summer of 1762 that work on two of the ships "totally halted."[49]

Wages were never high in the navy's arsenals, which led to the inefficient practice of training a great deal of the required labour. But security of employment, especially among *entretenus*, may have retained senior workers. The records contain enough requests to pension off old, infirm, nearly blind craftsmen to suggest that wages sometimes served in lieu of pensions.[50] In ordinary times workers' wages varied according to their trades, personal skill, and experience. Nailworkers employed on piecework in 1750 earned the equivalent of 40 to 50 sols a day.[51] Villeblanche obtained an increase in daily rates from 21 to 25 deniers for caulkers but kept the news from other workers.[52] Salaried employees earned considerably more. Senior carpenters received monthly stipends of between 50 and 80 livres, while other tradesmen obtained from 50 to 60 livres. Master smiths and founders earned up to 100 livres monthly while master mastmakers received supplements in addition to the same basic rate.[53] Bounties worth 150 livres, paid to foremen carpenters on ship launchings, went to *entretenus* to mark special contributions.[54] But daily wage rates generally rose rapidly in wartime while naval stipends remained fixed. By 1759, for instance, carpenters and drillers earned 45 sols a day, which was substantially more than the 40 livres monthly stipend paid to a junior carpenter *entretenu*.[55] The result was that men refused to accept promotion, preferring to remain *non-entretenu*, and work gangs lost junior supervisors. Proposals from Toulon's controller to increase wage rates to encourage skilled men to enter the service were inopportune, to say the least, for Berryer had recently refused a similar request from Brest.[56]

Methods of payment compounded the effect of low wages on workers and their families. Unless paid in cash, workers were quickly forced into a debtor economy, which fluctuated according to the price of bread and denied men the full value of their wages. During wheat shortages bakers demanded cash because they themselves needed to make cash payments for their own supplies.[57] As naval funds dried up following the outbreak of war, however, this once temporary situation became permanent, subjecting workers to extended poverty. Workers received scrip in lieu of wages, which bakers in turn accepted for bread. Grain merchants retired these notes by taking them as payment for wheat sold to the bakers. Naturally workers did not receive bread to the real value of their wages. At Toulon arsenal workers departed from the monied sector of the economy all through 1757. By December of the following year they had been without wages for ten to twenty-one months.[58] At that time, grain merchants, fearing for the security of scrip that remained unredeemed for so long, proved unwilling or unable to supply such long-term credit, and began demanding cash from the bakers. Thus, precisely when Berryer was enjoining intendants to spend current funds only on current expenditures, the latter had to redeem the oldest notes from previous fiscal years in order to secure the remainder. The web of credit survived but at great cost to workers. Three years later *Commissaire-général* Dasque reported that all naval scrip was being discounted from 15 to 20 per cent.[59] The loss of employment and heavy discounting of naval notes paid in lieu of wages during the Seven Years' War destroyed whatever job security may once have compensated arsenal workers for low wages. As early as the summer of 1758 activity began to decline in the arsenals, and following the severe deterioration of the next three years' operations ground virtually to a halt. Long before the end of hostilities, naval arsenals lost their ability to renew the losses incurred at sea or even to service the remaining ships. Neither organization and administration nor want of skill among workers were factors in the decline. The chief cause was lack of money.

An analysis of the different trades employed in the arsenals sheds light on the nature and complexity of arsenal labour and on the need for the extensive clerical staff employed in management duties. Table 5, constructed from a lengthy report by Lenormant de Mézy, gives an estimate of the workforce at Rochefort required to build one 74-gun and two 64-gun warships and three 24- to 30-gun frigates or a flute of 700 or 800 tons in place of one of the frigates. The 1,946 workers are assumed to be repairing two other vessels and annually fitting out twenty more. Presented as an idealized collective portrait – not a nominal census – of Rochefort's workforce, table 5 is a useful guide to the work and workers in French naval

TABLE 5
Workers at Rochefort, c. 1750–1754

| Craft | Salaried Workers | | | Day Workers |
	Masters	2nd Masters	Foremen	
Shipwrights & carpenters	7		13	440
Blacksmiths & ironworkers	2		4	100
Borers	2		4	50
Sawyers				60
Caulkers	3		6	130
Ropemakers	1	1	4	180
Mastmakers	1	1	2	15
Sailmakers	2	2		30
Carvers	1		1	12
Painters	1		1	15
Joiners	1	1	2	26
Blockmakers	1	1	1	40
Heavy carpenters	1		2	20
Small workshops	1		1	20
Armourers & gunsmiths	1	1	1	30
Gun-carriage & patternmakers	1	1	1	22
Founders	1	2		4
Coopers	1	1	1	18
Oakum boys			2	40
Ox-drivers				20
Casual labourers			4	120
Apprentice-gunners			4	100
Riggers	1	2	4	240
Watchmen				96
Gatekeepers				12
Total	29	14	63	1,840

Source: BN, n.a.f., no. 126, ff. 238–58, "Mémoire sur le service et l'administration du Port et arcenal de la marine à Rochefort."

arsenals. Though lacking a pay scale, it has the twofold merit of identifying trades and the proportion of workers, *entretenus*, and day-workers employed in each one.

Although some labour was paid for on a job basis (*à prix fait*), most workers received straight time (*à la journée du roi*) regardless of production. Sawyers, three men to a saw, were an exception. Whenever possible they were paid by prearranged contract (à l'entreprise). The Naval Ordinance stipulated that whenever possible ships were to be built on a job basis, but lack of skilled labour meant that the opportunity seldom occurred. By the middle of the eighteenth century wages so paid amounted to less than 10 per cent of the total paid for time. Although work à l'entreprise was considered cheaper, in 1748 Maurepas ordered two of the ships at Toulon to be built à la journée in order to train workers to meet the scarcity.[60] Poor pay, however, meant that the demand was never met, for, once trained, skilled workers sought employment in private yards, as was the case in 1751 of caulkers at Toulon.[61] Rouillé approved Lenormant's efforts to have harbour craft built and repaired à l'entreprise, but the practice had its limitations.[62] Joiners, who made the panelling, bulkheads, ladders, benches, and other ship's fittings, had once been paid in this manner, but poor workmanship led Lenormant to recommend that eighteen of the twenty-six men indicated in table 5 be paid on straight time to ensure work of better quality.

Provincial intendants were reluctant to levy anyone for naval service. A request for thirty armourers to work at Brest during the winter of 1754–5 had to be followed up by orders from the naval minister to the intendant of Brittany.[63] Appeals to provincial intendants of Lyon, Dauphiné, and Provence for 500 carpenters to work at Toulon in the spring of 1756 proved fruitless; a levy had to be ordered throughout France to meet the demand.[64] Later in the war, the intendant of Limousin and Angoumois predicted failure to levy 200 dayworkers for Rochefort; he argued that constraints and violence would not succeed and refused to use force except on the minister's explicit orders.[65] Naval requests for workers from areas distant from the arsenals invariably placed strains on local economies and forces of order.

At Rochefort each warship was entrusted to a master shipwright or constructeur who directed one or two foremen and sixty or eighty carpenters depending on the hull size. Frigates were entrusted to a single master shipwright with a foreman on each hull who supervised a hundred carpenters. Another master shipwright, foreman, and ninety carpenters were assigned to refits and repairs while a smaller team of forty carpenters under similar direction constructed and maintained craft employed in the arsenal itself. Finally, ten carpenters, also directed by a master shipwright and foreman, handled the receipt, arrangement, and delivery of timber. Master shipwrights possessed some initiative for they distributed carpenters and workers according to their own choice.[66]

Craft labour imposed a key limitation on the speed of work. Although the Naval Ordinance assumed that any ship could be completed in eight months, the employment of more than the above numbers on any one hull was counterproductive. Additional men obstructed one another while supervision became next to impossible.

Drillers bored the thousands of holes for the oak treenails and iron bolts that secured a warship's timbers. Under the immediate direction of several foremen small teams moved about the stocks and hulls wherever they were needed. Caulkers, who comprised a much larger portion of the workforce, were among the arsenal's most skilful and dextrous workers. A new ship was best caulked quickly on two sides at once which accounts for their number. When time pressed heavily, some carpenters also worked as caulkers. Both trades were required to train apprentices, one for every ten master carpenters or ten master caulkers, but more than one apprentice for five masters appears to have been normal.[67] Masters were explicitly forbidden to demand any payment from their apprentices, who received 5 sous daily, but the injunction was undoubtedly ignored.

The proportion of blacksmiths and ironworkers – locksmiths, edge-toolmakers, and nailmakers – at Rochefort may not have been typical of other arsenals. As the chief reception centre for the navy's cast-iron ordnance, Rochefort may have required a larger than usual complement. Moreover, the wide distribution of forges at Rochefort may have led to some unavoidable duplication of work.

The ropeyard was the largest single work area in the arsenal. Eighty of the workers were spinners and the remainder were employed as hacklers and layers to clean, break, and prepare hemp, spin and tar yarn, and form and lay rope and cables. Good spinners were of critical importance, for next to hemp of fine quality, well-twisted yarn was the prime requirement for good cordage. Sailmakers were employed in two separate shops for old and new sails. Painters pulverized and prepared colours as well as applying paint. The blockmakers' and pulleymakers' shop employed a large workforce requiring skilled labour and close supervision. Wheelwrights, cartwrights, and oarmakers are included in the designation heavy carpentry, but most workers laboured on construction and repair of wharves, bridges, cranes, and the maintenance of graving docks and slipways. "Small workshops" included tinsmiths, lanternmakers, mattressmakers, plumbers, and braziers.

Since no convicts were employed at Rochefort, a greater proportion of casual labourers worked there than elsewhere. The port's heaviest work was carried out by men and oxen. Lenormant de Mézy claimed that sleds hauled by ox teams were incomparably superior to horses and carts in moving timber and cannon. Causual labourers unloaded, inspected, and arranged timber, planks, iron, hemp, and other heavy stores; loaded, shifted, and unloaded ballast; loaded storeships for the colonies; cleaned slipways; closed locks; arranged and shifted stores in the warehouse; lent a hand cable-laying in the ropeyard; and performed an infinity of other tasks. Apprentice-gunners were similarly employed. Required to attend the arsenals to learn gunnery, these young sailors reinforced the casual labour each day after classes.

Riggers were sailors levied from the classes, but many had been rejected for sea duty and were of slight physique. Their poor quality and crucial importance to the arsenals' main activity demanded that they be closely supervised by the boatswain and his mates. The best riggers worked in the rigging-shop where everything relating to ship-handling was prepared. Others worked on the ships, while the dregs formed the crews of countless small craft that moved on the river and downstream to Basque Roads. Some twenty-eight masters were employed independently to guide these craft. Watchmen and shipkeepers were normally chosen from among old petty officers injured in the king's service and trustworthy carpenters and caulkers whose long service and advanced years left them unable to work. Three-quarters of them served in pairs on board ships in port and under construction or repair, and the remainder ashore in storehouses and workshops.

The sun and the seasons governed work. Delays at Rochefort in December 1751 were blamed on short days and snow that covered the ground; even Toulon was not spared – in January 1758 snow covered the ground there for two days.[68] Work proceeded six days out of seven in the week but religious and parish fêtes reduced the number of working days to about twenty-five a month. In winter, workers began at 7 A.M. and finished at 6 P.M., and in summer they laboured from 5 A.M. to 8 P.M. The work day was broken by half an hour in the morning and one hour for dinner between 11 A.M. and noon. A second half-hour break was allowed during the afternoon in summer. The ringing of a bell signalled the beginning and end of each working day. All workers were required to leave the park at the dinner hour. At noon and again fifteen minutes after the bell sounded in the evening scriveners made rounds to ensure that all workers had left. On Saturdays and holidays *commissaires* and general scriveners made morning and evening rounds preceded by an archer to ascertain whether watchmen and shipkeepers were at their posts, and whether unauthorized personnel were present. They possessed the power to arrest and imprison anyone unable to explain his presence.[69]

Workers were subject to two "appels" daily, when scriveners charged with details verified the real number of men on the job and noted absentees in their log-books, which contained workers' names, daily wage-rates, and days worked.[70] Whereas at British naval dockyards men were mustered at the clerk of the cheque's office only for *appels*, French workers remained under the eyes of naval officers as well as foremen throughout the working day.[71] Scriveners were physically present on ships being built or repaired, in the ropeyard and elsewhere, and were responsible for preventing idleness and accounting for materials.

Masters and foremen were charged with keeping men on the job, but with few incentives to do so they were unlikely truant officers. Scriveners were probably no better. Arsenals provided plenty of hiding places for idle workers nor were walls so high or so well kept that enterprising men could not leave the arsenals between *appels*. Sufficient complaints over the years concerning old sheds, lean-tos, and walls that served no purpose but as hideaways suggest that within the hive of activity of a busy arsenal many workers did as they pleased.

Discipline in the arsenals posed several thorny problems that were never resolved. Moreover, it is not clear whether the navy was capable of finding, or willing to seek, solutions. Much more than criminal activity was involved; worker discipline was intimately related to pay, worker custom, and security against theft and fire, as well as to efficiency and productivity. Insubordination and petty crime were difficult to handle because no clear disciplinary system was in place.

Whether a boot, fist, or rope's end resolved most problems between workers and foremen remains unknown, but more severe and arbitrary measures were not unheard of. On orders from a principal scrivener, Swiss guards at Rochefort once seized several workers, took them to a secluded timber hangar, and in an officer's presence, stripped and whipped them "comme des nègres." Despite the illegality of his actions, the authorities pleaded with the minister that the officer was too good to be made an example of; after two days' house arrest he returned to duty with a warning and the case was dropped.[72] The incident suggests that discipline was highly arbitrary and that workers possessed little or no collective security.

Officers of the pen were accused of depriving workers of advances, making them work for the officers' benefit, reducing their wages and pocketing the surplus, obstructing inspection of the care given to workers and sailors in hospitals, and disposing of custodial positions to servants and friends.[73] Although workers appeared to be closely supervised by administrators, successful management depended upon qualities of zeal and probity which were lacking among junior officers. Incentives to get maximum labour from the workforce appeared confined chiefly to salaried employees.

Discipline was chiefly maintained by deductions from wages and withholding payments. The performance of masters and other salaried employees was reviewed weekly and if absent they were deprived of a month's salary. Special regulations issued at Dunkirk for carpenters and sawyers lodged in the storehouses while building *bateaux plats* included fines of one-quarter of a day's pay levied against workers found in their rooms after *appels*, while those who had not returned there by 9:30 P.M. were required to pay 10 sols to the guard.[74] But the practice of levying fines was subject to multiple abuse and notoriously weak. Penalties fell not only on workers who left their jobs before the bells, but on men who fell sick or were injured on the job. The most serious abuse, however, lay in the practice of withholding salaries and wages from workers on the assumption that fear of losing unpaid amounts would keep workers in the arsenals.

Desertion meant forfeiture of all due payments. But as regularity of payments declined workers increasingly doubted that they would be paid at all.

Abuses and a certain job security provided by arsenal employment ate into efficiency. Charges that two wholesale wine merchants were on the cooperage rolls at Rochefort, and that other rolls contained the names of workers' children, were undoubtedly true. A review of the boatmen maintained at Toulon revealed that thirty of the fifty men on the rolls did not exist. Officers of the pen to whom they were assigned drew the monthly stipend of 18 livres themselves.[75] The scarce evidence probably reveals only the tip of an iceberg. But as financial exigencies forced increasing layoffs, major reductions in the workforce, and ever longer delays in payment of wages, efficiency became quite subordinate to the need to induce workers to remain in the arsenals.

Formal punishments were ineffective for several reasons. Before the war the intendant of Toulon had no reservations about hanging a watchman found guilty of theft of rope, or recommending that one of five men caught oyster fishing in the "New Port" be sentenced to the galleys.[76] A master carpenter arrested while trying to remove timber from Rochefort was banished from naval service.[77] But intendants became reluctant to award such punishments to men who remained unpaid, and towards the end of the war were even unwilling to convict. The single punishment of a life sentence to the galleys (living death), prescribed for theft exceeding 10 livres, was much too severe.[78] After arguing that many workers' misdemeanours did not warrant the death penalty or the galleys, in 1754 Lenormant de Mézy obtained permission to erect a *carcan* (an iron collar on a stake in which prisoners were exhibited) on the surrounding wall of the arsenal to punish dishonesty and insubordination.[79] Toulon already had a *carcan*. A carpenter caught in the act of stealing bolts from a workshop ought to have been sentenced to the galleys for life, but *Commissaire-général* Michel pleaded for a reduced sentence of three days in the *carcan* at the last hour of the working day and banishment from the arsenal. Arrested in January, the poor man's sentence was finally determined in August: six months in prison, already served, and banishment.[80] This more temperate attitude on the part of the authorities hardly improved the situation.

In the early 1750s theft had assumed epidemic proportions. Night patrols were introduced at Brest and Rochefort to improve security but with limited effect.[81] The new prison at Rochefort was the scene of so many escapes that the jailer was suspected of collusion.[82] The chief problem, however, appeared to be the sentries who were under military authority. Ruis-Embito trusted them less than the workers. The only solution, he claimed, was to give responsibility for security to the intendant. Ruis also blamed criminal elements in Rochefort, charging that some two hundred branded convicts chiefly occupied in maintaining cabarets lived in the town. If entrusted with security, he proposed to employ English mastiffs and their handlers in place of sentries and patrols.[83]

If theft was difficult to halt, negligence raised more complex problems. In 1755 Machault ordered Rochefort's mastmaker imprisoned for negligence and poor workmanship, after L'Inflexible, 64-guns, arrived at Brest and had to have her bowsprit, foremast, and mainmast replaced. During the brief voyage from Rochefort play in the butt-joints of the masts' "fishes" resulted in displacement of the iron bands in the "assembled" masts that revealed faulty manufacture. L'Eveillé and L'Aigle, both 50-guns, had sailed in company and the captains of all three warships also complained of bad quality cordage in the shrouds and rigging. In this instance the boatswain's competence was questioned. Machault demanded to know whether his activities arose from negligence or ignorance, or if he had followed usual standards at Rochefort. Naturally the minister's queries reflected upon the entire establishement; both intendant and commandant leaped to the mastmaker's defence.[84] Three years later authorities at Brest indignantly rejected charges from Rochefort that ships leaving port were poorly outfitted and sloppily stowed.[85] Charges of negligence and incompetence were usually resolved by diffusing blame. In the case of the mastmaker at Rochefort blame was apportioned between him and the ship's crew. Defects in the masts were said to have increased during the voyage to Brest owing to too much hauling on the shrouds. The mastmaker was criticized for failing to draw and sufficiently tighten the bands on the masts and imprisoned for one month. Negligence in ship construction and ship outfitting could not be adequately dealt with because so many vested interests in the arsenals moved to their own defence when accusations occurred.

Negligence leading to fire was a different matter and was severely dealt with. Rochefort suffered two disastrous fires in 1756. On 4 April fire broke out on the hulk, L'Elizabeth, which burned and sank. The fire jumped to Le Hardy, 66-guns, moored alongside. Five or six men were killed, about a score injured, and Le Hardy sank to her fore-stays. Tried by court martial, one shipkeeper from L'Elizabeth was sentenced to the galleys for three years, another, who was not on board Le Hardy on the night of the fire, was given three months in prison, deprived of pay, and banished for life from Rochefort. Three others were discharged.[86] Three months later a devastating fire consumed a wing of the General Stores containing paint shop, wood-carving shop and its contents, sailmaker's shop, the sail storehouse, all the material in the joiner's shop, and the gunroom, musket stocks, and timber for gun carriages. Total damage was rumoured to amount to 1,200,000 livres.[87] Cause of the fire was given as arson but Ruis-Embito, who joined in fighting it, found no one to blame for treason or carelessness. Failure to find the guilty party or parties of course may indicate negligence of a far more serious order.

Security and disciplinary problems in the arsenal should not be allowed to overshadow other aspects of worker behaviour, but very little is known about working-class customs. Whether craftsmen and workers could protect their jobs from others remains unknown, but as they were apparently encouraged to recruit their own children into the labour force, and children abounded on the pay rolls, it is reasonable to believe that workers enjoyed, at least in normal times, a certain security of tenure.[88] Indeed, Toulon's controller listed the "prodigious" number of children – exceeding the number of mastercraftsmen in some shops – on the pay rolls as a major abuse. But custom could not be abolished, only controlled. He recommended that children be at least ten years old and required to present baptismal certificates in order that three and four-year old "enfants à la jaquette" should no longer be seen in the arsenal.[89] Current worker customs, he claimed, were responsible for one-fifth to one-quarter of all superfluous expenses in the arsenal. But since these customs, including feather-bedding, were not illegal, alterations had to be carefully handled. The delicacy with which authorities confronted working-class custom is well illustrated by reference to removal of wood scraps from the arsenals.

Custodians were the worst offenders, frequently cutting up good timber and selling it in town. Nine months after arriving at Brest, Hocquart issued an ordinance designed to control removal. Abuses persisted and he issued a sterner ordinance in February 1756. Custom was too strong to forbid carrying wood scraps out of the arsenal; the intendant merely attempted to regulate the practice. Baskets not sacks were to be used, and only at the dinner hour. Nothing was to be carried away in the evening. Only carpenters and other woodworkers had the privilege; others, if caught, were to lose one month's pay and spend eight days in the cells on the first offence, and to be expelled from the arsenal in the second instance. The ordinance was reissued in August 1760, which suggests that its clauses had been ineffective.[90] Special regulations at Dunkirk also reflected a policy of control rather than prohibition; "chips" could be gathered daily, but only after the hoisting of a white flag to signal commencement of such activity, and could be carried out of the arsenal, but only twice a week.[91] Berryer was insensitive to worker custom; less than three weeks after Hocquart's second ordinance appeared, he issued a general ordinance forbidding any removal of pieces or scraps from the arsenals. Hoping to achieve another economy, he recommended that wood scraps be used to heat administrators' offices.[92] The measure was ineffective. While Ruis conformed to the ordinance at Rochefort, *Commissaire-général* Dasque at Toulon informed the minister that much of the scrap was inconsequential and insufficient to heat offices, adding that the old custom had the virtue of keeping the arsenal relatively clean.[93] With authorities reluctant to enforce them, such orders to shipwrights and woodworkers became a dead letter. Shipwrights, however, were probably the strongest group of workers in the arsenals and conservation of their prerogatives reflected their superior position in the workforce. Nevertheless, arsenal authorities recognized these worker "rights" and defended them from bureaucratic injunctions from on high.

Collective protest was something else. Strikes by French workers were rare. Daniel Baugh has noted that with a single exception none of the strikes in British naval dockyards during the 1740s was concerned with delays in paying men their wages. English strikes were for lost privileges concerning working hours, special pay allowances, and the "right" to work extra.[94] John Ehrman, on the other hand, found the opposite to be true half a century before and such was the case in France during the 1750s.[95] Group actions, which can scarcely be called strikes, arose from failure to pay men their wages and salaries or from increases in the price of bread.

In the spring of 1748 wheat collections to relieve famine at Bordeaux drove Brest bread prices to 3 sous a livre; "the worker ... had barely enough to live on."[96] A proposal to sell naval provisions at lower than market prices and give flour to workers in partial payment of wages was rejected, but the initiative suggests that as in the case of "chips" arsenal authorities were more conscious than the minister of worker realities.[97] Workers normally depended on credit and when bakers refused to give it owing to their own need to pay cash in times of scarcity, authorities made special appeals for funds. In 1751 at Rochefort *Commissaire-général* De Givry took cash from the colonial chest when the treasurers-general of the navy refused his appeal.[98]

Workers rarely threatened authorities effectively, but at Rochefort in the summer of 1750 a threat went unpunished owing to the anticipated damage to two hulls that had been on the stocks for four years; a fifth winter would destroy the ships. Lenormant de Mézy reported that several workers had mutinied and more would follow if advances were not forwarded.[99] Threatened job actions became more serious as wage payments declined during the war. Foreign workers rioted at Toulon in the summer of 1757, and authorities attributed their action entirely to delayed payments.[100] The most serious events occurred a year later. Early in August 1758 at Brest, Hocquart reported that workers everywhere had left their jobs, "to portray to me their poverty. Today," he added, "I am in the cruellest position that an intendant can be in."[101] Two weeks later, while dining alone, three hundred wives besieged his door demanding that their husbands be paid. "They and their children are perishing from hunger and poverty; hopelessness was written on their countenances," to which, he noted cryptically, "they joined quite indecent expressions, to say nothing more."[102] Claiming a conspiracy to confront him daily, Hocquart arranged for armed protection, but the workers appeared undeterred. A month later thirty sawyers gathered at his office protesting their poverty. But the intendant could neither help them nor hold them; "Sailors and workers absent themselves without leave or permission whether to seek subsistence elsewhere or support their families by loose living (*libertinage*) or work in the harvest."[103]

The situation was equally serious at Rochefort. On 1 August workers in many shops downed tools and refused to continue working. After receiving a promise of at least four of the ten and twelve months' wages owing, workers refused to return to work and requested their discharge even at the risk of losing all that was owed them. Some had already left the arsenal; *Commissaire-général* Du Teillay saw no means of relief. The ultimate sanction of holding back wages had failed.[104] Unrest and desertion continued. A few days later men thronged outside his quarters three times in one day. Soon, he thought, the port's own services would be abandoned; "if they are not given money and their discharges they will dismiss themselves by the soles of their shoes."[105] Violent fevers which struck the port in the late summer killed seventy-three, filled the hospitals with hundreds of sailors and workers, and added to the workers' misery.[106] Their poverty obtained no relief, however, for funds remained unavailable. Abandoning hope of ever seeing their back wages, men continued to desert. Collective action of this kind was generally ineffective because it posed no real threat in the face of lack of funds. Instead, it contributed to the destruction of the workforce, crippling the navy's chief production units.

In June 1760 the chevalier de Mirabeau described the heartbreaking scene that met his eyes every morning on opening his window overlooking Brest's arsenal: "The air of death and desolation that reigns there makes me groan. A ghastly silence! A wilderness laid waste."[107] Five years before, the naval minister had exulted that Brest stood ready to carry out any task, lacking for nothing in matériel or workshops.[108] The same contrast developed at Toulon and Rochefort. In 1755 Ruis-Embito had advised Machault that in five years Rochefort could build twenty-five ships-of-the-line and other ships in proportion. Availability of timber and masts rather than productive capacity was the crucial factor.[109] But five years later Rochefort was closing down. The size and strategic importance of each arsenal was partly responsible for their terrible state, for as funds declined one could not be closed in order to conserve the others; all ran down. While the British naval blockade is usually viewed as the primary cause of the deterioration of the naval arsenals, doubts remain about such a conclusion.[110] Financial clouds leading to worker layoffs had appeared on the naval horizon even before hostilities commenced; the arsenals experienced serious difficulties long before a close blockade of Brest occurred in 1759.

Moreover, lack of funds ensured the effectiveness of enemy action when the close blockade appeared.

How is one to assess the efficiency of the naval arsenals during wartime? Daniel Baugh used three questions to test the efficiency of British naval dockyards. Was the work done at moderate expense? Was it done right? Was it done on time? There can be no precise answers, he adds, because there were no precise standards, and there is no reason to fabricate arbitrary ones.[111] Answers to Baugh's questions appear to assume that sufficient funds were available to continue production whether efficiently or not, but French naval arsenals were starved for funds. Constant admonitions from naval ministers to reduce payments for day wages in the arsenals did not mean that too much was spent on wages, but that they were the most visible expenditures in the arsenals and their reduction was the easiest means to achieve short-term savings. On the other hand, large warships could not be built elsewhere and construction of smaller vessels, such as frigates and corvettes, in private shipyards produced no savings for the navy. Privately built ships were probably more costly. Frigates constructed at Nantes and Bayonne diverted skilled workers and required the dispatch of iron, sails, and cordage from Rochefort.[112] The duc d'Aiguillon charged that ships could be built at St Malo for 25 per cent less than the cost of Brest-built ships, but he was neither a sailor nor a disinterested critic, sending a proposal from that port's principal merchants along with his criticism to court.[113] Moreover, while the duke may have been correct, he ignored all of the limitations that prevented the naval arsenals from ever achieving the efficiency of commercial shipbuilders.

The strategic location, large size, and self-sufficiency of French naval arsenals prevented specialization, required large clerical staffs to manage them, and undoubtedly contributed to naval shipbuilding costs. The need to train and retain skilled workers and provide for the old and infirm in lieu of paying them pensions also contributed to these costs. But the high quality of French warship construction was generally acknowledged and wage costs were not excessive, merely visible. Complaints of substandard materials were far more common than those of poor workmanship. Indeed, the latter were too few to warrant serious consideration. Charges of poor quality work derived from a multitude of sources, including critics of unfamiliar innovations, ships' officers and petty officers whose poor seamanship led to damages at sea, and authorities in other arsenals who were quick to find fault with work that originated elsewhere.

The question whether arsenals fitted out ships efficiently and as quickly as possible after receiving ministerial orders is more difficult to answer. Months of endless delays often dogged departures of French squadrons during the Seven Years' War and even in peacetime. But lack of funds, provisioning and manning problems derived from the former, and the misbehaviour of officers did more to create delays than indolence or poor supervision of workers. In one respect, a serious problem in British naval yards did not occur in their French counterparts. Whereas in British dockyards ships' companies were supposed to clear incoming ships of guns, stores, and a good part of the rigging, these tasks were the responsibility of port captains in French arsenals.[114] The same difference held for rerigging, restowing, and reprovisioning ships at sea. Seamen from the French levies were not mustered into ships' companies until after ships completed careening, and afterwards they remained under arsenal authorities until the final review occurred. Common delays related to clearing and rerigging ships in British yards did not occur.

French officers sometimes complained that sailors arrived on board exhausted from working in the arsenals, but intendants denied that men were fatigued by their labours there. Any exhaustion, they claimed, was due to unnecessary and unauthorized journeys and work forced on the men by the officers themselves.[115] The establishment of stationary port commandants after 1745 reinforced the growing independence of ship captains from arsenal officers and fostered lack of cooperation in readying ships for sea. Far from assisting port officers in their duties, sea officers held them in contempt and impeded their work. It is difficult to see how the conflict between sword and pen could have led to innovations to improve efficiency.

The independence of intendants from any body with collective responsibility, on the other hand, may have contributed to efficiency in the arsenals. Intendants were able to establish priorities within the arsenals and could quickly shift their workforce to meet sudden demands from the court.[116] A major defect in the arsenals appeared to be the inadequate training of junior administrative officers who were directly involved in supervising workers and managing their activities. Their relations with workers and how much attention they paid to their immediate responsibilities remain uncertain, but so much arsenal management was taken up by accounting that when their registers fell into disorder delays were bound to follow. Nevertheless, the navy's major problems lay elsewhere than in the organization, employment, or management of arsenal workers.

CHAPTER EIGHT

Ships and the Fleet

Eighteenth-century French warships were the finest in the world. Their attributes became apparent as early as the War of the Spanish Succession when inferior French forces proved almost impossible to intercept, while at the end of the century they continued to display innovations that showed the French still in the forefront of naval ship design and construction.[1] Evolving throughout the century, French warships became larger, swifter, and more heavily armed. The crucial changes between the penultimate and final stages occurred in the development of the square-rigged warship between 1748 and 1762.

Well-built warships could last for more than a third of a century but only a few did so.[2] In 1748 nine ships remaining in the navy were twenty-one to thirty-six years old but most of the remainder were less than eight.[3] Two years later only five ships built before 1740 remained.[4] French naval planners assumed a ship's longevity to be twelve years, an arbitrary figure based on estimates that well-built ships constructed of carefully selected timbers lasted ten years in the Atlantic and twenty years in the Mediterranean. Few existing ships met these criteria in 1748.[5] Poor methods of construction, use of improper or green timber, and atmospheric conditions were three very general causes of premature deterioration in warships. These factors often combined to render newly built ships unfit in a very short time. Le Conquérant, 74-guns, was so filled with dry rot as to require rebuilding in 1750, only four years after launching; Le Fier, 60-guns, built the same year, also needed repair; and Le Caribou, a storeship, was converted to a hulk only five years and three voyages after launching.[6] French warships were also likely to be lost through enemy action or peril of the sea. While twenty-seven ships became unfit for service between 1741 and 1748, twenty-three were captured and eighteen frigates, sloops, and storeships were lost.[7] During the Seven Years' War ninety-three naval vessels of all types, about one-third of which were ships of the line, were captured, wrecked, burnt, or otherwise destroyed.[8] So many factors affected the life of a ship that statistical lifetime averages only made planners aware of the need to replace the fleet at a rate of one-twelfth annually, and of the fact that, at any one time, one-quarter of the ships in the fleet were unfit for sea or needed rebuilding or repair.[9]

After 1748 the navy not only had to build ships at a constant rate to maintain existing numbers, but had to double the number of ships of the line during the next five years. Increased innovation accompanied this development, and at the beginning of the Seven Years' War the French fleet was practically new. Between 1748 and 1758 the French built fifty-two ships of 64 guns or more.[10] The ability to innovate, growing timber shortages, financial constraint, and opportunities provided by the large number of orders encouraged new developments in shipbuilding that gave rise to significant, rapid changes in the proportions and characteristics of French warships.

The French generally did not make the same mistake as the British who took advantage of every increase in ship size to increase the number and calibre of cannon with little or no net gain in operational efficiency.[11] British practice finally unravelled in the 80-gun three-decker, which held the distinction of being the worst designed ship in the British navy.[12] Instead, the French tended to place fewer, larger guns in ever larger ships whose proportions gradually became finer in order to achieve greater speed. By mid-century these developments had brought about greater distinctions between ships of the line and frigates, and between new and old ships of the same rate, than existed in the navy of Louis XIV. But standardization remained more apparent than real. Despite fewer rates and fewer distinctions between ships of each rate than in the past, a critic claimed that no two ships in the navy were alike and consequently the cost of maintenance remained high.[13]

Past practice and present reality governed the manner of rating French warships. The Naval Ordinance of 1689, whose Book 13 contained ship specifications, was an end rather than a beginning. Its terms represented the culmination of fifteen years of research under Colbert and Seignelay, and laid down rates and dimensions of ships on the eve of a new war when demand for innovation was so great that the new ordinance was tossed aside. In many respects the terms regulating shipbuilding were a dead letter from the moment of their appearance.[14]

French warship ratings were based on a combination of heaviest calibre of gun on board and number of gun-decks rather than the number of guns alone. French first-rates were three-deckers, mounting 36-pounders in their main batteries. Second-rates, carrying 74 or 80 guns, also carried 36-pounders but possessed only two decks. Third-rates also came in two sizes or orders, 60 and 64 guns, but were considerably smaller than second-rates for they mounted only 24-pounders in their main batteries. By 1750 the presence of 24-pounders determined whether a ship was carried above or below "the line."[15] Fourth-rates, 50 to 56 guns, carried 18-pounders in their main armament. The old twin-decked fifth-rate, or heavy frigate, was virtually dropped from the fleet. Only four existed by 1750, and no more were built. The French did not rate their light frigates which carried 20 to 30 guns. Corvettes, like British sloops of war, included all square-rigged ships of less than 20 guns. They usually carried 4- or 6-pounders mounted in single tiers of from 10 to 16 guns.

Both navies employed 12-, 18-, and 24-pounder cannon, but the French livre weight of 489.5 grams was 8 per cent heavier than the British pound. The heaviest French gun, the 36-pounder, fired a ball more than one-fifth heavier than one fired from the largest British naval gun, the 32-pounder. The French 8- and British 9-pounders were virtually equivalent. Carrying twenty-eight and thirty 36-pounders, French 74- and 80-gun ships were larger and more powerful than British ships of similar armament.

Large ships obviously cost more money than small ones but it is difficult to determine whether the financially constrained French navy achieved economies of scale. The new, more powerful ships, particularly the new frigates, could be deployed with greater flexibility, but the frigates were costly to maintain because their heavy ordnance place a great strain on the relatively lighter timbers used in their construction. Unit costs increased but there seems no way to determine whether the navy achieved more "bang" for its livres. The following costs were estimated in 1744 for second-, third-, and fourth-rates and frigates: 74-guns, 350,000 livres, 60- and 64-guns, 300,000 livres, 46 to 50 guns, 200,000 livres, and 26-guns, 130,000 livres.[16] These very conservative figures include only the cost of the completed hull and standing rigging. Another estimate placed the cost of a 74-gun ship armed for war, but without provisioning, at between 700,000 and 800,000 livres and a 50-gun fourth-rate in a similar state at about 300,000 livres.[17] Even these estimates may be low if we accept one in 1758 that claimed a 60-gun warship provisioned for six months with a crew of 500 cost the crown 900,000 livres. By contrast, a 66-gun vessel with 540 men equipped for the Guinea slave trade with a year's supplies cost 640,000 livres.[18]

Costs probably increased during the 1750s. In 1750 the navy budgeted 1,500,000 livres for day wages alone in order to complete eight ships of the line and continue work on seven others.[19] Ten years later 500,000 livres were needed to purchase a 64-gun, fir-built, Genoese warship, which required another 100,000 livres to put her and two similar ships in condition for the service. Small-ship costs did not increase appreciably. In January 1758 the navy bought two 30-gun frigates for 200,000 livres each.[20] Privately built, these were undoubtedly very sound vessels.

TABLE 6
Comparative Firepower of French and British Warships, 1764 (in livres wt)

	French Gun Batteries						British Gun Batteries				
Type	1st	2nd	3rd	Weather	Total Wt of Shot	Type	1st	2nd	3rd	Weather	Total Wt of Shot
100 guns	30–36	32–24	32–12	6–6	2,268	100 guns	26–42	28–24	28–12	18–6	2,045
90 "	30–36	32–24	32–12	–	2,184	90 "	26–32	26–18	28–12	10–6	1,571
80 "	30–36	32–18	–	18–8	1,800	80 "	26–32	26–18	28–9	–	1,438
74 "	28–36	30–18	–	16–8	1,676	70 "	24–32	26–18	–	20–9	1,312
64 "	26–24	28–12	–	10–6	1,020	60 "	24–24	26–12	–	10–6	878
50 "	24–18	26–12	–	–	744	50 "	22–18	24–9	–	4–6	589
32 "	26–12	–	–	6–6	348	32 "	24–12	–	–	8–9	333
26 "	26–8	–	–	–	208	26 "	22–9	–	–	4–6	206
20 "	20–6	–	–	–	120	20 "	20–9	–	–	–	167
16 "	16–6	–	–	–	96	16 "	16–6	–	–	–	80
12 "	12–4	–	–	–	48	12 "	12–4	–	–	–	44

Source: Marine B⁵, 11, "Comparaison des vaisseaux français avec les vaisseaux anglois en dimentions principales, en artillerie et en equipage en 1764."
Note: The weight of shot of English ships has been determined in French livres weight of 489 grams. In 1764 French officials determined the equivalents on the following basis: 42-pound shot = 39⅞ livres; 32-pound shot = 29¼ livres and 24-pound shot = 21¹¹⁄₁₆ livres. They did not determine equivalents for shot of less weight.

Eighteen months earlier the intendant of Le Havre had claimed frigates cost only 115,000 livres, but this figure excluded internal joinery, carving, and masts. Merchants at Caen agreed to build two 30-gun frigates for 180,000 livres each.[21] The crown paid 226,540 livres for another 30-gun frigate built at Marseilles in 1760, but this vessel mounted 12-pounders.[22] These figures give only a notion of relative costs; ships were so individual that unit costs are incalculable.

Rebuilding costs were probably higher. Ships had to be carefully dismantled before new materials could be incorporated into old hulls. The intendant of Rochefort concluded that rebuilding always cost more than new construction. In his view the practice continued only because of false hopes of preserving qualities admired in the original. "It is a prejudice absolutely contrary to the King's interests," he wrote, for the original dimensions could never be preserved after a major rebuilding. By way of demonstration he pointed to La Zéphyr, a frigate rebuilt at Rochefort in 1753. The finished ship was several inches wider than the original so that her deck beams were too short and her deck lacked sufficient camber.[23]

Longevity, evolution, rating, and costs of warships reveal little about the navy's strategical requirements. Although the French are sometimes thought to have had no conception of naval strategy in the middle of the eighteenth century, armament, choice of type, and ship design do provide some indication of strategical intention. French shipbuilding during the 1750s demonstrated that the navy had no intention of meeting their enemies in a battle of annihilation and that ships were intended increasingly for operation in distant waters. Traditional requirements for Mediterranean-based ships to suppress Barbary pirates and to escort the Levant trade blurred the latter intention for one-third of the fleet was normally based at Toulon. But the high priority given to constructing 74s and 64s, and the continuing absence of first-rates, indicate that naval planners aimed to fulfil Maurepas' policy, developed during the recently concluded war, of creating a convoy system for the protection of trade.[24] That they did not succeed is not a demonstration of lack of intent, but of the difficulty of implementation.

Two former types of third-rates, highly esteemed as cruisers half a century before, were dropped from the line and quickly phased out of the fleet. With much less in masts and rigging, carrying only 18-pounders in their primary batteries and sometimes 8- and 4-pounders in second batteries and on weather decks, these ships of the old navy were no longer able to meet the demands of empire or the need for greater firepower.[25] The last two 56-gun cruisers were launched in 1745. During the next decade, however, L'Oriflamme and L'Arc-en-ciel mounting only 50 guns were classed as "heavy" frigates. The need to carry seven months' supplies and water for three months in order to cruise in the Caribbean reduced the usefulness of these small ships. Lack of firepower led to the disappearance of 60-gun third-rates. The 36-year-old *Le Toulouse* was broken up and *L'Heureuse* went to Rochefort to serve as a transport in 1750. Still seaworthy after twenty-three years, the latter's small size militated against her use in the line.[26] The same year, the four-year-old *Le Fier* was rebuilt to carry only 50 guns and sent to Toulon. The navy's last 60-gun ships were built at Quebec. *Le Saint Laurent* launched in 1748 was deemed unfit for service two years later; and, as if acknowledging her redundancy, *L'Orignal*, the final ship in her class, sank on launching in September 1750.[27]

Expediency appeared the chief reason for continuing to build a few 50-gun warships. In 1750 Rouillé acknowledged the relative uselessness of ships mounting only 18-pounders in their main battery but owing to large quantities of suitable timber on hand, he authorized their construction.[28] Even so, the new ships were much larger than before. *L'Amphion*, designed to carry twenty-four 24-pounders, was laid down at Brest in 1749 and served as a model for *Le Sagittaire* launched at Toulon in 1761. Expediency also accounted for its construction. Toulon had on hand only sufficient nonappropriated timber to build such a warship, and as the timber was four to five years old, it had to be utilized or wasted.[29] The new ships threw a broadside that far surpassed the weight of shot fired by the same class of cruiser of Louis xiv's day, and could still play a useful role in the eastern Mediterranean.[30] By the end of the war the few remaining 50-gun ships in the navy were based at Toulon.

From the beginning of the peace, the French concentrated almost exclusively on building 64s and 74s which best combined firepower and mobility. The 74 was the finest ship of the line ever built; for details of its construction and much else the superb work of Jean Boudriot must be consulted.[31] In 1748 the fleet contained six 74s and a 70. During the next three years six additional 74s were launched and six more laid down. A hybrid 72, *L'Algonquin*, was also laid down at Quebec. Nine 64s were also launched by the end of 1750 and six more were laid down. By October 1751 twenty-nine of the forty-four ships of the line were either 64s or 74s.[32] During 1753 six more of both rates were added to the fleet and six remained to be completed in 1754 and 1755.[33] By November 1754 forty-five of the fifty-five ships of the line were of these two classes.[34] During 1755 the navy ordered six more of each type.[35] War losses in these two classes were substantial and it is difficult to determine the status of the fleet at any one moment. *L'Alcide* and *Le Lys* ("en flûte"), both 64s, were lost in 1755 as was *L'Espérance*, a 32-year-old 74 mounting 70 guns. None was lost during the next two years but at least seventeen were destroyed, captured, or wrecked in 1758 and 1759.[36] Even so, by June 1761 the only ships available for service in the Atlantic were eight 74s and six 64s.[37]

The few large, powerful 80-gun ships in the fleet were built as flagships. Only one, the recently built *Le Tonnant*, remained in the navy in 1748.[38] *Le Soleil Royal* was launched in the first year of peace, and during the next two years Toulon, Brest, and Rochefort launched *Le Foudroyant, Le Formidable,* and *Le Duc de Bourgoyne* respectively.[39] A sixth and seventh, *L'Océan* and *L'Orient*, were launched at Toulon and Lorient in 1756. Two more were laid down late in the war but remained unfinished when hostilities ended.[40]

All three classes of ship increased in size and firepower during the period. The greatest absolute and relative increase occurred in the 74 which no longer mounted the same variety of cannon as in the past. By mid-century it was more powerful than an 80-gun ship of the War of the Spanish Succession. The 64 of 1759 was as large as the 80-gun ship of half a century before, and though lacking equivalent firepower, master shipwrights were busily designing plans to mount 18-pounders in the second batteries of new 64s.[41] The English rated the twin-decked, 80-gun ships, whose length surpassed those of earlier first-rates, as equivalent to their own three-decked second-rates of 90 guns. The dismal fate of this largest class of French warship during the Seven Years' War, when four were lost in action, is a reflection on their commanders and crews rather than on the qualities and merits of the ship (as well as being evidence of the enemy's superior numbers), for *Le Foudroyant*, captured early in 1758, provided the British with the form and dimensions of their two-decker, 84-gun ship and no three-decker of less than 90 guns was ever built again in Great Britain.[42]

The navy had no first-rate ships of the line in 1748, and did not intend to build any until after the authorized number of sixty of the line were completed in 1754.[43] Completion was slow and the navy ordered the first of five only in May 1757. By the spring of 1758 the keel, stem- and sternposts of *Le Royal Louis*, 116-guns, had been laid down at Brest and frames were being mounted, but the ship was only completed late in 1761.[44] The incomplete hull of *L'Impétueux*, 92-guns, remained on the stocks at Rochefort for five years, and the ship, renamed *La Ville de Paris*, was launched only after the war.[45] Authorities at Toulon planned to begin construction of *Le Majestueux*, 114-guns, and *L'Indomptable*, 112-guns, in the spring of 1758, but little activity occurred.[46] Timber acquisition went ahead but in February 1759 Berryer called a halt, there being by then no question of commencing their construction.[47]

Good reasons abounded for not completing these first-rates. The sole naval purpose of these huge ships, the navy's "ultimate" weapon, was in the event of a showdown to stand against the best that the enemy could offer. First-rates served no other useful purpose and were seldom employed. As a class of warship they were expensive to build, maintain, and operate. In brief, the navy did not need them unless its chiefs planned a battle of annihilation.[48] The cost of construction, maintenance, and operation, and the lack of versatility and opportunities for regular employment made them a poor investment for a numerically inferior fleet.

The influence of tradition and demands of prestige accounted for the laying down of two or three of these first-rates and the planning of others after the war began. Ruis-Embito strongly favoured building three-deckers, proposing as early as 1752 that one be built at Rochefort. Lenormant de Mézy curbed his enthusiasm but after Ruis became head of the arsenal he began reserving "bois d'élite," encouraged master shipwrights to produce plans, and begged the naval minister for permission to begin construction.[49] The preferences of a forceful man like Machault, demands for more second- and third-rates, and the need to increase the capacity of the arsenals to fit out a large proportion of the fleet in 1755 and 1756 reduced the priority of first-rates for a while. But naval officers, feeling keenly the absence of these monstrous vessels, successfully persuaded Peyrenc de Moras to order them. The marquis de Massic did not rescind the orders, but soon after assuming office Berryer called a halt to construction in Toulon and ensured that no funds were available to complete two already under construction at Rochefort and Brest. In 1762 the duc de Choiseul expressed doubts about the armed might of *Le Royal Louis*, arguing that no more ships of this type should be constructed; he favoured building larger 80-gun ships capable of mounting 24-pounders in their second batteries.[50]

During the Seven Years' War ships of the line frequently sailed to America *en flûte*, with their main batteries removed entirely or stowed in the hold, gunports sealed, and lower desks transformed into cargo holds. The 64s and 74s that transported eight battalions of troops to Canada in 1755 mounted 22 and 24 guns respectively.[51] The risks were great – two of the three ships lost in action that year were *en flûte* – but several reasons account for the practice. Unlike past wars the present one created a tremendous demand for troops, stores, and munitions to be sent overseas. The Minorca expedition alone contained 176 transports.[52] But the greatest challenge came from the colonies where the risks of the voyage were large and the cost to the navy from shippers crippling. Freight rates to Canada eventually rose to 350 livres a ton.[53] Warships fitted out *en flûte* possessed several advantages under these circumstances. First, the cost of transporting troops and supplies was reduced; second, a ship of the line *en flûte* could carry as much as four merchantmen, and third, it outsailed ordinary commercial vessels. Finally, warships, even *en flûte*, could protect themselves from all but the capital ships of the British navy, which obviated the need for escorts, and when their mission was completed the stowed guns of their main batteries could be remounted for the return voyage.[54] But while true enough, these reasons given at that time disguised the lack of ordnance to arm the ships that sailed to Canada that year. The same thing occurred in 1756 despite the loss of *L'Alcide* and *Le Lys*. Three warships carried two more battalions to Quebec. The second-rate *L'Héros* mounted only 36 guns and two third-rates, 26 and 22 guns respectively. One of the latter was left at Quebec to be broken up and her ordnance transferred into the two remaining ships. After mounting 56 guns carried as ballast, *L'Héros* and *L'Illustre* reemerged fully armed into the Atlantic, but the truth remains that even *en flûte* the three ships had carried only sufficient ordnance for two.[55]

Superior in size and speed, at least in light breezes, to their British counterparts, French frigates also evolved. Large, twin-decked frigates of an earlier age, mounting 32 to 46 guns, were no longer built after 1748. In 1751 the navy possessed only three of more than 30 guns.[56] The practice of carrying two different calibres of cannon, usually 8- and 12-pounders, was not abandoned but shipwrights favoured single-decked frigates with one calibre of gun on board. Frigates mounting 24 or 26 guns, usually 8-pounders, were most common, but several were built to carry 12-pounders. *La Gracieuse*, built in 1749 at Toulon, became the first 24-gun frigate designed to carry a single tier of 12-pounders;[57] *La Hermione*, 26-guns, the first of its class, joined the fleet the following May. As soon as she left the ways at Rochefort, a second, *La Nymphe*, was laid down.[58]

Some debate surrounds the qualities of these new frigates. The traditional view ascribed a superiority of design to characteristics not seen in British frigates of the same period. Captured French frigates are often touted as models for British frigates still employed more than thirty years later.[59] Whereas older, more heavily armed fifth-rates carrying 32 to 46 guns were forced to keep their lower gunports closed in heavy seas, the new single-decked frigates might be more able to fight in all weathers. But their long decklines, shallow draft, and light construction which gave them speed also limited their seaworthiness, a quality much sought after in enemy construction. Recent study suggests that French frigate design was not inherently superior to British design but intended for quite different purposes.[60]

Expediency also influenced frigate construction. Lack of ordnance and sufficiently large timbers, governed Rouillé's decision to construct two 20- or 24-gun frigates mounting 6-pounders in place of a single 26-gun vessel with 12-pounders.[61] Nevertheless, when possible, larger ships indicated the trend. Once the war began consideration was even given to building 24- and 26-gun frigates mounting 18-pounders. One such privately built vessel, however, was found unsuitable for the needs of the service.[62] The 30-gun frigate was probably the finest frigate design at mid-century, and like new ships of the line was imitated by the enemy who appreciated its fine qualities.[63] While some continued to carry a mixture of 8- and 12-pounders, others mounted a single battery of 12s. One such frigate built at Le Havre displaced nearly 1,100 tons which was greater than the 50-gun *L'Hippopotame* and only 50 tons less than *Le Lion* and *Le Sage*, two 64s laid down in 1749.[64]

Frigate construction never received high priority in the navy's own dockyards. *La Pléiade* lingered for two years on the stocks at Toulon before being launched in November 1755.[65] But these ships could be built quickly. *La Danaé* was launched at Le Havre less than six months after being ordered; and the same shipyard launched three sister ships during the interval.[66] Commercial shipbuilders possessed considerable experience owing to traditional demands for privateers and the easy availability of appropriate timbers. Twelve 30-gun frigates, six corvettes, and two flutes were ordered in 1756 from yards at Bayonne, Caen, and Nantes as well as Le Havre. After 1757 the department favoured acquiring already completed privateers. *L'Echo*, 26-guns, *L'Arethuse*, 30-guns, *La Terpsicore*, 22-guns, *La Favorite*, 32-guns, *La Fortuné*, 26-guns, *La Chimère*, 26-guns, and *La Diligente*, 30-guns, were all purchased by the department.

Barbary pirates continued to plague Mediterranean coastal shipping and xebecks and galleys continued to perform useful roles. But even here the navy introduced new xebecks of a type never before employed. In 1750 four of the new types were laid down at Toulon, the larger mounting twenty-four 8-pounders and the smaller sixteen 6-pounders. At first some difficulties occurred with broken lateen yards made of ordinary fir, but the problem was soon solved and the large xebecks proved very suitable at sea.[67] Indeed, by the end of the war the strength and sea-keeping qualities of the large xebecks led naval officers to recommend 20-gun xebecks mounting 8-pounders as minimum size for the service.[68]

Sixteen galleys remained in service when the galley corps was united to the sailing navy in 1748. They also continued their customary roles, transporting French ambassadors and princes of the blood from Antibes to Genoa and protecting coastal shipping and the mouth of the Rhone River from corsairs and pirates.[69] Indeed, new galleys continued to be ordered during the decade, *L'Amazonne* in 1751 and *La Bretonne* in 1755.[70] During the last three years of the war two to four galleys constantly escorted merchantmen carrying naval stores to Toulon.

During 1759 the department ordered between two and three hundred *bâteaux plats* or flatboats constructed at several Norman ports.[71] Intended to transport troops during the proposed invasion of England, the flatboats were to be 100 feet long, mount two heavy guns, and carry about 200 men.[72] In July the department also ordered twelve larger craft called *prames* designed to carry a crew of 250 or 300 men and built at Dunkirk, Bordeaux, and Nantes.[73] Original specifications called for a craft 130 feet long, 36 feet abeam and 9 feet deep, able to carry twenty 36-pounders and two mortars, but some were larger.[74] *La Louise*, completed at Bordeaux in April 1760, resembled a ship of the line above the waterline; nearly 160 feet from stem to sternpost and 44 feet abeam, she was rigged as a man of war with three masts and top masts and armed with a single tier of twenty-four 24-pounders, two mortars, and 23 swivels. But though she drew nine to ten feet of water, the *prame* was quite flat-bottomed, possessing three keels. Nevertheless, she sailed reasonably well, being described as stiff and a good seaboat.[75] There was little of real significance about these craft, but their construction, together with several *chalouppes canonniers* or gunboats, signalled an important shift in naval policy whose chief consequence was the virtual cessation of ship construction before the end of the Seven Years' War.

Only thirty ships of the line and nineteen frigates remained in the French navy after hostilities ceased in April 1748, and six months later when peace was finally signed the number fit for sea had declined to twenty-four.[76] Ship construction joined the naval debt as the most important concerns of naval policy during the early 1750s. The effect of an all-out construction program on other areas of the department, decisions concerning the number and types of ships to be built, and the speed of their construction crucially affected other naval policies. The degree to which other concerns affected decisions about shipbuilding created a tension in naval planning which, when combined with the brevity of tenure of ministerial office-holders, made it impossible to achieve a stable policy. In the confusion some important questions were lost from sight or given a secondary priority. Nevertheless, between 1748 and 1758 the navy successfully built a well-balanced, well-constructed fleet, although it was one that remained by no means ready for war.[77]

Losses were not serious during the first three years of the Seven Years' War, three third-rates in 1755 and one old-fashioned 50-gun cruiser during each of the next two years. But from the spring of 1758 until the end of 1759 the navy lost nearly half its total fighting strength.[78] Financial problems came to the fore after three years of war and the navy could not replace these serious losses. By and large, government bankruptcy in October 1759 confined the navy to the ports, unable to recover from its two major defeats of the year. Few ships put to sea during the next two years. In June 1761 only twenty-one ships of the line were available for naval operations.[79] A replacement program appeared later that year, but any ships that came down the ways before hostilities ended had been on the stocks for four and five winters, the last of the ships ordered in 1757.

At the beginning of 1748 Louis xv ordered twenty warships, two frigates, and a 600-ton storeship to replace the vessels lost during the recent war. Half of the ships were to be completed in the current year, the other half by the end of 1749.[80] But this first initiative ignored the exhausted state of the dockyards, the absence of naval stores, and the naval debt. The intendant of Brest seriously doubted whether he could fit out five ships and four frigates owing to the absence of stores; thirty thousand livres were needed to complete rebuilding a ship just to get it out of a slip needed for new constructions. In April workers were dismissed from the ropewalk owing to the lack of hemp.[81] The navy's debt, conservatively estimated at 14 million livres on 1 January, was acknowledged to be 26 million livres a year later. Nevertheless, by the end of 1749 ten of the line and two 50-gun cruisers had been launched.[82]

Maurepas planned to have fifty ships of the line in service by the end of 1750 and hoped to increase the fleet to 110 ships and 54 frigates during the decade following the Treaty of Aix-la-Chapelle, but his aspirations were unrealistic and his planning faulty.[83] Under his successor the king established the fleet at sixty of the line and forty frigates, but no date was set for their completion. Rouillé spent considerable time considering ways and means to achieve the new goal. Deterioration of existing ships was so great that the current rate of new construction could not replace them and double the number in the fleet at the same time. Moreover, Maurepas had not foreseen the demand for new naval ordnance. Without greatly increased production the new ships would have few guns to mount. Lack of cannon was a key factor in Rouillé's decision to extend the completion date of the new fleet to some time after 1753; this was combined with a decision to build slowly and at the same time commence work on as many ships as possible. Forgoing any but minimal frigate construction, Rouillé hoped to be only one unit short of the authorized number of ships by the end of 1753. Nearly the entire 10.5 million livres available for variable expenses in the navy's ordinary funds in 1750 went into construction and acquisition of naval stores and material. The price was paid in reduced training and few operations. Less than three-quarters of a million livres were destined to fit out ships for sea duty, a niggardly policy that continued for as long as Rouillé remained in office.[84]

The stimulation and reinvigoration of the naval arsenals produced the wanted results quite quickly. By October 1751 there were even some grounds for optimism. Recent comparison showed that the French navy stood in the same numerical relation to the British as in 1740; 38 to 116 ships in 1750 as compared to 44 to 120 in 1740, and whereas ten years earlier three-quarters of the French ships had been old, the present fleet was almost new.[85] But although the French matched British rates of construction and the newly invigorated dockyards could increase the rate of building, they refused to engage in an arms race.

The question had been considered since 1749. Lack of ordnance made it virtually impossible to expand the fleet beyond its authorized number. In

1750 the new secretary of state decided to make a virtue out of the need to increase the military establishment in Canada and the shortcomings of cannon manufacture in France. La Galissonière, Rouillé's confidential adviser and interim governor of New France for the past three years, developed a radically new concept of North American defence. Insisting that Canada was the key to all French influence in North America, he persuaded Rouillé to double the number of *troupes de la marine* in the colony and argued strongly against a policy of increasing the fleet rather than strengthening Canada. France, he argued, could never win an arms race with Great Britain, but could achieve a stronger imperial and maritime position by arming Canadian colonists. Although his argument was mechanistic, measuring the colonial balance of power solely in military and strategic terms and ignoring the demographic and economic power of the American colonial population, La Galissonière hoped, by developing a strong military threat in the colonies, to divide British naval resources between European and North American waters. Acceptance of this thinking was confirmed in October 1751 when the question of future naval building policy was carried to Louis xv for discussion and decision.[86] The authorized number of the fleet remained unchanged.

Twenty-six warships had been constructed or rebuilt since the peace. Eight had become unfit for service, but fifteen more were on the stocks and two more were to be laid down before the year's end. Twenty-one frigates were in service and three were to be launched in the next three months. With only sixteen needed to complete the authorized number and no special requirement for them in peacetime, the previous decision to ignore frigate construction was confirmed. The heavy pace of construction brought together large labour forces in the dockyards and in Rouillé's view no physical or technical impediment existed to complete the authorized fleet by the end of 1753. Two and a half years after taking office, Rouillé's regime had transformed the arsenals. The lethargy, insubordination, malversation, and even outright theft that marked the last years of Maurepas' regime had been largely overcome. The dockyards hummed with well-coordinated activity. A comparison of naval construction during this three-year period and the five years of the American War of Independence is very revealing. The twenty-six ships built from late 1748 to late 1751 compare most favourably with the twenty-nine new and eleven rebuilt ships constructed between 1779 and 1783.[87]

But early in 1752 financial constraints began to affect the pace of construction. Day wages, the single most expensive levy on the navy's ordinary funds, were the first to be affected. As a result, completion dates for eight of nine ships on the stocks were advanced to 1754. But while postponement permitted reduction of annual funds set aside for daily wages, new hulls had to be laid down at the beginning of 1753 to replace ships becoming unfit for service the following year. Once begun, however, the decrease in the pace of construction had a snowballing effect, and commencement of the first three-decker scheduled for 1755 was delayed until 1757.

Events at Rochefort and Toulon illustrate clearly the loss of momentum after 1752. Timber supplies were so great at Rochefort in December 1751 that the intendant requested suspension of further shipments; more than 300,000 cubic feet of timber were expected to arrive during the coming year and the dockyard lacked additional storage space.[88] In April 1752, however, the minister forbade commencement of a third-rate until the next year owing to lack of funds.[89] Shortage of funds also influenced types of construction. In September Rouillé rejected a proposal to build three of the line during 1753, ordering that only one ship and a frigate be built.[90] Two weeks later he ordered new construction to be carried out over two years in order to carry half the expense in the *projet* for 1754 and the other half the following year. By the beginning of November the financial situation was clearly spelled out: "It is sufficiently indifferent to the service whether a ship of 74-guns or 64-guns be placed on the stocks next year, and you may decide on one or the other construction according to the assortment of timber that is in the port. But if all things are equal, it will be best to build a ship of 64-guns rather than a stronger ship considering the lesser expense. I strongly advise you always to retain only the number of workers whom you consider are absolutely needed, in order to eliminate as much expense as possible."

The intendant decreased construction as ordered to a modest program to build one 74, a 26-gun frigate, and a storeship during 1753. But lack of funds forced a further slowdown. It became out of the question to place any new warship on the stocks. The frigate and storeship would be completed, but new work was to be laid down only after all other expenses had been met. Rouillé left to the intendant's discretion whether to complete the 74 or carry construction of her hull into the following year.[92]

At Toulon during the spring of 1754, work was suspended on L'Hector, 74-guns, Le Vaillant, 64-guns, and L'Océan, 80-guns, in order to allow the reduced labour force to fit out a small division of two ships and two frigates for sea.[93] The first two ships had been exposed to the elements for more than two years, but current plans called for them to remain on the stocks for another year before launching. Fearing for the quality and integrity of their work, the shipwrights successfully obtained approval to launch the ships before the year's end.[94] But the pace of construction decreased on other ships in order to keep wages constant. The decline in funds, however, had another unforeseen effect. By November it was acknowledged that lack of seasoned timber would prevent the launching.[95] L'Hector and Le Vaillant were launched only in July and October 1755, and L'Océan in June 1756.

The declining priority of construction also affected innovation. In April 1754 two regular 26-gun frigates were ordered to carry 12-pounders. The new-style frigate was eventually built in 1757, but only after the Chamber of Commerce of Marseilles arranged for a private entrepreneur with his own materials to undertake construction.[96]

The decline in construction well before hostilities began was one of the costs of improving the department's financial outlook. But it is difficult to criticize Rouillé. The controller-general had substantially reduced the funds available to the navy in 1753 and 1754. Rouillé gave chief priority to reconstructing the fleet to its authorized number. During his tenure of office thirty-eight ships of the line were built or rebuilt. He was probably right to postpone the completion dates of the last ships in view of the revised priorities of the department and the government's desire to remain at peace. He was undoubtedly wise to refuse to be drawn into an arms race that he could not win. His realistic if conservative policy after 1752 of concentrating on the long and short-term benefits to be achieved by reestablishing the navy's credit with its suppliers was perhaps the wisest decision of all. When he left the ministry in July 1754 the French navy stood at its greatest strength since the death of Louis xiv.

When Machault planned his major reinforcement of New France in the coming year he had fifty-seven ships of the line: twenty-seven second-rates, twenty-three third-rates, and seven fourth-rates. Six ships remained under construction but the same number in service required refits. The number of frigates had not increased from three years before, but eight were on the stocks and the authorized number of forty could easily be achieved during the next two or three years.[97]

Although he employed twenty-seven ships and frigates in the Atlantic in the spring and summer of 1755, Machault did not anticipate British reaction. Only in August, after learning of the loss of L'Alcide and Le Lys off Newfoundland, did he give serious consideration to increasing the fleet. Notes prepared by the naval secretariat indicated that material and human resources in the dockyards were sufficient to build forty more ships of the line, raising the number in the fleet to one hundred and increasing the number of frigates to fifty or sixty by the end of 1756. New yards for warships could be established at Genoa and Lorient, and for frigates at Bayonne and Le Havre. The sole obstacle was lack of funds.[98] The intendant of Toulon reinforced the need for funds. Responding to the minister's request for an estimate of the cost of completing all current construction and refits, building five new ships, and readying the whole Mediterranean fleet for sea, he replied that 21,396,000 livres to the end of 1757 would do the job. He gave no hint that the task was impossible or even difficult; the key was money.[99]

As leader of a faction in the Royal Council and former controller-general of finances, Machault produced increased funds during his tenure of office. In 1755 and 1756 he was authorized to spend 31,326,000 and 40,006,000 livres, respectively, increases of 76.5 per cent and 125.4 per cent over the combined ordinary and extraordinary funds granted to Rouillé in 1754.[100] Such increases, especially in unencumbered extraordinary funds, permitted vigorous action. Within days of receiving reports from the intendants, Louis xv received a proposal to increase the number of ships of the line by 20 per cent. Less than two months later the dockyards received approval to begin work on six new 74s and six 64s.[101] Fifteen ships were completed or built within the next twelve months.[102] But the cost was great. Total expenditures exceeded authorized funds. Costs of levying crews and provisioning ships rose beyond all estimates, far surpassing expenses under Rouillé. Increased emphasis on repairs and refits in the arsenals also increased costs. The reduction of labour and material in the dockyards and increased demands for refits, repairs, and outfitting meant that after an initial spurt of activity work proceeded very slowly on new construction. Two of five ships ordered at Toulon were launched in 1757, but only one ship was launched during each of the next three years. L'Orient, 80-guns, and Le Brillant, 64-guns, were launched at the India Company's shipyard at Lorient by the end of 1757, but only three of five ships ordered at Brest were launched during the same period. Le Raisonable, 64-guns, completed in 1756, was the last ship of the line to be launched at Rochefort during the war.

At the time of Machault's disgrace in February 1757, the fleet probably stood at its highest number for the entire period. Serious losses did not commence until the following year. The impulse to increase construction continued for a few months under Machault's successor. Five first-rates were included among twelve new ships ordered at Brest, Rochefort, and Toulon in May.[103] This last major decision to increase the fleet represented a failure in policy. Of the twelve ordered in May, only four were launched before the war's end.[104] Inclusion of so many first-rates also reflected a serious decline in policy-making. The plans had been drawn under Machault but he had refrained from ordering the vessels. But Peyrenc de Moras appeared unable to resist and gave in to traditional demands and the corps' search for prestige.

Ships ordered previously were only slowly completed as workers increasingly abandoned the dockyards. Ruis-Embito halted all construction at Rochefort in order to speed repairs and refits.[105] The frame timbers of the 92-gun L'Impetueux, begun in 1756, stood exposed to the elements until after the war. La Thesée, 74-guns, was launched at Brest in January 1759, but Le Duc de Bourgogne, 80-guns, remained two years in the dockyard for want of funds. Two hulls on the stocks were launched only after the war. Berryer halted construction on two first-rates at Toulon early in 1759; only a second- and a third-rate remained on the stocks. By the following May the two ships had been launched, and Berryer allowed work to commence on a new ship only to keep a few of the most skilled workers in the dockyard. At the beginning of 1761 Intendant Hurson entreated Berryer to order some construction at Toulon.[106] But dockyard personnel had been so reduced that after the minister agreed to build two warships, the intendant estimated that work could not begin before December.[107]

That money was the crucial obstacle to further construction after 1758 seems clear. Expanding on the need to build a second- and third-rate at Lorient in the spring of 1759, Berryer explained to the controller-general that the abundance of ship timber there and at Nantes was not the major justification for his request. The real reason, he wrote, was to avoid charging the cost to the navy's current funds, presumably by having it borne by the Indian Company.[108]

Growing awareness of weakness overseas finally led to a radical alteration of policy. Under the impetus of the duc de Choiseul and Marshal de Belle-Isle preparations proceeded to assault the centre of enemy power. The navy used current funds to build invasion barges and supporting vessels for the "expedition particulière" of the duc d'Aiguillon. Construction of 200 flatboats (*bâteaux plats*) was ordered at Le Havre and Dunkirk at an estimated cost of over five million livres.[109] Orders went out to naval officials at Brest, Lorient, and St Malo to send 1,000 workers to Le Havre, and Berryer dispatched Joseph Pellerin, *premier commis*, to aid Intendant Ranché with the project.[110] The department also arranged for *prames* to be built at Dunkirk, Nantes, and Bordeaux and in July ordered a further fifty-four flat-boats.[111] Costs escalated until the court banker, Jean-Joseph de Laborde, complained that 30 millions, sufficient to construct thirty ships of the line, had been expended on the craft and the aborted expedition.[112]

Little wonder that the arsenals were starved for funds for the next three years. The damage was considerable. Although the duc de Choiseul ordered new construction in December 1761 no new ships appeared before the end of hostilities. Workers trickled into Toulon so slowly that in July 1762 the intendant reported work on *Le Zélé*, 74-guns, and *Le Provence*, 64-guns, "has absolutely stopped."[113] At Rochefort, Ruis-Embito acknowledged the change of name of *L'Impétueux* to *La Ville de Paris* but lacked the timber and iron necessary to finish the vessel.[114] Throughout the fourteen years from 1748 to 1762 the naval dockyards were entirely capable of building whatever was demanded. Despite numerous and sometimes vicious disputes among personnel, no material, technical, or human impediment in their organization or administration stood in the way. The chief, indeed, the only cause of the collapse of the dockyards after 1758 was financial starvation preceded by five years of malnutrition.

CHAPTER NINE

The Ordnance Problem

The navy lost nearly 4,000 guns during the Seven Years' War and such staggering losses suggest at least that at the beginning of hostilities France possessed a full complement of naval ordnance.[1] Yet the truth of the matter is that the navy probably did not have 4,000 guns on the day the first shot was fired in 1755 – in fact, had struggled with inadequate and desperate measures to fill a gap that had existed since the signing the Treaty of Aix-la-Chapelle seven years before.[2] The secretary of state for the navy had been fully aware of the shortage of ordnance since May 1750 and had initiated a massive rearmament program before the end of the year. Failure to maintain regular transfers of funds to the treasurers-general of the navy played little or no part in the ordnance problem.[3] Suppliers of ordnance obtained generous advances and never complained that funds were insufficient or unpaid.[4] Only in 1758, after the ordnance program had failed, did the authorities express fear that forge workers might quit because they lacked money to buy bread.[5] Considerable savings actually resulted during the decade from the introduction of new technology in the production of ordnance. Between 1753 and 1757 the navy let contracts worth 7,884,500 livres, which represented a 13.8 per cent reduction in the price of the same weight of iron ordnance had it been let under the old prices, and towards the end of the war the duc de Choiseul claimed to have saved 1,348,000 livres when he negotiated new contracts in 1761.[6]

French cannon prices may have been too low to provide sufficient incentives to manufacturers for they were lower than English prices even though that industry was more efficient, technically advanced, and faced fewer overhead costs.[7] Between November 1748 and February 1763 the British Board of Ordnance paid approximately 21.6 pounds sterling per tonne for approximately 15,413 tonnes (16,975 English tons) of cast-iron guns received at Woolwich.[8] By comparison the French navy contracted

TABLE 7

Naval Gun Contracts, 1748–1762

Date of Contract	Supplier	Quantity (quintals)	$1.t./q^{tl.}$	Price (in livres) Total
15 Feb. 1748	De Voizé	68,400 (est)	30	2,052,000
26 June 1748	Reix des Fosses	45–50,000	20–30	1,100,000
30 June 1750	Bertin et Associés	11–12,000 (est)		
Nov. 1750	Montalembert	46,680	25.5	1,193,400
11 May 1751	Ségonzac	3,000 (est)	26.5–28	65,862
14 Dec. 1753	Montalembert	80,000	25	2,000,000
30 Sep. 1754	Ruffray	40,000	25	1,000,000
4 Aug. 1755	Bertin	40,000	27	1,080,000
18 Jan. 1756	Ségonzac	6,000	18	108,000
31 Jan. 1756	Bainaud	17,000	16	272,000
15 Feb. 1756	Laulanie	10,000	16	160,000
5 July 1756	Reix des Fosses	8,000	17	136,000
6 July 1756	Reix des Fosses	15,000	17	255,000
8 July 1756	La Pouge	15,000	17	255,000
16 July 1756	Reix des Rivières	5,000	14	70,000
21 Jan. 1757	Laulanie	16,500	17	280,500
20 Sep. 1757	Godet de Pontramé	19,000		
7 Feb. 1758	Reix des Rivières	15,000	16	240,000
1758	Damon	30,000	20	600,000
1758	Cherral	20,000	18	360,000
1762		150,000	16–18	

Sources: Marine B[4], 78, f. 198; BN, Mss. frs., 11,336, ff. 71–2, 91–1v; Marine B[2], 334, f. 308; 341, f. 559; 356, f. 454; and 358, f. 519; ibid, B[3], 549, ff. 52–3v; Marine D[4], 9; Rochefort, 5E[2], 19, and 1E, 410, no. 392.

over a much briefer period, from December 1753 to September 1757, for 13,290 tonnes (271,500 quintals) at an average price of 545.3 livres tournois or 19.6 pounds sterling a tonne.[9] Between 1748 and 1758 the French navy contracted for about 22,708 tonnes or 463,000 quintals of cast-iron guns. This quantity, when added to the thirty to forty thousand quintals of other ironware needed annually, leaves no doubt that the navy was the largest consumer of iron in the state. The sheer size of the demand accounts for many problems faced by the navy, but additional difficulties also existed. Technical imperfections of cannon manufacture, rivalries between manufacturers, tensions arising between different jurisdictions of the royal government, and the structure of the French iron industry itself all hampered cannon production.

During the first half of the eighteenth century the sole right to supply cast-iron guns to the navy fell into the hands of the Landouilette de Logivière family who owned Rancogne and Planchemenier. The decline of the fleet after 1715 and the quasi monopoly enjoyed by Landouilette's heirs led to the loss of skilled labour at other forges and failure to develop additional production capacity elsewhere. [10] By 1748 the forges were badly neglected owing to lack of orders during the previous quarter century and the owners were anxious to sell. Two smaller ironworks in Périgord, one at Ans owned by Henri Bertin, intendant of Roussillon and later controller-general, and the other at Plassac, owned by François-Louis de Bardon, baron de Ségonzac, also produced naval cannon but their forges had suffered as well. Once "the queen of Périgord's forges," the forge of Ans "was in a lamentable state." [11]

In the spring of 1748 the comte de Maurepas negotiated new contracts with the navy's traditional suppliers in Périgord, and in June contracted with the lessee of the forges in Angoumois to deliver 1,200 cannon to the Atlantic arsenals commencing in 1749 and thereafter for four years. [12] The minister also expanded the navy's sources of supply at Toulon, arranging to obtain ordnance from Joseph de Voizé, an entrepreneur of Grenoble and lessee of the royal forges at St Gervais in Dauphiné where naval guns had never been cast before. [13]

These arrangements did little to meet immediate shortages, but the next year Maurepas accepted an offer from Gabriel Michel, a wealthy Nantes slave trader and director of the India Company, to ship between 140 and 150 thousand quintals of captured French naval guns from Great Britain for 5 per cent below the lowest price being paid for new guns; by early 1750 the navy had taken in nearly 350 repatriated cannon. [14] A few cannon, perhaps twenty, were rejected and twenty British "11-pounders [sic]" were included. Michel was cautioned about possible fraud and the British guns were rebored. [15] The navy also accepted thirteen British "8-pounders [sic]" from a Havre merchant toward the end of 1750, but no further purchases of British ordnance occurred. [16]

Maurepas' arrangements and traditional reliance upon private enterprise appeared to satisfy the navy's current and future needs. Even before accepting Michel's offer, the secretary of state turned down a request for an ordnance contract from a merchant at St Jean de Luz. [17] Six months later, in October 1749, his successor also rejected an offer to supply 1,000 cannon because all of the contracts had been let, "and there is no question of increasing them." [18]

The ordnance problem that quickly appeared was twofold: first, the navy needed far more guns than Maurepas and his advisers had determined, and second, the traditional means of acquiring cannon *par entreprise* collapsed under pressure of the sudden increase in demand. By December 1749 the administration acknowledged that no guns could be expected from St Gervais before 1751 and that De Voizé needed 100,000 livres to assemble charcoal and iron ore.[19] Also, the lessee of the forges in Angoumois, Sieur Reix des Fosses, delivered only sixty-eight guns to Rochefort during the first year of his new contract; thirteen failed during proofing.[20] There was little likelihood that major alterations could be quickly made to the ironworks owing to their deterioration and nowhere else in France could the navy's heaviest guns be cast. Rouillé had no alternative but to renegotiate Reix des Fosses' contract to deliver the remaining guns by the end of 1754, and turn elsewhere to fulfil the navy's needs.[21]

Before negotiating additional cannon contracts, however, he had to reestablish the navy's ordnance requirement. After doing so, he confirmed his view that Maurepas had planned for an impossibly large fleet. In addition to the 3,399 guns on hand, Maurepas had called for 4,099 more cannon; although this figure included 388 cannon for harbour and coastal defence, it omitted 569 guns needed in the colonies.[22] Colonial demands could not be ignored; 526 guns had been transported to the colonies between 1739 and 1747. In 1750 Louisbourg alone received one hundred cannon, and at the year's end a demand for 110 of the navy's heaviest guns for St Domingue suddenly confronted the intendant of Rochefort.[23] The total number of cannon sent to the colonies after 1748 remains unknown, but on the eve of the Seven Years' War they required some seven hundred.[24]

At Toulon, which lacked 1,309 cannon, only 254 could be expected from St Gervais during the next four years. The remainder would have to come from the Atlantic arsenals or forges in Angoumois and Périgord. Taking into account the 2,790 cannon lacking in the west, these ironworks would have to produce 3,845 guns, nearly half of which were the three largest calibres employed in the navy.[25]

In 1750 the navy had only about two-thirds of the guns required to arm the authorized fleet of sixty of the line and forty frigates.[26] In June the unavailability of eighty-four 24-pounders and one hundred and twenty 36-pounders for ships at Brest revealed the seriousness of the current situation.[27] The navy could not mount primary batteries in four second-rates *and* three third-rates when the entire number of these ships in the fleet was only twenty-nine. Rouillé realistically abandoned Maurepas' earlier grandiose plan for 4,099 guns and concentrated on arming sixty of the line and forty frigates. After reducing the navy's minimal requirement by 30 per cent, he concluded that 1,600 new guns had to be manufactured in the west in addition to 1,145 cannon expected from Reix des Fosses. He immediately sought someone willing to develop new manufacturing facilities to cast large numbers of the heaviest cannon employed in the navy.[28]

At mid-century the French iron industry still lived off its old, indeed, medieval legacy of widely dispersed forges, small enterprises, rural settings, scarce capital, and narrow horizons. Of feeble capacity, badly designed, and provided with only primitive bellows driven by water power, the iron smelter was truly a rustic implement. The rhythm of work was slow and irrregular, punctuated by long delays brought on by depletion of ore and charcoal, variable water levels of rivers, and seasonal demands on the labour force to work in the fields. Though in theory a smelter operated one year in two, more often the period was one in three or four.[29] Production methods were inexact and extremely wasteful. No scientific theory directed the ironmasters' methods. Materials were combined by tradition, blast pressure was arbitrarily determined, and no one knew what chemical reactions occurred during the course of operations so that the quality of castings varied from one to the next. Routine guided the founders and forgers and luck governed their success. The yield was small. A casting of 2,000 livres-weight required 4,500 livres of ore and 2,070 livres of charcoal. Moreover, the average furnace could not cast any of the navy's four heaviest guns: founders normally employed three furnaces to cast 36-pounders.[30]

Rouillé planned to limit the size of contracts in order to encourage as many private manufacturers as possible but realistic offers were not forthcoming.[31] After accepting the comte de Roffignac's offer to produce 400 guns, the navy found him incapable of fulfilling the terms of his contract owing to debt, and when Marc-René, marquis de Montalembert submitted an offer to supply 800 of the three largest guns used in the navy in July 1750 the secretary of state accepted.[32] Montalembert was left alone in the field when Roffignac ceded his contract to him, and by November, after leasing the forge of another possible supplier, he agreed to provide 1,400 cannon to the navy.[33] Rouillé signed only two other agreements, contracting with the forge owners at Ans and Plassac for about 440 cannon.[34] Thus the navy's chief supplier of ordnance became the marquis de Montalembert, who had never manufactured a cannon in his life and who, as yet, did not own any forges.[35]

Producing cannon *par régie* (i.e., by a government body responsible to the Royal Council), as was the case in the army, could not be done. Lack of sufficient funds in the department's current revenues, Rouillé's drive for economy and reduction of the navy's debt, the enormity of the ordnance requirement, and the fortuitous appearance of Montalembert's proposal all inclined the secretary of state and his advisers to rely, as in the past, upon private entrepreneurs to supply the navy's guns. Initial successes appeared to confirm the wisdom of this policy. Before the end of 1750 Montalembert received authorization to establish a new ironworks at Ruelle, purchased the fief of Forge-Neuve in Périgord, and leased five additional forges.[36] Progress at St Gervais, where ninety-three guns were cast ahead of

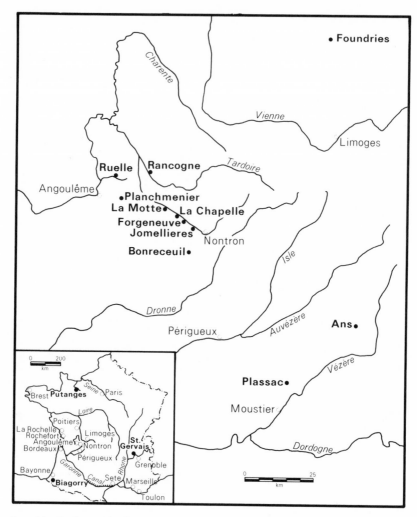

Foundries Producing Naval Cannon, 1748–1762

schedule, even provided grounds for optimism.[37] During 1751 Montalembert build new forges at Bonreceuil which were producing cannon by the
end of the year, added to his holdings at Ruelle, and delivered 100 guns to
Rochefort from the ironworks at Jomellières.[38]

But Montalembert's activities dealt a hard blow to the rickety operations
of Reix des Fosses, who complained that Montalembert debauched his
workers and enticed his suppliers.[39] Riex des Fosses had formerly obtained
cannon from Jomellières and Montalembert's acquisition of the lease did
not increase the navy's supply of ordnance.[40] The dilapidated state of the

forges at Planchemenier and Rancogne and the character of the entrepreneur himself also contributed to the lack of deliveries. Complaints in
1750 that Rancogne lacked a fourth furnace to permit continuous casting of
36-pounders and that Planchemenier lacked a third furnace for similar
production of 24-pounders suggest a reason why only thirty-seven cannon
of both calibres were on hand at Rochefort.[41] By 1754 the two ironworks
were in such a state of disrepair that the furnaces and waterways needed
rebuilding, and, added the intendant of Rochefort, "Sieur Reix des Fosses is
absolutely incapable of carrying out the work that must be done to effect
the repairs; it is scarcely possible to find a more inept and less suitable man
to occupy these forges."[42] From the beginning of 1749 to the end of 1754,
Reix des Fosses himself admitted delivering only 485 of the 1,200 guns in
his contract.[43] In July 1754 the intendant recommended that Reix des
Fosses be evicted from his lease and a new tenant be located. A buyer for
Rancogne was found and in September he signed a new contract to supply
40,000 hundredweight of cannon over five years commencing in 1755.[44]
Reix des Fosses himself had earlier purchased Planchemenier and though
he was authorized to deliver 167 guns still at the ironworks, Machault
refused to consider giving him a new contract.[45] It was a wise decision; later
on 71 of 103 of Reix's guns were rejected on reaching Rochefort.[46] After
hostilities broke out, with the navy no closer to achieving its demands, even
Reix des Fosses was pressed back into service as a naval gun-founder. But
the years of peace had been irretrievably lost.

At Brest the situation remained desperate. Eighteen months after
Gabriel Michel had repatriated nearly 350 guns, two third-rates, Le Lys and
Le Léopard, had to delay sailing until 24-pounders could be transferred
from ships still at sea.[47] At Toulon in 1752 two hundred cannon were
ordered from Rochefort, but of 153 actually sent, 90 were rejected on their
arrival.[48] At Rochefort at the end of 1753 so few 12-pounders remained that
L'Eveillé, 64-guns, could not be armed for the coming season unless
L'Hermione, a frigate, was stripped and armed with "eights."[49] A year later
there were still insufficient 12-pounders to arm a third-rate and a frigate
being fitted out.[50] By June 1755 the arsenal entirely lacked 6-pounders. La
Valeur, a frigate, went to sea with 4-pounders, and Machault approved a
proposal to arm five storeships with rejected 4-pounders from Reix des
Fosses's deliveries if necessary.[51] In 1755 the navy's major arsenal could
arm eighteen of the line and seven frigates only because eleven warships
were fitted out en flûte; of 829 cannon remaining at Brest there were
insufficient 36-pounders to arm an additional second-rate, and only enough
24-pounders to arm three more third-rates.[52] There can be little wonder at
French reluctance to go to war, for in addition to the slowness of Reix des
Fosses, the marquis de Montalembert's behaviour had led to chaos in naval
ordnance production.

Between 1752 and 1754 Montalembert had cast 1,100 cannon, or so he claimed. He also increased his holdings at Ruelle, obtained letters patent to cut timber in royal forests, and put additional forges into production.[53] But during the first quarter of 1752 only thirteen of thirty-six guns delivered to Rochefort were accepted; in April Montalembert halted further deliveries on the ground that the navy's ordnance inspectors employed unfair standards and methods to proof his guns and because he refused to accept the navy's custom of breaking the trunnions of all rejected guns.[54] Deliveries briefly resumed in May of the following year, but more than half of the small shipment of twenty-six cannon was rejected, and in July Montalembert reimposed his embargo on additional shipments.[55] The naval minister called a halt to any further payments, ordered Montalembert to await the arrival of an expert gun borer at his forges, and directed that a new contract be negotiated.

Montalembert's production efforts had been disastrous. According to naval ordnance inspectors the barrels of rejected guns were badly reamed, cannon had been cast too rapidly, the smelt was neither sufficiently molten nor pure enough, earthen cores used during casting were too large and deadheads or "gunheads," which closed the top of the casting to prevent penetration of air, provide for contraction of the metal while cooling, and receive slag and other impurities, were too small. A fine glaze disguised pits in the barrels, indicating fraud; the patterns of the guns had been altered by the addition of two iron bands round the barrels, "in order to give a more pleasing appearance to the guns of his supply."[56] Montalembert's guns were often three, four, and five hundred livres overweight, which in view of payments based on the weight of each gun compounded his shortcomings.[57] Montalembert had also cast cannon by a new, untried method, solid casting, and had ignored Rouillé's warnings to cease the practice and improve the quality of his core-cast pieces. By June 1754, 716 solid-cast guns lay scattered about his several forges, for his attempt to drill them with an apparatus of his own invention had failed.[58] Yet by November 1753 the navy had advanced 1,200,000 livres to Montalembert and received less than 200,000 livres worth of guns.[59]

Two and a half years passed before Rouillé halted Montalembert's activities and he had been slow to remedy the faults in Reix des Fosses's operations. But there was no point in moving against these entrepreneurs until alternatives could be found. The minister's long delay was also due to the system of administering the navy's supply of cannon. Following traditions developed half a century before under *Commissaire-général d'artillerie* René Landouillette, who had also produced guns, the administration of supply had fallen into the hands of ordnance officers. By mid-century they were no longer just technical personnel to be consulted; they had so infringed on the intendant's function as to reduce his duties simply to signing receipts and pay ordinances. Moreover, the controller in the arsenal no longer witnessed the receipts. But while ordnance officers inspected newly manufactured guns and authorized their rejection or acceptance, they had no authority to order changes from the manufacturers. Consequently, in order to preserve their independence, they refused to report deficiencies, leaving the intendant in the dark, unable to react swiftly to defects and defaults in the guns, or adjudicate properly protests from manufacturers whose guns had been rejected. Attempts by the arsenal authorities to resubordinate these officers and regain control of ordnance supply were frustrated by the confusion, ill-natured interference, and delays everywhere evident in the handling of the ordnance problem.[60]

The large number of rejected guns, large number required, scarcity of raw materials, and failure to find additional entrepreneurs did, however, provide incentives to seek technical innovations in order to increase savings and the number of acceptable guns. The need to cast guns round an earthen core (actually a mixture of clay, horse dung, and horse hair layered over greased rope), imperfections that arose from the primitive nature of smelting, and the quality of the raw materials caused many defects. Hollows and bubbles appeared in castings owing to slag and other impurities in the molten metal failing to rise into the deadhead. Complete castings often lacked regular density and strength throughout the piece. According to Marchant de la Houilière, reporting on the superiority of English naval ordnance, French guns burst so frequently that "our sailors fear the guns they are serving more than those of the enemy."[61] Such accidents caused carnage on gundecks and inspired mistrust among crews. In two actions fought by the Le Souverain during 1759 as many men were killed or wounded by five burst guns as by the enemy.[62]

The chief means to obtain greater solidity and density, using coke-iron and remelting pig-iron in a reverberatory or air furnace (i.e., by secondary fusion), were unknown to the French and known only to a few in England.[63] Solid-casting, however, offered a greater chance of improved solidity and regular density than before, although drilling the barrel raised a serious problem. Customary reliance upon private contractors and the capital cost of new, untried machinery with only limited application in the service of the state militated against the new technology ever being independently introduced into rural ironworks where naval ordnance was manufactured.

Jean Maritz, a Swiss gun-founder, had solved the technical problems while director of the French army's foundry at Lyon. His youngest son, also named Jean, accompanied his father to France and in 1743 succeeded him as director of the army's casting operations. In place of the old method, which required very careful calculations and complex machinery to keep the reamer and the gun vertically aligned for a considerable period of time, Maritz placed the cannon horizontally on a bed of his own design and turned the gun rather than the drill, as on a lathe. It was easier to keep the cannon turning about its own axis and the bore centred in the barrel. The new method gave cannon a regularity that was the most essential requirement for constant fire; solid casting reduced the number of flaws in the metal, increased strength, and permitted up to 5 per cent reduction in the amount of iron in the guns.[64]

Maurepas learned of Maritz's new techniques as early as 1742, but it was Rouillé who directed the gun-founder's attention towards naval ordnance problems.[65] Maritz cast a 4-pounder and successfully bored it in his workshops at Strasbourg during the summer of 1752, but an offer to supply 1,000 guns to Toulon from Franche-Comté in eastern France did not meet the navy's needs in the Atlantic, and his admission that he would earn between two and three hundred thousand livres from the transaction also discouraged its immediate acceptance. But a year later Maritz's technique was seen as a means to resolve the chaos created by Montalembert's behaviour.[66] Naval ordnance officers, drafting new ordnance specifications and fostering their own techniques, resented outside interference and opposed Maritz's early efforts, but the situation was so serious that in December 1753 Rouillé arranged for Maritz to build six boring and turning machines at forges in Angoumois.[67]

The marquis de Montalembert could not be abandoned for there was nowhere else to turn; moreover, he had the protection at court of the prince de Conti, the duchesse de Chaulnes, and through her Madame de Pompadour.[68] Montalembert signed a new agreement to supply 80,000 quintals of solid-cast ordnance, and agreed to have the guns bored and turned according to Maritz's method within five years, commencing immediately. Montalembert's claim to have cast 503 cannon weighing 21,827 quintals during the next six months is false.[69] Between 14 December 1753 and 1 June 1754 his forges produced 351 cannon, which, when added to the number cast during the previous season, amounted to 716 solid-cast cannon scattered about his several forges. None was delivered to Rochefort during the period.[70]

When Machault replaced Rouillé at the naval department, he immediately got rid of Reix des Fosses and reassessed Montalembert's activities. He also authorized purchase of 3,238 cannon from forges in Angoumois and Périgord.[71] This energetic action, however, only followed preconditions established by his predecessor. In February 1755 two of the new boring machines were finally erected at Ruelle and work commenced to reduce the enormous backlog of cannon at Montalembert's forges. Eighty-one guns were delivered to Rochefort in May but after fifty-one were rejected, twenty-one put aside for reboring, and only nine accepted, all payments to Montalembert were halted.[72] He was found to be 1,900,000 livres behind in his deliveries. On the grounds that the crown had paid for the new works at

Ruelle, Machault placed them directly under crown control and turned them over to Maritz, whom he had recently made inspector-general of naval ordnance, with powers to order entrepreneurs to carry out whatever he deemed necessary.[73]

Machault also expanded the navy's sources of supply. Between August 1755 and January 1757 the department contracted for an additional 132,500 quintals from several ironworks in Périgord and Angoumois (see table 7). Additional boring machines were installed at all forges producing naval cannon until by June 1757 they numbered twenty-one. By that time Maritz claimed that 1,665 guns had been bored on his lathes.[74] The magnitude of this effort compares very favourably with that of the British Board of Ordnance which received into stores just over 400 guns in 1756.[75] The outbreak of hostilities further stimulated Machault's sudden burst of energy, and Maritz's success relied to a great extent on the hundreds of solid-cast guns already at Montalembert's ironworks. But the naval ordnance problem was no nearer solution. From the day hostilities began at sea the navy lacked sufficient guns, and production never satisfied the growing demand.

At Toulon in December 1755, 714 cannon of all calibres were wanting for La Galissonière's squadron. A month later the lack of ninety 24-pounders and 12-pounders forced substitution of a third- and a fourth-rate for two second-rates in the force.[76] In February 351 guns were listed as unfit for service, and the port commandant complained that not a single gun on the coast could protect local shipping. Even batteries around Toulon were lacking; "The English," he reported, "can come up to the Grand Tower without coming under fire."[77] Clearly Maritz's later claim that he had provided sufficient cannon to arm all the ships ready for sea by the spring of 1756 needs qualification.[76] In September La Jumon, a frigate, was armed only by taking cannon from coastal batteries and from Fort Saint Louis that guarded Toulon itself.[79] The following spring twenty-six eight-pounders were put into L'Oriflamme, 50-guns, by disarming a xebeck; shortages had become so serious that six 18-pounders were cast in bronze in the arsenal's own foundry.[80] In August little more than one-third of the required 290 8- and 18-pounders were on hand to arm five second-rates being readied for sea.[81] Later, when the intendant began to fit out the twelve ships that would sail under La Clue for Brest, he noted bluntly that 390 guns had to be shipped to Toulon if the ships were to sail in the spring of 1759; more than 500 guns were needed to arm all the ships in port.[82]

The situation was no better in the Atlantic arsenals. During 1755 and 1756 Ruis-Embito continually asked Maritz to send small-calibre guns, especially 8-pounders, to Rochefort. But in June he had to put ten 6-pounders into La Fidelle, a frigate, to complete her armament.[83] Great guns were equally difficult to obtain. In September only twelve

36-pounders were on hand after arming the second-rates at Rochefort.[84] Ordered to ship seventy-two guns to Lorient for the new 80-gun flagship, Ruis could send only six of the required twenty-six 12-pounders.[85] A year later he had just fourteen 36-pounders and could send only sixteen 24-pounders to Brest where the situation was even worse.[86]

There, two third-rates were effectively removed from fighting in the line after being armed with 18-pounders; no 24-pounders were available. *Vice-amiral* Conflans went so far as to order that thirty-nine ancient guns from the walls of the port be put into the ships of the fleet together with their gunnery officers.[87] In February 1758 Rochefort lacked 129 guns including ninety-six 24-pounders to complete arming ships on hand.[88] The next month the port was lacking 137 guns, and Ruis planned to put 18-pounders into a third-rate to get it to sea.[89] Small-calibre guns continued to be unavailable, especially for hard-pressed corvettes escorting vital coastal convoys bearing stores, provisions, and munitions to the arsenals.[90] At Rochefort, a third-rate went to sea that spring with 4-pounder deck guns in place of the usual 6-pounders, but the intendant derived considerable satisfaction from reporting that at least the ship had a complete complement of ordnance.[91] At Brest more than half the ordnance was wanting for two second-rates in July, and a month later twenty-two English guns from the *Greenwich* were the only 12-pounders on hand.[92]

If anything the enormity of the ordnance problem had grown. Hastening to obtain as many guns as possible, Machault had authorized very general contracts specifying only the total weight of metal in each. As a result, entrepreneurs busily shipped a wide assortment of guns from wherever they could find them; the navy rarely benefited. In June 1757 Peyrenc de Moras acknowledged receiving fewer than 800 guns from the contracts authorized by his predecessor and intervened to reimpose discipline on contractors' activities, specify terminal delivery dates, and regulate the number and calibre of cannon that each was to deliver.[93] Including those already received, Moras expected 5,410 cannon to be delivered by the end of 1761. Yet this number proved insufficient. In September he contracted for 900 more cannon, chiefly 8-pounders, from Godet de Pontramé in Normandy, in order to meet the needs of frigates being built at Le Havre; the following January he renegotiated Reix des Rivières's contract, adding 500 heavier-calibre guns; and finally, he arranged for the Comte Damon to begin manufacture of 1,400 cannon in the Biagorry valley in Lower Navarre.[94] In less than a year Moras authorized the accession of 8,210 cannon, 71 per cent of which were 8-pounders and larger. To be sure, Machault had authorized purchase of 3,238 cannon in September 1754, but Moras' regulation of the navy's ordnance requirement bore little relation to prewar planning.

Moras' efforts and Jean Maritz's work, however, began to have an effect in 1759. Where once Rochefort was starved for 24-pounders, Ruis-Embito had 229 such cannon to ship to Le Havre in July.[95] Not only were guns reaching the arsenal but the quality of new, solid-cast pieces was markedly superior to the old. After firing up to twelve proofing charges in some guns, 100 shots in others, and using six of the new guns to train gunners for a year and a half without an accident, Ruis recommended abandonment of the core-cast method of manufacture.[96] Numbers of rejected cannon also declined considerably. Whereas between one-third and one-half of guns produced by the old method were normally rejected, in 1760 only twelve of 401 cast-iron guns of all calibres presented at Rochefort for inspection and reception into stores were rejected.[97] Indeed, by 1760 Jean Maritz claimed to have bored, recast, and rebored 2,300 cannon.[98] But though the figure can be accepted, it still amounted to little more than 70 per cent of Machault's schedule of purchases authorized in September 1754 and only 28 per cent of Moras' more recent figure. Despite technological innovation, reducing the number of rejected guns and improving their quality, the challenge was not met.

In October 1760 Toulon still lacked 12-pounders; after providing 362 guns to ships during the first three-quarters of the year, the arsenal had a mere 147 guns on hand. Fifteen months later the intendant needed 352 guns to complete arming ten ships, five frigates, and four xebecks ordered for April 1762.[99] A general inspection of ordnance at Brest in July 1761 found only 148 guns on hand. A month later the intendant reported that British "17-pounders [sic]" might be needed to complete arming a second-rate. Coastal batteries finally yielded twenty French guns, but in September captured British 9-pounders went into La Zéphyr.[100]

But if the tradition of producing naval cannon par entreprise, the choice and supervision of manufacturers, and the conduct of its own ordnance inspectors were at least theoretically subject to modification and correction by naval administrators, several additional obstacles remained larely beyond the navy's ability to influence. Cannon contractors constantly complained to the secretary of state about the lack of assistance and outright subversion of their efforts by royal provincial intendants. Despite requests from the minister, intendants often proved reluctant to support the navy's work. They frequently ignored requests for exemptions from the taille and corvée for forge workers, improvements to roads leading from ironworks to navigable waterways and public labour to haul iron ore to furnaces and cannon to riversides. Intendants and their sub-délégués often raided workforces for forced labour and harassed skilled workers. Six months after the intendants of Bordeaux and Limoges received instructions to exempt Reix des Fosses's foremen from the taille as agreed in his contract, the sub-délégué at Nontron made one of them collector of the tax.[101] The marquis de Montalembert complained that it was not enough to assemble a force of "masons, carpenters, miners, carters and labourers," but that some were conscripted for labour on the roads of Périgord. [102] These roads were so impassable in 1751 that cannon could not be hauled from Ans to the head of navigation at Moustier on the upper Vezère River whence they were shipped to Rochefort and Toulon. [103] Such was the weight of a reluctant intendant's inertia that in 1753 and 1755 the naval minister was still requesting repairs to the road. [104] Demands for public labour to haul iron ore to the forges and transport cannon to the waterways were never greater than from Montalembert, but when he himself used public authority to commandeer wagons from as far away as the *généralité* of Poitiers the provincial intendants were furious. [105]

With the owners and lessees of ironworks making large demands upon the human resources of such a vast area the hostility of provincial intendants is not surprising. Peasants in Périgord were liable to twelve days of forced labour every two and a half months and exempting those working at the forges drew labour away from the fields, devastated the pool of labour that other rural employers drew upon, and deprived the region of vital public improvements not to say revenues; once in the king's service many workers became exempt from the *taille*. The intendant of Bordeaux, Aubert de Tourny, replied to requests for aid that he well understood the navy's pressing needs, but that people scarcely bothered their heads about *corvées* when it was a question of public utility and in the present case the peasants believed they were being forced to work for the private profit of the cannon manufacturers. [106] Tourny, who had his own road-building priorities, probably agreed with the peasants. Royal provincial intendants might well embrace the royal will when dealing with local juridical bodies, but correct conduct on their part was very difficult to determine when they differed from other agents of the central government who also viewed themselves as acting on the king's business. Rouillé acknowledged this in December 1753 when he asked the naval intendant at Rochefort for advice on how to reconcile the navy's interest with that of the rural populace. [107]

The question of conflicting jurisdictions was particularly apparent regarding the declining forest resources of the kingdom and the constantly growing demand of industrial producers for fuel during the eighteenth century. The problem was especially acute in the iron industry whose blast furnaces consumed so much charcoal as often to deprive rural and urban populaces of fuel for heating and baking and material for industry. In 1760 a naval report claimed that scarcity of wood was the major problem facing the industry. [108] The seriousness of forest depletion led to demands to close factories near urban centres, riots among the lower clases in the countryside, and hostility from intendants anxious to preserve social order and economic stability. Pleas from ironmasters for wood to turn into charcoal left the intendant of Bordeaux unmoved; since 1748 he had worked steadily to reforest the region.[109]

Hostility from the *Grand maître des eaux et forêts,* whose carefully guarded jurisdiction came under the direction of the controller-general of finances, aided the obstructiveness of provincial intendants. Forest officers had longstanding rivalries with naval commissioners who interfered with their jurisdiction. The appearance of ironmasters and entrepreneurs with naval gun contracts weakened the navy in its contentions with local *maîtres des eaux et forêts.* Disputes also extended to river navigation. Naval authorities at Rochefort complained about the *maître* at Angoulême, whose laxity in maintaining a navigable channel in the Charente frequently left the river impassable for heavily laden barges transporting cannon.[110] *Maîtres* had the support of provincial intendants and local commercial and industrial interests who had also purchased timber rights in the forests and feared the rapacious effect of ironworks and requests that naval contractors be allowed to acquire timber by negotiated rather than auction purchase. Among seventeen objections to the forges at Ruelle by the town council of Angoulême were claims that the new ironworks would take work from other industries, damage the brandy industry at Cognac, poison the fish in the Charente, and destroy the timber trade on the river which annually employed thirty barges to carry firewood and charcoal downstream to Cognac, Saintes, Rochefort, and La Rochelle.[111]

Naval cannon contracts normally included terms that allowed entrepreneurs to obtain extraordinary cuttings in the royal forests, but Gabriel Taschereau de Baudry of the office of the controller-general, intendant of finances having the direction of streams and forests, proved extremely reluctant to authorize them. Soon after Reix des Fosses obtained his contract in 1748 Maurepas requested Taschereau de Baudry to prepare an *arrêt* authorizing two extraordinary cuttings in the forest of La Brancone north of Angoulême, but he was refused.[112] Three months later, when Maurepas asked the controller-general to intervene, the previous correspondence had been lost. When Rouillé took up the task all he received for his pains was a lecture from the controller-general on naval administrators who exceeded their authority. Later the controller-general agreed "with difficulty" to one extraordinary cutting but did nothing to overcome the animosity of the local *maître des eaux et forêts* at Angoulême.[113] Rouillé continued to complain of the "mauvais humeur" of that official.[114] Montalembert and other gun contractors faced similarly reluctant, partial agreement to requests for cutting rights. Throughout the period only the controller-general could counter the baneful influence of the *Grand maître des eaux et forêts,* whose animosity reinforced the obfuscation of the intendant of finances and provincial intendants.

The structure of the iron industry is a factor that deserves consideration together with the tensions and rivalries among naval and other royal officers and officials in accounting for the failure to produce sufficient ordnance in the years preceding and during the Seven Years' War. The absence of a national iron market probably doomed the navy's reliance upon private contractors to failure. French ironworks generally produced for local and regional markets that demanded neither quantity nor quality, moreover, they were relatively inflexible in their ability to respond to sudden demand.[115] Naval ordnance, on the other hand, required both quantity and quality. Its producers also needed flexibility to respond to sudden increases on the eve of war and equally swift decreases at the conclusion of hostilities in order to be successful. A national market might have allowed such producers to emerge, but French internal trade was surrounded by such a multitude of customs barriers, *péages*, *octrois*, and *douanes*, increasing the already high price of iron and discouraging the development of broad market horizons or improved production techniques, that its appearance awaited the next century. In addition, aristocratic forge owners, like the heirs of Landouillette de Logivière, Montalembert, Ségonzac, and Bertin were normally interested only in maximizing current rents, and remained blind to appeals for capital improvements to increase long-term benefits to themselves and their lessees. Finally, the fact that the state was the largest consumer of iron also hindered greater production; at the least crisis orders halted and entrepreneurs could not anticipate long-term benefits.

The surge in demand for naval ordnance in 1748 and 1750 could not be met. Acceptance of the marquis de Montalembert's proposals ensured the navy's continued reliance upon private contractors for its guns. The shift to partial production *par régie* in 1755 with the seizure of Montalembert's ironworks was an act of desperation and the subsequent signing of additional contracts was sheer expediency. The multiplication of contracts later criticized by Choiseul was a move away from reliance on a few contractors, but with war at hand and the failure of both major suppliers, no alternative existed but to obtain cannon from anyone offering to produce them. Choiseul's reduction of their number in 1762 was not a reform but a return to the situation of ten years earlier. Ministerial neglect and incompetence are awkward charges to lay before Rouillé, Machault, and Moras. All three strove to resolve the problems of production and became entangled in a web of interjurisdictional rivalries within the government. Neither technological improvement nor funds were obstacles to obtaining ordnance. The seriousness of the crisis probably hastened adoption of new methods of manufacture; cannon prices decreased throughout the period. But traditional methods of smelting, inflexible market structures, and ingrained acceptance of the existing order could not be overcome in such a brief period of time. Turning over Montalembert's ironworks to Jean Maritz was a significant step toward reform. Naval authorities acted rather swiftly, all things considered, but their action marked only the beginning of a long process that eventually saw Ruelle become the state's major producer of naval ordnance during the nineteenth century. But before that occurred the prosecution of the state's interest at local levels had to be clarified and decided, and centralization of naval administration and organization reestablished.

CHAPTER TEN

Naval Stores

Naval stores can be divided into two categories according to origin, or three basic commodities used in ship construction, timber, iron, and hemp. The navy consumed countless other materials but these three comprised 80 to 90 per cent of the value of all naval stores excluding victuals and cannon. French forests provided much of the ship-timber, but masts, spars, and a great deal of oak plank came under the rubric of northern or Baltic stores. Iron came entirely from France, but the navy consumed both domestic and foreign hemp. Sailcloth was manufactured from domestic supplies, while Russian hemp went into the best naval cordage.

After finances, the acquisition of naval stores confronted the navy with its greatest problems. The variety and magnitude of demands would have strained the resources of any eighteenth-century organization, but flawed structure and lapses in administrative procedures compounded the effect of a chronic shortage of funds in impairing naval acquisitions. Not that other arrangements only awaited discovery by intelligent men, or that more far-sighted statesmen might have imposed effective reforms; rather the historical legacy of royal finances and traditional methods of acquiring matériel for the crown weighed heavily on the navy department's ability to build ships and service the fleet. The absence of any central purchasing agency or a central bureau to keep records of orders and deliveries and a balance of receipt and expenditure was entirely in keeping with the crown's traditional practice of contracting with private persons and groups for services.

The diversity and irregularity of naval acquisitions prevented government production of any one commodity. The navy's auxiliary position to the army meant that demands for stores, munitions, and provisions fluctuated wildly before, during, and after wars. Naval manufactures could not operate on a profitable long-term basis. Moreover, geographical separation of the arsenals in a country lacking economic unity forced each to forgo savings from aggregating demand in favour of seeking self-sufficiency. Regions of specialized manufacture appeared, but manufacturing remained in private hands. More important factors reenforced the decentralized system of stores acquisition. First, the department's personnel lacked the requisite skills to initiate and manage the wide variety of industrial enterprises and commercial operations necessary to fulfil its needs. Second, the department lacked financial resources. In the past some naval stores had been acquired *par régie*, but such arrangements had been abandoned for want of managerial skills and lack of financial strength to support them.[1] This final reason is the key to understanding the organization of naval supply.

Naval officials did not normally acquire matériel directly because the government possessed insufficient credit. The navy needed commercial credit that salaried officials did not possess, and which was available only from private sources. Had the corps of the pen been composed of venal officeholders, each possessing real property in their offices, a potentially vast amount of private credit might have been available to the crown. But such was not the case. Naval stores were normally acquired *par économie*, a system that left the ownership and responsibility for delivery of goods to the arsenals in the hands of the private merchants and entrepreneurs who supplied them.

Circumstances sometimes forced naval officials to acquire stores directly *par économie*, engaging a commission-agent to buy stores in the open market on the navy's behalf. But the procedure forced naval officers to assume the same commercial risks as any merchant and the practice remained confined to sudden emergencies. When naval intendants or *commissaires-généraux* acquired stores *par économie*, they engaged their own personal credit to secure the transaction. Of course they sought ministerial approval beforehand and usually acted only on the minister's promise to pay for the goods, but in law naval officers remained personally liable for nonpayment. Without real property in their positions, they used their own credit or, more likely, appealed to patriotism or opportunities for extra profit to persuade merchants to fulfil such undertakings. Not surprisingly, then, the *entreprise* system remained the common form of stores acquisition. Access to private commercial credit was as crucially important to the conduct of naval operations as were manpower and cannon.

Contracting procedures ensured that the navy paid exorbitant prices and remained open to sharp, often fraudulent, business practices, especially after 1748 when the amount and value of naval purchases rapidly increased. Naval stores had always attracted entrepreneurs and merchants capable of handling large orders but the decision to rebuild the fleet in 1748 appeared to introduce a new order of naval contractor that included wealthy financiers and nobles as well as merchants. Traditional patterns of naval supply broke down and court influence, though present in the past, exercised an increasingly baneful influence on the awarding of contracts, which were sought by men more anxious to lend their credit than supply commercial expertise.

Naval rearmament created difficulties from the beginning. For it was not a question of replacing ships unfit for service, whose furnishings as well as most of their masts and tackle could be reused, but of providing new ships together with everything required for their fitting out. Moreover, the arsenals were denuded of stores. More than a year after the signing of the Treaty of Aix-la-Chapelle Brest continued to require hundreds of masts and spars, a million livres weight of hemp, 20 thousand livres weight of pitch, not to mention the nearly 1,000 cannon without which all the rest was meaningless.[2]

From the beginning, financial constraints bore heavily on the program. During the winter of 1747–8, naval intendants demanded nearly 13 million livres worth of munitions and stores, but Maurepas slashed their requests to 6.5 millions.[3] Uncertainty that allotted funds would be paid added to the burden. By April 1748 the department had requested 6.7 millions, encumbered 5 millions, while the treasurers-general of the navy received only one million livres from the year's extraordinary funds. Throughout the ensuing period naval suppliers often found themselves carrying heavy financial burdens. Payments were not only delayed and uncertain, but often made in long-term paper that was difficult, indeed, at times, almost impossible to negotiate profitably.

Five commodities have been selected to illustrate several features of the commercial and financial relations between the navy and its suppliers. Timber, iron, sails, cordage, and victuals were the material attributes (together with cannon) of any eighteenth-century navy. All were consumed in very large quantities. With the exception of timber, they were also produced more or less exclusively by a small group of men. Fewer than five companies manufactured the navy's wrought iron. A similar number of companies produced almost all of the navy's canvas. Sailcloth manufacture also reveals many of the complexities in the relation between business and government that limited the latter's freedom of action. Rope was manufactured chiefly in naval arsenals but so necessary was private credit that manufacturing was carried our *par entreprise* rather than *par régie* despite potential savings from the latter. Finally, a powerful syndicate of wealthy financiers supplied naval victuals. The victualler-general of the navy was a surrogate for a private consortium that enjoyed an exclusive monopoly largely beyond naval supervision or control. Its activities remain shrouded in mystery; a brief discussion is included to suggest the size of its operations, and, in yet another way, the department's need to rely on private purveyors for organization and management as well as credit and material.

TIMBER

Timber provisioning was at once the most expensive, most important, and most abused area of naval supply.[4] The difficulties arising from providing masts, plank, and ship-timber to the navy have been admirably treated by Paul Bamford, but shifting from his emphasis on strategic and logistical considerations to an organizational and financial perspective of limitations on the exercise of power suggests a modest revision is in order.[5] In the first place, Bamford's emphasis on logistics and on the external difficulties that affected the department's acquisition of timber — ineffective forest laws, poor resolution of administrative conflicts, overlapping jurisdictions between naval commissioners and masters of waters and forest in France, and subordination of commercial to dynastic aims in northern and eastern European foreign policy — tends to underestimate the internal difficulties that hindered naval timber acquisition. Second, the size of timber acquisitions in the first half of the 1750s indicates that the navy was more important in royal policy-making than previously thought, and third, severe timber shortages during the Seven Years' War were really a permanent condition owing to the department's financial difficulties and procedures for acquiring stores. These endemic features of acquisition turned the enemy's effective blockade of naval arsenals into a crippling blow from which the navy could not recover during hostilities.

While royal provincial intendants normally resisted attempts to exploit peasant labour for the naval service, correctly viewing timber contractors as the chief beneficiaries of forced labour on the navy's behalf, they were not major obstacles to acquiring domestic timber. Intendants usually conformed to ministerial directives to cooperate with the department. In Touraine in 1753, the intendant strongly supported naval contractors in a running dispute with local land, road, and mill owners over river levels; the latter wanted to hold water back while the entrepreneurs sought to put it through the system to carry their log trains into the Loire.[6] When the "fermier" of the bridge over the Marne attempted to levy duties on barrels used to support timber trains floating downstream from Champagne the intendant of Paris intervened on the contractor's behalf.[7] The intendant of Moulins successfully mediated a contractor's free passage through a private sluice erected on the Aron River to move his timber into the Loire.[8] Unless naval activity threatened economic or social stability in a region, provincial intendants appeared willing assistants to the navy.

Hundreds of domestic suppliers sold timber to the navy for amounts ranging from a few hundred to hundreds of thousands of livres, from single, once-only sales of a few trees to contracts for more than half a million cubic feet to be delivered over four to six years. It is very difficult, however, to estimate naval timber consumption between 1749 and 1758 in order to compare it with that of other periods in the eighteenth century. There can be no guarantee that all contracts are known; moreover, contractors abused royal passports for timber shipped to naval arsenals. Contracts were rarely fulfilled and timber merchants often included wood of such inferior quality in shipments that they clearly had no intention of delivering it to the navy downstream.[9] In 1752 passports designated 154,000 cubic feet for Toulon, yet by November only 26,588 cubic feet had entered the port during the previous twelve months.[10] Contractors who agreed on the eve of the Seven Years' War to supply the port with 300,000 cubic feet over six years still owed 176,000 cubic feet long after their agreement had expired.[11] The same conditions prevailed elsewhere. After agreeing to deliver 20 to 25,000 cubic feet annually to Le Havre, one entrepreneur shipped only 12,604 cubic feet during seventeen months; another who agreed to deliver 80,000 cubic feet annually to Bordeaux sent a mere 8,249 cubic feet during the same period.[12] Much of the timber in passports was never intended for the navy. The deliberate inclusion of unsuitable timber in naval shipments – a "commonly observed phenomenon" – allowed intrepreneurs to pocket the duties on rejected timber. In at least one instance, a contractor shipped timber downstream in the full knowledge that the navy would reject it all.[13] Such practices led Nicholas Berryer to wonder why the departments did not deal with monopolists. But for every abuse removed or placed under control, a new one would appear and several crucial demands could not be met by a monopoly.[14] No single domestic supplier could provide the thousands of cubic feet required for wartime refits and rebuilding. Such a supply was less likely to be properly seasoned, costs would be excessive, and loss of quality control would quickly follow. Moreover, such a system would allow timber monopolists to control acquisitions by withholding crucial pieces to obtain demanded prices and acceptance of unsuitable timber.[15] Having numerous small suppliers allowed naval intendants certain initiatives and local patronage opportunities, enabling them to obtain required pieces and recommend offers of supply to the secretary of state. Most important of all, however, the current system helped naval intendants to overcome serious defects in the arrangements for timber delivery.

The navy's system of entrepôts rather than contractor practices led to the most serious abuse in the domestic system of timber supply. Most contracts required provisioners only to ship to these entrepôts at Le Havre, Indret at the mouth of the Loire, Bordeaux, Bayonne, and Arles at the mouth of the Rhone, where their supplies received provisional reception. Failure to apply the elaborate procedures laid down in the 1689 ordinance for timber reception allowed contractors to supply whatever they wanted, whenever they wanted, and guaranteed them payment.[16] The system, in the words of one critic, "injures all reason."[17]

Brest and Rochefort suffered less from lack of domestic timber than from arrangements for its delivery. Aside from costs involved in stowing, unloading, and reloading timber at entrepôts, merchants made no effort to get it to the arsenals. This almost guaranteed a poor assortment reaching the entrepôts and an even worse selection arriving at the arsenals where only local officials knew the requirements to keep shipbuilders employed.[18] The key to the Atlantic arsenals' timber supplies lay at Le Havre, where millions of cubic feet of ship-timber arrived via the Seine from Champagne and Picardy. While the dangerous exposure of the sea routes to the arsenals is well known, an equally detrimental condition prevailed in peacetime. The intendant at Le Havre contracted for most of the timber delivered to the port. This excluded the intendants at Brest and Rochefort, who might be expected to have accurate knowledge of their own requirements, from the process of acquisition. Lack of major construction and the slow pace of activity during the first half of the century placed no severe burdens on this arrangement. But rapid building during the early 1750s, and the sudden, erratic demands of wartime for repairs and rebuilding, left the system in a shambles.

Most timber also reached Le Havre without contracts, and, consequently, without the minister's specific approval or even his knowledge. The largest timber supplier in Upper and Lower Normandy customarily signed an open contract in order to reduce departmental paperwork when dealing with petty contractors, who accepted the major contract's terms. The open contract mentioned quality, type, and dimensions, but naturally contained no mention of quantity.[19] Many provisioners who delivered timber on verbal agreements as to prices obtained certificates of receipt from Le Havre's storekeeper without even provisional inspection. These certificates often failed to mention species or proportions, and contained only number and cubic measure. Officials in the central bureaux were left in complete ignorance of the state of timber inventories.[20] Contracting "à la mode du Havre" also left intendants struggling to enforce delivery dates.[21] Placed at arm's length from the major purveyors of naval timber, intendants of Brest and Rochefort had little or no power to influence the quality and assortment of timber arriving at Le Havre and Indret. Dealing with local suppliers became a necessary concomitant of the entrepôt system for it allowed intendants to search for needed assortments and quality.

Timber quality was mixed. Brest officials happily received timber from Champagne and Picardy whereas at Rochefort it was despised. Brest's importance and proximity to Le Havre may have ensured that better pieces went there, but lack of exactitude during their reception also played a role.

Brest authorities classified timber into only three grades whereas fifteen categories prevailed at Rochefort.[22] Authorities there commonly rejected thousands of cubic feet of timber after its delivery. In 1752 they arranged for all 302 thousand cubic feet required that year to come from local sources.[23] Rouillé once agreed to suspend timber shipments from Champagne and Picardy to Rochefort, but on second thought instructed his officials to be less fastidious during inspections; scarcity, he insisted, prevented too much rigour.[24]

Assortment only increased the problem of quality. In the spring of 1751 when Rochefort was overwhelmed with timber, the arsenal lacked sufficient compass timber to continue ship construction.[25] Naval officials found some at Bayonne and Bordeaux, but the problem returned at the year's end in complaints that the greatest portion of timber from Le Havre and Indret was of little utility, "ordinarily consisting only of very common pieces."[26] In December 1752 officials again sent to Bayonne for main-deck beams for a 74, and three months later work on two 64s halted completely owing to lack of proper timber.[27] Few contractors could supply a complete assortment, which required different forests of varying ages and densities, while the entrepôt system kept the intendants of Brest and Rochefort at arm's length from major contractors and forced them to explore reduced areas to fill their needs. Securing the required pieces from the steadily shrinking forests of France was simply a never-ending task.[28]

Attempts to secure domestic masts had failed since the seventeenth century and renewed efforts during the early 1750s failed again.[29] Brest officials contracted to receive 450 fir masts from Auvergne late in 1749, but the products proved unsuitable; two years later Rochefort authorities consigned 225 domestic masts of white spruce for use as wharf pilings.[30] Paradoxically, then, the navy's success in obtaining masts from the Baltic is perhaps the greatest indicator of the renewed importance of the navy in royal policy-making at mid-century. In June 1750 Rouillé signed one of the largest single contracts for northern stores ever undertaken during the Old Regime. Worth nearly 6 million livres, the contract called for more than 8,000 masts and spars and more than 900 thousand cubic feet of timber and plank, together making up 58.3 per cent of the contract's total value, all to be delivered during the next four years. All evidence suggests that despite many difficulties, the contractors filled the terms of their agreement.[31] In 1751, 36 per cent of all masts exported from Riga went to France, and by mid-1753 Rochefort officials reported that 90 per cent of the northern stores designated for their arsenal had been delivered.[32] The supplying of northern masts and plank did not fare so well during wartime. Complaints of scarcities began soon after hostilities broke out. But the chief difficulties in acquiring both domestic and foreign timber were financial and organizational; administration was not so much lax as often pointless. Failure to solve these problems before war broke out reinforced the disastrous effect of the enemy blockade of the Atlantic arsenals.

The blockade provided justification for changes in the inadequate organization of timber acquisition; they can scarcely be labelled reforms. In addition to moving closer to Dutch suppliers for Baltic masts and plank, the duc de Choiseul reduced the number of domestic contractors and relied more heavily than in the past on quasi-monopolists with greater financial resources.[33] But these arrangements were designed as much to accommodate the growing interests of financiers in naval contracting as to correct flaws in the system of timber supply. Moreover, the limited political influence of naval secretaries of state and the very short financial leash that kept them in check account for the apparent short-sightedness of most who held the office.

IRONS

The navy consumed two kinds of ironware, cast and forged. The former went chiefly into ordnance. Arsenals received some cast-iron pigs for ballast, but normally it was too brittle to be futher worked by smiths. The bulk of naval iron was semifinished, malleable wrought iron delivered in rounds, bars, rods, hoops, and sheets. Anchors weighing up to three and a half tonnes were only the most obvious pieces of ironware in wooden warships. An astonishing amount or iron went into their construction. Nor was this a uniquely French phenomenon. The British navy's purchases of wrought iron dwarfed all others, with payments for ironware exceeded only by those for timber and masts.[34] Each French arsenal annually consumed hundreds of thousands of livres weight of forged iron including millions of nails up to two feet long.

France was self-sufficient in iron production, but large naval orders during the 1750s strained the expanding facilities of naval suppliers and forced officials to reduce their demands. As the naval shipbuilding program got seriously under way after 1750, annual demand rose to more than 3 million livres weight of irons, excluding anchors.[35] On the eve of the Seven Years' War annual aggregate demand rose to 4 million livres and remained there during each of the next three years.[36] By the end of 1757 naval demand exceeded the capacity of iron producers.[37] Soon afterwards, a growing credit shortage squeezed producers who soon found themselves in advance to the navy. Suddenly their shipments were suspended; naval iron producers moved to the edge of bankruptcy in the wake of inadequate payments and wildly fluctuating orders.

Anchors were a special case. While their total weight comprised only a small proportion of annual consumption, limited facilities and enormous waste during manufacture ensured slow deliveries. Forged from tightly strapped packages of iron bars, one each for shank and arms, each anchor was composed of 75 or 105 separate bars; shanks and arms were forged separately a foot or so at a time in successive heatings, before being welded together. One hundred thousand livres of iron bars yielded only half their weight in anchors.[38]

Most iron produced for the navy during Louis xiv's reign had been *par régie*. But this system of industrial organization had failed from lack of capital and credit, insufficiently large markets, inadequate consumption, and poor transportation.[39] By the mid-1730s the comte de Maurepas decided to leave production to others and fifteen years later the navy's sole supplier of great anchors and chief provider of irons was Pierre Babaud de la Chaussade. Already known as an important timber supplier, holding part-interest in the monopoly to provide northern masts and timber to the navy in 1750, Babaud de la Chaussade is best remembered as the first "iron king" to emerge in eighteenth-century France.[40]

He began his career under the tutelage of his father and elder brother, naval timber contractors in central France. A closer look at his complex business arrangements must await P.W. Bamford's forthcoming study, but, briefly, during the 1730s Babaud and his associates acquired the former naval forges at Cosne and a twelve-year contract to supply naval anchors, and began to build an iron empire along the upper Loire river in Nivernais. Babaud also raised himself into the society of new wealth and nobility associated with financiers, purchasing the ennobling charge of *secrétaire du roi* in 1743, marrying the sister of the marquis de Pierrecourt the following year, and calling himself baron de Guérigny where he built a vast industrial establishment.[41] His enterprises experienced a boom tied to the rise of Maurepas, the War of the Austrian Succession, and the growing influence of the Pâris brothers. According to Herbert Lüthy, Maurepas' disgrace damaged Babaud's connections, but the evidence scarcely supports the contention.[42]

The new shipbuilding program provided greater opportunities than ever before, leading Babaud to expand production more than ten times beyond the original terms of the anchor contract which expired in 1748. In 1751 he undertook to deliver two million livres weight of irons to Le Havre and Brest, and anchor production grew to 200,000 livres.[43] Expansion continued apace. By 1755 his iron works alone produced annually two million livres weight of iron and anchors weighing 400,000 livres. Machault endowed Guérigny with the title and privileges of a royal manufacture the same year.[44] Babaud's labour force had probably reached 3,500 men employed at ten forges, two furnaces, four anchor forges with seven tilt hammers, and 6,400 arpents of forest. None of his production appeared on commercial markets; Babaud's establishment was equivalent to a fourth naval arsenal.[45]

Although Babaud may have ruled over the largest iron empire in France, his establishment was not on a sound financial basis. Insatiable naval demand had led to very rapid expansion entailing heavy investment. Moreover, demand never ceased. The same day that Babaud signed a new three-year anchor contract, dated 6 September 1755, the intendant of Toulon demanded an entire year's production of anchors over the next two years.[46] Earlier the same year, the intendant of Brest had demanded even more, 600,000 livres weight of anchors in addition to nearly three million livres weight of irons for 1755 alone.[47] In March 1756, with his regular irons contract up for renewal and less than one quarter of the previous year's order delivered to Brest, Babaud forced the naval minister to face facts. One and a half millions remained to deliver on the 1755 order; three millions were ordered for the current year; and 4,855,000 livres weight were wanted for 1757. If, as expected, Brest demanded four to five million livres again in 1758, more than twelve million livres would have to be delivered during the next three years to Brest alone. Babaud could provide only four millions of irons in addition to anchors. The minister must seek alternative sources for the remainder.[48] The minister agreed. Knowing that he could never obtain the required quantity himself, however, he supported Babaud's credit in the market-place with regular payments rather than sign new contracts, and had the entrepreneur subcontract for as much iron as possible, placing the onus for delivery on him.[49]

To a considerable degree, Babaud had become a prisoner of the navy. During the War of the Austrian Succession, Babaud had been paid in "rescriptions" on which he lost 6 per cent through discounts. During the early 1750s Rouillé paid him one million livres in 3 per cent Post Office contracts at par.[50] In view of the low interest, payment at par amounted to a discount, really a forced loan exacted by the naval minister, for such paper could not be readily negotiated. Babaud enjoyed certain exemptions from duties and privileged assistance in transporting his iron to Brest in the king's ships, but these did not compensate for payment in paper that was nearly impossible to negotiate.

As the war progressed naval payments became more difficult to obtain. Between October 1756 and September 1757 a mere 200,000 livres weight of irons reached Brest, whereas Babaud shipped nearly 2 million livres weight of irons and anchors downstream to Nantes.[51] The enemy blockade off the mouth of the Loire encouraged Babaud's diversion of irons to the India Company, but naval officials used nondelivery at the arsenals to justify their diminished support. Babaud had no option during 1758 but to continue to ship irons downstream to Nantes. Nicolas Berryer was quite unsympathetic to the entrepreneur's difficulties, contending that Babaud had sufficient funds and warning that only a minimum order of indispensable irons would appear in 1759.[52] Babaud produced only 441,000 livres weight which he delivered to Nantes that year, but their failure to go beyond the mouth of the Loire became Berryer's excuse not to pay him. By the year's end Babaud claimed to be owed 500,000 livres and that he had never received the promised advances for the current year's production.[53] By then the navy had experienced a "kind of bankruptcy" and in February 1760 Berryer suspended all iron shipments as part of his solution of the larger problem.

A man of his times, the naval minister viewed the government's financial crisis as chiefly due to fraud, malversation, and profiteering by men like Babaud, who subsequently remained for several months without payment. In May he received an inadequate 30,000 livres in *rescriptions*; but paper of the farmers-general on the *gabelles et traites* of Moulins and *aides* and *tabac* of Nevers was expensive to negotiate and no substitute for cash to pay his workers. Berryer refused a minimum level of support, and by July Babaud had cut his labour force by nearly two-thirds.[54] In desperation Babaud sought to sell his anchors on commercial markets, but foreign anchors used in commercial shipping were cheaper and with French maritime commerce all but cleared from the seas his proposal remained highly academic.[55] At the end of 1760, having received only 15,000 livres from the navy during the past four months, with new debts incurred to produce 200,000 livres weight of irons in order to keep his reduced labour force together, and, finally, threatened with seizure of his property by tax collectors, the "iron king" was reduced to pleading. "In the name of God, Sir, take pity. Give me 25,000 livres; every moment is ruining my establishment and the basis of my fortune."[56]

The controller-general of finances tried to arrange a Dutch loan with manufactured irons as collateral and asked the Royal Council for a monthly payment of 15,000 livres. But Berryer opposed the proposal and no one would overrule the minister.[57] To all intents and purposes Babaud was ruined. The duc de Choiseul's appearance at the head of the ministry brought no relief. Taking advantage of depressed market conditions, he forced Babaud to accept lower prices in a new anchor contract and substantially reduced the navy's demand for irons.[58] Failure to receive monies owed to him for shipments during the Seven Years' War forced him finally in 1769 to offer his properties to the king.[59] Babaud de la Chaussade owed both his rise and fall to the same source, naval contracting.

The fate of the other major iron suppliers is less well known but available evidence suggests generally the same story. Claude Leblanc of Marneval and Company, the largest iron producer in Berry and source of the best iron in France supplied Rochefort. But after 1758 he suffered an even worse fate than Babaud. In addition to nonpayment he lost the lease on his best and largest establishment, Clavières, which employed about 1,500 workers.[60] Producers for Toulon's needs fared little better. In January 1760 Pierre

Aguillon, a small local contractor, had not received a sou on his account more than eighteen months after his last shipment and Nicolas Pleny, an ironmaster at St Jullien in Lyonnais experienced similar if less severe difficulties.[61]

Poor drafting of contracts initially gave entrepreneurs opportunities. As with timber, iron contracts were normally signed on a time basis, specifying only agreed prices and total quantities to be delivered over several years. Advantages lay with contractors who ignored the annual assortment requested by naval intendants and shipped the largest quantity of irons as quickly as possible. The procedure practically ensured that a great deal of unwanted iron arrived at the arsenals and left intendants unable to enforce delivery dates.[62] On the other hand, these contractors invested in large plants in order to meet sudden, sharp increases in demand for products often of such superior quality that they could not be sold on commercial markets in the event of declining demand. The long delays between orders, deliveries, and payment also meant that producers granted long-term credit for which the navy paid in the prices charged. Experienced contractors built these considerations into their prices. It might be argued that manufacturers of naval ironware could hold the navy to ransom by refusing to enter into further contracts, but such large industrial operators had nowhere else to turn in an age of poor transportation and undeveloped markets. Far from holding the navy in fee, iron manufacturers were prisoners to be paid when possible but certainly not ahead of anyone else. The navy exploited the entrepreneurial skills and credit resources of its contractors, engineered their ruin if necessary in order to confine government financial failure as close to home as possible, and moved on with promises of generous advances and favourable prices to encourage new sources of credit in order that the department might continue.

CANVAS

Until the middle of the century the navy acquired canvas from entrepreneurs who searched the producing provinces and bought up supplies for sale to the navy. But such sailcloth usually failed to meet naval standards of quality. Beginning in the 1740s the navy encouraged establishment of several manufactures devoted to production of naval canvas. The success of a royal manufacture founded at Darentel on the outskirts of Brest in 1746 freed the French from the need to import premium-grade canvas from Holland for their largest warships. Under the direction of the lessee, Sieur Vallet de la Touche, Darantel achieved a high level of quality using hemp from Champagne and Russia; a spinning mill erected at Tonniens prepared all the yarn employed at the manufacture.[63] The navy seemed assured of complete satisfaction, but Vallet lost the *ferme* in 1750 and the new lessee,

Jean-François Le Boucher, ran down the manufacture until Berryer closed it after suspending further canvas shipments to the navy in 1760.

Le Boucher, a hemp supplier from Rennes who possessed a canvas manufacture there, obtained subsidized prices for supplies from the royal manufacture, a commission to purchase local hemp for the navy, and, in case Darantel's production proved insufficient, authorization to purchase canvas elsewhere.[64] Darantel quickly became a front behind which he delivered canvas acquired elsewhere. As early as October 1751, naval authorities at Rochefort rejected 8,000 *aunes* (ells) of sailcloth: in the words of one official, they were "détestables."[65] Nevertheless, Le Boucher soon obtained two price increases: for Darantel canvas and for cloth from his Rennes manufacture.[66] In less than two years naval canvas came to cost more than under Vallet. He also had a good part of his canvas manufactured at Rennes in order to reduce inspections, and in June 1753 received permission to reduce the number of looms at Darantel, which soon led to closure of the spinning works at Tonniens.[67] Finally, fraud proved so profitable that Le Boucher also ran down his own manufacture at Rennes. The *aune* of Brittany of 50 *pouces* provided the basis for naval payments to Le Boucher, but he began to buy canvas by the *aune* of Paris, which was one-eighth shorter, and deliver it to the arsenals at Darantel prices.[68]

Le Boucher was the chief purveyor of canvas to the Atlantic arsenals and the navy's largest supplier of sailcloth. He claimed to have shipped 782,382 *aunes* worth 1,275,543 livres from Darantel to Brest, Rochefort, and Le Havre between July 1756 and May 1758. But the royal commissioners established to verify and liquidate naval debts discovered that he had falsified delivery dates and doubted that weavers at the royal manufacture had produced more than 120,000 *aunes* during the period. They also charged that no Darantel cloth had entered naval stores at either Rochefort or Le Havre.[69] Later on, 44,000 *aunes* in his warehouse at Brest officially shipped from Darantel were found to have been made at Rennes.[70]

According to the head of the royal commission appointed in 1758, Gaspard-Moise de Fontainieu, the navy's purchasing system, or rather the lack of one, was as much to blame as entrepreneurial dishonesty. "These kinds of things would be easily uncovered," he reported to Berryer, "if there was a general balance established at Paris that could correct the one that ought to be ordered every six months in each port."[71] With no reference to original purchase orders, semiannual reports of deliveries to the arsenals or general inventories of stores on hand had only limited effectiveness. In addition to underdeveloped administrative procedures and immature management, however, geographical separation of the arsenals and sources of supply, and each arsenal's need to become self-sufficient, militated against establishment of a central purchasing bureau. The appearance of new canvas manufactures for Rochefort and Toulon reflected the force of these factors and the arsenals' search for self-suffi-ciency.

About the same time as Le Boucher obtained his first lease on Darantel in Brittany, the intendant of Rochefort proposed that a new manufacture be established on the Charente to meet the arsenal's needs, but Rouillé demurred in favour of two groups of entrepreneurs who started up separate manufactures at Angers and nearby Beaufort. Efforts of the intendant of Tours to stimulate the weaving and textile industry and new naval demand for high quality canvas encouraged the entrepreneurs; one group later claimed that Rouillé had inspired them to start their establishment.[72]

Sometime in 1749 Pierre Deshayes and his two sons, Pierre-Jean and Nicolas, opened a modest establishment at Beaufort outside Angers. On 30 March 1750 he received a ten-year exclusive privilege to manufacture sailcloth "façon de Russie" in the Elections of Angers and Baugé, and fifteen months later he formed a company of which he became director.[73] At Angers, three local cloth merchants, proceeding in ignorance of Deshayes' undertaking, installed several looms in the Faubourg St Michel, which were seized by bailiffs as the latter sought to protect his privilege.[74] But the Angevins had the financial support of the *receveur des tailles* in the Election of Angers, the backing of the town council which supplied the land for their establishment, and the favour of the intendant of Tours.[75] They began again and by June 1751 their establishment, described as eight or ten months old, was producing canvas for sale to the India Company.[76] Both companies petitioned the naval minister for orders and after meeting naval specifications signed contracts to supply 25,000 *aunes* of canvas annually to Rochefort.[77] Le Boucher protested against the new arrangement, but soon *Commissaire-général* De Givry wanted to draw all the arsenal's canvas from Beaufort: "The manufacture of Larenthal [*sic*] is often unable to supply us with canvas," he reported, "and those from Rennes are never any good."[78]

Despite support from naval authorities at Rochefort, Deshayes' Beau-fort manufacture lost money in 1753 and 1754 and he appealed for an advance, really an interest-free loan, for the life of the contract. The controller-general's department favoured payment of a bounty, and thereafter Beaufort canvas gave complete satisfaction to authorities at Rochefort.[79] From October 1754 to September 1755 deliveries rose to 57,700 *aunes* and during the subsequent twelve months to 96,721 *aunes*.[80] By May 1758 the Beaufort producer had shipped over a quarter of a million *aunes* to Rochefort.[81] The Angers manufacture, however, failed to achieve similar success. Although 180,000 *aunes* of canvas was shipped to Rochefort during the four years after 1753, arsenal authorities judged it to be "very inferior," and charged the producers with paying scant attention to specifications, delivering unordered cloth, and favouring commercial buyers at Lorient, La Rochelle, and Bordeaux.[82] Indeed, the Angevin manufacture may have ceased deliveries to the navy soon after the outbreak of war.

During the 1750s both companies struggled to meet problems of liquidity and profitability. Insufficient naval orders may have been a major cause of weakness. Competition from Brittany and introduction of cheaper, inferior canvas from Russia were given as reasons for the Angevin company's apparent lack of interest, but unpaid naval accounts and naval orders spread between two competitors may also have deterred the Angers merchants.[83] In 1759 naval authorities substantially reduced their canvas orders and virtually cancelled them for the next two years. By the beginning of 1762 both companies begged for naval orders but the duc de Choiseul refused to place any, and towards the year's end, continuing paucity of orders, financial constraints, and constricted markets forced the two companies to amalgamate.[84] Attempts to sell canvas to the arsenal at Brest were opposed by the Estates of Brittany and, bowing to pressure, the naval minister rejected the reformed company's offer.[85] The decade-long attempt at Angers to develop a naval canvas industry for Rochefort had failed, a victim of local and regional competing interests involving the producers themselves, naval and provincial intendants, financial constraints, and insufficient markets. The story at Toulon appeared much the same.

The poor reputation of canvas and reliance upon the old discredited purchase system of naval acquisition probably account, as at Beaufort and Angers, for the appearance of a new manufacture at St Jean de Bournay in Dauphiné. By 1749 Etienne Faure had established fifty looms and in November he formed a partnership with the Lyon firm of Rivail, Durand and Company to manufacture sailcloth. A year later the associates formed a second company with Toulon's most important naval purveyors, Portaly and Legier, and the latter contracted for canvas with Toulon's intendant.[86] A falling out among the partners led to legal struggles during 1753 and 1754 and delayed payments undoubtedly exacerbated the dispute.[87]

Delays were not a product of wartime finances but a chronic condition of doing business with the government. In January 1754, well before the outbreak of hostilities, Portaly and Legier possessed 400,000 livres worth of naval pay orders (*ordonnances*) for which they had received little more than a quarter of their value.[88] Two years later their situation remained unchanged, perhaps worse; with only three months to fit out La Galissonière's squadron, they had begun to supply canvas to the navy, but 300,000 livres in promised advances remained unpaid and the entrepreneurs could not provide the desired quantities.[89]

Unable to help their suppliers with monies for their accounts, naval authorities turned to another, Claude Sadoul, "entrepreneur de la manuf[actu]re de Strasbourg."[90] Sadoul's offer of canvas at 5 per cent below prices granted to Portaly and Legier undoubtedly attracted Toulon's intendant, but naval indebtedness was equally important. The need to find new sources of credit probably accounts for the navy's apparent policy of encouraging an excess of suppliers, for the department lacked the resources to support those it already had. Indeed, the navy's treatment of its chief suppliers at Toulon destroyed them.[91]

As early as August 1757 Toulon had exhausted the canvas most heavily in demand, and Portaly and Legier had neither yarn to manufacture nor credit to buy.[92] The following March, *Commissaire-général* Michel arranged for the treasurer to provide the exhausted partners with 30,000 livres in bills of exchange to acquit several notes and stave off their closest creditors.[93] But during the early months of 1758 they delivered canvas worth a mere 10,000 livres in contrast to sailcloth worth 310,000 livres shipped the previous year; by the end of 1758 they claimed to have advanced more than 550,000 livres to the navy.[94] After Berryer suspended all shipments to the arsenals, they closed their doors. Naval authorities, however, had already signed a nine-year contract with Sadoul the previous September.[95] These blows probably contributed to Legier's death in April 1761.[96]

Late that year, with sails wearing out, Portaly refused to buy canvas for the navy; authorities reverted to the old discredited practice of purchasing on the open market, paying twice the normal commission to a Marseilles merchant to buy 40,000 *aunes par économie*.[97] Canvas had become so scarce that the intendant requested 8,000 *aunes* from far-off Brittany and proposed stripping sails from ships in port to be resewn into studding sails and substituting lighter than normal canvas for lower courses to meet his needs.[98] The sorry account of sailcloth acquisition illustrates clearly how several features of stores acquisition severely limited the naval department's ability to organize, control, or even manage its own purchasing system.

HEMP AND CORDAGE

Several factors encouraged the manufacture of cordage in naval arsenals. The enormous quantities required, the need to renew much of a warship's cordage after each cruise, and the natural desire of ships' officers to equip their vessels with more than the two complete gangs of rigging allowed by regulations, together with abuses in its use and care at sea ensured that producing sufficient supplies was a continual occupation. Only the navy required cables of the size demanded by first- and second-rates, and private ropeyards were generally too small, incapable of meeting sudden naval demands or surviving in the face of equally sudden contractions in orders.

Moreover, the wide separation of arsenals and great variety of hemp sources encouraged self-reliance and self-sufficiency at each arsenal. Contemporary naval officials claimed that safety at sea depended upon good quality cordage and its manufacture could not be entrusted to entre-preneurial greed.[99] But this was an ambiguous claim to say the least; for although naval rope was manufactured in the arsenals, financial weakness led officials to rely on production *par entreprise* rather than *par régie*.

The navy's annual consumption of hemp is unknown, but it is beyond question that warships required enormous amounts of rope and cordage. Fully rigged third- and second-rate ships of the line required 140 and 190 thousand livres weight of hemp respectively, while first-rates consumed a staggering 300,000 livres, nearly 150 tonnes. As a similar weight of tar ideally replaced waste from hemp's manufacture into cordage, these figures give a rough idea of the weight of rope in each rate.[100] Six hundred quintals of hemp, sufficient to manufacture two gangs of rigging for a frigate, yielded only five cables for a 74-gun ship of the line.[101] In 1750 the department contracted for 63,000 quintals of Riga hemp during the next four years.[102] But if the navy annually consumed nearly 16,000 quintals of northern hemp, it probably used about the same amount again of domestic hemp.[103] In wartime, however, demand exploded and the navy purchased both tarred rope and spun hemp yarn (*fil de carret*) in commercial markets.[104] Assessing the arsenal's needs for 1756, Rochefort authorities requested 60,000 livres weight of hemp.[105]

Assuring quality was the most serious problem in acquiring hemp. First-grade Ukrainian or Riga hemp was the best in the world, but it was also the most expensive.[106] Second-grade Riga was no better than the domestic product and was two or three livres a quintal cheaper, but suppliers often passed it off as first-grade or baled it with inferior material.[107] Faced with easy opportunities for fraud, in 1751 Rouillé ordered naval officials henceforth to acquire only first-grade hemp from the north, encouraging greater reliance on domestic production.[108] Nevertheless, even after the outbreak of war threatened northern supplies, naval officials remained suspicious of French hemp and reluctant to buy it.[109] Domestic quality varied widely and cultivation in Berry, Guienne, Champagne, and Lyonnais could only be encouraged at prices higher than second-grade Riga.[110] While naval authorities regarded Berry hemp as equal or superior to premier Riga, they considered Burgundy and Auvergne hemp inferior to Riga's second-grade. Southern producers also faced stiff competition from Italian hemp, a decidedly superior product, the best of which came from Piedmont, Bologna, Ancona, and Naples.[111]

Naval contracting practices did little to encourage greater production. Producers in Brittany were forbidden to sell to anyone other than naval purveyors who paid them too little to bother cultivating the crop. The intendant of Burgundy feared that naval buying practices would lead to the disappearance of hemp cultivation in the province. In the past naval purveyors had purchased hemp *par entreprise*, by separate, annually renewed contracts (*traités particulières*). Since 1748, however, one supplier had held a six-year contract with the exclusive privilege of acquiring his provision before any hemp could be sold or exported. This arrangement allowed the supplier to purchase cheap in abundant years, not at all after scarce harvests, and dally all year, buying a bit of hemp here and there in order to control prices and indeed the entire hemp trade. Moreover, in Franche-Comté and Dauphiné, where his contract called upon him to obtain one-third of his provision, he bought nothing because he did not hold an exclusive privilege.[112] In 1754 the contractor's demand for a monopoly on the entire hemp trade of Burgundy, Dauphiné, Franche-Comté, and Bugey led to changed procedures and for the next few years naval officials purchased hemp in open markets *par économie* and refused offers of supply.[113] But although the system of acquiring domestic hemp *par économie* treated producers more fairly than the *entreprise* system, it did not advance the department's interests. The intendant of Alsace, who sought to encourage rope-hemp cultivation, failed to find an entrepreneur to organize the project until naval authorities agreed to a fixed supply.[114] Without *par entreprise* contracts that secured quantities and terms, merchants remained reluctant to invest in accumulating stocks and landowners refused to cultivate a special crop. This is probably why naval officials in Burgundy succeeded in pursuading the minister to return to the *entreprise* system a few years later.[115]

Each of the three qualities sought in naval cordage, strength, durability, and flexibility, can only be obtained at the expense of the other two; and only skilled workers can ensure their appearance at all.[116] After deposit in an arsenal's General Stores, hemp was dressed, combed, and spun into yarn. A good scutcher dressed sixty to eighty livres weight of hemp a day, cleaning it of foreign matter, splitting, and removing the longest fibres. A hackler combed about the same amount daily. A poor hackler, however, could reduce first-grade hemp fibres to tow fit only for mattress ticking.[117] The chief disadvantage in the work came from the clouds of lung-choking dust arising from the workers' labour; each quintal of hemp produced four to six livres weight of dust. Hacklers prepared the combed fibres into small packages weighing from one and a half to three livres and sent them to the spinners, who spun a thread of 180 to 190 spans (*brasses*) of five French feet each. A spinner's skill lay in producing a fine, even yarn which gave it strength.[118] Though light, the work was tedious, requiring miles of walking backwards each day. Ideally eleven spinners could produce 700 livres weight of yarn daily, but a wartime naval estimate indicated a much lower rate of production, perhaps less than half.[119]

After spinning, workers tarred the dry hemp yarn, up to 300,000 livres weight at a time, employing 600 quintals of tar and taking two months to complete the task.[120] Tarring operations required careful supervision by the arsenals' master ropemakers, especially where manufacture was *par entreprise*. An entrepreneur would add as much tar as possible, up to 20 per cent of total weight, whereas 14 to 16 per cent was thought ideal for long conservation. Too much tar burned the yarn and caused it to swell after seven or eight months in stores.[121] Afterwards the yarn was ready for the ropewalk where it was formed into strands and laid into rope.[122] Laying shortened strands by as much as one-fifth of their length and hence the length of the ropewalk was crucial to the length of finished rope. Rope or cable varied from 120 to 150 spans in length and was designated by its circumference and an agreed weight per span. Naval ropeyards manufactured forty-two sizes of cordage varying half an inch in circumference from three to twenty-four inches and weighing two to 107.5 livres a span.

While the navy always paid premium prices for hemp and these rose during the Seven Years' War, they never reached the levels of the previous war.[123] However, some reduction occurred in the quality of rope manufactured in the arsenals. At Rochefort, authorities approved manufacture without separating first- and second-grade fibres in order to reduce the amount of tow and increase the quantity of yarn by 12 to 15 per cent.[124] They sought additional savings by reducing the number of strands in rope. A perfectly laid twenty-four-inch cable contained 3,600 strands, but by the middle of the Seven Years' War it was likely to have only 2,400.[125] But the navy never suffered a serious shortage of hemp. In July 1758 the intendant of Brest complained of hemp yarn being harbour-bound at Nantes, but Dutch vessels carried northern hemp into naval arsenals as long as funds remained available to pay their freight bills.[126] In 1759 naval arsenals were sufficiently well stocked for Berryer to be able to refuse an offer of domestic supply, and officials at Toulon had more than enough tarred yarn and hemp on hand to rig all the ships in port.[127] Nevertheless, the navy department could not achieve substantial savings by aggregating demand or manufacturing rope *par régie*. Each arsenal's aim to achieve self-reliance and self-sufficiency prevented recourse to the former system, while the department's need for private, commercial credit hindered adoption of the latter.

VICTUALLING

The navy turned to private enterprise, as with all other suppliers, to obtain its victuals. But unlike the others, naval provisioners not only prepared but also embarked and distributed sailors' rations at sea. Moreover, the interested parties had long been organized into a strong syndicate that enjoyed a jealously guarded monopoly. The arrangement to provide victuals appeared to be the nearest to a *ferme* in naval organization. The syndicate, operating behind a surrogate or *prête-nom* known as the victualler-general of the navy (*munitionnaire-général de la marine*), did not feed officers, but did provision the king's forces in America, an arrangement which was to prove a terrible drain on its credit during the Seven Years' War. Animal slaughtering and salting occurred at the arsenals or places designated by naval intendants, while biscuit and fresh bread were prepared and stored in ovens and warehouses belonging to the king. But the victualler-general maintained his own employees in the arsenals and even on board ships of war. Clerks, stewards, and cooks to the number of six in second- and third-rates and four in smaller ships prepared and distributed sailors' daily rations. Although included in ships' muster-books and paid according to rates set down in the Naval Ordinance these men were the victualler's private employees and, as such, were exempted from punishment by captains for infractions.

The monopolistic organization of victualling enshrined in the Naval Ordinance represented a vast improvement over previous arrangements, when captains, entrusted to victual their own ships, had permitted frightful abuses. The terms of Book Ten of the ordinance, confiding all provisioning of ships' crews to a victualler-general, marked a clear administrative advance over previous practices.[128] But in spite of the care expressed in the ordinance for the quality of biscuit, wine, cheese, dried legumes, salt fish, and fresh and salt meats, and for the preparation, preservation, distribution, and composition of sailors' rations, provisions were often of the worst sort: salt meats mediocre, legumes spoiled, and live animals incapable of supporting life itself.[129]

The reason was twofold: first, of the four components of naval victualling, planning, buying, preserving, and packing and distributing, the third faced technical limitations that could not be overcome in the eighteenth century no matter how well organized or well intentioned the victualling personnel;[130] second, the supervision of the victualler-general's employees by naval officials in an arsenal's victualling bureau had distinct limits. Appointed to inspect the quality of incoming provisions and the care exercised in their preparation and packing, naval officials dealt with the victualler's own employees rather than subordinate naval personnel. In the light of the numerous inspections required by the terms of the Naval Ordinance, the victualling offices were undermanned and inspections haphazard. Who was to say that provisions acquired hundreds of miles away from the arsenals by subcontractors and commission-agents of the victualler-general were from the most recent harvest as the Naval Ordinance required? Was every hogshead of salt meat to be opened in order to ensure that sufficient salt had been employed in meat preparation, or that pickle was properly composed, or too much bone was not packed in sea rations, or if the heads and feet of slaughtered animals had been excluded? Chiefly accountants, the naval officials concerned appeared to devote most of their time to keeping accurate records of entry and exit of provisions from warehouses, preparing statements of quantities of needed stores, and supervising embarkation of provisions into warships fitting out.[131]

On the other hand, all things considered, including geographical separation of the arsenals, widely varying agricultural conditions in their hinterlands, lack of a national agricultural economy or transportation network, and weakness of naval supervision, the central organization of naval victualling under private monopoly control appeared remarkably successful. The absence of any large correspondence concerning victualling problems in naval archives confirms the private nature of the victualler-general's activities, but also that the syndicate performed its duties with few complaints and encountered few obstacles.

The very success of the victualling monopoly has kept the parties in the shade. Little is known about its members. Contracts of six years' duration had become roughly standardized since the 1690s and were handled directly by the Royal Council or naval secretary of state. Earlier contracts indicate that syndicate members were numerous; thirty-six appeared in one and fifteen in another.[132] Several receivers-general of finances were interested parties, and their growing power and influence during the eighteenth century suggest that these *officiers* probably continued to be involved. Unfortunately, no contracts have been located for the years covered by this study; only one, signed in December 1762, was located in naval records.[133] Scanty additional evidence reveals the surrogates for the mid-century contracts: Thomas Sauvalle (1745–50), Claude Fort (1751–6), and Nicolas Perney (1757–62), and the names of one or two syndicate members, Sieurs Hébert and Brémond.[134] Members had strong connections at court. The duc d'Estissac reportedly received 30,000 livres annually from naval victuallers in return for his support.[135]

The victualler-general held far and away the largest single naval contract. In 1750, a year of moderate activity at sea, naval planners scheduled 1.3 million livres, or one-eighth of the department's variable expenditures, for seamens', convicts', and hospital rations.[136] The syndicate's importance naturally increased in wartime as the number of sailors grew and additional ships put to sea. According to a very conservative estimate, the victualler-general received 19,460,000 livres, 16.9 per cent of total naval expenditures, during the first three years of hostilities from 1755 to 1757.[137] With such enormous sums involved, the financially constrained government obviously relied on the wealth, credit, and influence of members of the provisions monopoly. The syndicate normally agreed not to accept advances and to receive payment in twelve equal instalments during the calendar year regardless of the quantity of provisions supplied at any particular time. But while the victualling monopoly represented an administrative advance over previous arrangements, and its particular organization and relationship to the navy reflected the Bourbon monarchy's need to tap private sources of credit, centralized food provisioning also arose from the requirements of nature and demands of logic.

Sea rations were based on salt meat which could only be prepared during temperate months. With the creation of a standing navy and increased ship construction during Louis XIV's reign, requirements had to be known in advance of the killing season which began generally after All Saints' Day (1 November). Each October the victualler-general normally received a detailed, confidential statement from the secretary of state containing the number and order of ships to be fitted out in each port, number of men in their crews, and number of months they would spend at sea. As the French made no attempt to keep ships constantly at sea, a simple calculation quickly gave the number of sea rations per man per month. During the first three years of the Fort contract, 1751–3, naval authorities required on average 21,100 man-month rations annually.[138] for 1754, however, they called for nearly three times the recent annual average.[139] But early in November of that year, Machault demanded only 22,680 man-month rations for 1755, interesting evidence that the government had yet to determine the degree of its support for Canada in the face of hostilities in the Ohio Valley.[140] A month later, however, Machault requested 75,761 man-month rations, nearly three and a half times the previously ordered quantity.[141] In September and October 1755 Machault advised the provisioners to anticipate an even greater demand for the coming year, more than 100,000 man-month rations; in the following July he ordered 136,100 man-month sea rations and 54,100 harbour rations for the final three months of the year.[142] Regardless of increases or suddenness of demand, however, the victualler-general produced what was needed; heavy requirements posed only minor difficulties.[143]

Greatly increased demands during wartime placed a strain on salt-beef provisions, especially since most supplies came from Ireland. British embargoes on salt-beef exports to France, Ireland's largest consumer, appeared ineffective. But after the British government removed prohibitions on Irish exports to Britain in 1756 the victualler-general had to seek out new sources of beef. In August Machault urged the syndicate to explore Danish resources.[144] And after some initial difficulties that saw naval officials condemn the entire first shipment of 10,000 quintals of salt-beef from Denmark, the new source filled naval needs admirably.[145] In 1758 the victualler-general signed an eight-year contract with Danish suppliers;

during the year fifty-one foreign vessels, chiefly Dutch but some Spanish, all fully equipped with bogus charter parties and lading bills, carried provisions into Brest and Rochefort from Bordeaux, Nantes, and Cherbourg, but also from Cork, Copenhagen, and Aalbourg.[146] By 1762 the victualler-general was vigorously defending his Danish salt-beef contract against Turgot's insistence that he purchase salt-meat from Limousin.[147]

The chief problems were financial. One source of difficulty may have been rates of payment that were insufficient to cope with wartime expansion of demand. In the 1751 contract the navy agreed to pay 10 sols for the first three million rations and 9 sols, 6 deniers, for any surplus requirement. Convict and hospital rations drew lower and higher rates respectively, but the syndicate expected to be paid the top rate for the bulk of its provisions. In 1757, however, the victualler-general supplied nearly fifteen million rations and with costs invariably mounting as a result of greater demand and inflation, the syndicate claimed to be subsidizing the navy.[148] Since the first postwar contract allowed the basic rate to rise to 11 sols on four million rations, this may well have been true.[149] In any case, the victualler-general demanded the ten sol rate for the entire amount delivered in 1757, and thereafter during the life of the new contract. The minister feared the effect of failure to meet the victualler-general's demand on the syndicate's suppliers and the departments' other creditors, yet was unable to find the extra money. The syndicate claimed to have had to make payments of its own in April amounting to 1,726,834 livres. Unable to authorize payments of such magnitude, the controller-general of finances stalled.[150] Pâris de Marmontel, the court banker, refused to help and Moras turned to Louis xv himself. The king accepted the losses claimed by the syndicate, acknowledged his government's need to support their credit, annulled the year-old contract, and agreed to a new one to run for the original term at a revised rate of 10 sols for the first nine million rations and 9½ sols for any surplus. It was not quite what the syndicate wanted, but by way of compensation, the new agreement included increased payments for hospital rations.[151] Unfortunately, the new financial agreement may not have aided the syndicate; condemnation of the first shipment of Danish salt meat was a short-term disaster and probably cancelled any benefit from the renegotiated victualling contract.[152] But much worse, the government soon found itself unable to meet its obligations. The syndicate's receipt of large regular monthly payments became a thing of the past. The navy's demand for provisions remained high in 1759 but payments became delayed and difficult to negotiate. Berryer proposed to pay for the last four months of 1760 with one-third in cash and the remainder in previously matured, unredeemable *rescriptions*, the only form of government paper being supplied to the treasurers-general of the navy by the controller-general of finances.[153]

These financial difficulties are what gave effect to the British blockade of the seaports during the final three years of the war. Here, as elsewhere, serious complaints of delays and undelivered cargo did not result from the appearance of enemy vessels off the French coast, but from the financial collapse of the government.[154] Even the navy's largest contractor could not remain immune from the financial disaster that befell the service in 1759. Indeed, while the victualler-general and other naval suppliers had struggled against financial constraints since the end of 1757, the collapse in October 1759 brought low the treasurers-general of the navy themselves.

CHAPTER ELEVEN

Naval Finances

The navy's financial position was precarious at the best of times and its financial starvation has been viewed as among the chief causes of Britain's naval victories during the Seven Years' War.[1] But if there is agreement about French financial weakness, historians too often reveal a predilection to link it to human incompetence rather than to the impersonal organization of the financial system itself.[2] According to J.F. Bosher, contemporaries and historians have identified fraud, foreign bankers, faithless royal servants, defects of character, and deficient policy as causes of France's financial difficulties. But such explanations, he argues, encourage the unwarranted assumption that others more enlightened, more active, more faithful, or stronger willed might have developed different policies and taken steps to overcome the Old Regime's financial difficulties. This was not so, for "the financial system was not anyone's to change."[3] With this injunction in mind, this chapter focuses on the workings of the financial system, the problems that the system posed for naval officials, and the consequences, both administrative and organizational, for one of the government's major spending departments. We will then be able to appreciate the important differences between the theory and reality of the government's financial practices, assess their impact on naval organization, especially for acquiring stores and munitions. In this way short-term financial demands, important political constraints, and the financial system itself, stand revealed at the heart of the navy's financial difficulties. These features arose less from a lack of funds, that were always wanting, than from a sudden constriction of credit following financial and political developments of which the navy was victim rather than instigator.

The navy, like other spending departments of the Bourbon monarchy, did not have an income, nor, in the strict sense, did it spend government revenue. Notions of naval income, expenditure, and accounting imply a directness of relation between the collection, management, and spending of government monies that did not exist. The cardinal rule of French financial administration authorized naval officials solely to order payments on naval business. They never saw a sou of the funds assigned to the department's expenses, nor did they control those who received, held, managed, and paid those funds.

Nor did naval officials operate within a budget in the sense of estimating their expenses within financial limits imposed by some previous notion of revenue.[4] Indeed, in the absence of an annual naval revenue the naval secretaries of state did not really exercise a budgetary function. Each year between August and October they requested forecasts of the coming year's expenses from intendants and other *ordonnateurs* in the arsenals, ports, and colonies. Naval officers drew up draft plans of expenditures, *projets de dépenses*, and forwarded them to Versailles during the final quarter of the year. There, the *premier commis*, Joseph Pellerin, and the secretary of state reviewed them and afterwards drew up a *bordereau-général des dépenses* or general schedule which they returned to the intendants accompanied by injunctions to seek additional economies. The sums listed therein, however, were not authorized expenditures; indeed, sometimes the sums on the *bordereau* were *not* to be paid during the current fiscal year. Returning a *bordereau-général* to the intendant of Brest, Maurepas once noted that "this is less an authorized statement (*estat arreté*) of expenses to be made than a copy of your draft (*projet*) in the form that I have settled on."[5] Authorization came only after an *Etat général des fonds* for the year was prepared and carried to the king, who, together with the controller-general of finances and the secretary of state for the navy, reviewed the items, and after further paring, signed it. Clearly the controller-general who had the best general notion (that is all he had) of the government's revenues and not the naval secretary of state was the key person to decide the total amount of authorized annual naval expenditures. In crucial budgetary decisions affecting the navy the power of naval secretaries was illusory. Plainly and simply the naval secretary was not responsible, either in law or in fact, for his department's expenses. The king alone was responsible in law and the controller-general in fact.[6] But the controller-general lacked the knowledge to assign government revenues to naval expenditures.

The *état général des fonds* possessed a certain legal and fiscal force. It was the basis of the navy's fiscal year or *exercice*; carried the signatures of the king and his foremost advisers with secondary fiscal powers affecting the navy; established the original discharge for the treasurers-general; and, finally, represented a pay order to the keeper of the Royal Treasury. In a juridical sense it allowed the treasurer-general to begin to manage his accounts for the coming year.

Of approximately 9 million livres that comprised the navy's ordinary funds before 1748, about 7.4 millions were encumbered by fixed, invariable expenses, of which 1.5 and 2.5 millions were earmarked for galleys and colonies and the remainder to officers' appointments, troops' pay, pensions, arsenal employees' wages, hospitals, building leases, and secret expenses. Only 1.6 million livres remained available for variable expenditures, chiefly running costs in the arsenals, warship construction, repair and maintenance.[7] No ordinary funds at all were designated for sea operations.[8] The structure of naval finances reflected a very old notion that the navy could be kept in being (i.e., in ordinary) by remaining in the arsenals. But for all its age, the decision to pay for all naval armaments from extraordinary funds was taken only after Louis xiv's death. Maurepas blamed a desire to seek détente with the Maritime Powers during the regency and the growing attraction of controllers-general to the India Company during the subsequent period for the severe reduction of naval funds and constraints on armaments. He successfully argued on behalf of increasing the ordinary funds from 8 to 9.5 million livres, but further the controllers-general would not go.[9] Separation of naval funds into ordinary and extraordinary components at a time of rapidly growing French maritime, especially colonial, commerce was quite unrealistic; but the first important rearrangement of naval finances appeared only after 1748.

Three alterations to the ordinary funds radically changed their nature: the first followed the abolition of the galley corps; the second divided colonial and naval finances into separate chests; and the third increased the authorized amount of the ordinary funds. Together they reversed the previous relation between fixed and variable categories of ordinary expenditure, permitted vigorous reconstruction of the navy, and allowed a degree of operational planning not seen since the reign of Louis xiv. None of these developments, however, altered the financial system itself in any way. Short-term credit demands rather than long-term strategical aims continued to dominate the concerns of secretaries of state.

The union of the galley corps with the sailing navy cut more than 600,000 livres from pay and appointments of galley officers and petty officers, and reduced by 100,000 livres the cost of galley construction and repair. Nearly half the fixed expenses of the old corps were extinguished, and most of the remainder shifted to the variable portion of the ordinary funds.[10] Certain fixed costs remained; convict rations, the conduct of chain gangs, and hospital maintenance still required about half a million livres. But the movement of convicts into the arsenals enabled intendants to release unskilled labourers, keep wage rates stable, and reduce their forecasts for day wages.[11] The division of colonial and naval funds into separate chests transferred colonial expenses right out of naval accounts. Along with savings from suppression of the galley corps, it reduced the fixed portion of annual ordinary expenses to about 4.5 million livres.[12]

Finally, in 1749 the navy's ordinary funds dramatically increased to 15 million livres. This enormous increase was perhaps Maurepas' greatest achievement. From having less than 17 per cent of the ordinary funds free for variable expenses, the navy suddenly found itself with 10.5 millions or 70 per cent of the funds available to rebuild the fleet. Maurepas' successor found himself able to decide on spending priorities, plan construction of the new fleet, and acquire stores as far ahead as 1754.

Before the middle of the century extraordinary funds had been designed to meet the contingent demands of the sea service in wartime. They were only rarely provided under the regent and Cardinal Fleury. Though authorized from 1739 to the end of the War of the Austrian Succession, none was granted in 1749. Thereafter, however, extraordinary funds were regularly allotted for naval expenses. The total amounts were inadequate, but Lacour-Gayet missed the significant point that they appeared at all and continued on a regular basis in peacetime.[13] The enormous increase in extraordinary funds in 1755 demonstrated the government's willingness to employ the navy. Machault obtained the largest extraordinary fund ever authorized for naval expenditures, 16.3 million livres, which, when added to the ordinary funds, totalled 31,326,000 for the year's anticipated expenses. Increased authorizations appeared in 1756, declined slightly in 1757, and increased again in each of the next two years (see Appendix). During the last three years of the Seven Years' War the king and the controller-general drastically cut the extraordinary funds. But the important question is, why was the navy so financially weak between 1755 and 1759 when government revenues had been made available on a scale never before seen in the navy's history? To answer this question we must go back to the financial system to see how payments were made on the navy's behalf.

Naval funds, like other government revenue, were handled by treasurers-general, venal office-holders who, though legally mere accountants, were *de facto* private bankers possessing royal authority to carry on the financial business of the navy.[14] They did not simply manage government chests, but controlled their own private chests in which funds belonging to the crown were held on account together with other private accounts.[15] As *officiers comptables*, treasurers-general acted virtually independently of naval or, indeed, any government control. They were accountable only to the Paris Chamber of Accounts whose members saw themselves as watchdogs of the financial probity of individual accountants and had nothing to do with budgetary questions.[16]

Originally the treasurers-general of the navy had been accountants, keeping the department's books and paying out funds on receipt of payment orders (*ordonnances*) signed by authorized naval officials. But long before the middle of the eighteenth century their accounting and paying functions had been subordinated to finding the necessary funds to meet authorized expenses. Royal letters patent exempting naval treasurers-general from all penalties levied by the Chamber of Accounts for delayed presentation of their accounts acknowledged the permanent nature of this development.[17] But the change in function so altered the relation of the treasurers-general to the naval department that by mid-century they had become linch-pins of the navy's existence.[18]

The entire arrangement for financial administration of naval payments was built on a false assumption that treasurers-general of the navy had funds previously authorized for payments in their chests. The preparation of naval estimates, their careful review in the department's central offices, and the rigorous definition of who could sanction payments mattered little in the cold light shining on the inadequately supplied chests of the treasurers-general. Yet it was precisely the absence of funds that gave the treasurers-general their great power and influence. Since they lacked government funds to effect authorized payments yet were solely responsible for making them, the rigorous separation between *ordonnateur* and *payeur* became a legal fiction. Nor could it be otherwise. The continued operation of the navy, indeed, its very existence, required treasurers-general to find the funds. They did so by issuing their own notes or borrowing on the credit of their office in which they possessed real property. At no time did they appeal to anything like royal or public credit.

The government's receipts were scattered throughout France in the chests of hundreds of accountants, particularly receivers-general and farmers-general and their employees. The keeper of the Royal Treasury, also an accountant and private banker, handled only a portion of the government's revenues, but only he could order a holder of receipts to release funds to a payer of expenses.[19] After presenting payment orders to the keeper of the Royal Treasury, the treasurer-general *en exercice* obtained *assignations* or assignments from the former on one or more of the hundreds of chests belonging to accountants who collected the government's revenues. No document reveals the location of the chests on which the navy's funds were assigned during the middle of the eighteenth century, but during Colbert's day the chests for obvious reasons were located in the coastal regions where the bulk of naval expenditures were expected. Some chests were also near Paris where the treasurers-general centred their own activities and paid out large sums on the navy's behalf.[20]

The first problem concerned the ability of various revenue chests to provide funds at the appropriate moment. It was important to smooth operation that high levels of naval expenditure during the first and third quarters of each year when warships were normally fitted out be matched by *assignations* that fell due on a receiver's chest at the same time. If, as most likely, treasurers held notes for later in the year, they borrowed short-term *anticipations* from receivers or advanced their own long-term bills to meet the demand. Receivers-general of finances issued *rescriptions*, notes drawn on their own cashiers, which naval treasurers-general held to support their own notes. Negotiable only at lower than current lending rates, *assignations* failed to provide for a treasurer's immediate requirements. Treasurers-general fulfilled their needs by delivering bills of exchange to local lenders in return for their short-term paper on Paris. Such bills allowed provincial merchants and financial officers to avoid the cost of remitting specie to Paris and earned quick profits by disposing of notes that would have been heavily discounted if negotiated locally. No public credit was involved in any of these private transactions. Naval funds commonly appeared in the form of private, short-term notes, *rescriptions*, *anticipations*, *billets*, and so on. It is not unreasonable to suppose that at any time but especially during wartime naval treasurers-general might have several million livres worth of their own notes in circulation. For if they were financially sound, their paper continued in the market long after the maturities on the notes. It is here, in the issuing of short-term loans between bankers, that the profits of all accountants lay. [21]

A second problem derived from the keeper of the Royal Treasury's poor accounting. It was not unusual for him to issue *assignations* on a receiver's chest that was inadequately supplied, empty, or had no hope of being filled with the required amount. [22] The treasurer still had to find funds to pay naval expenses, but if the *assignation* remained unpaid beyond his fiscal year it ceased being a charge on him and became his charge against the government, as he advanced his own funds to cover the required amounts. [23]

The administrative consequences of the navy's reliance upon a system of private banking are fairly clear. Whereas royal administration "was founded upon the confusion of public power and private property," nowhere was this distinction more sharply drawn than in naval administration. [24] In the absence of venal office-holding there could be no confusion between power and property within the navy itself. Whether of sword or pen, naval officers were royal servants subject to royal orders and directly responsible through the secretary of state to the king for their every action. Yet royal naval administration depended on a private financial system for its continued daily existence. The existence of these two separate institutional structures, fundamentally different from one another, was bound to create confusion. The financial system left naval officials responsible only for issuing payment orders to meet naval expenditures; they had no liability to ensure that payments actually were made. No naval official, including the secretary of state, had the slightest legal obligation to see that naval creditors received their due. Concern for unpaid creditors pervades official naval correspondence, reflecting awareness of the eventual consequences of such a state of affairs, but also helplessness and frustration at being tied to a private financial system, unable to effect remedies. In a legal sense, this concern was none of their business; naval treasurers might even view it as meddlesome interference. At the same time, officials had a direct interest in seeing that payments were made because future goods and services depended on present payments (i.e., "naval credit" was at stake). A final consequence of this archaic mixture of royal and private systems was that payment orders could easily exceed amounts in the *état général des fonds* despite injunctions to *ordonnateurs* to prevent such a situation from occurring. In 1751, for example, Lenormant de Mézy spent in excess of one-third of a million livres more than was carried on the year's approved *bordereau*.[25] Under pressure to get ships to sea, intendants correctly viewed exhortations to live within their means as ambiguous rhetoric. In modern parlance cost overruns were normal, not only because no one really knew the costs until long afterwards, but because those who authorized excess expenditure had no responsibility to meet it.

Without a budget the navy had neither a formal, organized, annual deficit nor the means to establish one. The department normally carried unpaid expenditures from one year to the current expenses of the next.[26] But these had amounted to a small proportion of each year's payments and could be safely carried over. During the Seven Years' War, however, the amount of unpaid expenses grew steadily until by 1758 they surpassed the authorized funds for the current fiscal year. So that although treasurers-general had lacked sufficient funds for half a century this new situation developed quite rapidly and left the navy more exposed to the icy blasts of political and financial winds of circumstance than before.

The outbreak of war between Britain and Spain in 1739 brought all of the potential strains on naval finances to the fore. By January 1743 about 3 million livres remained unpaid on the expenditures of the last five fiscal years.[27] A large extraordinary fund was authorized, partly to acquit unpaid expenses, and thereafter such funds became increasingly devoted to this object rather than to expanded sea operations. The cumulative debt mounted quickly. By the end of 1746 unpaid expenses totalled 14.8 millions.[28] Thereafter even the crude system of estimating naval expenditures collapsed. No *état des fonds*, and hence no statement of authorized expenses, appeared for 1747 or 1748.[29] Expediency governed naval finances. The total unpaid expenses from the War of the Austrian Succession remain uncertain. One estimate of January 1748 was wholly fictitious.[30] Another reported between 20 and 22 million livres.[31] But three retrospective reports written in 1758 indicate that the debts contracted during the war amounted to between 26 and 27 millions, "and was believed to be more than thirty millions including the cost of liquidation."[32]

Maurepas requested a thirteen-year moratorium on repayment of noncurrent expenses, for naval suppliers had threatened to cease dealing with the department except on a cash basis.[33] And though he obtained a greatly increased ordinary fund in 1749, failure to obtain an extraordinary fund limited its effectiveness. Rouillé, too, sought to remove the naval debt from current expenses, but although he may have been promised 5 millions in each of three years from 1749 to 1751, no such fund ever appeared.[34] After being refused an extraordinary fund in February 1750, however, he obtained royal approval for each treasurer-general to borrow 2 millions in order to secure a portion of the unpaid expenses.[35] The borrowing appeared to be fully subscribed. The controller-general made no arrangement to repay the loan so with his approval each man issued his own, annually renewable notes (*billets*) while the navy agreed to pay the interest.[36] But the navy had only consolidated a multitude of debts to its suppliers into a greater one to its two treasurers-general whose private notes were nothing more than a from of short-term credit. About 21 millions in unpaid expenses remained, but the same year Rouillé obtained the first of five annual, peacetime, extraordinary funds, which totalled a little over 18 million livres by 1754. These funds, it appears, were devoted exclusively to paying off old expenses.[37] With 4 millions secured by a private note issue and about 18 millions paid off, the war debt had been very substantially reduced. But current expenditure annually exceeded funds by about 500,000 livres. When added to the outstanding wartime debt, this brought the burden of unpaid expenses on the 1755 *exercice* to 9 or 10 million livres. About one-third of the amount, however, was in notes of the treasurer-general, quite different from unpaid bills.[38]

Reduction of the mass of old, unpaid, wartime expenses was not accomplished easily; it interfered with rebuilding the fleet and prevented realistic planning for the future. In the middle of 1752 Treasurer-general Mouffle de Georville began to delay making exact remittances to the arsenals.[39] *Rescriptions* were reaching Rochefort six months late and had to be discounted to meet recent expenses.[40] Similar difficulties arose in 1753 when the treasurers at Toulon and Marseilles could not meet bills of exchange drawn on themselves. By August only 350,000 of 600,000 livres normally authorized had been sent on the current *exercice*.[41] By early 1754 the treasurer-general was holding back the greater portion of monthly remittances to Rochefort in favour of making payments on previous *exercices*.[42] Treasurers-general also found it increasingly difficult to remit funds on time and in notes sufficiently short-term to be easily negotiable. In 1754 Treasurer-general De Selle remitted nothing at all to Toulon on his 1753 *exercice*. In June the intendant borrowed 60,000 livres on his own signature to meet day-workers' wages, and persuaded the new naval minister to let him borrow 80,000 livres from Marseilles' Chamber of Commerce.[43] At the beginning of April the treasurers-general also borrowed 1.2 million livres which they turned over to the treasurers-general of the colonies to meet unexpected bills of exchange arriving from Canada. Colonial finances failed to improve and the borrowing continued to be annually renewed.[44] The treasurers-general had 5.2 millions of their own notes circulating in the market, money was cheap, and their notes appeared to be a good investment for other financiers and bankers.

During the early 1750s Rouillé, with the cooperation of the controller-general and assistance of the treasurers-general, had wrought a minor miracle, assembling large quantities of naval stores, nearly doubling the number of ships-of-the-line in the fleet, and substantially reducing unpaid expenses only six years after Maurepas had pleaded for a thirteen-year moratorium on repayments. In the summer of 1754 money was cheap. The farmers-general were borrowing at 4 per cent and Pâris de Montmartel at 4.5 per cent. [45] As long as the economy remained active little reason existed for treasurers-generals' notes to be presented for redemption on maturity. Continued circulation was a compliment to a sound financier. Any sudden increase in interest rates or contraction of credit brought about by rumours of war, however, placed the naval treasurers-generals' notes in a precarious position subject to wartime panic and increased speculation. Late in 1754 the treasurers-general probably began to withhold funds in reserve to be able to redeem notes from nervous holders refusing to renew them.

Machault continued Rouillé's policy during his first year in office, concentrating on debt reduction, controlling expenditures, and ordering no new ships to be laid down. At Toulon news of Machault's intention to liquidate the unpaid expenses of 1745, 1746, 1747, and 1748 "spread joy throughout the public."[46] By the spring of 1755 Toulon's intendant reported only half a million livres owing on the three exercices, 1746 to 1748, and all expenses paid on the exercices of the next four years.[47] Fortunately several opportunities enabled the government to increase revenues without heavy borrowing in 1755, opportunities that the controller-general was quick to seize.[48] After Machault estimated the cost of fitting out the large fleet that sailed to Canada at just over 5 million livres, Controller-general Séchelles immediately signed pay orders transferring one million livres each for December through March to meet expenses; the fifth million was to meet laying up expenses in the summer.[49] Funds continued to flow after news of the loss of L'Alcide and Le Lys reached France. By October the treasurer-general of the navy was reported receiving 4.5 millions worth of assignations a month from the keeper of the Royal Treasury, and the amount was to grow to 5 millions in January.[50] Treasurer-general De Selle remitted funds to Toulon on the current exercice in excess of the monthly états de distribution, and Mouffle de Georville transferred more than one million livres to the arsenal's previous exercice.[51] As yet there appeared to be no serious difficulty.

The total naval debt stood at just under 14.5 million livres on 1 January 1756.[52] Unpaid expenses worth less than 10 millions did not threaten the department; but with more than one-third of the total in highly speculative, private, short-term notes, issued by the treasurers-general, the financial structure of the department had few defences against political and financial vicissitude. The bulk of the debt was in unpaid wages owed to sailors and workmen and payments due to provisioners and manufacturers. France's formal declaration of war on Great Britain forced the government to reintroduce wartime income tax, the *dixième*, and impose the second *vingtième* in order to raise revenues and secure new borrowings. New perpetual *rentes*, however, were only taken up at 5 per cent.[53]

Unfortunately, borrower confidence was seriously undermined, first, by opposition to wartime financial edicts that culminated in the king's *lit de justice* in December followed by the resignation of almost the entire Paris parlement, and second, by the physical attack on Louis xv in January followed by the dismissal of the ministers of war and the navy. As early as 2 January 1757 money was drying up; Pâris de Montmartel complained of being unable to find funds on the market with his own notes; "Disrepute and mistrust are so great since the resignations in the parlement that everyone is withdrawing money [left] with notaries to place."[54] Bearing no greater interest than recent perpetual *rentes* and with no provision for their redemption, the notes of the naval treasurers-general declined in value. Their annual renewal was in question. The controller-general's admission into the Royal Council as minister of state and his assumption of the naval secretaryship did not restore confidence. Indeed, the need to restore confidence in the notes of the naval treasurers-general may have been the chief reason why Peyrenc de Moras replaced Machault. Unrest abroad in the money market led some note-holders to demand reimbursement. Pâris de Montmartel had no option but to buy them up. How many and of what amount is unknown. But he purchased notes to secure the credit of the remainder. As supplier of funds to the Royal Treasury, Montmartel gave them to Treasurer-general De Selle, as part of the assigned naval funds which amounted to a forced redemption, further diminishing the funds available to the treasurer-general.[55]

The feeble returns from war taxes forced Peyrenc de Moras to move from one expedient to another during the spring and summer of 1757, raising funds through lotteries, life annuities, advances, and the creation of new offices. The king had authorized an extraordinary fund of 24 million livres to meet the navy's current expenses. Together with the ordinary funds the department had 33 millions. But by 1 August when the navy had been assigned 18.3 million livres, 4.7 millions had been transferred to previous fiscal years and total anticipated expenses had grown to 38 millions. In brief, 24 million livres remained to be paid, but only 14.7 livres remained to be assigned. The department's total unpaid expenses were thought to be 20 million livres.[56] By August, however, the treasurers-general had ceased to remit funds to their *commis* in the arsenals and had forbidden the latter to draw on them for any more.

Also in August Abbé de Bernis negotiated a short-lived peace with the Paris magistrates. Louis xv withdrew his edict of exile and the parlement its resignation; Moras' removal from finance sealed the bargain, and on 24 August Jean de Boullongne replaced him as the new controller-general.[57] Expedients became ever harder to find, and naval intendants sought local financial aid. Marseilles' Chamber of Commerce became a major support at Toulon.[58] The *consuls* of Toulon also lent funds.[59] At Le Havre the intendant borrowed sums at half a per cent monthly to meet his most pressing needs.[60] Local aid had dried up at Rochefort, the port being, in the intendant's words, "exhausted by the considerable credits that it has made to the King, and [its merchants] unable to lend us the slightest sum for the most pressing needs."[61] The keeper of the Royal Treasury was unable to assign funds on the government's receivers and in September Treasurer-general De Selle borrowed half a million livres on his own account to meet the department's most pressing expenses.[62] Indeed, during the last three months of 1757 Moras appeared not to authorize any funds at all.[63]

The coming year's operational plan required an extraordinary fund of 34 millions, but after passing to the controller-general's office in December it died.[64] One estimate placed unpaid naval expenses at the beginning of 1758 at 36 millions.[65] Although the king approved an extraordinary fund of 27 millions for 1758, the treasurers-general received only 14 millions during the year. Delays obtaining *assignations* from the Royal Treasury dogged the treasurer-general's business throughout the year.[66] Only one million livres each was made available in January and February. The latter payment went entirely to the victualler-general.[67] Moras pleaded with Boullongne for help, sending along Lenormant de Mézy's report on the department's debts, repeating portions of it verbatim, demanding payment of one-third, or at least one-quarter, of the total debt, and insisting that payment for current expenses remained absolutely crucial. Fear of bankruptcies among provisioners mingled with Moras' lack of influence. In his opinion almost all naval suppliers were at the point of abandoning the service if not given strong assistance in March; but he had almost ceased to care.[68] Demands grew so great that the Royal Treasury was on the point of closing. The government lived on advances from Pâris de Montmartel, but his means, too, were not inexhaustible.[69]

The constraints devastated the arsenals. At the end of January the Rochefort treasurer owed 600,000 livres on already authorized *états de distribution*, and the *commis* of La Rochelle's receiver-general of finances refused to negotiate a matured *rescription*.[70] In March Ruis-Embito sent bills of exchange worth 200,000 livres to Bordeaux for negotiation because such sums could not be obtained at La Rochelle.[71] Finally, Ruis began to issue bills of exchange drawn on the treasurers-general before requesting the required authority.[72] At Brest, *Commissaire-général* Robert obtained funds to pay off three warships by having *rescriptions* heavily discounted in the port. Needing additional funds, he drew on the treasurer-general and had such drafts discounted as well. Robert succeeded in raising 157,000 livres in April and 262,000 livres in May, but by early June there was not a sou in the treasurer's chest.[73] Payments for cargo arriving from St Domingue in Kersaint's squadron provided a brief respite, but in August "there remained not an *écu* in the chest."[74] The situation was just as bad at Toulon. At the beginning of August *Commissaire-général* Michel diverted over 700,000 livres in specie to pay expenses incurred in 1756, and neither treasurer-general had remitted any funds to fill the current *états de distribution*.[75] The lack of funds was due to the steadily growing need to transfer the greatest portion of any remittance to meet the unpaid expenses of 1757 and to retain additional sums at Paris to meet the growing number of bills of exchange being drawn in the ports.[76]

Bills of exchange drawn by intendants on the treasurers-general procured only temporary aid and were ultimately an important cause of the collapse of naval finances. In order to acquit the bills in the ports and at Paris, treasurers in the ports retained the few notes (*effets*) they had on hand rather than spend them in accordance with the *états de distribution*. The effect was threefold. First, the oldest invoices became viewed as already paid because the amounts were carried on the *états*, and second, the treasurers-general sent their remittances to the ports in forms increasingly difficult to negotiate.[77] As difficulties in negotiating paper grew, intendants turned more and more to issuing bills of exchange on the treasurers-general, thereby creating a vicious circle. The treasurers-general retained their short-term notes in order to redeem intendants' bills of exchange, which had been issued in the first place because insufficient short-term notes reached the treasurers in the ports. Finally, recent invoices were being paid although they were not always listed on the *états*. Without sufficient funds, the separation of *états de distribution* from remittances of the treasurers-general was complete, destroying the crude accounting system between the navy and its bankers.

The creation on 18 October of a special commission to verify and liquidate the debts of naval creditors was not surprising in view of such longstanding conditions. The Royal Council initially considered postponing payment of bills of exchange from the colonies, but settled on the commission as less drastic.[78] Nevertheless, the commission's appearance further restricted the department's access to credit.[79] While Abbé de Bernis viewed the commission as reflecting the government's desire to attack fraud

TABLE 8
Naval Debt, 1 June 1758

Items	Amounts (livres tournois)	%
Principal on 1750 loan	4,000,000	9.5
Principal on 1754 loan	1,200,000	2.9
Principal on 1757 loan	500,000	1.2
Subtotal outstanding loans	5,700,000	13.6
Interest on loans, discounts, and exchange on assignations and rescriptions negotiated between 1754 and 1758	1.102,230	2.6
Unpaid expenses pre-1756	974,721	2.3
Unpaid expenses 1756	5,430,715	12.9
Unpaid expenses 1757	17,505,598	41.7
Unpaid expenses to June 1758	11,290,454	26.9
Subtotal unpaid expenses	35,201,488	83.8
Total debt on 1 June 1758	42,003,718	100.

Source: Marine B[4], 78, ff. 172–3, untitled report labelled "Marine," dated November 1758; Legohérel, Les Trésoriers généraux, 206, presents similar data taken from BN, Mss. frs., 11,340.

and wartime profiteering, naval creditors could only wonder whether the government had a similar will to meet their demands. The commission's mandate covered unpaid expenses only to 1 June 1758 when the navy's debt totalled 42 million livres. A report prepared for the Royal Council and supplied to the new commission claimed that the debt consisted of 12 million livres unpaid from the previous war, 3 millions unpaid on *exercices* from the subsequent peacetime interval, and 27 millions unpaid on the *exercices* of the current war.[80] But the burden on the current and two most recent fiscal years was actually closer to 35 million livres. The report's author, Lenormant de Mézy, was attempting to separate unpaid prewar expenses in order to support a plea, made and approved fourteen months earlier, for an extraordinary debt reduction fund of 12 to 15 million livres. As table 8 shows, less than one million livres actually remained unpaid on all fiscal years prior to 1756.

In human terms the debt consisted of approximately 16.8 millions in appointments, pay, and stipends for naval personnel, 13 millions owed to naval suppliers, 7 millions for warehouse leases, hospital care, subsistence for sick and prisoners, and freight, lightering, and travel costs, and 5.2 millions owed to the treasurers-general.[81] By 1758 the total unpaid expenses had become greater than the entire fund allotted to the current fiscal year. In theory and in practice there was no money for current expenses, and under existing constraints there would not be any. The archaic financial system was breaking down. No attempt was made to remit funds in accordance with the *états de distribution* which were the only real point of contact between the naval administration and the navy's financial agents. Current pay orders no longer bore any relation to current remittances.

It is common knowledge that Bourbon kings borrowed at least as long as the personal, private credit of their bankers held out, but we need to be reminded of the additional invidious practice of exacting forced loans from thousands of sailors, workers, and naval officers but most especially from hundreds of merchants and entrepreneurs who supplied millions of livres worth of stores to the department. During 1757 and 1758 these forced loans deteriorated. Unpaid appointments were the least important for officers could be expected to remain at their posts. By 1758 the navy was being borne largely on the backs of its personnel and its suppliers. Sailors and workingmen, however, were abandoning their posts, writing off, in effect, their bad debts to the crown, which reduced the numbers from whom the crown could continue to borrow.

Since becoming controller-general in August 1757, Jean de Boullongne with the support of Abbé de Bernis had sought to introduce Jean-Joseph de Laborde into the financial milieu as a new source of funds. But Boullongne only achieved success a year later when Laborde took up residence in Paris. A self-made man of thirty-five, Laborde, came to Paris with the understanding that Pâris de Montmartel wanted his support. Montmartel, however, claimed not to have been consulted by Boullongne or Bernis, and refused to have anything to do with him.[82] Nevertheless, the new arrangement coincided with two important developments at the naval department. First, Nicolas Berryer succeeded to office in November and insisted on a new policy that subsequent payments on old accounts be made only from surpluses arising after meeting current expenses.[83] The Fontanieu Commission became, then, an important device to stall payment of old debts. Second, towards the end of December Pâris de Montmartel put together a syndicate or consortium of five financiers to supply funds to the treasurers-general of the navy.

The syndicate, known as Beaujon, Goossens and Company, was composed of the suppliers of northern masts and stores to the navy for the past three and a half years: Gabriel Michel, who had recently acquired the office of treasurer-general of artillery and engineering, Nicolas Beaujon, since 1756 receiver-general of finances for La Rochelle, and Pierre-François

Goossens. The other members were Joseph Micault d'Harvelay, grand-nephew of Montmartel and his successor since 1755 as keeper of the Royal Treasury and Jean Le Maître de la Martinière, Montmartel's personal friend and later Michel's fellow treasurer-general of artillery and engineering.[84] The syndicate agreed to provide 36 million livres to the navy, thereby relieving the treasurers-general of the navy from having to issue their own bills of exchange to obtain funds, at least to the tune of 3 million livres a month. Owing to the growing length of their maturities, *rescriptions* no longer filled the treasurers' need for short-term funds. The syndicate would do all this and supply the naval treasurers with funds rather than long-term paper.[85] Like Laborde, members of the syndicate received *rescriptions* on the chests of the receivers-general, which could be held until their maturities or negotiated in the money markets in return for the funds they supplied. To raise their own funds they circulated their own bills of exchange due twelve or fifteen months later. According to Laborde, this practice of issuing medium- to long-term notes doomed their enterprise from the start. Dutch capitalists normally credited French borrowers for much shorter terms, two and three months, and for three or four hundred thousand florins (approximately 660 to 880 thousand livres tournois).[86]

The new arrangements put together during the winter of 1759 did not help Controller-general Boullongne. The antipathy between Montmartel and Laborde probably contributed to his downfall. On 4 March Etienne de Silhouette, whose name has become synonymous with shadow images of reality, replaced him. During his first few months in office, he achieved great popularity by brilliantly portraying a new borrowing as an opportunity for everyone to make money. But beyond his shares in the united tax farms, neither life annuities nor other borrowings were fully subscribed; new loans could not be floated. Taxation remained the only alternative. "Any credit operation today," Silhoutte reported in September, "will only produce the fatal effect of revealing our powerlessness to the enemy and making peace more difficult."[87]

The delicate, already precarious web of poorly organized paper and credit needed only one more blow to disintegrate. Admiral La Clue's defeat off Lagos in mid-August had already weakened government notes on the money market, and when news of the fall of Quebec reached Paris in mid-October it brought the edifice down. These blows had a multiplier effect: first, by threatening the future success of the "expédition particulière," which had been heavily supported with funds supplied by Beaujon, Goossens and Company, and second, by announcing the end of France's North American empire, which threatened colonial bills of exchange.

Government finances wavered. Only a few days earlier, Laborde had noted laconically to Choiseul: "It is absolutely impossible to wage war during all of 1760."[88] News of the fall of Quebec killed Treasurer-general De Selle before the day was out, on 15 October.[89] Berryer asked Jean-Nicolas de Boullongne (not to be confused with his father, the former controller-general) to assemble Laborde, Beaujon, Goossens, and the two treasurers-general of the colonies to obtain their opinion on proposals to suspend all colonial bills of exchange and report in five days.[90] The following day Beaujon and Goossens informed Berryer that they must suspend payments to the victualler-general's cashier. Berryer replied that they must continue to meet payments required for De Selle's current état de distribution.[91] Reporting the results of his meeting with the financiers and bankers to Berryer on the 20th, Boullongne's news was the blackest. The following day the Royal Council rushed through four draconian measures. The first arrêt, backdated to the day of De Selle's death, suspended payment on all colonial bills of exchange for the duration of the war, and the second, third, and fourth suspended the rescriptions of the receivers-general of finances, notes of the General Tax Farm, and all capital payments by the royal treasurers and the caisse d'amortissements.[92] It was, recorded Barbier, "a kind of bankruptcy," a comment echoed by the duc de Choiseul.[93] The suspension totally discredited colonial paper, and seriously impaired government obligations in any form.[94]

Suspension of receivers-generals' rescriptions struck Beaujon, Goossens and Company a deadly blow for their entire arrangement to supply funds was based on their holding the equivalent amount in receivers' paper that had been delivered but on which they could no longer draw. Laborde supplied them with 3 millions in Silhouette's shares on the united farms, which the syndicate used to obtain fifteen-day pledges on the bourse.[95] Berryer and Boullongne scrambled to keep the company afloat but by mid-November Beaujon, Goossens and Company ceased its service to the navy and closed its doors. Etienne de Silhouette retired amid universal opprobrium, the capital value of his shares having fallen 35 per cent.[96] Knowledgeable men of business estimated that about 200 million livres in government obligations were affected; money practically ceased to circulate.[97] The government moved again to confine the crash, this time protecting Beaujon, Goossens and Company; on 30 November the Royal Council suspended payment of the company's obligations to its own creditors, retroactive to the 14th, the day the company failed.[98] Designed to enable the syndicate to acknowledge its obligations to the crown (i.e., its outstanding paper with reconnaissances or I.O.U.s), the action extended the damage; companies abroad began to fall.[99]

The crash profoundly affected naval activities ashore and afloat. Provincial agents of the syndicate as well as the cashier of the naval victualler at Rochefort closed their doors.[100] On the same day that Admiral Conflans met defeat in the waters of Quiberon Bay, the commis of the receiver-general of finances at La Rochelle protested 300,000 livres worth of bills of exchange; in all nearly 800,000 livres in bills of exchange and notes drawn on the port treasurer, naval treasurers-general and Beaujon, Goossens and Company were lost in Rochefort's November crash.[101] At Le Havre an even greater sum appeared at risk. Treasurer-general De Selle had arranged to meet the year's expenses with 120 notes, each with a face value of 10,000 livres, five maturing each week from April onwards. With the entire amount matured and in circulation, and no payments made since De Selle's death, Berryer demanded funds for De Selle's cousin to meet any obligations, in order "not to discredit entirely the Treasurer's signature."[102] Indeed, in the light of the financial catastrophe, the navy's defeat at sea was an anticlimax. The latter certainly did not bring about the collapse of French credit nor even the cessation of seaborne operations.[103] It was financial collapse, not defeat at sea, that reduced naval operations for the next year and a half.

Naval operations continued only because actions of the Royal Council enabled Beaujon, Goossens and Company to acknowledge its debts and the bills of the treasurers-general of the Navy to be backed by bullion. Louis xv sent the royal plate to the mint at the beginning of November. Courtiers followed suit. The India Company's plate made a similar journey from Lorient soon afterwards.[104] The Royal Council named César-Luc-Marie De Selle de la Garejade to complete his late cousin's fiscal year, and the new treasurer-general obtained one million livres worth of *assignations* on the mints of Paris, Rennes, and Nantes to support his cousin's notes. Treasurer-general De Georville drew 16,000 *marcs* of plate from Paris for transportation to the two provincial mints in order to back his payments to Bompar's squadron returning from the West Indies.[105] Funds were also assigned on the chest of the director of the mint at La Rochelle to pay off and lay up the ships from Conflans' fleet that sought refuge at Rochefort. While awaiting delivery, Ruis-Embito inventoried the arsenal's plate, including all of the silver from the chapels on board warships in the port, anticipating that it would make the same journey as the king's plate a month before.[106] Ships at Brest and in the Vilaine river were paid off similarly and laid up only after the directors of the mints at Rennes and Nantes received 600,000 livres in gold and 500,000 livres in silver respectively.[107] Through the use of its enormous legal powers to block pursuit of its financial agents by creditors, and massive use of bullion to back payments to wind up existing naval operations, the government gradually returned to its normal financial state. But without new credit the navy remained a useless weapon, a wooden sword in the hands of anyone attempting to wield it.

Early in December the Royal Council read and approved the coming year's plan of naval operations. Department officials requested 40 million livres for both navy and colonies. [108]Berryer reported to the Royal Council on actions taken to reduce naval expenditures: half the *troupes de la marine* placed on half pay, naval establishments at Port Mahon and Marseilles and in the French interior suppressed; hospital care and administration reduced; many officers of the pen placed on half pay, all *haute paye* and pensions suspended; and no new increase allowed the corps of the sword. Supply shipments were suspended, storehouses left empty and three-quarters of the navy's arsenal workers let go. Daily wages at Brest, previously amounting to between 250 and 300 thousand livres a month, were reduced to 50 or 60 thousand livres. "In a word," he concluded, "we have cut into the quick as much as possible, maybe even more than necessary, and more quickly than circumstances allowed."[109] But he failed to move his fellow ministers. Three months later the new controller-general, Henry-Léonard-Jean-Baptiste Bertin, authorized only 30 million livres including 9 millions for the colonies.

No funds appeared for further sea operations. At the beginning of March, faced with grim news from the West Indies, Berryer appealed to his fellow ministers, the marquis de Puysieulx, duc de Belle-Isle, and duc d'Estrées, to find 12 million livres to mount a relief expedition to Martinique.[110] But in vain; fellow ministers would not release money from their own funds which, in the army's case, had been even more drastically slashed.[111] The controller-general held to the authorized 30 million livres: additional funds could not be found. The relief expedition was postponed for fourteen months and when it finally sailed from Brest in January 1762 it was too late to relieve the island which fell into English hands before its arrival. The delay has been commonly condemned as an unparalleled example of French incompetence, weakness, and moral bankruptcy, but just as commonly, the judgment is made with little or no awareness of the financial system or the recent bankruptcy of the government.[112] Indeed, between March 1760 and October 1761, when preparations for the expedition were renewed, the navy did little but mark time. Economy became its watchword while the minister sought out malfeasance and maladministration.

Berryer's often criticized efforts had one valuable effect, for by the fall of 1760 the surviving treasurer-general of the navy and Beaujon, Goossens and Company had struggled back on their feet. While failing to persuade his fellow ministers to release their funds for naval operations, he had induced the controller-general of finance to aid the navy's bankers. By May no vestige of the two large borrowings of 1750 and 1754 by the treasurers-general remained, and by July they had been reimbursed even for all the loan interest and costs of discounts on rescriptions.[113] Beaujon, Goossens and Company had been so successful in acknowledging its debts that by October Berryer offered to restore the company's old function. As the controller-general could only obtain the assigned sums on anticipated *assignations* on the General Farm, Berryer invited Beaujon and Goossens to supply a monthly fund of one million livres for the navy and 250,000 livres for the colonies.[114] By the beginning of the new year the syndicate actually arranged to provide the full amount of the new authorized ordinary fund, 1.5 millions monthly.[115] But while Berryer and the controller-general's agent, Boullongne, shored up naval finances through rigorous retrenchment and payment of old debts, chiefly unpaid wages to facilitate dismissals in the arsenals, they could not obtain extraordinary funds for sea operations. Berryer proposed to employ authorized funds for 1761 only to protect the French coast and prevent the entire destruction of the fleet.

Berryer continued his economies, suppressing the post of *ordonnateur* at Bayonne, reuniting the departments of Bordeaux and Nantes to Rochefort and Brest, ordering sales of munitions and equipment in the arsenals, laying off more personnel, and demanding even greater reductions of the monthly wage bills in the arsenals.[116] Lack of funds made it impossible, he informed Choiseul, to arm *prames* and gunboats for the defence of Dunkirk and Maritime Flanders; nor could the navy fit out craft to transport cannon needed for Norman coastal batteries to Le Havre.[117] Only after Choiseul recommended that the War Department meet the expense could Berryer order a levy of seamen and the fitting out of coastal defence vessels.[118] Choiseul rather than Berryer also ordered the squadrons fitted out at Brest and Rochefort for the attempted riposte to the British invasion of the Island of Belle Isle in the spring of 1761. The naval minister appeared merely as a conduit for Choiseul's instructions. But instructions have a limited effect without funds. Four million livres were ordered for the fitting out, but none was assigned before the end of May, and the ships failed to get to sea before the island fell to the enemy.[119] Replying to another of Choiseul's requests, Berryer claimed that naval funds were so exhausted that not even two frigates could be fitted out to escort four battalions to Minorca.[120] Such a state of affairs could not continue unresolved, and perhaps these events forced Choiseul to think more seriously about the navy.

On 1 June the king revived plans for the Martinique expedition, authorizing a new extraordinary fund of 15 million livres. Ships fitted out for the attempted riposte in May remained ready for sea and new ships were fitted out later in the summer and fall.[121] These were the first important actions to affect the department in more than eighteen months, during which time Canada was surrendered and Lally-Tollendal defeated in India. The first half of 1761 was devoted to the financial rescue of the army.[122] The summer was taken up with intense diplomatic activity that culminated in the Franco-Spanish *pacte de famille* signed on 15 August. Thereafter came the turn of the navy.

Earlier Choiseul had sublimated the traditional antagonism between merchant bankers and financiers that often made cooperation impossible. The key to finding a solution lay in Jean-Joseph de Laborde, whom Etienne de Silhouette had previously forced to become a farmer-general and member of the General Farm's *grand comité* and *comité des caisses*. Laborde was proud of his mercantile background, hostile to the financial interest in the farm, and vigorously promoted and defended the trading interest. But as Choiseul's most devoted "creature," he became the minister's intermediary between the monied interests and the General Farm, informing the latter of the court's desire and doing little to defend the interests of those who leased the king's revenues.[123] In addition, Choiseul sought to reconcile Pâris de Montmartel and Laborde and shore up the pro-Austrian party which he continued to lead at court.[124] Choiseul's efforts to reconcile the two families continued years later when Laborde's son succeeded Montmartel's grand-nephew as keeper of the Royal Treasury.[125] From 1759 onwards Choiseul successfully exploited Laborde's powerful mercantile connections and positions as court banker and farmer-general to reestablish the government's credit.

Such activities cemented financial and diplomatic connections in the government's support, but required time to affect the navy's creditors. Moreover, the Royal Commission to validate and liquidate naval debts had not produced the desired political and financial benefits, and the suspension of payment of all colonial bills of exchange had had a negative effect. Both undermined credit and blocked its restoration. The Fontanieu Commission's judgments, week after week for nearly three years, revealed an unwillingness to admit that wartime inflation, high demand, and scarce materials had led to legitimate cost increases for naval entrepreneurs and merchants. Established to investigate allegations of fraud and profiteering, the commission was feared by naval creditors. Commissioners had leave to pay 5 per cent interest on unpaid accounts, but granting it as a grace rather than a right alienated many creditors.[126] Shipowners and outfitters at La Rochelle objected strongly to the commission's decision to allow wartime freight charges only at peacetime rates and protested the lack of procedures to appeal commission rulings. The commissioners, on the other hand, claimed that such protests demonstrated the justice of their actions and proved the existence of *armateurs'* illegitimate profits.[127]

On 24 September 1761 the Fontanieu Commission adjourned to begin its annual break from its labours, but on its return after Saint Martin's Day (11 November) it found a new minister and a new task designed specifically to produce political benefits. The king halted investigation of naval debts and on 28 November Choiseul ordered the commissioners to begin to investigate colonial debts.[128] Berryer had earlier set forth a plan for a court of investigation and criminal procedure, but he had a judicial rather than a political end in view. Choiseul had no doubt of the need to alter

Berryer's policies and capitalized on growing public support for the king's beleaguered navy and increasing opprobrium of naval administration.[129] On 12 December he moved to have a special judicial commission of the Paris Châtelet established to investigate those persons most prominently connected with the loss of Canada and the expenditure of its funds.[130] The records of the Fontanieu Commission were placed at the disposal of the commission of the Châtelet, which began an investigation, chiefly for public consumption, that would continue for the next two years. Two days later Choiseul had the Royal Council agree to add all the interest on unpaid colonial bills to the end of 1761 to the capital amounts of the bills and to assign 5 per cent interest to the total sums.[131] Choiseul's new moves were politically astute, focusing mounting anger on Canada, already lost and a long way from Versailles, and simultaneously restoring life to colonial bills of exchange that had been "dead in the hands of their holders" for more than two years. Suddenly restoring value to millions of livres worth of paper gave temporary hope to a large number of people who could not know, though they might suspect, that the government would repudiate much of its colonial debt. The Châtelet's commission shifted public attention away from naval ignominy and charges of excessive expenditures at home to financial malversation, fraud, and corruption practised by a small group of not very influential administrators and their cronies from across the sea. Together with restoration of colonial bills of exchange it took the heat off the administration.

A third development, also Choiseul's doing, ensured the success of the first two. Shortly after becoming secretary of state for the navy, Choiseul proposed to the president of the Estates of Languedoc, Cardinal de La Roche-Aymon, archbishop of Narbonne, that the Estates offer a warship to the king. The Estates were meeting and on 26 November unanimously offered their gift to Louis xv. Other provincial estates, municipal and corporate bodies, including the church which alone pledged one million livres, quickly picked up the example.[132] Early in December Montmartel, Laborde, and several others offered an 80-gun ship to the king, the receivers-general of finances presented a similar ship, and the farmers-general even threw in a frigate with their major gift. Paris wits said that the city's archbishop was going to donate a fireship because of his stubbornness against the Jansenists. In mid-December the corps of merchants and aldermen of Paris donated a 74-gun ship and the city's *receveur* made arrangements to accept individual donations, such as one from the *trésorier des parties casuelles* who sent 12,000 livres. That some gifts were inspired by patriotism or a sense of outrage is beyond question, but others, especially from financiers, were perhaps a reaction to news that the Châtelet commission had been established. Other donations were exacted. According to Barbier, Controller-general Bertin summoned the syndics of the *payeurs des rentes* of the Paris Hôtel de Ville and taxed each one 1,000 livres or 2.5 per cent of the capital value of their office for a ship.[133]

Merchants, of course, were not easily taken in by political manipulation. The following May the new intendant of Toulon cautioned the minister that "the provinces and especially provençals" would regain confidence in the navy only after all old debts were paid. Moreover, Choiseul's success sometimes worked against him; merchants feared that the enthusiasm generated in the government and its citizens would disappear when the ministries of war and navy ceased to be united under his direction.[134] But Choiseul's initiatives were more than an exercise in public relations. In a lesser known move, Choiseul also looked to the king's sailors; another *arrêt du conseil*, dated 19 December, permitted the treasurer-general of the *Invalides de la Marine*, backed by the enormous wealth in his chest, to borrow 3 million livres in order to meet hospital expenses and *la demi-solde*, which had not been paid for three years, and to provide for wounded veterans and the heirs of seamen killed in the service.[135] Moreover, the warships donated to the king were not built in some cases for years, but the funds, soon totalling 14 million livres, were pledged within a few weeks. As early as December Choiseul dispatched 4 million livres to Brest, with strict instructions to acquit unpaid expenses on the 1760 and current *exercices*.[136] The following April, the king authorized just over 6 million livres to be spent at Brest; in May Toulon's expenses were revised from 1.8 to 5 millions.[137] The new funds were free and clear of usual encumbrances and they provided the resources for the brief flurry of activity during the next nine months, fitting out the expeditions to Newfoundland and St Domingue, the Rochefort and Toulon squadrons, and the transports for the planned attack on Rio de Janeiro.[138] The funds were insufficient to restore the navy, but enough to bring suppliers back, and allowed Choiseul some time before more bad news forced him to the peace table.

Capitalizing on public revulsion against France's maritime defeats, Choiseul had painted the navy as a victim, which was in part true, pointed to the victimizers, which was also partly true, restored once-dead credit notes, and sought and obtained a massive subsidy from the public. Financial reform was out of the question. The financial interests were approaching the apogee of their power. Reform was neither intended nor attempted. But the navy's success during the next two decades was a reflection of Choiseul's restoration of the government's credit among its naval suppliers. That achievement cannot, however, be counted among his reforms.

CHAPTER TWELVE

Conclusion

Although much has been written about the organization and administration of Louis xv's navy, historians continue to deal in generalities. The naval disasters of 1759 remain commonly identified with poor organization, disorderly administration, ministerial negligence, corrupt officials, unpreparedness for combat, and deplorable conduct of operations. Few go beyond anecdote to explore these issues. The normative approach continues to abstract the navy from its environment and fails to explore the links between naval organization and its activities and the social, political, economic, and financial realities of the day. Although revisions have been in progress for more than thirty years, many continue to view the navy as a clinical instrument in the hands of a political will rationally selecting from objective goals and options. Naval organizational processes receive monolithic treatment and administrative procedures continue to be rationally perceived, leading to misunderstanding.

Money and credit remained the foundation of naval power throughout the eighteenth century. Although this was vigorously denied by A.M. Wilson many years ago, the inadequacy of the funds assigned to French peacetime naval expenditures prior to 1739 seriously threatened the survival of the Colbertian heritage, the permanent organization of the navy.[1] Failure to provide for the sea service in the navy's ordinary funds was not a vestige of an earlier arrangement, and Cardinal Fleury's failure to remove the impediment frustrated the development of French naval power. Reduction in numbers of administrators and officers of the sword followed. Insufficient ship construction kept the fleet below authorized strength. Inadequate accumulation of stores left arsenals unable to fulfil later wartime functions, notably the refitting, repairing, and replenishing of sea-worn ships. Peacetime conditions disguised defects in the system of naval conscription. The War of the Austrian Succession quickly revealed the fundamental relationship between money and credit and naval power.

Money made all the difference between previous anaemia and rebirth during the years following 1748. The sudden influx of funds allowed reform and renewal of the navy's permanent organization as well as rebuilding of the devastated fleet. The allocated sums may well have guaranteed the navy's survival as an instrument of power, but remained inadequate within the existing organization of naval finances that failed to extinguish past and current debt, threatened continuation of credit, and limited naval preparedness for a war that all expected to come. At the outbreak of hostilities at sea in the spring of 1755 the navy possessed a fine fleet of new battleships and frigates but no staying power. Training of officers and men had been sacrificed to reconstruct the fleet. Stores still needed to be assembled to allow arsenals to shift to their wartime tasks. Encumbered by debt, long a permanent condition of naval finances, naval organization became unduly sensitive to changing domestic and international circumstances.

The organizational processes of naval finances were secondary but no less significant. Responsible only for supplying estimates, with no liability for payment of approved naval expenditure, naval administrators, from secretary of state to the most junior *commissaire-ordonnateur*, remained powerless to influence the outcome. Formal links between naval organization and its financial environment were too tenuous to guarantee improved activities. Yet, paradoxically, money and credit ended by becoming an end in themselves. Rather than being the foundation of naval power, money became the foundation of naval administration.

Naval defeats of minor importance threatened consequences of great significance; naval victories, moreover, would likely have had little beneficial effect. Relying upon an ever-growing mountain of credit, naval strength became dependent more than ever before on private financiers and court bankers caught up in the meshes of factional struggles during an unusually sensitive period of domestic politics. Sources of funds ebbed and flowed according to public confidence, which fell prey to far more than naval operations. Louis xv's navy strove to find its destiny within a vicious circle circumscribed by limited availability of funds, fluctuating credit, and volatile public opinion continually shaken by a decade of domestic political crisis.

The connection between financial power and naval power is conspicuous everywhere one looks. Corruption, too often singled out in order to account for French naval disasters, does little to explain shortages of funds or administrative inefficiency; it may better be seen as normal wartime cost overruns brought on by increased demand, scarcity, and price inflation. This is not to claim that naval officers of both corps were not corrupt; they probably were, but no more than other groups of eighteenth-century government officials, and probably a good deal less than some others.

While able to use their positions to advance their own interests, naval officials did not handle naval funds or pocket funds intended for naval expenses. High prices charged to the navy department for goods and services were the costs demanded for the forced loans exacted from suppliers and officers who remained unpaid for years.

Disorderly administration is another convenient scapegoat with little explanatory power, especially when the argument is confined to anecdotal accounts of inter-corps rivalry between officers of the sword and of the pen. Such disputes only infrequently affected naval administration in any significant manner. Moreover, the notion of disorderly administration is ambiguous; it is built on the equation of order with rationality. While options may be rationally arrived at, choice seldom is. Far more serious weaknesses in naval administration originated in the organizational processes of the monarchy that led to clashes between naval agents and members of other government organizations, few formal instruments existing for their resolution. Here, however, the smallness of the government and personal relations between officials counted for more than regulations and powers. Increasing recruitment of naval intendants from members of the magistracy was positively beneficial under such conditions, breaking down the isolation of naval and other government administrators, integrating naval organization more closely into the larger absolutist system of government. Weaknesses leading to the deplorable conduct of operations and unpreparedness for combat so characteristic of the navy during the Seven Years' War also had less to do with current organizational processes and administrative procedures than the absence of professionalism and group identity among officers of the sword and lack of training at sea, characteristics more distinctly attributable to cultural and social differences and a lack of money than to other causes.

But if lack of money lay at the heart of French naval weakness, men and matériel remained no less fundamental components of naval power. The inadequate manning of the fleet that was the most obvious navy weakness throughout the Seven Years' War, giving rise to insoluble problems, occurred not because France lacked a sufficiently large seafaring population or because privateering continued to be attractive, but because of failure to pay French sailors in the naval service. The chief immediate causes of a lack of seamen were capture and desertion; both can be attributed to lack of money. Capture too often followed after undermanned warships with inexperienced, untrained sailors put to sea with inept officers in command to confront an enemy honed to a fine edge of effectiveness by long periods spent at sea under a wide variety of conditions. Sailors were not brutes conditioned to perform relatively simple tasks. The giant wind-powered warships of the period had achieved their penultimate form as the most sophisticated machines ever invented by preindustrial western man. Possessed of staggering complexity and capable of a wide variety of manoeuvres, eighteenth-century warships could be efficiently operated only by well-disciplined teams of highly skilled sailors under command of professional officers. The want of seamanship common to many French naval crews had no other origin than the diversion of money from training cruises during the years of peace to debt reduction, ship construction, and stores acquisition, and the king's failure to pay his sailors. The same can be said of desertion. Sailors' privileges had always been ignored in part because in the past the king's sailors had been better paid. The reconfirmation of sailors' privileges during the Seven Years' War was a hopelessly inadequate substitute for failure to pay their wages; not all the privileges in the world or renewed protection afforded sailors' families could stop desertion and flight from the realm. The sole remedy was regular payments. Whether by cash or scrip was immaterial, as long as the latter could be negotiated. When the scrip became worthless, however, credit had gone. To continue in this vein concerning other naval personnel, matériel, and topics dealt with in detail in earlier chapters would only belabour the point. More important considerations lie in the nature of French naval organization and administrative procedures, for these, at least in theory, were subject to modification from within the organization itself. Or were they?

Considering the government as a system rather than a will, where information was processed rather than acted upon, clearly reveals the nonrational forces behind government decisions. The fundamental weakness of senior appreciation and advisory channels in naval organization increased opportunities for political negotiation and administrative politics. The indirect nature and general weakness of senior control of Bourbon naval organization ought to remove any vestige of Mahanite notions of the principles of sea power discoverable by a rational intelligence. The eighteenth-century French navy, like today's navies, was not a disembodied will but an organization made up of men. Unlike today's navies, however, the Bourbon naval organization possessed few mechanisms or instruments for exercising control over its processes and activities.

Organization of strategic direction of the naval war was defective. No precise chain of command had developed through which royal authority flowed downward to senior officers, bureaux, and arsenals. Instructions to commanders were prepared in the Royal Council or by the king and naval secretary of state, but no senior body of experienced sailors appreciated or advised on their feasibility. Bureaux continued to remain appendages of their *premiers commis*, whose influence waxed or waned according to the identity of the secretary of state. Maurepas' dismissal and the appearance of outsiders, Bernard Pallu and Sébastien Lenormant de Mézy, broke any developing chain of command in the 1750s. The marquis de la Galissonière's presence as Rouillé's confidential adviser permitted what a later age would call staff appreciation and professional advice to be made available to the minister, but this was a personal arrangement involving the most junior flag officer in the navy. Moreover, lack of unity among naval officers militated against the officer corps itself ever influencing the planning of naval operations. Outsider penetration continued to manifest itself throughout the 1750s until by the end of the decade even the treasurers-general of the navy had been partially supplanted by Beaujon, Goossens and Company, contractors become naval bankers. Without a chain of command, subordinate naval personnel and intendants in the arsenals were not forced to concentrate on their own duties. The weak linkages between the centre and the periphery of naval organization guaranteed the survival of local initiatives, but also inhibited policy coordination.

Although often viewed as the greatest weakness in naval organization, the failure to bring forward naval officers with sea experience to positions of administrative responsibility requires qualification. Naval officers did not exhibit any general desire to become administrators. Maurepas' appointment of permanent commandants in each arsenal attempted to fill the lack of permanent shore-based appointments for senior officers but the two-headed direction of naval organization was too fundamentally embedded in Colbert's legacy to reform. Port commandants corresponded regularly with the naval secretaries of state but daily events in their commands rather than strategic and tactical matters remained their chief concern. Moreover, senior admirals had no experience with large squadrons. None was held in universal respect throughout the service. The marquis de la Galissonière's death removed one hope that such a development might occur. La Galissonière was not a great fighting admiral, but he was an intelligent sailor with a demonstrated concern for a French imperial strategy and an obvious competence to carry out tasks entrusted to him. As things stood, naval strategy, if anything worthy of such a name existed, achieved shape and form in royal and ministerial instructions issued to naval commanders, but their substance derived from a king with little or no interest in the sea and ministers who, with the exception of the duc de Choiseul, were not statesmen. Neither king nor secretaries of state knew very much about navies. Without a concern for naval strategy or the appreciation of practical sailors, French naval organization became caught up in questions of matériel and finances. Financial constraints reinforced this development. The crucial role of sailors was ignored unless the sailors were courtiers; naval organization contained no provisions to bring any forward. While lack of formal linkages between sailors and royal advisers did not preclude informal bonds, it was also true that no safeguards existed against conflicting opinions coming forward to the king and council from naval officers and even from soldiers. Thus the seizure of Minorca originated with Marshal de Richelieu and the proposed invasion of England with Marshal de Belle Isle.

The absence of collective responsibility also weakened senior naval efficiency. French absolutism's consitutional structure denied collective responsibility. *Premiers commis* and naval intendants remained specialists in particular areas of naval administration or of a single arsenal, individually responsible for their conduct. Moreover, naval organization destined them to remain so. Just as it failed to advance sailors to senior administrative positions, so too naval organization left a gap in communications and understanding by failing to provide for the transfer of experienced arsenal administrators to the central bureaux. Even consultation remained idiosyncratic. The absence of collective responsibility left naval organization with no person or body, except the secretaries of state themselves, to maintain pressure on naval administrators to get things done quickly and efficiently. When secretaries of state changed rapidly and remained entangled in court politics, as between the years 1748 and 1762, this deficiency assumed increased significance.

The question of whether French naval organization was over- or undercentralized relates to the degree of control or management from the centre. The organization itself was not highly centralized. Each arsenal remained an entity unto itself directed by an intendant who desired a self-sufficient instrument under his command and who remained individually responsible to the king for his administration. But lack of centralization may have been beneficial in view of the growing exhaustion of naval suppliers and the increasing paucity of credit available to the naval department. Ordnance, timber, naval stores, victuals, and manpower procurement were organizational processes that functioned under varying degrees of central control. Victuals procurement was the most centralized, for as far as the navy was concerned the entire process remained in the hands of a private syndicate. This arrangement appeared entirely satisfactory. But ordnance procurement, the next most centralized organizational process, met with serious setbacks. Control of all naval ordnance produced in Angoumois and Périgord was exercised through Rochefort, first through the intendant and later through a specially appointed inspector, Jean Maritz. But effective planning, efficient production, and close management appeared defective due to the naval department's lack of control over its funds, but also its inability to resist outside influence from the court and flaws in its own organization, namely the two-fold involvement in inspection and control by members of two corps of antipathetic naval officers. Whether more or less centralization would have contributed to more effective, efficient gun production remains moot. When left in the hands of intendants, a wide variety of stores appeared as required. Without exception intendants displayed creative imagination, innovation, and seriousness of purpose in overcoming scarcities induced by contracting credit, exhausted suppliers, and enemy blockade. Arsenal intendants were much better placed than *premiers commis* to observe and react quickly to changing circumstances in diverse, widely separated areas of France. The absence of a central purchasing office in the organization of the central administration acknowledged this fact.

Conversely, sending domestic irons and timbers to various entrepôts at La Charité-sur-Loire, Rouen, or Ile d'Indret, thereby inserting additional links between arsenals and naval contractors in the organizational processes, obstructed effective control over assortment. But the procurement of foreign naval stores benefited from greater centralization, since there was the likelihood of problems that could be overcome only by expertise that was commercial and diplomatic rather than naval. Additional centralization, however, could not resolve other difficulties. The fundamental weakness of French naval influence in Italy and Baltic markets lay in the failure to coordinate French foreign policy and naval policy. French commercial weakness and naval requirements encouraged adoption of monopolistic contracting, but administrative linkages in naval organization marginalized benefits. Contracting procedures that allowed suppliers to deliver unwanted, overdue stores without penalty weakened control and did not improve accounting when conducted from the central bureaux. Intra-administrative cooperation and weak management were causes as well as symptoms of the growth of naval intendants' authority. Attempts to increase centralization were misdirected.

In the light of the foregoing considerations, did naval organization change significantly, enabling the department to respond more effectively to current challenges of empire and public interest than before? Or was the navy incapable of undergoing reform before reaching its nadir due to the dead weight of the Colbertian legacy? Traditional answers indicate the latter, agreeing with the duc de Choiseul's self-congratulatory encomiums on his successful naval reforms of the 1760s. Any reader might infer that little or no change had occurred in naval organization during the previous seventy or eighty years.[2] Choiseul's favourable press is based to a great degree upon two naval memoranda drawn up in 1763 and 1765.[3] According to a recent essay, "the French navy received a far greater share of attention and available resources [than before] in the early years of the peace," but the evidence does not bear the weight of the claim.[4] At no time between 1764 and 1769 did the navy obtain significantly greater funds than during the period from 1750 to 1754; on average the funds granted during the earlier period exceeded those of the later one by nearly one million livres annually.[5]

To agree with Choiseul's own view of his ability is relatively easy because he acknowledged frankly that his colonial reforms had failed.[6]

Moreover, his great naval ordinance of 25 March 1765 represented the first systematic rethinking of naval organization since Seignelay consolidated his father's work in 1689. But in the light of the present study Choiseul cannot be seen as a great naval reformer for two fundamental reasons. In the first place, significant changes had been occurring in naval organizational processes at least since 1748, and several were more important than anything introduced by Choiseul after 1762.

The most important of Choiseul's reforms, concerning the reorganization of the two naval officer corps, amounted to little more than recognition of current reality and continued recent developments, submerging but not abolishing distinctions among officers of the sword, increasing their emoluments to encourage better performance and reducing numbers; all had been initiated by Berryer. Moreover, in organizing the military hierarchy along geographical lines, Choiseul only acknowledged his inability to reform significantly the officer corps. Suppression of the galley corps and unification of officers of the sword in one corps under Maurepas were more significant accomplishments than Choiseul's, while the most important development, the breaking of the generational connection with Louis XIV's navy, was due to time and the Seven Years' War itself. Other more significant developments, evolving a personnel bureau, altering the recruitment of intendants, rationalizing ordnance production and acquisition of northern stores, opening new areas in the Pyrenees and Albania for mast and timber exploitation, had all first occurred under his predecessors. Few developments in the 1760s showed such a marked improvement over previous conditions as did those of the peacetime years during the previous decade. Arsenals were in worse shape in 1749 than 1762, despite the dismal descriptions of desolation in the latter year. Deterioration was recent, largely financial in nature, and the infrastructure built up during the early 1750s remained in place, as evidenced by the very rapid renewal begun in 1762 before hostilities ended. Choiseul's predecessors were as vigorous or more so even in shipbuilding. With less matériel on hand at the start, thirty-eight ships of the line were built under Rouillé and Machault in a shorter period than Choiseul required to increase the fleet by twenty-four ships.[7] Indeed, some sixty-nine warships and forty-two frigates were built during the entire fourteen-year period studied here.

Second, and more importantly, Choiseul failed to deal with naval finances. The great changes effected during 1749 and 1750, namely, the provision of extraordinary funds in peacetime, the increase in ordinary funds, and the separation of colonial and naval funds, continued unaltered until Choiseul's dismissal in 1771. Clearly a clever politician and an astute statesman, Choiseul successfully capitalized on public humiliation and outrage to generate sympathy and financial support for the navy in 1761–2, and, incidentally, to deflect criticism of the government. He also successfully linked naval policy to French foreign policy in a manner not seen before, enabling a naval strategy to emerge.[8] But political expediency is no substitute for reform. Without financial reform, which some historians believe to have been impossible, the foundations of French naval power remained subject to all the recently revealed weaknesses, ready to take effect when the appropriate conditions arose. Changes in naval organization became matters of technique, inadequate in themselves to permit the navy to meet effectively the challenge of empire. Nevertheless, significant events in the internal development of naval organization marked the years between 1748 and 1762. Changes and attempted changes occurred in processes that would affect naval developments during the next quarter-century. Indeed, the period was a valuable, perhaps necessary, precursor to the subsequent period of naval domination of French foreign policy. But government inability and unwillingness to confront directly the question of naval finances severely limited long-term aspirations concerning naval power and effectively denied France fulfilment of the dream that she might one day be mistress of the seas.

Appendix

Several documents purport to be records of French naval funds and expenditures during the middle of the eighteenth century. Legohérel's discussion, by far the most complete, advises caution; it is wise to be sceptical of all such data.[1] They are presented here to allow others the opportunity to confirm or deny their veracity and clarify their significance; to provide an order of magnitude and a notion of trends in naval financing and expenditure; and to add to Legohérel's discussion. Several caveats need to be made. It is not clear what most of the data represent, given the vague notions of naval revenues and expenses and the nonexistence of a naval budget. Did the amounts authorized annually by the king, controller-general, and secretary of state for the navy, or those assigned by the keeper of the Royal Treasury to the treasurers-general of the navy constitute naval funds? Did the pay orders of naval administrators or the funds paid out by naval treasurers and treasurers-general constitute naval expenses? Considering that naval expenses were generally acquitted with privately borrowed funds, do the figures on any of these lists constitute a record of reality at all? Archival sources are also insufficiently precise to furnish answers to questions concerning annual global amounts. Keeping track of global figures is a challenge to modern governments despite their greatly expanded powers of supervision and control of state finances. It was beyond the capacity of Old Regime administrators.

The first document, "Tableau général des dépenses effectives de la marine, des Galères et des Colonies, ... depuis l'année 1678 jusques et compris l'année 1810," from a collection of documents "pour servir à l'histoire financière de la Marine jusqu'en 1811," was published and discussed by Henri Legohérel.[2] The document provides a continuous run of annual naval expenses from 1690 to 1782 alongside a record of the date of

TABLE 9

Naval Expenses, 1748–1762

	Sources		
Year	BN, n.a.f., no. 5399 (Doc. no. 1)	Marine, E, 208, No. 110; and AN, G⁷, 1830 (2) (Docs. 2 & 3)	A. Duchêne, Histoire des finances coloniales, 43–5 (Doc. no. 4)
1748	18,414,669 l.t.	32,107,957 l.t.	
1749	15,562,455 l.t.	25,695,969 l.t.	
1750	18,217,772	25,240,841	
1751	16,510,653	24,672,280	
1752	16,278,498	27,644,634	the same
1753	14,603,542	23,527,565	
1754	15,424,262	21,785,968	
1755	24,897,472	34,494,972	
1756	42,959,888	49,293,901	
1757	49,712,985	60,269,589	
1758	40,949,164	55,306,482	
1759	51,800,243	77,000,000	66,645,015 l.t.
1760	17,289,289	33,770,579	42,957,115
1761	16,722,415	–	–
1762	30,529,650	–	–
Total	389,872,957	490,810,737	489,642,288
Avg.			
1749–54	16,099,530	24,761,208	24,761,208
1755–60	37,934,840	51,689,253	51,494,511

judgments in the *Chambre des Comptes* of each fiscal year's "true" account (*état au vrai*). The data for years from 1748 to 1762 are produced in table 9 (col. 1). Nothing indicates the document's origin but Legohérel suggests that it originated within the Chamber, which became the *Cour des Comptes* in 1811.[3] Several problems arise in attempting to use the document. First, it did not originate in the navy department. Second, it is not clear what the figures represent. According to Legohérel, they may represent expenses forecast at the beginning of the fiscal year, those recorded at the end of the fiscal year, or the expenses established years later during judgment before the *Chambre des Comptes*.[4] In eleven of fifteen years between 1748 and 1762, however, the figures are lower than the total amounts authorized annually for naval expenditure (cf. table 10). Claiming to be from a General Table of "dépenses effectives," they may be the actual results of payments and receipts of the Royal Treasury as shown by the records of the keepers of the Royal Treasury after the fiscal year had ended, and not the records of the navy's treasurers-general at all. Legohérel notes the general correspondence between the figures given in the first document and those showing the funds granted to the navy department.[5] The latter, however, do not appear to be the funds actually assigned to naval expenditures by the keeper of the Royal Treasury. The following figures found among miscellaneous documents in the archives of the controller-general's department give amounts assigned by the keeper of the Royal Treasury to the treasurers-general of the navy: in 1756, 34 million livres; in the first eleven months of 1758, 38,571,085 livres; in 1759, 49,763,321 livres; in 1760, 21,295,843 livres; and in 1762, 21,507,733 livres.[6] Unfortunately, these sums include between three and ten million livres annually assigned on the previous fiscal year. While accurately revealing the funds assigned during a calendar-year, they do not relate directly to the fiscal expenses of the same year.

The second source, heretofore unpublished, "Dépenses de la marine et des Colonies depuis 1740 jusques et compris 1760," is an incomplete document for our purposes.[7] Located in the naval archives with no indication concerning its origin, it contains the same figures as are found in a third document, already published by Legohérel.[8] This third document from the archives of the *Contrôle-général des finances* is entitled "Comparaison des dépenses de la Marine sur les registres du Tresor Royal et sur les registres de la Marine," dated by Legohérel as 1782. The second document was unknown to him, but on the basis of additional information may be preferred over the third, for it is probably the source of the latter, can be dated some twenty years earlier, and came from naval archives. The data for the years between 1748 and 1762 are given in column 2, table 9. A fourth document appears to be the source of both previous ones. Thus, while the third source is found in the archives of the *Contrôle-général*, it did not originate in that department.

Nearly half a century ago Albert Duchêne located another document containing nearly identical data and published some of the figures. Unfortunately, he did not provide a complete run of data and his reference to sources is useless.[9] But the data given for 1749, 1754, and 1755 are the same as in the second document. Moreover, the annual expenses for 1744, given separately for the navy and colonies, equal the figure in the second document. The fourth document's figures are for the years between 1737 and 1760 but differ for 1759 and 1760; Duchêne gives 66,645,015 l.t. and

TABLE 10
Funds Granted to the Navy, 1748–1762

Year	Ordinary	Extraordinary	Total
1748	9,500,000 l.t.	15,300,000 l.t.	24,800,000 l.t.
1749	20,000,000	nil	20,000,000
1750	15,000,000	2,650,000	17,650,000
1751	"	3,700,000	18,700,000
1752	"	7,256,000	22,256,000
1753	"	2,394,575	17,394,575
1754	"	2,746,000	17,746,000
1755	"	16,326,000	31,326,000
1756	"	25,006,000	40,006,000
1757	"	24,006,000	39,006,000
1758	"	27,370,149	42,370,149
1759	"	41,903,954	56,903,954
1760	"	8,713,060	23,713,060
1761	12,200,000	18,000,000	30,200,000
1762	17,800,000	6,700,000	24,500,000
Total	224,500,000	202,071,736	426,571,738

Source: Marine, E, 208, no. 111; and G, 47–9.

42,957,115 l.t. respectively.[10] The confusion over figures for 1759 and 1760 suggests that final years of the Seven Years' War as the time of authorship.[11] Unfortunately, we are left with no figures for 1761 and 1762. While the data appear to concern naval expenses, it is unclear what they include or what they mean.

Global funds allotted to the navy are difficult to arrive at. A document in the naval archives, "Fonds accordées à la Marine depuis 1750 jusques et compris 1770," appears quite straightforward; the data come from retrospective reports on naval administration by Du Trousset d'Héricourt and continued by Sieur Bertrand, and were produced some time after 1770.[12] They give both ordinary and extraordinary funds for the twenty-one-year period, which covers the entire time of the separate colonial and naval funds.[13] Almost all extraordinary funds were assigned to naval expenses, but the figures appear to show only the naval portion when any separation occurred. The king, controller-general, and secretary of state did not sign états des fonds for 1747, 1748, or 1749.[14] I have assembled data for 1748 and 1749 from other sources of poor quality. Generated inside the navy's central bureaux, the figures were used by naval administrators; whether they are accurate may not matter as much as that naval officials believed in them.

Naval expenses comprised a significant proportion of the government's annual expenditure and an even greater share of its war expenses. Between 1690 and 1700 naval expenses made up between 13 and 23 per cent of the government's total military expenditure; the proportion fell to between 11 and 18 per cent during the next decade, and the quarter-century of peace from 1715 to 1739 saw a further decline to 4 or 5 per cent of military expenses.[15] Other figures for 1722, 1734, and 1739, however, suggest that naval expenses amounted to 5, 6.6, and 8.5 per cent of total government expenses respectively.[16] The naval proportion of military expenses was much higher. Available statistics for the middle of the century are very dubious, being little more than gross approximations of income and expenses. But during the early 1750s naval expenses probably consumed a greater proportion of government revenue than during any other peacetime period in the first three-quarters of the eighteenth century.

Taking Marion's figure of 222 million livres as the government's revenue in 1749, the navy's ordinary funds alone encumbered 9 per cent of the total.[17] Five years later total naval expenses (excluding the colonies) came to 9.4 per cent of the government's total expenditures of 232,701,000 livres; adding colonial expenditures, to compare with earlier in the century, brings the proportion to 16.4 per cent.[18] A more accurate figure for 1755 is 18.5 per cent of all government funds issued by the keeper of the Royal Treasury. The keeper actually assigned and paid 25,600,000 livres, or 15.9 per cent of the government's projected expenses, to the treasurers-general of the navy, who also received 6,762,400 livres, or nearly half of the payments not included in the *projet*.[19] The total amount, 32,362,400 livres, is remarkably close to that given in table 10. For the first eleven months of 1758, however, the keeper of the Royal Treasury assigned only 14.1 per cent of his total funds to the treasurers-general of the navy, though in absolute terms the treasurers received 38,571,085 livres.[20] In 1758, when the government's ordinary revenues amounted to 236 million livres, the navy's ordinary funds fell to 6.4 per cent of the total; this share doubled as a proportion of military expenses of 109 million livres; including allocations for the colonies, the proportion rose to about 23 per cent.[21] The naval share was probably even greater the following year. With 285 millions in receipts, and expenses forecast to reach 418 millions and actually totalling 503 millions, naval expenditure accounted for between 13 and 15 percent of total government expenses. Again, as a proportion of military costs, these percentages may well have doubled.[22] It must be repeated that the figures are dubious ; they serve to suggest, however, that the navy was not starved for the benefit of the army. Indeed, in 1759 the keeper of the Royal Treasury assigned just under 50 million livres to the treasurers-general of the navy.[23] Nevertheless, the Bourbon monarchy's revenues and borrowing capacity were incredibly low and naval warfare had become unbelievably

TABLE 11

Funds Authorized and Assigned to Naval Treasurers-General, 1748–1762

Year	Funds Authorized (from Table 10)	Funds Assigned (from Table 9)	Difference
1748	24,800,000	18,414,669	− 6,385,331
1749	20,000,000	15,562,455	− 4,437,545
1750	17,650,000	18,217,772	+ 567,772
1751	18,700,000	16,510,653	− 2,189,347
1752	22,256,000	16,278,498	− 5,977,502
1753	17,394,575	14,603,542	− 2,791,033
1754	17,746,000	15,424,262	− 2,321,738
1755	31,326,000	24,897,472	− 6,428,528
1756	40,006,000	42,959,888	+ 2,953,888
1757	39,006,000	49,712,985	+ 10,706,985
1758	42,370,149	40,949,164	− 1,420,985
1759	56,903,954	51,800,243	− 5,103,711
1760	23,713,060	17,289,289	− 6,423,771
1761	30,200,000	16,722,415	− 13,477,585
1762	24,500,000	30,529,650	+ 6,029,650
Total	426,571,738	389,872,957	− 36,698,781
Avg.	Authorized	Assigned	Difference
1749–54	18,957,763	16,099,530	− 2,858,233
1755–62	36,003,145	34,357,638	− 1,645,507

costly. With little power to supervise and control expenditure, governments could only deal with problems by throwing money at them. The Old Regime administration simply did not have sufficient money to throw.

Just how expensive naval warfare had become can be seen from table 11, which assumes that the first of the aforementioned documents (table 9, column 1) contains a record of assignments from the keeper of the Royal Treasury to the treasurers-general of the navy and compares them with the funds authorized by the king for naval expenses in table 10. In eleven of fifteen years the king authorized more than was assigned; the treasurers-general received only 91.4 per cent of the authorized funds for the entire period. The actual shortfall between amounts assigned to the treasurers-general and naval expenditure, then, was far greater than the difference between authorized funds and expenses. Between 1748 and 1760 the king authorized 361.8 million livres but the keeper of the Royal Treasury

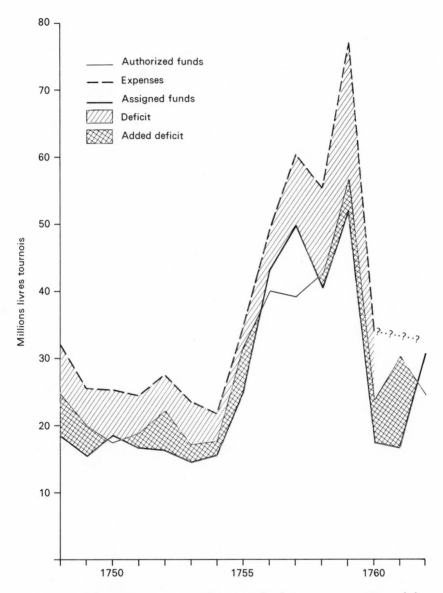

Naval Funds and Expenses, 1748–1762 (after H. Legohérel, *Les Trésoriers-généraux de la marine, 1517–1788*, p. 181)

assigned only 342.6 millions and the navy spent about 490 million livres (table 9, column 2). The official deficit might be said to be 119 millions, but the true deficit was about 25 per cent higher. The deficit for 1761 and 1762 only increased the total; naval expenditure remains unknown, but the shortfall between authorized and assigned amounts grew by 7.4 million livres.

The figures are not very satisfactory. We can tentatively conclude, however, that during six years of peace prior to the Seven Years' War naval expenditures approached 25 million livres annually. But authorized funds averaged only 19 million livres, while assigned funds were closer to 16 millions. During the next six years of war naval expenses and assigned funds doubled and the annual average shortfall declined, but the structure of naval finances prevented it from accumulating.

Notes

ABBREVIATIONS

AN	Archives Nationales
BN	Bibliothèque Nationale
BSHM	Bibliothèque du Service Historique de la Marine
Brest	Archives de la Marine at Brest
Colonies	Archives des Colonies (Archives Nationales)
Marine	Archives de la Marine (Archives Nationales)
PRO	Great Britain, Public Record Office
Rochefort	Archives de la Marine at Rochefort
Toulon	Archives de la Marine at Toulon

PREFACE

1 Dale K. Van Kley, *The Damiens Affair and the Unravelling of the Ancien Regime 1750–1770* (Princeton, NJ: Princeton University Press 1984).
2 The works of Roland Mousnier and François Bluche are too well known to require mention, but the following titles well illustrate the trend. V.R. Gruder, *The Royal Provincial Intendants: A Governing Elite in Eighteenth-Century France* (Ithaca, NY: Cornell University Press 1968); Y. Durand, *Les Fermiers généraux au XVIIIe siècle* (Paris: PUF 1971); J.F. Bosher, *French Finances, 1770–1795: From Business to Bureaucracy* (Cambridge: The University Press 1970); M. Bordes, *L'Administration provinciale et municipale en France au XVIIIe siècle* (Paris, SEDES 1972); M. Antoine, *Le Conseil du roi sous le règne de Louis XV* (Paris: Droz 1970); C.H. Church, *Revolution and Red Tape: The French Ministerial Bureaucracy, 1770–1850* (Oxford: Clarendon Press 1981).
3 P.W. Bamford, *Forests and French Sea Power, 1660–1789* (Toronto: University of Toronto Press 1956); E.L. Asher, *The Resistance to the Maritime Classes: The Survival of Feudalism in the France of Colbert*

(Berkeley and Los Angeles: University of California Press 1960); H. Legohérel, *Les Trésoriers généraux de la Marine, 1517–1788* (Paris: Editions Cujas 1965); D. Ozanam, *Claude Baudard de Sainte-James: trésorier-général de la marine et brasseur d'affaires (1738–1787)* (Geneva: Droz 1969); G. Symcox, *The Crisis of French Sea Power, 1688–1697: From the "Guerre d'escadre" to the "Guerre de course"* (The Hague: Martinus Nijoff 1974).

4 G. Lacour-Gayet, *La Marine militaire de la France sous le règne de Louis XV* (Paris: Honoré Champion 1902) and Capitaine de Vaisseau E. Chevalier, *Histoire de la marine française depuis le début de la monarchie jusqu'au traité de paix de 1763* (Paris: Hachette 1902).

5 Jean Egret, *Louis XV et l'opposition parlementaire* (Paris: A. Colin 1970), is a valuable exception.

6 Richard Pares, *War and Trade in the West Indies, 1739–1763* (Oxford: Clarendon Press 1936) is exceptional for several reasons, notably its use of French sources.

7 The Seven Years' War normally applies to the period from May 1756, when Great Britain declared war against France, to March 1763, when the belligerents signed the Peace of Paris. From the point of view of this study the term applies to the period from December 1754, when the French navy began moving towards a war-footing in response to British aggression in America, to November 1762, when, driven to the peace table after learning of the fall of Havana, the French signed a ceasefire; the period might be called more accurately the Eight Years' War.

8 See J.R. Dull, *The French Navy and American Independence: A Study of Arms and Diplomacy, 1774–1787* (Princeton, NJ: Princeton University Press 1975).

CHAPTER ONE

1 M. Antoine, *Le Conseil du roi sous Louis XV* (Paris and Geneva: Droz 1970), 124–7.

2 Ibid., 441.

3 The belief that Mme de Pompadour exercised a baneful influence on French history was chiefly a judgment of the eighteenth and nineteenth centuries. Those historians who have reassessed her role during the last fifty years deny that she influenced any important decisions of Louis XV and his ministers. See especially Pierre de Nolhac, *Madame de Pompadour et la politique d'après des documents nouveaux* (Paris: L. Conard 1928), 350–1, cited in Lee Kennett, *The French Armies in the Seven Years' War: A Study in Military Organization and Administration* (Durham, NC: Duke University Press 1967), 7; also Antoine, *Le Conseil du roi*, 622.

4 See J.F. Bosher, *French Finances, 1770–1795: From Business to Bureaucracy* (Cambridge: The University Press 1970), 4–6.

5 Although superficial, the best attempt at biography remains Pierre Gaxotte, *Le Siècle de Louis XV* (Paris: 1933), trans. J.L. May, *Louis the Fifteenth and His Times* (London: Cape 1934); see 74–102 and 141–91; also G.P. Gooch, *Louis XV: The Monarchy in Decline* (London: Longmans Green 1956). Olivier Bernier, *Louis the Beloved, the Life of Louis XV* (Garden City, NY: Doubleday 1984) is a sympathetic reexamination of a misjudged monarch.

6 Antoine, *Le Conseil du roi*, 601.

7 P. Vaucher, *Recueil des instructions données aux ambassadeurs et ministres de France*, 25, pt. 2, *Angleterre* (Paris: CNRS 1965), 366.

8 Alfred Cobban, *A History of Modern France*, 3 vols. (Harmondsworth: Penguin Books 1961), 1: 50–1.

9 Gaxotte, *Le Siècle de Louis XV*, 145–7.

10 Antoine, *Le Conseil du roi*, 120; see 118–27, 132–5 for the operations of the councils.

11 J.F. Bosher, "French Administration and Public Finance in Their European Setting," *The New Cambridge Modern History*, vol. 8, *The American and French Revolutions, 1763–1793*, ed. A. Goodwin (Cambridge: The University Press 1965), 568.

12 C. Rousset, éd., *Correspondance de Louis XV et du maréchal de Noailles*, 2 vols. (Paris: P. Dupont 1865), 2: 291–3.

13 J.F. Bosher, Introduction, *The French Prerevolution, 1787–1788* by Jean Egret, trans. W.D. Camp, (Chicago: University of Chicago Press 1977), xi. Henry Kissinger made the latter point in *White House Years* (Boston and Toronto: Little, Brown 1979), 20; see also Cobban, *Modern France*, 1: 58.

14 H. Carré, *Le Règne de Louis XV, 1715–1774* (Paris: Hachette 1909), 163, 221, 223; and S. Wilkinson, *The Defence of Piedmont, 1742–1748: The Prelude to a Study of Napoleon* (Oxford: Clarendon Press 1927), 271.

15 Charles-Philipe d'Albert, duc de Luynes, *Mémoires du duc de Luynes sur la cour de Louis XV, 1735–1758*, 17 vols., éd. L.E. Dussieux et E. Soolie (Paris, 1865–7), 9: 394; René-Louis de Voyer de Paulmy, marquis d'Argenson, *Journal et mémoires du Marquis d'Argenson*, éd. E.J.B. Rathery, 9 vols. (Paris: J. Renouard 1859–67), 5: 448–9; and Edmond-Jean-François Barbier, *Chronique de la régence et du règne de Louis XV (1718–1763); ou Journal de Barbier*, 8 vols. (Paris: Charpentier 1857), 4: 366.

16 Argenson, *Journal et mémoires*, 5: 415–16.

17 Ibid., 423.

18 Ibid., 451.

19 Mouffle d'Angerville, *Vie privée de Louis XV, ou principaux evénements, particularités et anecdotes de son règne*, nlle éd., 4 vols. (London: J.P. Lyton 1781), 2: 340–2.

20 On Pallu see J.N. Dufort, *Mémoires sur les règnes de Louis XV et Louis XVI et sur la Révolution par J.N. Dufort, comte Dufort de Cheverney*, éd. R. de Crevecoeur, 2 vols. (Paris: Plon 1909), 1: 105; E. de Croy, *Journal inédit du*

Duc de Croy, 1718–1784, 4 vols. (Paris: Flammarion 1906–7), 1: 274n1; also Luynes, *Mémoires*, 10: 299, 308, 441–2; and M. Antoine, *Le Gouvernement et l'administration sous Louix XV: dictionnaire biographique* (Paris: CNRS 1978), 197.

21 E.g., J. Tramond, *Manuel d'histoire maritime de la France des origines à 1815*, 2e éd. (Paris: Société d'éditions géographiques maritimes et coloniales 1947), 398; Cobban, *Modern France*, 1: 74; and G. Lacour-Gayet, *La Marine militaire de la France sous le règne de Louis XV* (Paris: Honoré Champion 1902), 210–11.

22 De Croy, *Journal inédit*, 1: 274; 3: 273–86; Argenson, *Journal et mémoires*, 8: 329.

23 Rousset, éd., *Correspondance de Louis XV*, 2: 334–66.

24 Charles-Jean-François Hénault, *Mémoires du Président Hénault* éd. F. Rousseau (Paris: Hachette 1911), 205.

25 See A. Lambert de Sainte-Croix, *Essai sur l'administration de la marine, 1689–1792* (Paris: Lévy 1892), 169–70; Lacour-Gayet, *La Marine militaire*, 235; and Tramond, *Manuel d'histoire maritime*, 398.

26 P.V. Malouet, *Mémoires de Malouet publiés par son petit-fils le Baron Malouet* 2 vols. (Paris: Didier 1868).

27 Cobban, *Modern France*, 1: 58–9.

28 Archives des Colonies B, 101, Machault to Bompar, 17 February 1755; and ibid., ff. 165–5v.

29 Identified and discussed in Z.E. Rashed, *The Peace of Paris, 1763* (Liverpool: The University Press 1951), 12–13.

30 D'Argenson, *Journal et mémoires*, 9: 52.

31 Cited in P. Boulle, "The French Colonies and the Reform of Their Administration during and following the Seven Years' War" (PH D thesis, University of California, Berkeley 1968), 91n70.

32 Argenson, *Journal et mémoires*, 9: 222; and Du Croy, *Journal inédit*, 1: 349.

33 See J. Egret, *Louis XV et l'opposition parlementaire* (Paris: A. Colin 1970), 68–83.

34 Cardinal de Bernis, *Mémoires et lettres de François-Joachim de Pierre, cardinal de Bernis, 1715–1758*, 2 vols., éd. F. Masson (Paris: E. Plon 1878), 1: 303–8, discusses the options in great detail.

35 Egret, *Louis XV et l'opposition parlementaire*, 85.

36 Lacour-Gayet, *La Marine militaire*, 224.

37 Curiously, Antoine, *Le Conseil du roi*, 215, fails to note this double appointment.

38 Luynes, *Mémoires*, 15: 441–2; and Marine B³, 536, f. 93; ibid., 534, f. 301; also ibid., 533, f. 37.

39 Marine B³, 535, ff. 18–119 (see esp. f. 34); and Marine B⁴, 78, ff. 19–21v.

40 Malouet, *Mémoires*, 2: 275; and Lacour-Gayet, *La Marine militaire*, 225–6.

41 See Richard Pares, *War and Trade in the West Indies, 1739–1763* (Oxford:

Clarendon Press 1936), 359–75, for discussion of the neutral passports and differences between Machault's and Moras' policies.

42 Lacour-Gayet, *La Marine militaire*, 224.

43 BN, Mss. frs., no. 11,340, ff. 89–90, 94–5. "Mémoire sur l'état present de la marine du Roy," February 1758.

44 Marine B², 358, f. 575, also Luynes, *Mémoires*, 16: 453–4; and Malouet, *Mémoires*, 2: 275.

45 Antoine, *Le Conseil du roi*, 211.

46 Marine C¹, 165, cited in D. Neuville, *Etat sommaire des archives de la marine antérieur à la révolution* (Paris, 1898; Krause Reprint 1977), 179n4.

47 Marine B³, 521, f. 22.

48 See especially Marine B⁴, 78, ff. 19–21; also Marine B³, 535, f. 120.

49 Barbier, *Chronique*, 7: 28–9; Mouffle d'Angerville, *Vie privée de Louis XV*, 3: 185.

50 Joseph-Hyacinthe de Rigaud de Vaudreuil had been governor of St Domingue from 1753 to 1757, and Pierre de Rigaud de Vaudreuil-Cavagnal had been governor-general of New France since 1755; Comte de Vaudreuil's appointment would have appeared to turn the French empire in America into a family fief.

51 Massiac's West Indian fortune was estimated at 1.5 million livres. P. Sagnac, *La Formation de la société française moderne*, 2 vols. (Paris: PUF 1945–6), 2: 226.

52 Antoine, *Le Conseil du roi*, 212.

53 Ibid.

54 Luynes, *Mémoires*, 16: 434; and Marine C⁷, 180, "dossier Lenormant de Mézy."

55 Ibid.

56 Mouffle d'Angerville, *Vie Privée de Louis XV*, 3: 185; Barbier, *Chronique*, 7: 54; Bernis, *Mémoires*, 2: 272.

57 Mouffle d'Angerville, *Vie privée de Louis XV*, 3: 186.

58 Du Croy, *Journal inédit*, 1: 433; Bernis, *Mémoires*, 2: 268, 272; also Lacour-Gayet, *La Marine militaire*, 228–9.

59 Antoine-Rigobert Mapinot de la Chapotte, *Sous Louis le bien aimée, correspondence amoureuse et militaire d'un officer pendant la guerre de Sept-ans, 1757–1765*, éd. J. Lemoine (Paris, 1905), 163, 204–5, 209, 233; Bernis, *Mémoires*, 2: 85; Barbier, *Chronique*, 7: 79–87.

60 Luynes, *Mémoires*, 16: 491; 17: 1; and Barbier, *Journal*, 7: 70.

61 M. Marion, *Histoire financière de la France depuis 1715*, 5 vols. (Paris: Rousseau 1914–19), 1: 187–8.

62 Bernis, *Mémoires*, 2: 85.

63 Marine G, 121, quoted in G. Dagnaud, *L'Administration centrale de la marine sous l'ancien régime* (Paris: Revue Maritime 1912), 27n5.

64 AN, AD VII, 3 no. 120; and Brest IE, 511, f. 334; also F. de Veillechèze de la

Mardière, *L'Evolution historique du contrôle de la marine* (Poitiers: Société française d'imprimerie et de librairies 1912), 77.

65 Lacour-Gayet, *La Marine militaire*, 77; Bernis, *Mémoires*, 2: 268; and Louis de Loménie, *Les Mirabeau, nouvelles études sur la société française au XVIIIe siècle*, 8 vols. (Paris: E. Dentu 1879), 1: 227–52.

66 Luynes, *Mémoires*, 17: 1; Barbier, *Chronique*, 7: 70; and Antoine, *Le Gouvernement et l'administration*, 30.

67 Dufort, *Mémoires*, 1: 264. Bernis, *Mémoires*, 2: 303, 322, is chiefly responsible for Berryer's later reputation; see Lacour-Gayet, *La Marine militaire*, 247. But the historian can take his pick in the contemporary stakes for worst minister; Mouffle d'Angerville, *Vie privée de Louis XV* (cited in Dumon, *Une carrière*, 164) opted for Peyrenc de Moras, whereas Voltaire (cited in Lacour-Gayet, *La Marine militaire*, 210–11) chose Rouillé.

68 Marine G., 121, ff. 271–3; Marine B^4, 78, ff. 58–61v, 65 [marginalia in the hand of Bernis].

69 See Dufort *Mémoires*, 1: 264; also Tramond, *Manuel d'histoire maritime*, 411.

70 Marine B^1, 66, ff. 243–5v; ibid., 67, ff. 68–96; and Marine B^3, 552, ff. 473–86.

71 Carré, *Le Règne de Louis XV*, 268.

72 Max Savelle, *Diplomatic History of the Canadian Boundary, 1749–1763* (New Haven: Yale University Press 1940), 90–102.

73 Marine B^1, 66, ff. 218.

74 One sentence scarcely does justice to a period of intense French diplomatic activity. For a compelling argument that Choiseul genuinely sought peace in the summer of 1761, see Rashed, *The Peace of Paris*, 73. See also Vaucher, éd., *Recueil des instructions*, 25, pt. 2: 372–84, for his instructions to François de Bussy, minister plenipotentiary to the British court, 23 May 1761.

75 Marine B^4, 104, "Plan de campagne par mer pour l'Année, 1762."

76 Argenson, *Journal et mémoires*, 6: 455–6.

77 Lacour-Gayet, *La Marine militaire*, 210.

78 Tramond, *Manuel d'histoire maritime*, 361.

CHAPTER TWO

1 N.M. Sutherland, *The French Secretaries of State in the Age of Catherine de Medici* (London: Athlone Press 1962), 29–98.

2 O. Ranum, *Richelieu and the Councillors of Louis XIII: A Study of the Secretaries of State and Superintendants of Finances in the Ministry of Richelieu, 1635–1642* (Oxford: Clarendon Press 1963), 72, 98–9.

3 Marc Perrichet, "Plume ou épée: problèmes de carrière dans quelques familles d'officiers d'administration de la marine au XVIIIe siècle" in *Actes du quatre-vingt-onzième congrès national des sociétés savantes*, Rennes, 1966 (Paris, 1969), 2: 149; also Albert Duchêne, *La Politique coloniale de la France: le ministère des colonies depuis Richelieu* (Paris: Payot 1928), 27.

4 R. La Roque de Roquebrune, "La direction de la Nouvelle-France par le ministère de la marine," *Revue d'histoire de l'Amérique française* 6 (1952–3): 474, gives the names of nine.

5 G. Dagnaud, "L'administration centrale de la marine sous l'ancien régime," *Revue maritime*, no. 193 (1912): 17–19; Neuville, *Etat sommaire des archives de la marine antérieur à la révolution* (Paris, 1898; Krause Reprint 1977), 250.

6 Neuville, *Etat sommaire*, 308, 633; Duchêne, *La politique coloniale*, 31.

7 Donald G. Pilgrim, "The Uses and Limitations of French Naval Power in the Reign of Louis XIV: The Administration of the Marquis de Seignelay 1683–1690" (PH D thesis, Brown University, 1969), 38.

8 See Marine B[8], 18, f. 16, "Mémoire de Pontchartrain, 9 novembre 1690;" cited in Pilgrim, "The Uses and Limitations of French Naval Power," 40.

9 Neuville, *Etat sommaire*, 30n5, 451; and Duchêne, *La politique coloniale*, 35.

10 J.C. Rule, "Colbert de Torcy, an Emergent Bureaucracy, and the formulation of French Foreign Policy, 1698–1715," in (American edition only) *Louis XIV and Europe*, ed. Ragnhild Hatton (Columbus: Ohio State University Press 1976), 261–2.

11 See P. Goubert, *Louis XIV and Twenty Million Frenchmen*, trans. A. Carter (New York: Vintage Books 1966), 239–68, for a brief summary. Marcel Giraud, "Crise de conscience et d'autorité à la fin du régne de Louis XIV," *Annales, ESC.* 7 (1952): 172–90, 293–302; and "Tendances humanitaires à la fin du régne de Louis XIV," *Revue historique* 209 (1953): 217–37, contain brilliant treatments of this material and the moral crisis in the navy.

12 Dagnaud, "L'administration centrale," 23; and Neuville, *Etat sommaire*, 449, 451.

13 Neuville, *Etat sommaire*, 147, 648; H. Fontaine de Resbecq, "L'administration centrale de la marine et des colonies," *Revue maritime et coloniale*, no. 87 (1886): 413.

14 Maurepas remains a controversial figure; for two recent studies, see J.C. Rule, "Jean-Frédéric Phélypeaux, comte de Pontchartrian et Maurepas: Reflections on His Life and His Papers," *Louisiana History* 6 (1965): 365–77; and M. Filion, *Maurepas, ministre de Louis XV (1715–1749)* (Montréal: Leméac 1967).

15 Neuville, *Etat sommaire*, 28.

16 Marine C[2], 116 (1749), "Etat des payement à faire ... aux p[aux] commis des B[aux] de la M[e] ... pend[t] les 6 p[rs] mois, 1749."

17 Ibid., "Bureaux de la marine à la cour et à Paris," juin 1753.

18 Roland Mousnier, "La fonction publique en France du début du seizième siècle à la fin du dix-huitième siècle," *Revue historique*, no. 530 (1979): 332; also Dagnaud, "L'administration centrale de la marine," 35.

19 Marine A[1], 87, no. 22.

20 Marine C[2], 116 (1748), "Etat de payment, 1 juillet 1748;" and Neuville, *Etat sommaire*, 306–8.

21 See Lee Kennett, *The French Armies in the Seven Years' War: A Study in Military Organization and Administration* (Durham, NC: Duke University Press 1967), 12, for a similar situation at the War Office.

22 J.-P. Samoyault, *Les Bureaux du secrétariat d'état des affaires étrangères sous Louis XV* (Paris: A. Pedone 1971), 96.

23 Marine, C², 116 (1750), "Bureaux de la marine, 1750;" "Bureaux de la marine à la cour et à Paris, juin, 1753;" and "Etat des Appointemens des prem^{rs} commis et des commis subalternes des Bureaux de la Marine à la cour et à Paris 1757 [1759]."

24 Marine C², 117 (1761), "Etat des payements qui seront faits ... pour leurs appointemens et suplement d'appointemens ..."

25 Ibid., 40, "Liste générale ..." re: M. David "à la cour."

26 Marine B², 360, ff. 248–8v.

27 Marine C², 116, "Etat des appointemens de M. Pellerin et des commis de son bureau," janvier 1750.

28 Ibid., "Mémoire concernant les appointemens fixés et à fixer aux commis qui travaillerait sous les ordres de M. de Machault fils et qui passent sous ceux de M. Charron," March 1757; also René-Louis de Voyer de Paulmy, marquis d'Argenson, *Journal et memoires du Marquis d'Argenson*, éd. E.J.B. Rathery, 9 vols. (Paris: J. Renouard 1859–67), 9:81.

29 Marine C², 116, "Etat des appointemens ...," 1759.

30 Neuville, *Etat sommaire*, 5, citing Marine B⁸, 1, f. 176; see also Marine A¹, 20 to 33, for the eleven-volume collection and tables.

31 See Marine G, 39–46, for the history.

32 G. Lacour-Gayet, *La Marine militaire de la france sous le règne de Louis XV* (Paris: Honoré Champion 1902), 395.

33 See Neuville, *Etat sommaire*, 631.

34 Yvonne Bezard, *Fonctionnaires maritimes et coloniaux sous Louis XIV: Les Bégon* (Paris: Albin Michel 1932), 326–7.

35 *Almanach royale de 1762*, 167; and Marine C², 117 "Etat des appointements ...," 1763.

36 Marine C², 116, "Bureau de la Marine à la Cour et à Paris, juin 1753."

37 Marine G 33, 191, "Liste des officiers de la marine et des Vaisseaux et autres Batim^s du Roy," c. 1763.

38 Marine C², 117 [note], 1 January 1762.

39 Ibid., 116, "Bureaux de la marine à la cour, et à Paris, juin 1753."

40 Ibid., "Etat des appointmens des prem^{res} commis et des commis subalternes des Bureaux de la marine a la cour et a Paris 1757 [1759]."

41 Charles-Philippe d'Albert, duc de Luynes, *Mémoires du duc de Luynes sur la cour de Louis XV, 1735–1758*, 17 vols., éd. L.E. Dussieux et E. Soolie (Paris: 1865–7), 15:441–2; Neuville, *Etat sommaire*, 452; and Marine C², 116, "Bureaux de la marine, 1750;" also J.N. Dufort, *Mémoires sur les règnes de Louis XVI et sur la Révolution par J.N. Dufort, comte Dufort de Cheverney*, éd. R. de Crevecoeur, 2 vols. (Paris: Plon 1909), 1:105.

42 BSHM, no. 29, ff. 178–9.

43 Argenson, *Journal et Mémoires*, 9:81.

44 E.g., Toulon 1A¹, 209, f. 25.

45 Marine C², 117, "Bureaux dont est chargé M. Le Tourneur," 15 novembre, 1762; ibid., 40, "Liste général ... "; ibid., 116, Pallu à Moras, 23 May 1757.

46 G. Frégault, *François Bigot, administrateur française*, 2 vols. (Montréal: Institut d'histoire de l'Amérique française 1948), 2:97–8.

47 See Neuville, *Etat sommaire*, 314n2; Duchêne, *La Politique coloniale*, 43; and Frégault, *François Bigot*, 1:290–3.

48 Marine C², 116, "Appointemens suplement d'appointemens et gratifications ... année 1754;" ibid., C², 40 "Liste général des officiers de plume ... 1 janvier, 1750."

49 See Jean Tarrade, *Le Commerce coloniale de la France à la fin de l'ancien régime; l'evolution du régime de l'Exclusif de 1763 à 1789* (Paris: PUF 1972), 1:77n46.

50 James S. Pritchard, "French Charting of the East Coast of Canada," in *Five Hundred Years of Nautical Science, 1400–1900*, ed. D. Howse (Greenwich: National Maritime Museum 1981), 123.

51 J.-N. Bellin, *Atlas maritime, ou recueil des cartes réduites dressées au Dépôt des cartes et plans de la marine pour le service des vaisseaux du roi* ([Paris], 1751).

52 J.-N. Bellin, "Remarques sur les cartes du 'Neptune François' dont les Planches ont été remise au Dépôt des Plans de la marine, en 1753," in *Le Neptune françois* (Paris, many imprints).

53 Marine C², 117, "Appointemens ... avril 1761;" ibid., 41, *entreface*, 161–2.

54 J.-N. Bellin, *L'Hydrographie françoise, recueil des cartes générales et particulières qui ont été faites pour le service des vaisseaux du roy, par ordre des ministères de la marine depuis 1737 jusqu' en 1765 par le Sr. Bellin, ingénieur de la marine et du depost des cartes, plans et journaux de la marine*, 2 vols. (Paris: Chez M. Bellin 1756).

55 On Narbonne-Pelet see; Marine C¹, 165–8, 545; 178, 72v; 180, 140v, and C⁷, 224; see also *Dictionnaire de la noblesse*, 14 vols. (Paris: La Chenaye-Desbois 1770–84), 10:678.

56 Rule, "Colbert de Torcy," 262.

57 Max Weber, *The Theory of Social and Economic Organization*, trans. A.M. Henderson and Talcott Parsons (New York, 1947), 331, cited in Peter M. Blau, ed., *Bureaucracy in Modern Society* (New York: Random House 1956), 31.

58 J.F. Bosher, "Government and Private Interests in New France," *Canadian Public Administration* 10 (1967): 254.

59 C.H. Church, *Revolution and Red Tape: The French Ministerial Bureaucracy, 1770–1850* (Oxford: Clarendon Press 1981), 308; see also chapter 1, 1–22.

60 Marine C², 116 (1757), "mémoire" (signed) Pellerin, 15 March 1757.

61 Michel Antoine, "L'entourage des ministres au XVIIᵉ et XVIIIᵉ siècles," in *Origines et histoire des cabinets des ministres en France* (Geneva: Droz 1975), 17–21.

62 M. Antoine, *Le Conseil du roi sous le règne des Louis XV* (Paris: Droz 1970), 310.

63 J.F. Bosher, "The Premiers Commis des Finances in the Reign of Louis XVI," *French Historical Studies* 3 (1964): 485.

64 E.g., Marine B², 361, f. 252; P. Masson, *Histoire du commerce française dans le levant au XVIIIe siècle* (Paris, 1896; New York: Burt Franklin 1967), 341, reports that Berryer sent Le Guay to Marseilles to negotiate with the Chamber of Commerce on arrangements for the protection of commerce. Earlier he sent Pellerin, the younger, to Le Havre to assist the intendant with construction of 150 *bateaux plats* in 1759 (see Marine D¹, 1, ff. 1–2).

65 Cf. Samoyault, *Les Bureaux du secrétaire d'état*, 60–1; also Pierre Boulle, "The French Colonies and the Reform of their Administration during and following the Seven Years' War," (PHD thesis, University of California, Berkeley, 1968), 32–3.

66 Mousnier, "La fonction publique," 334.

67 Duchêne, *La Politique coloniale*, 55.

68 Marine C², 116, "Etat des payements a faire … aux p^aux commis des B^aux de la M^e pour leurs app^s du Tresor Ro^al pend^t des 6 p^rs mois 1758," 30 juin 1758; also ibid., 29 octobre 1748.

69 Marc Perrichet, "Plume ou epée," 145–83.

70 Marine, C², 117, "Appointemens," April 1761; ibid., 58, f. 244, "Officiers de plume sans destination actuelle," 23 March 1762; ibid., 116 (1752), "divers demandes pour augmentation d'appointments," July 1752.

71 J.F. Bosher, *French Finances, 1770–1795: From Business to Bureaucracy* (Cambridge: The University Press 1970), 278.

72 Marine C², 57, f. 213.

73 Marine C⁷, 180, "Lenormant de Mézy."

74 Marine B², 347, f. 352; ibid., 349, ff. 196, 353; ibid., 350, f. 40; Marine, D³, 34 Lenormant to Machault, 22 July 1756; and B³, 528, f. 222.

75 Argenson, *Journal et Mémoires*, 9:243–4.

76 BN, n.a.f., no. 126, f. 300.

77 See Marine B³, 547, ff. 378–9 [minister's marginalia].

78 Marine C², 117, "Appointemens des premiers commis et commis subalternes des Bureaux de la marine, … avril, 1761."

79 Ibid., Etat des app^temts … 1763; also *Almanach Royal*, 1762, 167.

80 Cf. Antoine, *Le Conseil du roi*, 423–4; also Duchêne, *Le Politique coloniale*, 64–5.

CHAPTER THREE

1 Cornell University, Maurepas Papers, "Mémoire [sur les abus qui se sont glissés dans la marine]," [c. 1745–6].

2 G. Dagnaud, *L'Administration centrale de la marine sous l'ancien régime*

(Paris: Revue Maritime 1912), 20, who cites "Etat abrégé de la marine," and R. Mémain, *La Marine de guerre sous Louis XIV, le matériel, Rochefort arsenal modèle de Colbert* (Paris: Hachette 1937), 361, 471.

3 See W. Fischer and P. Lundgreen, "The Recruitment and Training of Administrative and Technical Personnel," in *The Formation of Nation States in Western Europe*, ed. C. Tilly (Princeton, NJ: Princeton Uiversity Press 1975), 497.

4 R. Mandrou, *La France aux XVIIe et XVIIIe siècles* (Paris: PUF 1967), 203–4.

5 V.R. Gruder, *The Royal Provincial Intendants: A Governing Elite in Eighteenth-Century France* (Ithaca, NY: Cornell University Press 1968), 19, 37.

6 See André Corvisier, "La société militaire française au temps de la Nouvelle France," *Histoire sociale / Social History* 10, no. 20 (1977): 222.

7 E.g., Marine B³, 548, f. 237; ibid., 547, f. 330; and ibid., 550, ff. 231–4.

8 M. Bordes, *L'Administration provinciale et municipale en France au XVIIIe siècle* (Paris: SEDES 1972), 13; and J. Phytiles et al., *Questions administratives dans la France du XVIIIe siècle* (Paris: PUF 1965), also G. Vedel, *Droit administratif* 6eme éd. (Paris: Cours de droit 1976 [1958]), 779.

9 Cf. Talcott Parsons, "Professions," in David L. Sills, ed., *International Encyclopedia of the Social Sciences* 17 vols. (New York: Macmillan 1968), 12:536–47.

10 Marine B², 343, ff. 246–6v; and Toulon 1A¹, 214, ff. 106–8. See also Dagnaud, *L'Administration centrale*, 20n5, citing Marine G, 74.

11 Toulon 1A¹, 208, ff. 263–3v.

12 Marine B³, 514, ff. 306–8v, 310–11v; ibid., B², 343, ff. 245–6v; also Toulon 1A¹, 214, ff. 106–8.

13 Rochefort, 1E, 381, 28 December 1753.

14 Gabriel de Bory, *Mémoires sur l'administration de la marine et colonies* (Paris: P.D. Pierres 1789–90), 7–8.

15 Rochefort 1E, 382, no. 153.

16 A. Deschard, "Notice sur l'organization du corps du Commisariat de la marine française depuis l'origine jusqu'a nos jours," *Revue maritime et coloniale*, nos. 59–61 (1878–9): 59, 499; and D. Neuville, *Etat sommaire des archives de la marine antérieur à la révolution* (Paris, 1898; Krause Reprint 1977), 445.

17 Rochefort, 1E, 379, no. 17.

18 See Marine B³, 529, ff. 345–7; ibid., 530, f. 310; and ibid., 536, ff. 60–5, 66–75.

19 Marine C², 58, ff. 151–6, 171–6.

20 Ibid., ff. 156–9v, 160–1v, 163–4v, 168–9, and 179.

21 Marine G, 128, f. 18.

22 Marine C², 40 "Liste générale des officiers de plume contenant leur avancement congés et autres mouvements, premier janvier 1750."

23 Marine A¹, 95, no. 23.

24 Marine G, 128, f. 18; see also Marine A¹, 92, no. 35.

25 Rochefort 1E, 416, no. 11.

26 Marine C², 58, ff. 223–4.

27 Ibid., ff. 168–9; also Marine B², 336, ff. 287–7v; and Marine B³, 538, ff. 225–6.

28 See R. Mémain, *La Marine de guerre*, chap. 8, 361–81.

29 Based on Deschard, "Commissariat," no. 60: 774–97, and Marine C⁷, "dossiers personnels."

30 Maurepas' new policy was clearly explained to François Bigot, quoted in J.F. Bosher and J.C. Dubé, "Bigot," *Dictionary of Canadian Biography*, vol. 4, *1771 to 1800*, 60.

31 For their earlier careers see D. Horton, "Hocquart," and J. Pritchard, "Lenormant de Mézy," *Dictionary of Canadian Biography* 4:354–65, 465–8.

32 Based on Deschard, "Commissariat," no. 61: 179–200, and "dossiers personnels" in Marine C⁷.

33 J.F. Bluche, *L'Origine des magistrats du Parlement de Paris au XVIIIe siècle 1715–1771* (Paris, 1956).

34 See Marine C⁷, 175, dossier "Lefebvre de Givry"; and Bluche, *L'Origine des magistrats*, 268–9.

35 Deschard, "Commissariat," no. 61, 193.

36 L.-P. May, "Le Mercier de la Rivière, intendant des iles du Vent, 1759–1764," *Revue d'histoire économique et sociale* 20 (1932): 47; also J. Egret, *Louis XV et l'opposition parlementaire* (Paris: Colin 1970), 60n37 and 85.

37 J.F. Bluche, *Les Magistrats du Parlement de Paris au XVIIIe siècle (1715–1771)* (Paris: les Belles lettres 1960), 316–18; F.L. Ford, *Robe and Sword: The Regrouping of the French Aristocracy after Louis XIV* (1953; New York: Harper Torchbooks 1965), 173–4; also M. Antoine, *Le Conseil du roi sous le règne de Louis XV* (Paris: Droz 1970), 251.

38 Mémain, *La Marine de guerre*, chap. 14, "Commissaires généraux et commissaires ordinaires," 466–91.

39 *Almanach royal de 1748* (Paris, 1748), 100.

40 Marine G, 244; and Marine C², 41.

41 Marine B³, 534; and Neuville, *Etat sommaire*, 270–4.

42 Based on Deschard, "Commissariat," no. 60: 777–97, and no. 61: 180–99; *Almanachs royaux*, 1748–62; Marine G, 33; and Marine C², 40.

43 Marine C², 58, ff. 120–2; and Marine B³, 530, ff. 202–20.

44 Marine C², 58, ff. 27–300.

45 Neuville, *Etat sommaire*, 381n3 and 385; Deschard, "Commissariat," no. 59: 498n1.

46 Neuville, *Etat sommaire*, 385–6.

47 Deschard, "Commissariat," 182–3.

48 Marine C², 58, f. 122.

49 Marine B³, 534, ff. 113–14.

50 Marine C², 40–1; and 58, ff. 163–4v.

51 Deschard, "Commissariat," no. 59: 495. See also Mémain, *La Marine de guerre*, chap. 16, 502–6.

52 Marine C², 58, f. 33.

53 Marine B³, 540, ff. 338–9, 340; and ibid., 545, ff. 6–8.

54 Marine G, 133, printed in Dagnaud, *L'Administration centrale*, 102–9.

55 Marine C², 58, ff. 93, 100–9, 120–2.

56 E.g., Rochefort 1L¹, 7, f. 23; Marine, C², 58, ff. 127–9. Rochefort, 1E, 382, no. 321; and ibid., 410, no. 662.

57 Mémain, *La Marine de guerre*, 509.

58 Marine C², 58, ff. 134–6.

59 Dagnaud, *L'Administration centrale*, 102.

60 Marine B³, 530, ff. 71v–2, 278.

61 Ibid., 543, f. 301.

62 Marine G, 224, ff. 77–108; and BN, Mss. frs., no. 14,286, ff. 47–64v.

63 Marine B², 338, [n.p.], 9 November 1749.

64 See *Considerations sur la constitution de la marine de France* (London, 1756), 27–8.

65 Deschard, "Commissariat," no. 59: 500; and Dagnaud, *L'Administration centrale*, 25n2.

66 Elizabeth Bégon, "Correspondance," ed. C. de Bonnault, *Rapport de l'archiviste de la province de Québec pour 1934–1935* (Quebec: Rédempti Paradis 1935), 95.

67 F. de Veillechèze de la Mardière, *L'Evolution historique du contrôle de la marine* (Poitiers: Société française d'imprimerie et de librairies 1912), 70n4.

68 Rochefort 1E, 382, no. 142.

69 Marine B³, 516, ff. 225 passim.

70 Printed in A. Lambert de Sainte-Croix, *Essai sur l'administration de la marine de France, 1689–1792* (Paris: C. Lévy 1982), 174.

71 E.g., Marine B², 345, ff. 278–8v; and Rochefort 1E, 406, no. 74.

72 E.g., Marine B², 347, f. 334.

73 Marine B³, 529, ff. 372–2v.

74 Ibid., 538, ff. 224, 243–2v.

75 Marine B², 349, f. 75.

76 Toulon 1A¹, 118, f. 232.

77 Brest 1, 45, ff. 203–4.

78 Cf. G. Lacour-Gayet, *La Marine militaire de la France sous le règne de Louis XV* (Paris: Honoré Champion 1902), 221–2.

79 According to Mouffle d'Angerville, *Vie privée de Louis XV ou principaux événements particularités et anecdotes de son règne*, nlle éd., 4 vols. (London: J.P. Lyton 1781), 2:305–6, Maurepas' major weakness had been his reluctance to punish anyone for serious breaches of naval discipline and questionable conduct during the war.

80 Marine B², 338, n.p., 9 November 1749.

81 Rochefort 1E, 382, no. 153.

82 Marine A^1, 92, no. 35.

83 See Dagnaud, *L'Administration centrale*, 33, citing Marine G, 122, "mémoire," 1762; also G, 127.

84 The argument is made in John Ehrman, *The Navy in the War of William III, 1689–1697; its State and Direction* (Cambridge: The University Press 1953), 171.

85 Mouffle d'Angerville, *Vie privée de Louis XV*, 1:300–1.

86 François Bluche, *Les Magistrats de la Cour de monnaies de Paris au XVIIIe siècle 1715–1790* (Paris: les Belles lettres 1966), 36.

87 The only work concerning the navy is the excellent essay by Marc Perrichet , "Plume ou épée: problèmes de carrière dans quelques familles d'officiers d'administration de la marine au XVIII siècle," *91e Congrès nationale des sociétés savantes*, Rennes 1966 (Paris, 1969), 1:145–83.

88 The stimulating monograph by Carl-Axel Gemzell, *Organization, Conflict, and Innovation; A Study of German Naval Strategic Planning, 1888–1940*, Lund Studies in International History, 4 (Lund: Esselte Studium 1973), contains a theoretical discussion of the historical dimensions of the topic; see especially 13–30 and 92–139.

CHAPTER FOUR

1 Rochefort 1A, 111, f. 13; see also Marine F^1, 47, ff. 1–32.

2 Marine G, 33, ff. 26–7; Marine F^1, 47, ff. 32v–48v; and BN, Mss. frs., no. 14,286, ff. 2–29.

3 M. Vergé-Franceschi, *La Royale du temps de l'amiral d'Estaing* (Paris: A. Pedone 1977), 97–9; also H. Carré, *Le Règne de Louis XV 1715–1744* (Paris: Hachette 1909), 172.

4 Eugene L. Asher, *The Resistance to the Maritime Classes: The Survival of Feudalism in the France of Colbert* (Berkeley and Los Angeles: University of California Press 1960), 41–2.

5 See P.W. Bamford, "The Knights of Malta and the King of France, 1665–1700," *French Historical Studies* 3 (1964): 429–53.

6 Marine F$_1$, 47, ff. 1–32; see also D. Neuville, *Etat sommaire des archives de la marine antérieur à la révolution* (Paris, 1898; Krause Reprint 1977), 340n1.

7 P.W. Bamford, *Fighting Ships and Prisons: The Mediterranean Galleys of France in the Age of Louis XIV* (Minneapolis: University of Minnesota Press 1973), 279; also Marine B^6, 145, ff. 176–7v; and Marine B^3, 547, ff. 169–72.

8 Marine G, 38; and BN, 77, Mss. frs., no. 14,286. See also R. Cavaliero, *The Last of the Crusaders: The Knights of St John and Malta in the Eighteenth Century* (London: Hollis & Carter 1960), 11, 16–17.

9 Brest 1L, 45, f. 193v; ibid., 1A, 151, f. 92v; and ibid., 1L, 46, f. 65. Also J. Godechot, "La France et Malte au XVIII siècle," *Revue historique* 206 (July

1951): 67–79; and François Bluche, *La Vie quotidienne de la noblesse française au XVIIIe siècle* (1973; Paris: Hachette 1980), 171.

10 BN, Fonds frs., no. 11,314, f. 58v.

11 Based on lists of general officers in the *Almanachs royaux* for 1749, when the ages of sixteen of twenty-five were known.

12 The average age on entry of thirty-six officers was fifteen; fifty-three officers spent an average of forty-five years in the navy and 15.8 years as *capitaine* before achieving general rank. The average age of thirty-seven officers on receipt of their flag was 59.9 years; and fifty officers lived for twelve years as general officers. The average age at death of thirty-six officers was 75.7 years.

13 Brest 1L, 44, ff. 241v–2v.

14 E.g., Rochefort 1L¹, 7 and 8, "registres du control."

15 See the interesting letter from marquis de Massiac to Machault (Marine B³, 529, ff. 74v–5). Also Bluche, *La vie quotidienne de la noblesse*, 164–5.

16 Vergé-Franceschi, *La Royale*, 111.

17 Cornell University, Maurepas Papers, "Liste des capitaines des vaisseaux suivant leur rang et ancienneté," [c. 1749]. Two colonial governors, Vaudreuil of Louisiana and De Clieu of Guadeloupe, are not included in this number.

18 Based on dates of entry and promotion to *capitaine de vaisseau* for 111 of these officers.

19 Brest 1L, 76, ff. 26v–41v.

20 See *Considerations sur la constitution de la marine de France* (London, 1756), 9; reprinted in J. Tramond, *Manuel d'histoire maritime de la France des origines à 1815*, 2e éd. (Paris: Société d'éditions géographiques maritimes et coloniales 1947), 399.

21 Marine B⁴, 68, ff. 3–5v.

22 BN, Fonds frs., no. 14,286, ff. 2–29.

23 E.g., Rochefort 1A, 111, f. 67v.

24 Marine B³, 550, f. 129; and ibid., 551, f. 41.

25 A. Doneaud du Plan, *La Marine française au XVIIIe siècle au point de vue de l'administration, et des progrès scientifiques* (Paris: Extrait Revue maritime et coloniale 1867), 24–5.

26 Jacques Aman, *Les Officiers bleus dans la marine française au XVIIIe siècle* (Geneva: Droz 1976), 38–9.

27 BN, Mss. frs., no. 14,286.

28 Marine B³, 350, f. 129.

29 Marine B², 369, f. 1.

30 Marine G, 33, ff. 134–6; also Vergé-Franceschi, *La Royale*, 111; and Neuville, *Etat sommaire*, 325, 357.

31 Aman, *Les Officieurs bleus*, 153–4.

32 See Rochefort 1E, 382, no. 194.

33 Marine D⁴, 8, ff. 109–11; also Neuville, *Etat sommaire*, 428.

34 Marine D⁴, 1, f. 42v; and Marine A¹, 85, no. 48.

35 Brest, 1L, 45, ff. 108v–9; bn, n.a.f., no. 136, ff. 227–8.

36 Neuville, *Etat sommaire*, 431.

37 bn, fonds frs., no. 14,286.

38 E.g., Marine B³, 531, ff. 35–6; and Brest 1L, 45, f. 140. See also G. Lacour-Gayet, *La Marine militaire de la France sous le règne de Louis XV* (Paris: Honoré Champion 1902), 358–9.

39 Marine B³, 350, f. 124.

40 Vergé-Franceschi, *La Royale*, 57.

41 Marine B³, 519, f. 184.

42 Marine A¹, 85, no. 15.

43 Vergé-Franceschi, *La Royale*, 71.

44 *Almanach royal de 1755* (Paris, 1755), 90–8.

45 Marine G, 38.

46 Marc Perrichet, "Plume ou epée: problemes de carrière dans quelques familles d'officiers d'administration de la marine au xviiie siècle," in *Actes du quatre-vingt-onzième congrès national des sociétés savantes* (Rennes, 1966; Paris, 1969), 2:166, 168.

47 Marine A¹, 86, no. 14, and Brest 1L, 45, f. 131v.

48 Jurien de La Gravière, *Souvenirs d'un amiral* (1860), vol. 2, 382, quoted in Y. Le Gallo, *Etudes sur la marine et l'officier de marine, Brest et sa bourgeoisie sous la monarchie de juillet*, 2 vols. (Paris: puf 1968), 1:96; see also Jean Meyer, *La Noblesse bretonne au XVIIIe siècle*, 2 vols. (Paris: sevpen 1966), 2:300–1, 1125–6, 1134.

49 See Lacour-Gayet, *La Marine militaire*, 483–9 and 499–507. Of sixty-six officers, *lieutenant de vaisseau* and above, in La Galissonière's squadron, fifty-five came from Provence, Languedoc, and Comtat d'Avignon. Paris, Normandy, and Beauvais accounted for six and Rochefort and the colonies for three. Three years later, when La Clue sailed from Toulon, twenty-six new officers were on board; twenty-one who have a known place of origin came from southern France. Conversely at Brest, only six of eighty-two *lieutenants des vaisseaux* and above who sailed in Conflans' squadron came from the south. Thirty-four were from Brittany, thirty-three from Saintonge, Poitou, Maine, and Normandy, and six from the colonies.

50 See M. Vergé, "Les officiers de marine d'origine provençal à Toulon au xviiie siècle" (Mémoire en vue de la maîtrise d'histoire, Nice 1973), 247. Also Marine B², 338, [n.p.], 9 November 1749.

51 C. Chabaud-Arnault, "La marine française sous la régence et sous le ministère de Maurepas," *Revue maritime* (July 1891): 62–3; Lacour-Gayet, *La Marine militaire*, 214–17; J. Tramond, *Manuel d'histoire maritime*, 370–1, and also R. Jouan, *Histoire de la marine française* (Paris: Payot 1950), 83.

52 Rochefort 1E, 379, no. 132.

53 See Roger Hahn, "L'Enseignement scientifique des gardes de la marine en xviiie siècle," in *Enseignement et diffusion des sciences en France au XVIIIe*

siècle, éd. R. Taton (Paris: Hermann 1964), 547–58. See also Vergé-Franceschi, *La Royale*, 64–94; and F. Russo, "L'Enseignement des sciences de la naviga-tion dans les écoles d'hydrographie aux xvIIIe et xvIIIe siècles," in *Le Navire et l'économie maritime du moyen age au XVIIIe siècle principalement en Mediterranée*, éd. M. Mollat (Paris: SEVPEN 1958), 161–72; and "L'Hydro-graphie en France au XVIIe et XVIIIe siècles, écoles et ouvrages d'enseigne-ment," in *Enseignmement et diffusion des sciences en France*, 436.

54 Toulon 1A¹, 198, f. 117v.

55 Ibid., 199, f. 20.

56 *Considerations sur la constitution de la marine de France*, 20; and Mouffle d'Angerville, *Vie privée de Louis XV ou principaux événements, particuliar-ités et anecdotes de son règne*, nlle éd., 4 vols. (London: J.P. Lyton 1781), 2:341.

57 Marine G, 86, to G, 91, contain several projects for reform of education sent to Choiseul. Hahn, "L'Enseignement scientifique," 550, notes that these plans are inseparable from the larger movement for educational reform in France, but they are striking because they reveal the idea of reform of education as a panacea for the ills of the navy.

58 Cf. D. Bien, "Military Education in Eighteenth-Century France: Technical and Non-Technical Determinants," in *Science, Technology and Warfare, Proceedings of the Third Military History Symposium*, United States Airforce Academy, 8–9 May 1969, ed. M.D. Wright and L.J. Paszek (Washington, DC: US Government Printing Office 1971), 51–60. See also G. Chaussinand-Nogaret, *La noblesse au XVIIIe siècle: de la féodalité aux lumières* (Paris: Hachette 1976), 23–38, for a stimulating discussion on how deeply notions of personal merit had penetrated noble thinking.

59 Cited in V.F. Brun, *Guerres maritimes de la France: Port de Toulon, ses armements, son administration depuis son origine jusqu'a nos jours*, 2 vols. (Paris: Plon 1861), 1: and Vergé-Franceschi, *La Royale*, 100.

60 See Rochefort 1L¹, 7–8, "registres du contrôle."

61 E.g., Marine B⁴, 64, f. 136; also Toulon 1A¹, 120, f. 241.

62 Cf. D. Baugh, *British Naval Administration in the Age of Walpole* (Princeton, NJ: Princeton University Press 1965), 109.

63 Vergé-Franceschi, *La Royale*, 234–5.

64 E.g., Marine B³, 511, ff. 338, 341; ibid., 547, ff. 186 –6v.

65 Rochefort 1E, 413, no. 170.

66 Brest 1E, 511, f. 157; and Marine B³, 548, f. 180v.

67 Rochefort 1A, 111, f. 13.

68 BN, Clairambault, no. 872, ff. 49–50, 51–2v, and 55–5v; also Vergé-Franceschi, *La Royale*, 136.

69 Marine B⁴, 68, f. 293v.

70 Ibid.,71, ff. 209–309.

71 Toulon 1A¹, 120, f. 241.

72 Brest 1A, 151, f. 106v.

73 Toulon 1A¹, 118, f. 135.

74 Louis-Guillaume de Parsçau du Plessis, "Journal d'une compagne au Canada à bord de *la Sauvage* (mars-juillet 1756)," *Rapport de l'archiviste de la province de Québec pour 1928–29* (Québec: Redempti Paradis 1929), 217.

75 E.g., Marine B⁴, 66, ff. 276, 283.

76 Rochefort 1E, 408, no. 541.

77 BN, Fonds frs., no. 14,286, ff. 2–29.

78 Lacour-Gayet, *La Marine militaire*, 346.

79 Mouffle d'Angerville, *Vie privée de Louis XV*, 4:84–5.

80 Lacour-Gayet, *La Marine militaire*, 409–11.

81 Marine C¹, 178, 15 June 1763.

82 Brest 1A, 153, ff. 88–9v.

83 Marine B³, 551, ff. 139–40.

CHAPTER FIVE

1 Eugene L. Asher, *The Resistance to the Maritime Classes: The Survival of Feudalism in the France of Colbert* (Berkeley and Los Angeles: University of California Press 1960), 9–14, for a brief summary of the institutional history. See also Jacques Captier, *Etudes historique et économique sur l'inscription maritime* (Paris: V. Giard et E. Brière 1907), and René Mémain, *Matelots et soldats des vaisseaux du roi, levées d'hommes du département de Rochefort (1661–1690)* (Poitiers: Hachette 1937).

2 See J.S. Bromley, ed., *The Manning of the Royal Navy: Selected Public Pamphlets, 1693–1873* (London: The Naval Records Society 1974), Appendix I, 330–6, for a 1740 translation of the first section (*titre premier*) of Book 8.

3 D. Neuville, *Etat sommaire des archives de la marine antérieurs à la révolution* (Paris, 1898; Krause Reprint 1977), 451–2.

4 Florian Cordon, *Les Invalides de la marine: une institution sociale de Louis XIV, son histoire de Colbert à nos jours* (Paris: Société d'éditions géographiques, maritimes et coloniales 1950), 23–4, 47–52.

5 T.J.A. Le Goff, "Offre et productivité de la main-d'oeuvre dans les armements français au XVIII⁰ siècle," *Histoire économie et société* 2 (1983): 457–73, is the best examination of the whole question of French manpower resources to date. I gratefully acknowledge Professor Le Goff's generosity in making his research concerning France's seafaring population in the eighteenth century available to me and criticizing earlier drafts of this chapter.

6 BSHM, no. 29, "Mémoire sur les classes fait au mois de Janvier 1750," 97–8; and Marine C⁴, 76, 189.

7 See Marc Perrichet, "Contribution à l'histoire sociale du XVIII⁰ siècle: l'administration des classes de la marine et ses archives dans les ports bretons," *Revue d'histoire économique et sociale* 37, no. 1 (1959): 97–8.

8 V.F. Brun, *Guerres maritimes de la France: Port de Toulon, ses armements, son administration depuis son origine jusqu'à nos jours*, 2 vols. (Paris: H. Plon 1861), 1:357–8.

9 BSHM, no. 29, "Mémoire sur les classes."

10 BN, Mss. frs.,11,341, ff. 1–46 [January 1760].

11 Marine C^4, 76, f. 189; and ibid., 78, f. 133.

12 Ibid., 78, ff. 134–5.

13 Ibid., 156, f. 133 [dated c. 1758–9 by T.J.A. LeGoff].

14 See ibid., 5, ff. 651–8.

15 BSHM, no. 29, ff. 66–7.

16 Ibid., ff.71–4.

17 Marine C^4, 80, ff. 136, 280.

18 Ibid., f. 133, "Mémoire sur les classes ... 1749."

19 Ibid., ff. 250–1.

20 BN, Mss. frs., no. 11,341, f. 617.

21 BSHM, no. 29, f. 75–7; also Marine A^1, 86, no. 22.

22 Rochefort E, 379, piè 263 et 294.

23 See Marine C^4, 36.

24 Marine B^2, 349, f. 10.

25 Rochefort 1E, 417, no. 324.

26 Marine C^4, 136, "Mémoire de Maureau," 1 May 1757.

27 Paragraph based on Marine B^1, 66, ff. 96–100; Marine B^3, 532, ff. 296–300; 542, ff. 172–82, 231–40, and 198–9; and Marine C^4, 136.

28 Marine B^3, 549, ff. 283–4.

29 Rochefort 1E, 420, no. 135.

30 Marine C^4, 136; also Perrichet, "L'Administration des classes," 93.

31 Marine C^2, 58, ff. 22–53v.

32 See Toulon 1L, 364, ff. 557–62v.

33 Marine G, 224; Marine C^2, 41; BN, Mss. frs., no. 14,286, ff. 46–64v; Marine C^4, 136; and Marine C^2, 58, ff. 223v–4.

34 BSHM, no. 29, f. 56; Marine C^4, 156; and Marine C^2, 58, ff. 184–5.

35 Marine C^2, 117, "Ordonnance du roi."

36 E.g., Toulon 1A^1, 205, f. 265v, 271; and ibid., 213, f. 238v.

37 E.g., Marine C^4, 133, summarized in Brun, *Guerres maritimes*, 1:354–62.

38 Marine D^2, 34, f. 235.

39 Toulon 1A^1, 212, ff. 180–0v.

40 Ibid., 209, f. 94; and 210, ff. 296v–97.

41 Perrichet, "L'Administration des classes," 100–9; also Rochefort 1E, 382, piè 397.

42 J.S. Bromley and A.N. Ryan, "Navies," *New Cambridge Modern History*, vol. 6, *The Rise of Great Britain and Russia, 1688–1715/25* (Cambridge: The University Press 1970), 822–3.

43 Cornell University, Maurepas Papers, anonymous "Mémoire," c. 1746; also Brun, *Guerres maritimes*, 1:354–62.

44 Marine B³, 340, f. 40.

45 Marine B², 355–5v; and Marine B³, 530, ff. 218–18v, 124.

46 Marine C⁴, 78, ff. 133–5.

47 Ibid. [inserted between ff. 132–3].

48 E.g., A.T. Mahan, *The Influence of Sea Power upon History, 1660–1783* (Boston: Little, Brown 1890), 318–19.

49 E.g., Jean Meyer, *L'Armement nantais dans la deuxième moitié du XVIIIe siècle* (Paris: SEVPEN 1969), 80, 89.

50 François Crouzet, "Economie et société (1715–1789)," in *Bordeaux au XVIIIe siècle*, éd. F.-G. Pariset (Bordeaux: Fédération historique du Sud-Ouest 1968), 295–7.

51 Patrick Crowhurst, "Bayonne Privateering, 1744–1763," in *Course et piraterie, Etudes présentés à la Commission International d'Histoire Maritime à l'occasion de son XVe colloque international*, San Francisco, août 1975 (Paris: CNRS 1975), 458.

52 Crouzet, "Economie et société (1715–1789)," 298; Henri Robert, "Les trafics coloniaux du port de la Rochelle au xviiie siècle," *Mémoires de la société des antiquaires de l'ouest*, 4eme série (1960) (Poitiers, 1960), 4:159; and R. Thomas-Lacroix, "La Guerre de course dans les ports des amirautés de Vannes et de Lorient (1744–1783)," *Mémoires de la société d'histoire et d'archéologie de Bretagne* 26 (1946): 167–8.

53 Pierre Dardel, *Commerce, industrie et navigation à Rouen et au Havre au XVIIIeme siècle* (Rouen: Société Libre d'émulation de la Seine Maritime 1966), 36.

54 Marine C⁴, 136, Magistrats et officiers de la Chambre de Commerce de Dunkerque à Massiac, 28 August 1758.

55 A. Corvisier, "Une enquête sur les inscrits maritimes au dix-huitième siècle: les pêcheurs havrais pendant la guerre de Sept Ans," *Revue des société savantes de Haute-Normandie*, no. 61 (1971): 42.

56 PRO, Adm 98/9, 222; A. Cabantous, "Gens de mer, guerre et prison: La captivité des gens de mer au xviiie siècle," *Revue d'histoire moderne et contemporaine* 28 (1981): 246–67, is disappointing because he failed to consult the very full and detailed records of the British Admiralty. He does, however, confirm the devastating effect in France of losses from capture.

57 PRO, Adm 98/6, 358.

58 Marine B⁴, 97, f. 165; cited in O. Anderson, "The Establishment of British Supremacy at Sea and the Exchange of Naval Prisoners of War, 1689–1783," *English Historical Review* 75 (1960): 77–89.

59 Toulon 1A¹, 210, ff. 302v–3.

60 PRO, Adm 98/6, 455; and Adm 98/7, 58–9.

61 See Adm 98/9, 318 and 338–9. The same number is also given in Affaires étrangères: Correspondance politique, Angleterre, no. 449, f. 386.

62 S.F. Gradish, *The Manning of the British Navy during the Seven Years' War* (London: Royal Historical Society 1980), 2, 212.

63 Rochefort 1E, 413, no. 317.

64 Several important studies on sailors' diets appear in J.J. Hémardinquer, ed., *Pour une histoire de l'alimentation,*Cahiers des Annales, 28 (Paris: A Colin 1970), Sec. D, "La Marine," 79–125. See also R.J. Bernard, "Peasant diet in Eighteenth-Century Gévaudan," in *European Diet from Pre-Industrial to Modern Times*, ed. E. and R. Forster (New York: Harper and Row 1975), 19–46; and Willem Frijhoff and Dominique Julia, "The Diet in Boarding Schools at the End of the Ancien Régime," in *Food and Drink in History: Selections from the Annales E.S.C.*, vol. 5, ed. R. Forster and O. Ranum (Baltimore and London: Johns Hopkins University Press 1979), 73–85.

65 Brest 1E, 503, f. 93.

66 Marine B², 349, ff. 158–8v.

67 Marine B⁴, 71, ff. 160, 164.

68 Louis-Guillaume de Parsçau du Plessis, "Journal d'une campagne au Canada à bord de la Sauvage (mars-juillet, 1756)," *Rapport de l'archiviste de la province de Québec pour 1928–29* (Québec: Rédempti Paradis 1929), 217, 225.

69 See J.-P. Goubert, *Malades et médecins en Bretagne, 1770–1790* (Rennes: Institut Amoricain de Recherches Historiques 1974), 336; J.-B. Fonssagrives, "Recherches historiques sur l'epidémie qui en 1758 ravagea l'escadre de l'amiral Dubois de la Motte et la ville de Brest," *Annales d'hygiene publique et le médecine legale*, série 2, 12 (1859): 243; and Amedée Lefevre, *Histoire de la service de santé de la marine militaire et des écoles de médecine navale en France depuis le règne de Louis XIV, jusqu' à nos jours, 1666–1867* (Paris: Baillière 1867), 162.

70 Marine B³, 534, ff. 221–5; and Marine B⁴, 76, ff. 93–3v.

71 Fonnsagrives, "Recherches historiques," 244.

72 Goubert, *Malades et médecins*, 327, 332–7.

73 Rochefort 2F¹, 539; see also Lefevre, *Histoire de la service de santé de la marine*, 157.

74 Brest 1A, 151, f. 38; and Marine B³, 542, ff. 157–8, 159–64v, 170–3.

75 Brest 1E, 511, ff. 13–14, 16, and 41.

76 Ibid., ff. 67, 188–9.

77 Ibid., ff. 325, 334.

78 Marine B², 361, ff. 127, 133.

79 Rochefort 1E, 416, no. 226.

80 Marine B¹, 67, ff. 138–8v.

81 Brest 1E, 512, ff. 150, 156.

82 Toulon 1A¹, 211, ff. 255–6.

83 Marine B², 366, f. 112v.

84 Brest 1E, 503, f. 66.

85 Captier, *Etude historique*, 154.

86 Toulon 1L, 365, ff. 638–40; and ibid., 1A¹, 211, f. 262.

87 Marine B³, 529, ff. 76, 215; and ibid., 530, f. 288v.

88 Toulon 1A¹, 209, ff. 129–9v, 227.

89 Rochefort 1E, 410, no. 541; and ibid., 383, 25 December 1756.

90 BN, Côte no. F 4756 (43); and Brest 1L, 46, ff. 123–3v.

91 Marine B³, 543, f. 156; and Marine A¹, 95, piè 31.

92 Toulon 1A¹, 213, ff. 238–8v; and ibid., 214, ff. 276–6v.

93 Marine B³, 531, ff. 69–72; and Brun, *Guerres maritimes*, 1:356.

94 Marine B², 359, ff. 109–10v, 260–0v; ibid., 361, f. 196; and Toulon 1A¹, 211, f. 256.

95 See Rochefort 1E, 378; and ibid., 382, piè 397; also Marine B³, 519, ff. 246–7; 542, ff. 94, 95, 216–17, 223; and 546, ff. 154–5.

96 See Brest 1L, 45, ff. 173–4; also Marine C⁴, 136.

97 Marine B³, 532, f. 280; and ibid., 542, ff. 100–5.

98 Toulon 1A¹, 209, f. 230v.

99 Ibid., 210, ff. 302v–3.

100 BN, Mss. frs., 11,340, ff. 100–1.

101 Brest 1E, 511, ff. 188–9, 249–51, and 350–1.

102 Toulon 1A¹, 211, ff. 261v–2v.

103 Marine C⁴, 137, "Mémoire sur les causes de la diminution du Nombre des Matelots en France et sur les moyens d'y rémedier," January 1760, is an exception to the general rule.

104 Brest 1E, 51, ff. 314–15.

105 BN, no. 11,340, f. 117.

106 Toulon 1A¹, 210, f. 300.

107 Marine B⁴, 74, f. 46v; and Toulon 1A¹, 214, f. 283v.

108 Marine B², 366, f. 9, 1760; and B³, 548, ff. 167–8.

109 Marine B³, 547, ff. 190–2.

110 Ibid., 550, ff. 108–11v.

111 Ibid., 547, ff. 148–9, 152–2v.

112 Rochefort 1E, 419, no. 452.

CHAPTER SIX

1 Cf. D. Baugh, *British Naval Administration in the Age of Walpole* (Princeton, NJ: Princeton University Press 1965), 264, table 16, "No. of Dockyard Workmen, 1711–1748."

2 John U. Nef, *Western Civilization since the Renaissance, Peace, War, Industry and the Arts* (1950; New York: Harper Torchbooks 1963), 84–8. See also Peter Mathias, *The First Industrial Nation: An Economic History of Britain, 1700–1914* (New York: Charles Scribner's Sons 1969), 121; and Jan de Vries, *The Economy of Europe in an Age of Crisis, 1600–1750* (Cambridge: Cambridge University Press 1976), 205.

3 Baugh, *British Naval Administration*, 263.

4 P.J. Levot, *Histoire de la ville et du port de Brest*, tome 2, *Le port depuis 1681* (Paris, 1864–6; Brionne, 1972), 96–100.

5 Brest 1E, 504, ff. 152–9.

6 Ibid., ff. 95, 109–10, 127–9, and 152–9.

7 Ibid., 505, ff. 172, 249.

8 Julian S. Corbett, *England in the Seven Years' War: A Study in Combined Strategy*, 2 vols. (London: Longmans, Green 1907), 1: 135.

9 M. Vovelle and M. Crook, "Du temps de la peste à l'ère des lumières," in *Histoire de Toulon*, dir. M. Agulhon (Toulouse: Privat 1980), 113–15.

10 Toulon 1A¹, 205, f. 55v.

11 V.F. Brun, *Guerres maritimes de la France: Port de Toulon, ses armements, son administration depuis son origine jusqu'à nos jours*, 2 vols. (Paris: H. Plon 1861), 2: 65–7, 276–7, 300, 319–20, 366, 373, 478, and 535–8.

12 René Mémain, *La Marine de guerre sous Louis XIV: le matériel, Rochefort, arsenal modèle de Colbert* (Paris: Hachette 1937), remains the classic study.

13 BN, n.a.f., no. 126.

14 Marine B², 337, f. 303.

15 BSHM, Ms. 195.

16 Rochefort 1E, 420, no. 218.

17 Marine B², 339, f. 243; also Rochefort, 1E, 379, no. 290.

18 A. Lefevre, *Histoire du service de santé de la marine militaire et des écoles de médecine navale en France depuis le règne de Louis XIV jusqu'à nos jours, 1666–1867* (Paris: Baillière 1867), 189–90.

19 P. Dardel, *Navires et marchandises dans les ports de Rouen et du Havre an XVIIIe siècle* (Paris: SEVPEN 1963), 237–8.

20 Marine B³, 547, f. 45; P.W. Bamford, *Forests and French Sea Power, 1660–1789* (Toronto: University of Toronto Press 1956), 60.

21 Marine D¹, 1, ff. 1–2, and 16–17.

22 Marine B³, 547, ff. 63–8v.

23 Ibid., f. 52; and Marine B², 364, ff. 252–2v.

24 Marine G, 49, f. 63, citing Marine B², ff. 364–5.

25 Marine B³, 550, f. 106.

26 E.g., Marine B³, 524, Dunkirk correspondence for 1755.

27 A. de Saint-Leger, *La Flandre maritime et Dunkerque sous la domination française, 1659–1789* (Paris-Lille: Ch. Tallandier 1900), 329–30.

28 E.g., Marine F², 67.

29 Y. Bezard, *Fonctionnaires maritimes et coloniaux sous Louis XIV, les Bégon* (Paris: Albin Michel 1932), 326–37, citing Marine B², 355, f. 251; 364, f. 348; and B³, 534, f. 11; also PRO, Adm 97/106.

30 Marine D¹, 1, f. 39.

31 D. Neuville, *Etat sommaire des archives de la marine antérieur à la révolution* (Paris, 1898; Krause Reprint 1977), 31n4.

32 Marine B³, 550, f. 106.

33 See Rochefort 1E, 410, nos. 624–99.

34 Marine B³, 550, ff. 236, 332 *bis.*

35 Ibid., 547, f. 240v.

36 Ibid., 527, f. 209.

37 Neuville, *Etat sommaire*, 118n2 and 665.

38 Marine B², 362, ff. 503–3v; Marine B³, 546, ff. 192–3v; also ibid., 548, ff. 391–2v.

39 Brun, *Guerres maritimes*, 1: 390, 431.

40 See Marine B², 369, f. 18v; ibid., 367, f. 412.

41 Marine A¹, 96, no. 12; also Brun, *Guerres maritimes*,1: 446–7.

42 Bamford, *Forests and French Sea Power*, 74–94, 97, 128.

43 Perrichet, "Plume ou epée," 155.

44 See Jacques Mathieu, *La Construction navale royale à Québec, 1739–1759* (Québec: Société historique de Quebec 1971).

45 See Richard Pares, *War and Trade in the West Indies, 1739–1763* (Oxford: Clarendon Press 1936), 269, 279–88.

46 E.g., Marine B², 339, f. 239; ibid., 347, ff. 340–1; and Rochefort 1E, 382, no. 153.

47 Marine B², 343, f. 231; Rochefort 1E, 405, pp. 141–4; ibid., 410 no. 408; and ibid., 412, no. 415.

48 Rochefort 1E 406, pp. 139–43.

49 Ibid., 413, no. 249.

50 Ibid., 410, no. 471.

51 F. de Veillechezé de la Mardière, *L'Evolution historique du contrôle de la marine* (Poitiers: Société françaises d'imprimerie et de librairies 1912), 78.

52 Rochefort 1E, 379, f. 213.

53 Marine B³, 534, ff. 295–300; and Rochefort 1E, 413, no. 63.

54 Rochefort 1E, 379, f. 229; Brest, 1E, 504, p. 143.

55 Marine B⁴, 63, ff. 166–7.

56 Brest 1E, 504, pp. 143, 265; also Marine B², 339, ff. 225–5v, 249v.

57 Marine B², 339, f. 264.

58 BN, n.a.f., no. 126, ff. 262–3; and Marine B³, 336, ff. 65v–75.

59 Marine B², 359, ff. 278–9v.

60 Naval Ordinance, 1689, Book 12, title 6, clauses 10 to 17.

61 BN, n.a.f., no. 126, ff. 258–76.

62 F. Dumon, *Une Carrière de commissaire de la marine au XVIIIe siècle, François de Magny, 1733–1800* (Lyon: Bosc Frères 1940), 88–9.

63 BN, n.a.f., no. 126, ff. 176–9.

64 BSHM, Ms. 195, ff. 5–6.

65 Toulon 1A¹, 205, ff. 61v–2.

66 Marine B², 347, ff. 334–5, 340–1; Rochefort 1E, 413, no. 249.

67 Marine G, 49, ff. 292–6.

68 Dumon, *Une Carrière*, 95.

69 BN, n.a.f., no. 126, ff. 271–2.

70 Marine D², 34, pp. 230–7.

71 Marine B³, 492, f. 279; and Rochefort 1E, 382, no. 10.

72 BN, n.a.f., no. 126, ff. 272–3.

73 Marine B³, 547, f. 240; ibid., and B², 366, f. 32.

74 E.g., Marine B³, 547, f. 174.

75 Marine D², 34, ff. 230–7.

76 BN, n.a.f., no. 126, f. 261.

77 Veillechezé de la Mardière, L'Evolution historique du contrôle, 70–1.

78 See J.F. Bosher, "Les trésoriers de la Marine et des colonies sous Louis XV: Rochefort et la Rochelle," Revue de la Saintonge et de l'Aunis 5 (1979): 95–108.

79 BN, n.a.f., no. 126, ff. 27–30.

80 Marine D³, 2, ff. 195–8v.

81 Ibid., 32, ff. 153–4v.

82 Ibid.

83 Cf. Baugh, British Naval Administration, 292.

84 Marine B², 363, ff. 217–18.

85 Marine B³, 547, ff. 278–9.

86 Ibid., 383.

87 Brest 1L, 46, ff. 77–7v.

88 Brest 1A, 153, f. 202v.

89 Rochefort 1E, 408, nos. 482 and 510.

90 Toulon 1A¹, 208, ff. 218v–19.

91 Ibid., f. 222v.

92 Marine B³, 543, f. 173.

93 Rochefort 1E, 379, f. 213; ibid., 382, no. 376; and ibid., 412, no. 417.

94 Marine B³, 336, ff. 66v–75, 207.

95 Ibid., 539, f. 139.

96 BN, Mss. frs., no. 11,338, ff. 114–16.

97 Rochefort 1E, 382, no. 297.

98 Rochefort 1L³, 46; and 1E, 417, no. 312.

99 Rochefort 1E, 386; ibid., 416, no. 5; ibid., 417, nos. 311 and 312.

100 Marine C², 58, ff. 223v–4.

101 Rochefort 1E, 420, no. 65 bis.

102 Marine B², 366, ff. 46, 55v, 80, and 89v; ibid., B³, 548, f. 263; and ibid., B¹, 67, ff. 128–9v.

CHAPTER SEVEN

1 A. Zysberg, "Galley Rowers in the Mid-Eighteenth Century," in Deviants and the Abandoned in French Society: Selections from the Annales E.S.C., vol. 4., ed. R. Forster and O. Ranum (Baltimore: Johns Hopkins University Press 1978), 83–110.

2 Marine B⁶, 134, ff. 394–404; Toulon 1A¹, 199, f. 18v.

3 Determined from monthly statements in Toulon 1A¹, vols. 199–211. These statements no longer appear after April 1759.

4 Toulon 1A¹, 211, ff. 152, 157, and 217.

5 V.F. Brun, *Guerres maritimes de la France: Port de Toulon, ses armements, son administration depuis son origine jusqu' à nos jours*, 2 vols. (Paris: H. Plon 1861), 1: 447.

6 Marine B², 337, ff. 244–4v; Brest 1E, 504, ff. 58–62.

7 Brest 1E, 504, ff. 94. 118.

8 Ibid., 508, f. 41.

9 Ibid., ff. 49, 79.

10 Ibid., "Chiourmes," 1758–65.

11 Marine B⁶, 134, ff. 399–404.

12 See note 10.

13 Toulon 1A¹, 118, f. 100; and Brest 1E, 508, f. 141.

14 Brest 1E, 504, f. 50; ibid., 512, f. 56.

15 Marine B², 337, ff. 109–9v.

16 Marine B⁶, 135, ff. 158–9; also Brest 1E, 511, ff. 207–8; and ibid., 512, f. 56.

17 Brest 1E, 504, ff. 58–62.

18 P.J. Levot, *Histoire de la ville et port de Brest, le port depuis 1681*, tome 2 (Paris, 1864–6; Brionne, 1972), 2: 105.

19 E.g., Brest 1L, 45, ff. 166v, 217.

20 Brest 1E, 508, f. 41.

21 Marine B³, 548, ff. 136–7.

22 Marine B², 349, ff. 142–2v, 172–2v.

23 Brest 1E, 511, f. 126.

24 Ibid., f. 293; and Marine B², 359, f. 178v.

25 Marine B², 364, f. 14v; and Marine B³, 547, f. 195.

26 Ibid., f. 212–2v.

27 Ibid., f. 234–4v.

28 Rochefort 1E, 382, no. 42; also Marine G, 48, 25–7.

29 Rochefort 1E, 414, no. 557.

30 Ibid., 417, 15 April 1760.

31 Ibid., 416, no. 158.

32 Ibid., 417, 21 June 1760.

33 Ibid., 13 June 1760.

34 Ibid., 2 August 1760.

35 Rochefort 1E, 418, no. 63.

36 Ibid., 417, 28 June 1760.

37 See Rochefort 2F¹, 539, "matricule mortuaire," 1748–62.

38 Rochefort 1E, 418, nos. 228, 271, 326, and 345.

39 Marine B², 367, f. 226v; and Rochefort 1E, 419, nos. 388 and 396.

40 Rochefort 1E, 419, no. 578.

41 Marine B³, 530, ff. 26v, 57, 77.

42 Toulon 1A¹, 210, ff. 160v–1v, 310v.

43 Ibid., ff. 82, 84–4v; and ibid., 211, f. 44.

44 Marine B², 544, ff. 183–5.

45 Ibid., ff. 59–60.

46 Marine B², 351, f. 148; ibid., 366, f. 35; Toulon 1A¹, 214, f. 285; and Marine B³, 551, ff. 176–6v.

47 Marine B³, 551, ff. 144–50v.

48 Ibid., ff. 189–90v.

49 Toulon 1A¹, 214, ff. 39v–40, 92; and Marine G, 48, ff. 18–19.

50 E.g., Rochefort 1E, 378, f. 173; also Marine B³, 545, ff. 263–7.

51 Rochefort 1E, 378, 28 February 1750.

52 Marine G, 48, ff. 18–19.

53 Marine B³, 343, f. 391.

54 E.g., Toulon 1A¹, 211, ff. 138, 140.

55 Marine B³, 545, ff. 311–13.

56 Ibid., 543, f. 152; also ibid., 545, ff. 263–7.

57 Rochefort 1E, 379, no. 480.

58 Toulon 1A¹, 210, ff. 191v–2.

59 Ibid., 213, f. 152.

60 Marine G, 47, ff. 480–2.

61 Ibid., 48, ff. 18–19.

62 Marine B², 243, f. 216v.

63 Ibid., 347, f. 542.

64 Marine B³, 530, ff. 26v, 57, 77; and ibid., 532, f. 319.

65 Ibid., 542, ff. 261–1v.

66 Naval Ordinance (1689), Book 12, title 9, clause 2.

67 Marine B³, 545, ff. 311–13.

68 Rochefort 1E, 379, no. 479; and Toulon 1A¹, 210, f. 7v.

69 Brest 1L, 45ff. 138–8v.

70 Marine D², 34, f. 233.

71 Cf. D. Baugh, *British Naval Administration in the Age of Walpole* (Princeton, NJ: Princeton University Press 1965), 311–12.

72 Rochefort 1E, 405, ff. 147–8.

73 Cited in Dumon, *Une Carrière de commissaire de la marine au XVIIIe siècle, François de Magny, 1733–1800* (Lyon: Bosc Frères 1940), 143–4.

74 Marine B³, 543, ff. 13–14.

75 Marine D², 34, ff. 178–85; Marine B³, 545, ff. 26–7v.

76 Toulon 1A¹, 205, ff. 24–4v.

77 Rochefort 1E, 382, no. 197.

78 Toulon 1A¹, 214, ff. 279–80.

79 Rochefort 1E, 302, no. 171; and Marine B², 347, f. 245.

80 Toulon 1A¹, 205, f. 29; and ibid., 210, ff. 8v, 20v, 64, 71.

81 Marine B², 341, f. 222; and Brest 1E, 504, ff. 109–10.

82 Marine B², 341, f. 220.

83 Rochefort 1E, 410, nos. 392 and 406.

84 Marine B², 349, ff. 253–3v.

85 Brest 1E, 511, f. 150.

86 Rochefort 1E, 409, nos. 182 and 279.

87 Ibid., no. 344; and René-Louis de Voyer de Paulmy, marquis d'Argenson, *Journal et mémoires du Marquis d'Argenson*, éd. E.J.B. Rathery, 9 vols. (Paris: J. Renouard 1859–67), 9: 297.

88 Marine G, 47, ff. 480–2.

89 Marine B³, 545, ff. 311–13.

90 Brest 1L, 45, ff. 179–80; ibid., 46, ff. 47v–8.

91 Marine B³, 543, ff. 13–14.

92 Ibid., 547, f. 138.

93 Rochefort 1E, 417, no. 488; and Marine B³, 548, ff. 274–7.

94 Baugh, *British Naval Administration*, 327.

95 John Ehrman, *The Navy in the War of William III, 1689–1697: Its State and Direction* (Cambridge: The University Press 1953), 91, 328, 475, 489, cited in Baugh, *British Naval Administration*, 327n272.

96 Brest 1E, 503, f. 89.

97 Ibid., ff. 100, 152v.

98 Marine B³, 503, f. 356; and Rochefort 1E, 379, no. 480.

99 Marine B³, 492, ff. 231–3.

100 Toulon 1A¹, 209, f. 57v.

101 Brest 1E, 511, f. 179.

102 Marine B³, 538, ff. 262v.

103 Ibid., f. 277.

104 Rochefort 1E, 414, no. 434.

105 Ibid., no. 444.

106 Rochefort 1E, 414, nos. 457, 474, and 487.

107 Quoted in G. Lacour-Gayet, *La Marine militaire de la France sous le règne de Louis XV* (Paris: Honoré Champion 1902), 390.

108 Marine B², 349, ff. 172–2v.

109 Rochefort 1E, 408, 16 September 1755.

110 E.g., P.W. Bamford, *Forests and French Sea Power 1660–1789* (Toronto: University of Toronto Press 1956), 61–7; P.M. Kennedy, *The Rise and Fall of British Naval Mastery* (London: Macmillan 1983), 100–1.

111 Baugh, *British Naval Administration*, 332.

112 E.g., Rochefort 1E, 412, no. 482.

113 Marine B³, 523, ff. 144–4v.

114 Baugh, *British Naval Administration*, 335.

115 E.g., Rochefort 1E, 416, no. 158.

116 Brest 1E, 504, f. 221.

CHAPTER EIGHT

1 See James Pritchard, "From Shipwright to Naval Constructor: The Profession-alization of Eighteenth-Century French Naval Shipbuilders," *Technology and Culture* 28, no. 1 (January 1987).

2 P.W. Bamford, *Forests and French Sea Power, 1660–1789* (Toronto: University of Toronto Press 1956), 12n10.

3 Marine B⁵, 3 May 1750.

4 Ibid., 11.

5 Marine B¹, 66, ff. 33–4.

6 J. Mathieu, *La Construction naval royale à Québec, 1739–1759* (Québec: Société historique de Québec 1971), 43, 102.

7 Marine B⁵, 3; slightly different figures are given in G. Lacour-Gayet, *La Marine militaire de la France sous le règne de Louis XV* (Paris: Honoré Champion 1902), 476.

8 Mouffle d'Angerville, *Vie privée de Louis XV, ou principaux événements, particularités et anecdotes de son règne*, 4 vols. (London: J.P. Lyton 1781), 4: 15, is the unacknowledged source used by A.T. Mahan, *The Influence of Sea Power upon History, 1660–1783* (Boston: Little, Brown 1890), 76; Lacour-Gayet, *La Marine militaire*, 391, and Alexandre Lambert de Sainte-Croix, *Essai sur l'administration de la marine de France* (Paris: C. Lévy 1892), 91.

9 Marine B⁵, 3, August 1755.

10 Marine G, 49, f. 53.

11 F.L. Robertson, *The Evolution of Naval Armament* (London: Constable 1921), 43–4; Brian Lavery, *The Ship of the Line*, vol. 1, *The Development of the Battlefleet 1650–1850* (Annapolis, MD: Naval Institute Press 1984), 64–95.

12 A. Baugh, *British Naval Administration in the Age of Walpole* (Princeton, NJ: Princeton University Press 1965), 250.

13 BN, n.a.f., no. 126, f. 132.

14 R. Mémain, *La Marine de guerre sous Louis XIV: Le materiél, Rochefort, arsenal modèle de Colbert* (Paris: Hachette 1937), 723.

15 Marine B², 337, f. 251.

16 Cornell University, Olin Library, Maurepas Papers, "Mémoire sur l'estat actuel de la marine, et sur les arrangements à prendre pour le service de l'annee 1745," n.d.

17 C.-P. d'Albert, duc de Luynes, *Mémoires du duc de Luynes sur la cour de Louis XV, 1735–1758*, 17 vols., éd. L.E. Dussieux et E. Soolie (Paris, 1860–5), 9: 431.

18 BSHM, no. 222, f. 9.

19 Marine B⁴, 63, f. 204.

20 Marine B¹, 66, f. 117.

21 Marine B³, 527, ff. 116–17; Marine B², 353, f. 4.

22 V.F. Brun, *Guerres maritimes de la France: Port de Toulon, ses armements, son administration depuis son origine jusqu'à nos jours*, 2 vols. (Paris: H. Plon 1861), 1: 423–4.

23 BN, n.a.f., no. 126, ff. 175–7; also Marine B², 341, f. 299v.

24 Richard Pares, *War and Trade in the West Indies, 1739–1763* (Oxford: Clarendon Press 1936), 311–25.

25 Rochefort 1E, 406, no. 85.

26 Brun, *Guerres maritimes*, 1: 349–50.

27 Mathieu, *La Construction navale*, 67.

28 Marine B², 339, f. 190v.

29 Toulon 1A¹, 210, ff. 103v–4.

30 Cf. Mémain, *La Marine de guerre*, 816.

31 Jean Boudriot, *Le Vaisseau de 74 canons: traité pratique d'art naval*, 4 vols. (Grenoble: Editions des Quatres Seigneurs 1973–7), vol. 1, *Construction du vaisseau*. See also Lavery, *Ship of the Line*, 1: 81.

32 Marine B¹, 66, f. 37.

33 Marine B⁴, 66, f. 3.

34 Marine B⁵, 3, November 1754.

35 Marine B⁴, 68, f. 17.

36 O. Troude, *Batailles navales de France*, 4 vols. (Paris: Challamel 1867–8), 1: 330, 371, 414.

37 Marine B³, 552, f. 474.

38 Brest, 1E, 511, ff. 104–5.

39 Marine B⁵, 3, May 1750; Marine B¹, 66, f. 39.

40 Marine B³, 551, ff. 524–6; and Brest 1E, 512, f. 119v.

41 Rochefort 1E, 412, no. 391.

42 Robertson, *Evolution of Naval Armament*, 44; Lavery, *Ship of the Line*, 1: 103.

43 Marine B¹, 66, ff. 33–4. Lacour-Gayet, *La Marine militaire*, 212, incorrectly claims five first-rates in the fleet in 1754.

44 Brest 1L, 45, f. 20; ibid., 1E, 511, f. 116.

45 Marine B¹, 66, f. 111; Rochefort 1E, 384; and ibid., 420, no. 88.

46 Marine B³, 536, ff. 162–3.

47 Toulon 1A¹, 208, f. 141; ibid., 211, ff. 123v–4.

48 Baugh, *British Naval Administration*, 249.

49 Rochefort 1E, 409, no. 242; ibid., 410; nos. 471 and 529.

50 Marine B², 371, ff. 58–60.

51 Marine B⁴, 68, f. 5.

52 Lacour-Gayet, *La Marine militaire*, 482.

53 E.g., see Colonies, F¹A, 42.

54 Brest 1A, 151, f. 3v.

55 Marine B², 352, f. 43v.

56 Ibid., 334, f. 574; and Marine B¹, 66, f. 37.

57 See Jean Boudriot, "L'Evolution de la frégate dans la marine française 1660–1850," in *Five Hundred Years of Nautical Science, 1400–1900*, ed. D. Howse (Greenwich: National Maritime Museum 1981), 229–40; also Brun, *Guerres maritimes*, 1: 348.

58 Marine B², 343, f. 163.

59 James Henderson, *The Frigates: An Account of the Lesser Warships of the Wars from 1793–1815* (London: Adlard Coles 1970), 17.

60 Robert Gardiner, "Frigate Design in the 18th Century," *Warship: A Quarterly Journal of Warship History*, nos. 9, 10, and 12 (1979): 2–12, 80–92, and 269–77.

61 Marine B², 339, ff. 253–3v.

62 Toulon 1A¹, 209, f. 104v; ibid., 210, f. 25.

63 Mathieu, *La Construction navale*, 68n5, notes the presence in the National Maritime Museum, Greenwich, of English draughts of *L'Abenaquaise*, built at Quebec and captured in 1758.

64 Marine B³, 533, 5 April 1756; and Lacour-Gayet, *La Marine militaire*, 480–1.

65 Toulon 1A¹, 205, f. 9v; and ibid., 207, f. 67.

66 Marine B², 352, ff. 14, 18; and ibid., 353, f. 7.

67 Brun, *Guerres maritimes*, 1: 348, 362.

68 Toulon 1A¹, 214, ff. 14–15.

69 E.g., Marine B², 366, f. 222; see Toulon 1A¹, 118, ff. 24, 86–7.

70 BN, Mss. frs., 14,286, ff. 66–75.

71 Marine D¹, 1, ff. 16–17, 39, and 175.

72 See Lacour-Gayet, *La Marine militaire*; Marine D¹, 1, ff. 16–17.

73 Marine B¹, 67, f. 112.

74 Marine D¹, ff. 134 b–e.

75 R.C. Anderson, ed. and trans., "The Reminiscences of Lieutenant Malmskold," *The Naval Miscellany*, vol. 4, ed. Christopher Lloyd (London: The Naval Records Society 1952), 262.

76 Marine B⁵, 3, 16 April 1748; also Lacour-Gayet, *La Marine militaire*, 208–9; and Marine B⁵, 3, May 1750.

77 P.L.R. Higonnet, "The Origins of the Seven Years' War," *Journal of Modern History* 40, no. 1 (1968): 81.

78 Troude, *Batailles navales*, 1: 330, 340, 347, 371, 414.

79 Marine B³, 552, f. 474; and ibid., 551, f. 226.

80 Marine B⁵, 3, 16 April 1748; also Marine B¹, 65, f. 129.

81 Brest 1E, 503, ff. 39, 56–9, 78; this volume is filled with letters calling attention to the lack of medicines, nails, coal, powder, cannon, lead, etc.

82 Marine B⁵, 3, May 1750.

83 Lacour-Gayet, *La Marine militaire*, 209.

84 Marine B⁵, 3, no. 2; Marine B⁴, 63, f. 204; Marine B², 339, f. 160.

85 Marine B⁵, 11, April 1751; Marine B¹, 66, ff. 33–4.

86 La Galissonière's arguments can be found in at least two places. An early

version, written while in New France, is in Colonies, C11A, 91, ff. 116–23; and the final version of December 1750, translated as "Memoir on the French Colonies in North America," is printed in E.B. O'Callaghan, ed., *Documents Relative to the Colonial History of the State of New York* (Albany: Weed, Parsons Printers 1853–87), 10: 220–32.

87 See Bamford, *Forests and French Sea Power*, 69n83.

88 Rochefort 1E, 379, no. 49.

89 Marine B², 343, f. 198v.

90 Marine B², 343, ff. 232, 236.

91 Ibid., ff. 237–7v and 249.

92 Ibid., 345, f. 268.

93 Toulon 1A¹, 206, f. 33.

94 Ibid., ff. 40v, 49v.

95 Ibid., f. 78v.

96 Ibid., ff. 30, 37; and ibid., 209, ff. 69, 87.

97 Marine B⁵, 3, November 1754.

98 Ibid., August 1755.

99 Toulon 1A¹, 207, ff. 38, 46–9.

100 Marine E, 208, no. 111.

101 Marine B⁴, 68, f. 17; also Toulon 1A¹, 207, f. 62.

102 Alfred Doneaud du Plan, *La Marine française au XVIIIe siècle au point de vue de l'administration et des progrès scientifiques,"* extrait de *Revue maritime et coloniale* (November 1867), 21.

103 Marine B², 355, f. 375.

104 Marine B⁴, 68, f. 17.

105 Rochefort 1E, 413, no. 70.

106 Toulon 1A¹, 213, f. lv.

107 Ibid., ff. 65v–6v.

108 Marine B², 361, f. 372.

109 Marine B¹, 1, ff. 16–17 and 39.

110 Ibid., ff. 1–2.

111 Ibid., f. 175; Marine B⁴, 94, f. 53.

112 Y. Durand, éd., "Mémoires de Jean-Joseph de Laborde fermier-général et banquier de la cour," *Annuaire-Bulletin de la Société de l'histoire de France, 1968–69* (Paris, 1971), 151.

113 Toulon 1A¹, 214, ff. 39v–40, 92.

114 Rochefort 1E, 420, no. 88.

CHAPTER NINE

1 Mouffle d'Angerville, *Vie privée de Louis XV ou principaux événements, particularités et anecdotes de son règne*, 4 vols. (London: J.P. Lyton 1781), 4: 15; and Alexandre Lambert de Sainte-Croix, *Essai sur l'administration de la marine de France* (Paris: C. Lévy 1892), 91.

2 Marine B⁴, 78, f. 190v.

3 Henri Legohérel, *Les Trésoriers-généraux de la marine, 1517–1788* (Paris: Editions Cujas 1965), 184.

4 See Marine B⁴, 63, ff. 175–5v; and Marine B⁵, 3, "Mémoir sur l'état de la marine," May 1750; Rochefort 4E, 7, "Sommaire des dépenses projettées," 24 December 1751; and Rochefort 1E, 410, no. 392.

5 Marine B³, 539, ff. 207–7v.

6 Marine B⁴, 78, f. 198; Marine B³, 549, ff. 52–3v.

7 L.J. Williams, "A Carmarthenshire Ironmaster and the Seven Years' War," *Business History* 2 (1959): 33.

8 Howard C. Tomlinson, "Wealden Gunfounding: An Analysis of its Demise in the Eighteenth Century," *Economic History Review*, 2nd ser. 29, no. 3 (August 1976): 397.

9 Marine B⁴, 78, f. 198. The rate of exchange of one pound sterling to 23.19 livres *tournois* is based on John J. McCusker, *Money and Exchange in Europe and America, 1660–1775* (Chapel Hill, NC: University of North Carolina Press 1978), 96–7. The French *livre* weight of 489.5 grams was approximately 8 per cent heavier than the English pound.

10 See René Mémain, *La Marine de guerre sous Louis XIV: le materiél, Rochefort, arsenal modèle de Colbert* (Paris: Hachette 1937), 809–62.

11 G. Bussière, "Henri Bertin et sa famille, la production nobiliaire du ministre, ses ancêtres, son intendance de Lyon, ses ministères," *Bulletin de la société historique et archéologique du Périgord* 33 (1906): 225.

12 Marine B², 334, ff. 283v, 293–3v, 623; and ibid., 335, f. 132.

13 Ibid., 336, f. 100 *bis*; Toulon 1A¹, 198, f. 38v.

14 Marine B², 337, f. 491; and ibid., 339, f. 68.

15 Ibid., 337, ff. 193–3v, 535–5v; and ibid., 339, f. 7.

16 Ibid., f. 143; ibid., 341, f. 33.

17 Ibid., 337, f. 245.

18 Ibid., ff. 532, 572.

19 Marine B⁴, 63, ff. 195–7.

20 Marine B², 339, ff. 196–6v.

21 Ibid., 337, f. 329v.

22 Marine B⁴, 63, f. 175.

23 Cornell University, Maurepas Papers, "Mémoire sur l'éstat actuel de la marine et sur les arrangements à prendre pour le service de 1747," f. 3; and T.J.A. LeGoff, "Artillery at Louisbourg," Manuscript Report No. 50, National and Historic Parks Branch [Ottawa, 1967], 84–5; also Rochefort, 1E, 378, no. 497.

24 Rochefort 1E, 408, no 515.

25 Marine B², 339, ff. 196–9v.

26 Marine B⁴, 63, f. 175; also Marine B⁵, 3 May 1750.

27 Marine D⁴, 8, f. 118.

28 Marine B⁴, 63, f. 175v.

29 See Pierre Léon, "La reponse de l'industrie," in F. Braudel et E. Labrousse, *Histoire économique et social de la France*, tome 2, *Des derniers temps de l'âge seigneurial aux préludes de l'âge industriel, 1660–1789* (Paris: PUF 1970), 231–7; and B. Gille, *Les Origines de la grande industrie métallurgique en France* (Paris: Editions Domat Montchrestien 1947), 33–54.

30 Marine B³, 521, ff. 119–20.

31 E.g., Marine B², 339, f. 383.

32 Ibid., f. 221.

33 Ibid., ff. 212, 246–6v, 233–3v, 485, and 490.

34 Ibid., 341, f. 559.

35 See E.M.Lloyd, *Vauban, Montalembert, Carnot: Engineering Studies* (London: Chapman and Hall 1887), 98–154; and the more important essay by R. Gaudin, "Marc-René, Marquis de Montalembert," *Bulletin et mémoires de la Société Archéologique et Historique de la Charente, 1938* (Angoulême, 1939), 49–127.

36 Marine B², 339, ff. 515, 523; and ibid., 341, ff. 308–8v.

37 Ibid., 340, ff. 22, 167v, 288.

38 AN, série K, 909, no. 48, *Extrait de divers mémoires imprimés sur les nouvelles forges établies en Angoumois par le Marquis de Montalembert & sur les fabrications d'artillerie qu'il y a fait executer pour la marine depuis l'année 1750* (Paris, 1768).

39 Marine B², 339, ff. 264–3v; and ibid., 345, ff. 359–9v.

40 Ibid., 203.

41 Rochefort 1E, 378, 24 March 1750.

42 Ibid., 382, no. 332.

43 Marine B², 349, f. 196.

44 Marine D⁴, 9, contract, 30 September 1754.

45 Marine B², 349, ff. 213–3v.

46 Rochefort 1E, 408, no. 268.

47 Brest 1E, 505, f. 378.

48 Marine B², 343, ff. 219, 464.

49 Rochefort 1E, 381, 22 December 1753.

50 Marine B², 347, f. 355; also Rochefort 1E, 406, 31 December 1754.

51 Marine B², 349, ff. 262, 277.

52 Ibid., 347, f. 174.

53 AN, K. 909, no. 848, *Extrait des divers mémoires.*

54 Marine B², 343, ff. 368, 383.

55 Ibid., 345, ff. 201, 259–9v.

56 Ibid., 341, f. 280v.

57 Rochefort 1E, 410, no. 513.

58 Marine B³, 521, f. 111.

59 Marine B², 345, ff. 259–9v; also Marine B⁴, 78, f. 189v.

60 BN, n.a.f., no. 126, ff. 226–33; also Rochefort 1E, 406, no. 74.

61 Marchant de la Houlière; "Report to the French Government on British methods of smelting iron ore with coke and casting naval cannon in the year 1775," translated with an introduction and notes, by W.H. Chaloner, *Edgar Allen News* 27 (December 1948–January 1949): 194–5, 213–15; cited in H.R. Schubert, *History of the British Iron and Steel Industry from c. 450 B.C. to A.D. 1775* (London: Routledge and Kegan Paul 1955), 270.

62 Rochefort 1E, 413, no. 68; and ibid., 415, no. 650.

63 M.A. Basset, "Essais sur l'historique des fabrications d'armement en France jusqu'au milieu du xviiie siècle," *Memorial de l'Artillerie française*, tome 14, 4e fascicule de 1935 (Paris, 1935), 1067; also Schubert, *British Iron and Steel Industry*, 269–70.

64 G. Monge, *Description de l'art de fabriquer les canons faite en execution de l'arrêt du Comité de Salut publique, du 18 pluviose de l'an 2 de la république française, une et indivisible* (Paris: Comité de salut public, an II), 87 ff.

65 Marine D³, 34, 5 May 1742; and Marine B², 341, f. 269.

66 Marine B², 343, ff. 403–3v; ibid., 345, f. 391.

67 Ibid., 345, ff. 63, 408–8v; and Marine B⁴, 78, ff. 181–85v.

68 Argenson, *Journal et mémoires*, 9: 156; also D.K. Van Kley, *The Damiens Affaire and the Unravelling of the Ancien Régime, 1750–1770* (Princeton, NJ: Princeton University Press 1984), 78–9, 91.

69 AN, série K, 909, no. 48; and B. Gille, *Les Origines de la grande industrie*, 180.

70 Marine B³, f. 111.

71 Rochefort 1E, 406, no. 66.

72 Marine B², 347, f. 331; ibid., 349, f. 450.

73 Ibid., 349, f. 500.

74 Marine B⁴, 78, ff. 191, 197.

75 Williams, "A Carmarthenshire Ironmaster," 32.

76 Marine B³, 527, ff. 25, 31–2; ibid., 530, ff. 13, 31.

77 Ibid., 530, f. 80; ibid., 529, ff. 23–3v.

78 Marine B⁴, 78, f. 150.

79 Marine B³, 529, ff. 391–1v.

80 Toulon 1A¹, 210, ff. 48, 74.

81 Ibid., 209, f. 46v; Marine B³, 536, f. 244.

82 Toulon 1A¹, 210, f. 112v; Marine B³, 544, f. 207.

83 Rochefort 1E, 408, no. 481; ibid., 409, no. 83, 306.

84 Ibid., 410, no. 513.

85 Ibid., no. 569.

86 Ibid., 412, no. 474.

87 Marine B⁴, 74, f. 106.

88 Rochefort 1E, 413, no. 68.

89 Ibid., 158, 161.

90 Brest 1E, 511, f. 118.

91 Marine B³, 539, f. 149.

92 Brest 1E, 511, ff. 137, 212.

93 Marine B², 355, ff. 331–8.

94 Ibid., 356, f. 454; ibid., 358, ff. 519–9v; and ibid., 355, f. 339.

95 Rochefort 1E, 415, no. 434.

96 Ibid., 413, no. 274.

97 Ibid., 417, several letters.

98 P.-M. Jean Conturie, *Histoire de la fonderie nationale de Ruelle, 1750–1940, et des anciennes fonderies de canons de fer de la marine,* 2 vols. (Paris: Imprimerie nationale 1951), 1: 134–5.

99 Marine B³, 548, f. 281; Marine B², 369, f. 197.

100 Brest 1E, 512, ff. 3, 16, 18, 29, and 63.

101 Marine B², 335, f. 297; ibid., 337, ff. 448–9.

102 Ibid., 341, f. 404.

103 Ibid., ff. 436, 470.

104 Michel L'Héritier, *L'Intendant Tourny (1695–1760)* (Paris: Felix Alcan 1920), 439n4; also Marine B², 345, ff. 381–1v.

105 Marine B², 343, ff. 436–6v; ibid., 345, f. 443; and Marine B³, 519, ff. 241–2v; see also Marine B², 349, f. 196; and ibid., 347, ff. 582–3.

106 Marine B², 341, f. 404.

107 Ibid., 345, f. 443.

108 Marine D³, 32, "Des fers pour la marine," 28 March 1760.

109 L'Héritier, *Tourny,* 381–4.

110 Marine B², 337, ff. 611–12; ibid., 349, f. 433.

111 Gaudin, "Marc-René, marquis de Montalembert," 57, 60.

112 Marine B², 335, ff. 329–9v.

113 Ibid., ff. 373–3v; ibid., 337, ff. 474, 517, 536; and ibid., 339, f. 176.

114 Ibid., 341, f. 208.

115 Gille, *Les Origines de la grande industrie,* 101–2.

CHAPTER TEN

1 For definition see M. Marion, *Dictionnaire des institutions de la France aux XVIIe et XVIIIe siècles* (Paris: A. Picard 1972), 477; also J.F. Bosher, *French Finances 1770–1795: From Business to Bureaucracy* (Cambridge: The University Press 1970), 121.

2 Brest 1E, 504, ff. 152–9.

3 Marine B⁵, 3, 16 April 1748.

4 Marine D³, 2, ff. 198–200.

5 P.W. Bamford, *Forests and French Sea Power, 1660–1789* (Toronto: University of Toronto Press 1956).

6 Marine B³, 519, ff. 338–61, several letters (see esp. ff. 342–9v).

7 Marine B², 349, f. 350.

8 Ibid., ff. 398, 420.

9 See Bamford, *Forests and French Sea Power,* 95–104.

10 Marine B², 344, ff. 381–3, 388, 396, 414, 424–5, and 430–0v.

11 Toulon 1A¹, 214, ff. 59–60, 79.

12 AN, V⁷, 344, no. 257, "titres et pièces de créances"; also ibid., 342, no. 47.

13 Toulon 1A¹, 213, ff. 81–2.

14 Marine D³, 2, ff. 191v–2v.

15 Toulon 1A¹, 211, ff. 125v–6.

16 Ibid., f. 191v; also Rochefort 1E, 417, 7 January 1760.

17 Marine D³, 2, ff. 194–5.

18 Bamford, *Forests and French Sea Power*, 60, discusses shipping timber from the entrepôts to the western arsenals.

19 Marine B², 349, ff. 305, 321, 324.

20 BN, Mss. frs., 11,337, ff. 97, 99–101, 174–4v.

21 Rochefort 1E, 382, no. 276; and ibid., 417, Conseil to Berryer, 8 May 1760.

22 Marine D², 3, ff. 196–8v.

23 Rochefort 1E, 379, no. 495.

24 Marine B², 345, ff. 173, 345.

25 Ibid., 341, f. 240.

26 Ibid., 263; and Rochefort 1E, 379, no. 526.

27 Rochefort 1E, 405, ff. 6–7, 31.

28 E.g., Marine D³, 2, ff. 189–91v.

29 Bamford, *Forests and French Sea Power*, 113–14, contains a full discussion of these attempts and failures.

30 Marine B², 337, f. 204; and rochefort 1E, 379, no. 377.

31 J. Pritchard, "Fir Trees, Financiers, and the French Navy during the 1750s" (forthcoming).

32 Marine B³, 509, f. 518; and Rochefort 1E, 405, f. 60.

33 See Rochefort 5E², 19, contract of Louis-Michel Petel of Paris to deliver timber to Brest and Rochefort for six years from 1763. According to Bamford, *Forests and French Sea Power*, 34n. Petel and Company was capitalized at 640,000 livres in 32 shares. Petel was a *prêt-nom* produced by the marquis de Puységur. Many former timber contractors from northern France and several financiers were also involved.

34 M.W. Flinn, *Men of Iron: The Crowleys in the Early Iron Industry* (Edinburgh: University Press 1962), 147.

35 Brest 1E, 505, ff. 15–22; and Marine B², 341, ff. 410–0v; ibid., 338, f. 473; and ibid., 340, f. 337.

36 Marine B³, 31, ff. 177–88.

37 Marine B², 357, ff. 170–0v.

38 Ibid., 334, ff. 592–2v; Marine B⁴, 63, ff. 176–6v; Marine B², 339, f. 428; ibid., 355, f. 345v; see also "Ancres" in *Encyclopédie ou dictionnaire raisonné des sciences des arts et des métiers*, vol. 1 (Paris: Briasson 1755), 442–6; and volume 7, "Planches," for thirteen plates illustrating operations at the naval anchor forges at Cosne; and Marine B³, 31, f. 181.

39 B. Gille, *Les origines de la grande industrie métallurgique en France* (Paris: Editions Domat Montchrestien 1947), 52–4.

40 Marine D³, 31, ff. 177–88; also Bamford, *Forests and French Sea Power*, 35; and his "Entrepreneurship in Seventeenth and Eighteenth Century France: Some General Conditions and a Case Study," *Explorations in Entrepreneurial History* 9, no. 4 (April 1957): 204–13; G. Richard, *Noblesse d'affaires au XVIIIe siècle* (Paris: Armand Colin 1974), 147.

41 M. Prèvost et R. D'Amat, dir., *Dictionnaire de biographie française* (Paris: Letouzey et Ané 1948), 4:990; Gille, *Les origines de la grande industrie*, 131; and Richard, *Noblesse d'affaires*, 149.

42 H. Lüthy, *La Banque protestant en France de la Révocation de l'Edit de Nantes à la Révolution*, 2 vols. (Paris: SEVPEN 1959), 2:413.

43 Marine B², 341, ff. 347, 409, 569–9v.

44 Marine D³, 31, ff. 218–8v.

45 AN, F¹², 1316, no. 136; and AN, F¹², 1302, "Mémoire particulière," 1769.

46 Toulon 1A¹, 207, f. 65; and Marine B³, 529, ff. 344–4v.

47 Marine B², 349, ff. 536–6v.

48 Marine D³, 31, ff. 177–88.

49 Ibid., f. 209.

50 AN, F¹², 1316, no. 141; also Marine D³, 31, ff. 210–20.

51 Marine B², 359, f. 447; ibid., 355, ff. 309–9v, 330; and ibid., 356, ff. 401, 410.

52 Ibid., 357, ff. 170–0v; and ibid., 359, f. 419.

53 AN, F¹², 1316, Babaud de la Chaussade to [Trudaine?], 24 December 1761; and Marine B³, 538, f. 422v; also AN, F¹², 1316, no. 141; Marine B³, 31ff. 210–20; Marine B², 361, f. 409; ibid., 362, f. 452; and ibid., 364, f. 431.

54 Marine B³, 364, f. 556; also AN, F¹², 1316, no. 7.

55 AN, F¹², 1316, nos. 11 and 39.

56 Ibid., nos. 16, 20, 14, and 7.

57 Ibid., nos. 138, 137, and 143.

58 Marine D³, 31, f. 209; Marine B², 370, f. 735; ibid., 371, ff. 614, 644, and ibid., f. 718.

59 AN, F¹², 1302, "mémoire particulière," 1769.

60 Eugene Hubert, "Le Château et les forges de Clavières," *Bulletin du musée municipale de Châteauroux*, 2e série (1895–9), 644–53; also Gille, *Les origines de la grande industrie*, 177–8.

61 Toulon 1A¹, 209, f. 109; and BN, Mss. frs., 11,335, ff. 69–70v, 71–2v.

62 Marine B², 343, ff. 314–4v; ibid., 345, f. 324; also Toulon 1A¹, 206, ff. 11v–6v; Marine B², 341, f. 375; and Rochefort 1E, 378, ff. 41, 45.

63 Marine B², 339, f. 265; and BN, Mss. frs., 11,337, ff. 348–9v.

64 BN, Mss. frs., 11,342, ff. 441–54.

65 Rochefort 1E, 379, no. 429.

66 Marine B², 343, f. 437.

67 Ibid., 345, f. 380.

68 BN, Mss. frs., 11,342, ff. 449–50.

69 Ibid., 11,334, ff. 179–82.

70 Ibid., 11,337, ff. 348–9v.

71 Marine D³, 24, ff. 146–6v.

72 V. Dauphin, *Recherches pour servir à l'histoire de l'industrie textile en Anjou* (Angers: G. Grassin 1913), 93–4; and Marine B³, 514, ff. 105–6v.

73 Dauphin, *Recherches*, 100–1.

74 Ibid., 101–4; also D. Ozanam, *Claude Baudard de Sainte James, trésorier-général de la marine et brasseur d'affairs (1738–1787)* (Geneva and Paris: Droz 1969), 19.

75 Dauphin, *Recherches*, 101–4.

76 AN, F¹², 564; and BN, Mss. frs., 11,334, ff. 28v–9.

77 Marine B³, 514, ff. 105–6v, 107–7v, and 336–7; also Marine B², 343, ff. 335, 428; and ibid., 345, ff. 208, 344.

78 Rochefort 1E, 405, p. 28.

79 Dauphin, *Recherches*, 112.

80 Marine B², 350, ff. 1–3; ibid., 355, ff. 380–3; and ibid., 359, ff. 441–5.

81 BN, Mss. frs., 11,334, ff. 180–2; and ibid., 11,335, ff. 82–4v; also AN, V⁷, 346, 20 December 1758.

82 Rochefort, 1E, 408, no. 293.

83 BN, Mss. frs., 11,335, ff. 80v–4v; and ibid., 11,336, ff. 112–2v.

84 Marine B², 370, ff. 721–1v, 724; ibid., 371, ff. 658, 717; also Toulon 1A¹, 214, f. 33.

85 Marine B², 371, ff. 204–5, 260.

86 Toulon 1A¹, 210, f. 106; and Marine B³, 523, ff. 236–41.

87 Marine B³, 519, ff. 368–71, 276–6v; also Toulon 1A¹, 205, ff. 65v, 83; and Marine B² 348, ff. 272–5v.

88 Toulon 1A¹, 206, f. 136.

89 Marine B³, 530, ff. 22–3.

90 Marine B², 354, f. 355; and Toulon 1A¹, 209, ff. 33v–4.

91 BN, Mss. frs., 11,334, ff. 179–93; and 11,335, ff. 80v–4, 182–4, and 204–6v.

92 Toulon 1A¹, 209, f. 68v.

93 Ibid., ff. 77v, 96–6v; and ibid., 210, ff. 151–2.

94 See Marine B², 541, 15 December 1757; and BN, Mss. frs., 11,335, ff. 204–6; and Toulon 1A¹, 210, ff. 100–4v.

95 Marine B², 360, ff. 182–2v; also ibid., 363, ff. 269, 271.

96 Toulon 1A¹, 210, ff. 16–6v; ibid., 213, f. 41v; and ibid., 214, ff. 120–0v.

97 Ibid., 213, ff. 110v, 119v–20; ibid., 214, f. 3v.

98 Ibid., 214, ff. 28–33, 43v–4.

99 BN, Mss. frs., 11,342; ibid., ff. 577–82.

100 Ibid., f. 244.

101 Toulon 1A¹, 214, f. 33v.

102 Marine B², 339, ff. 421–3.

103 E.g., Rochefort 1E, 378, no. 284.

104 Marine B², 349, ff. 151, 156; BN, Mss. frs., 11,335, ff. 61–3; and Marine B³, 527, ff. 305–6.

105 Rochefort 1E, 408, no. 511.

106 Marine D³, 24, ff. 36–41.

107 BN, Mss. frs., 11,342, f. 585; and Brest, 1E, 504, f. 232.

108 Marine B², 341, f. 216.

109 Rochefort 1E, 410, no. 600.

110 Marine B², 349, f. 355.

111 Marine D³, 26, ff. 84–95; also Toulon 1A¹, 208, f. 147v.

112 Marine B³, 519, ff. 301–8.

113 Ibid., ff. 309–11v, 312–16; also ibid., 523, ff. 289–95; and Marine B², 350, f. 17.

114 Marine B³, 542, ff. 258.

115 Marine B², 360, ff. 53–3v.

116 Marine D³, 26, ff. 96–110v.

117 See "Chanvre" in *Encyclopédie*, 3:153–5.

118 See S.E. Morison, *The Ropemakers of Plymouth: A History of the Plymouth Cordage Company, 1824–1949* (Boston: Houghton Mifflin 1950), 5–14, for the ropes required in sailing ships and the art of ropemaking.

119 "Corderie" in *Encyclopédie*, 4:215–38; and Rochefort 1E, 417, 21 June 1760.

120 Rochefort 1E, 378, no. 72.

121 Marine B³, 544, f. 193.

122 See *Recueil de planches sur les sciences, les arts libéraux et les arts mécaniques avec leur explication* (Paris, 1763), vol. 3, "Corderie," for five plates illustrating the work of spinners and ropelayers.

123 BN, Mss. frs., 11,335, ff. 111v–2v; also Marine D³, 24, ff. 116–6v.

124 Rochefort 1E, 408, no. 571.

125 Marine D³, 26, ff. 96–110v.

126 Brest, 1E, 511, f. 135; Toulon 1A¹, 209, f. 61; ibid., 210, f. 25, and ibid., 211, ff. 140–1v, 167v.

127 Marine B², 361, ff. 328–30; and Marine B³, 544, ff. 191, 193.

128 R. Mémain, *La Marine de guerre sous Louis XIV: Le matériel, Rochefort, arsenal modèle de Colbert* (Paris: Hachette 1937), 902–3, 939.

129 A. Lefèvre, *Histoire du service de santé de la marine militaire et des écoles de médecine militaire et des écoles de médecine navale en France depuis le règne de Louis XIV, jusqu'à nos jours 1666–1867* (Paris: Baillière 1867), 119–20.

130 D.A. Baugh, *British Naval Administration in the Age of Walpole* (Princeton, NJ: Princeton University Press 1965), 374, 422–4.

131 Clause 4 of Book 10 of the Naval Ordinance, 1689, is devoted entirely to the duties of the *commissaire* entrusted with the victualling office.

132 See [*Recueil de traités pour la fourniture des vivres de la marine, classés par ordre chronologique, 1692–1729*], BN, Côte no. Lf⁷³.2.

133 Marine D³, 43, ff. 105–34.

134 Marine B², 349, f. 502, passport, 6 March 1755, identifies Srs Hébert and Brémond as *munitionnaires-généraux de la marine;* ibid., 356, f. 442, Moras to President Ogier, 25 November 1757, refers to Hébert; also ibid., 358, ff. 549–51 *bis,* Hébert to Ogier, 14 March 1758.

135 Jean-Frédéric Phélypeaux, comte de Maurepas, *Mémoires du comte de Maurepas, ministre de la marine,* 3ème ed., 4 vols. (Paris: Buisson 1792), 4:215; and Marine B², 371, ff. 642, 644.

136 Marine B⁵, 3, "Bordereau général," May 1750.

137 BN, Mss. frs., 11,340, ff. 113–14.

138 Marine B², 339, f. 518; also ibid., 341, f. 527; and ibid., 343, f. 418.

139 Ibid., 345, f. 441.

140 Ibid., 347, f. 516.

141 Ibid., ff. 535–5v.

142 Ibid., 350, ff. 58, 85; and ibid., 353, f. 19.

143 Ibid., ff. 28–9v.

144 Ibid., also J. O'Donovan, *The Economic History of Live Stock in Ireland* (Dublin and Cork: Cork University Press 1940), 110–11.

145 Marine B², 356, ff. 424, 442, 443, and 446; also ibid., 358, ff. 549–51v; ibid., 359, f. 390; and Rochefort 1E, 414, no. 476.

146 Marine B², 359, f. 516.

147 Marine D³, 38, ff. 3–6v.

148 Marine B², 358; Toulon 1L, 365, ff. 1165–8v.

149 Marine D³, 43, ff. 133–4, clause 61, "Traité des vivres," 14 December 1762.

150 Marine B², 358, ff. 539, 554.

151 Ibid., f. 568; also Marine A¹, 90, no. 12.

152 Marine B², 359, ff. 395, 414.

153 Ibid., 365, ff. 585, 599.

154 E.g., Brest 1E, 512, ff. 60, 65; Rochefort 1E, 419, no. 628; and Toulon 1A¹, 214, f. 60v.

CHAPTER ELEVEN

1 Richard Pares, "American versus Continental Warfare, 1739–63," *The English Historical Review* 51 (1936): 451.

2 E.g., R. Harris, *Necker, Reform Statesman of the Ancien Regime* (Berkeley and Los Angeles: University of California Press 1979), 68.

3 J.F. Bosher, *French Finances, 1770–1775: From Business to Bureaucracy* (Cambridge: The University Press 1970), 4–6.

4 H. Legohérel, *Les Trésoriers-généraux de la marine (1517–1798)* (Paris: Editions Cujas 1965), 94–5; also M. Marion, *Dictionnaire des institutions de la France aux XVIIe et XVIIIe siècles* (Paris: A. Picard 1972), 58.

5 Marine B³, 337, ff. 37–8.

6 Etienne-François de Stainville, duc de Choiseul, *Mémoires du Duc de Choiseul, 1719–1785* (Paris: Plon 1904), 239–40; also Legohérel, *Les trésoriers-généraux*, 99.

7 M. Filion, *Maurepas, ministre de Louis XV, 1715–1749* (Montreal: Leméac 1967), 145; and A.M. Wilson, *French Foreign Policy during the Administration of Cardinal Fleury, 1726–1743: A Study on Diplomacy and Commercial Development* (Cambridge, Mass.: Harvard University Press 1936), 71, 72n87.

8 D. Neuville, *Etat sommaire des archives de la marine antérieur à la révolution* (Paris, 1898; Krause Reprint 1977), 615–16.

9 Marine G, 127, ff. 29v–32.

10 Marine B⁶, 135, ff. 7–8.

11 Brest 1E, 504, f. 203; ibid., 505, ff. 15–22, 60, 146, 153, 368–76.

12 Marine B⁴, 63, f. 203; B⁵, 3.

13 G. Lacour-Gayet, *La Marine militaire de la France sous le règne de Louis XV* (Paris: Honoré Champion 1902), 211.

14 Bosher, *French Finances*, 10–13.

15 A. Guéry, "Les finances de la monarchie française sous l'ancien régime," *Annales, ESC* 33 (1978): 222.

16 See Bosher, *French Finances*, 111–22.

17 Marine A¹, 86, no. 26.

18 Legohérel, *Les Trésoriers-généraux*, deals with the evolution of the office, but his emphasis on the two great crises in naval finance at the beginning of the eighteenth century and following the American War of Independence provides limited information for the mid-century period. The judicial or legal thrust of his discussion and limited use of naval sources are further limitations, but this work remains invaluable for an understanding of how the treasurers-general carried out their duties.

19 Ibid., 109–18, 264–8; also Bosher, *French Finances*, 73–81.

20 Legohérel, *Les Trésoriers-généraux*, 111–13, 275–6.

21 D. Ozanam, *Claude Baudard de Saint-James, trésorier- général de la marine et brasseur d'affaires, 1738–1787*(Geneva-Paris: Droz 1969), 144; also P. Butel, "Contribution à l'étude de la circulation de l'argent en Aquitaine an xviiie siècle: le commerce des rescriptions sur les recettes des finances," *Revue d'histoire économique et sociale* 52 (1974): 86–96; Bosher, *French Finances*, 92–4; and Legohérel, *Les Trésoriers-généraux*, 109–10, 248–50, and 254–5.

22 E.g., Toulon 1A¹, 207, f. 125.

23 Legohérel, *Les Trésoriers-généraux*, 115.

24 Bosher, *French Finances*, 11.

25 Marine G, 48, f. 21.

26 Legohérel, *Les Trésoriers-généraux*, 204.

27 Cornell University, Maurepas Papers, "Mémoire sur les depenses de la marine en 1743," April 1743.

28 Cornell University, Maurepas Papers, "Mémoire sur l'estat actuel de la marine

et sur les arrangements à prendre pour le service de 1747," November 1746. Neuville, *Etat sommaire*, 161–17, cited by Legohérel, *Les Trésoriers-généraux*, 204–5, gives 6 millions for 1745, but the figure is for new debts acquired during the year.

29 Marine G, 47, ff. 274, 300.

30 Marine B⁵, "Mémoire sur l'état present de la marine," 16 April 1748.

31 Charles-Philippe d'Albert, duc de Luynes, *Mémoires du duc de Luynes sur la cour de Louis XV, 1735–1758*, 17 vols., éd. L.E. Dussieux et E. Soolie (Paris, 1860–5), 9:431nl; 10:141.

32 Marine B⁴, 78, ff. 172–4; BN, Mss. frs., 11,340, ff. 73, 119–20.

33 E.g., Brest 1E, 503, ff. 70v–1.

34 BN, Mss. frs., 11,340, ff. 120–1.

35 Marine G, 48, ff. 11–12.

36 AN, F⁴, 1008, mémoire from Georville to D'Ormesson, February 1762, 10 February 1761.

37 BN, Mss. frs., 11,340, ff. 73–4; Marine E, 208, no. 111.

38 Legohérel, *Les Trésoriers-généraux*, 205.

39 Marine B³, 511, f. 337; also B², 343, f. 236.

40 Marine B³, 511, f. 555.

41 Toulon 1A¹, 205, ff. 52–3, 59v, 208v–11.

42 Marine B³, 520, ff. 343–4, 355/6.

43 Toulon 1A¹, 206, ff. 40v, 55v–6, 156v–7, 167v.

44 Marine B⁴, 78, ff. 172–4; also A. Shortt, ed., *Documents Relating to Canadian Currency, Exchange and Finance during the French Period*, 2 vols. (Ottawa: King's Printer 1925), 2:819–21.

45 René-Louis de Voyer de Paulmy, marquis d'Argenson, *Journal et Mémoires du Marquis d'Argenson*, éd. E.J.B. Rathery, 9 vols. (Paris: J. Renouard 1859–67), 8:277, 292.

46 Toulon 1A¹, 206, f. 165.

47 Ibid., 207, ff. 118–19, 123.

48 M. Marion, *Histoire financière de la France depuis 1715*, 5 vols. (Paris: Rousseau 1914–19), 1:184.

49 Marine B², 347, f. 534.

50 d'Argenson, *Journal et mémoires*, 9:102–3.

51 Marine B³, 530, ff. 7–8.

52 Marine G, 49, f. 37.

53 Marion, *Histoire financière*, 1:181, 186.

54 d'Argenson, *Journal et mémoires*, 9:378.

55 Marine G, 49, ff. 34–5.

56 Ibid., ff. 35–44.

57 Marion, *Histoire financière*, 1:186.

58 Marine B², 357, ff. 142–2v; and Toulon 1A¹, 209, ff. 84v–5.

59 Toulon 1A¹, 209, ff. 117, 124–5, 127.

60 BN, Mss. frs., 11,337, ff. 89–91; also Marine B³, 556, f. 59.

61 Rochefort 1E, 412, nos. 426, 533.

62 Marine B⁴, 78, ff. 172–4.

63 Toulon 1A¹, 209, ff. 136–6v.

64 BN, Mss. frs., 11,340, ff. 92–3.

65 Marine G, 49, f. 49.

66 E.g., Marine B¹, 66, f. 131.

67 BN, Mss. frs., 11,340, ff. 92–3.

68 Marine B², 358, ff. 538–38v.

69 Marine B¹, 67, ff. 13–19.

70 Rochefort 1E, 413, no. 37.

71 Ibid., no. 179.

72 Marine B³, 539, ff. 148v–9.

73 Brest 1E, 511, 6, 24, 30, 38, 55–6, 68, 140, 152, 157.

74 Ibid., 155, 190.

75 Toulon 1A¹, 210, ff. 167v, 168v, 182v–3.

76 Ibid., 185–7.

77 E.g., ibid., ff. 189v–90.

78 Marine A¹, 90, no. 42.

79 On the commission see H. Legohérel, "Une Commission extraordinaire du Conseil d'Etat du Roy: La Commission de liquidation des dettes de la Marine et des Colonies 1758–1763," *Faculté de droit et des sciences économiques de Dakar* (Paris, 1968).

80 BN, Mss. frs., 11,340, ff. 121–2.

81 Ibid., ff. 123–5.

82 Y. Durand, éd., "Mémoires de Jean-Joseph de Laborde, fermier-général et banquier de la cour," *Annuaire-Bulletin de la Société-de l'histoire de France, 1968–69* (Paris, 1971), 91, 141–2.

83 Marine B², 359, ff. 153–6v, 269–72, 323; ibid., 360, ff. 248–8v.

84 J.F. Bosher, "Financing the French Navy in the Seven Years' War: Beaujon Goossens et Compagnie in 1759," *Business History* 28, no. 3 (July 1986): 115–33, for the most recent identification of these men; see also his "The French Government's Motives in the 'Affaire du Canada,' 1761–1763," *The English Historical Review* 96, no. 378 (January 1981). See also Durand, éd., "Mémoires de Jean-Joseph de Laborde," 149; Mouffle d'Angerville, *Vie privée de Louis XV*, 4 vols. (London: J.P. Lyton 1781), 3:184; and J.M. Price, *France and the Chesapeake: A History of the French Tobacco Monopoly, 1674–1791, and Its Relationship to the British and American Tobacco Trades*, 2 vols. (Ann Arbor: University of Michigan Press 1973), 1:582–3, 1033–4, 1035–6.

85 Marine A¹, 92, no. 18; Marine B¹, 66, ff. 123, 125, and Marine B², f. 303.

86 Durand, éd., "Mémoires de Jean-Joseph de Laborde," 147; J.J. McCusker, *Money and Exchange in Europe and America, 1660–1775* (Chapel Hill, NC: University of North Carolina Press 1978), table 5.1, 310–11.

87 Marion, *Histoire financière*, 1:191–8; H. Carré, *Le règne de Louis XV*,

1715–1774 (Paris: Hachette 1909), 362–5; Silhouette's report, read before the King in Council in September, is printed in Charles-Joseph Mathon de la Cour *états et tableaux concernant les finances de la France depuis 1758 jusqu'en 1787* (Lausanne and Paris: Cuchet et Gattey 1788), 29–48.

88 See Durand, éd., "Memoires de Jean-Joseph de la Borde," 155.

89 Bosher, "French Government's Motives," 75.

90 Marine B², 362, f. 480.

91 Ibid., f. 482.

92 Shortt, *Documents*, 2:929–33; the first *arrêt*, dated 15 October, was clearly not issued on that day, indeed, Bosher claims it was issued on the 26th, the same day that a circular enclosing copies of the *arrêt* was sent for the chancellor's signature to the Chambers of Commerce of the French seaports. The second, third, and fourth *arrêts* were all dated the 21st and I have assumed that they are not backdated.

93 E.J.F. Barbier, *Journal historique et anecdotique du règne de Louis XV*, 4 vols. (Paris: Société de l'histoire de France 1856), 4:330; Bosher, "French government's motives," 75.

94 Shortt, *Documents*, 2:937n.

95 Durand, éd., "Mémoires de Jean-Joseph de Laborde," 154.

96 Barbier, *Journal historique*, 4:333, 335; also Bosher, "French government's motives," 75.

97 Barbier, *Journal historique*, 4: 331.

98 Marine A¹, 92, no. 18.

99 Price, *France and the Chesapeake*, 1:583–4.

100 Bosher, "French government's motives," 76.

101 Rochefort, 1E, 415, no. 707; ibid., 418, no. 66.

102 Marine B⁴, 94, ff. 7–7v.

103 Cf. J.S. Corbett, *England in the Seven Years' War: A Study in Combined Strategy*, 2 vols. (London: Longmans, Green 1907), 2:72.

104 Barbier, *Journal historique*, 4:333.

105 Marine B², 362, f. 510.

106 Rochefort, 1E, 415, nos. 742, 748.

107 Marine B², 364, ff. 8, 9–10, and 601.

108 Marine B⁴, 94, f. 43v.

109 Ibid., 43v–6.

110 Marine B¹, 67, ff. 12; also Marine B⁴, 94, ff. 52–3; Pares, "American vs Continental Warfare," 452n1.

111 Pares, "American vs Continental Warfare," 451–3.

112 E.g., L. Kennett, *The French Armies in the Seven Years War: A Study in Military Organization and Administration* (Durham, NC: Duke University Press 1967), 4.

113 Marine B¹, 67, ff. 26–30; 40, 42–2v; Marine B², 365, ff. 531–1v.

114 Marine B², 365, ff. 617–7v.

115 Ibid., ff. 623–3v; also ibid., 368, f. 463.

116 Ibid., f. 145; Rochefort 1E, 418, no. 3.

117 Marine B², 367, ff. 442–2v, 452.

118 Marine B¹, 61, f. 84.

119 Ibid., 67, ff. 56–7; also Rochefort 1E, nos. 221, 228, 271, 276, and 365.

120 Marine B², 369, f. 94.

121 Marine B¹, 67, ff. 74–7, 78; ibid., B³, 552, ff. 473–86.

122 Choiseul, *Mémoires*, 250–1.

123 Y. Durand, *Les Fermiers généraux au XVIIIe siècle* (Paris: PUF 1971), 80, 116, 140.

124 Ibid., 80; Bosher, *French Finances*, 91n1, 178n5.

125 Ibid., 329, 334.

126 BN, Mss. frs., 11,334, ff. 61–2.

127 BN, Mss. frs., 11,336, ff. 4–13v, 14–17.

128 Marine A¹, 94, no. 33; the registers of this part of the commission's activities are in AN V¹, vols. 342–5.

129 Shortt, *Documents*, 2:937, note, citing Colonies B, 113, ff. 286–92.

130 Ibid., 957n1.

131 Ibid., 947–9.

132 Choiseul, *Mémoires*, 504–6; Lacour-Gayet, *La Marine militaire*, 390.

133 Barbier, *Journal historique*, 4:414–16; Mouffle d'Angerville, *Vie privée de Louis XV*, 4:14–15; Marine B⁴, 100.

134 Toulon 1A¹, 214, ff. 49v–50v.

135 Marine A¹, 94, no. 42.

136 Marine B³, 550, ff. 108–11v.

137 Marine B¹, 67, f. 167; Marine, G, 49, 77.

138 Choiseul, *Mémoires*, 406–7.

CHAPTER TWELVE

1 A.M. Wilson, *French Foreign Policy during the Administration of Cardinal Fleury 1726–1743: A Study on Diplomacy and Commercial Development* (Cambridge, Mass.: Harvard University Press 1936), 71–2.

2 Etienne-François de Stainville, duc de Choiseul, *Mémoires du Duc de Choiseul, 1719–1785* (Paris: Plon 1904), 250; also G. Lacour-Gayet, *La Marine militaire de la France sous le règne de Louis XV* (Paris: Honoré Champion 1902), 416–20; H. Carré, *Le Règne de Louis XV, 1715–1774* (Paris: Hachette 1909), 375–8.

3 Marine G, 127, ff. 112–72 and 175–98.

4 H.M. Scott, "The Importance of Bourbon Naval Reconstruction to the Strategy of Choiseul after the Seven Years' War," *The International History Review* 1 (1979): 20.

5 Marine E, 208, no. 111 (see Appendix).

6 P. Boulle, "The French Colonies and the Reform of Their Administration during and following the Seven Years' War" (PH D, University of California, Berkeley 1968), 594–7.

7 Lacour-Gayet, *La Marine militaire*, 420; also Scott, "Bourbon Naval Reconstruction," 17–35.

8 L. Gershoy, *From Despotism to Revolution, 1763–1789* (New York, 1944), 165–74; M.S. Anderson, "European Diplomatic Relations, 1763–1790," in A. Goodwin, ed., *The American and French Revolutions*, The New Cambridge Modern History, vol. 7 (Cambridge: The University Press 1975), 253–9; also J.F. Ramsey, *Anglo-French Relations 1763–1770: A Study of Choiseul's Foreign Policy*, University of California Publications in History, vol. 17, no. 3 (Berkeley: University of California Press 1939), 143–264.

APPENDIX

1 Henri Legohérel, *Les Trésoriers-généraux de la marine, 1517–1788* (Paris: Editions Cujas 1965), 179.

2 BN, n.a.f., 5,399, ff. 306–14v; in Legohérel, *Les Trésoriers-généraux*, fp. 180.

3 Legohérel, *Les Trésoriers-généraux*, 177–8.

4 Ibid., 179.

5 Ibid., 178.

6 AN, F⁴, 1076–77, "Budgets divers; état et mouvement des fonds du Trésor public."

7 Marine E, 208, no. 110.

8 AN, G⁷, 1,830 (2); Legohérel, *Les Trésoriers-généraux*, 179 and fp. 180.

9 A. Duchêne, *Histoire des finances coloniales de la France* (Paris: Payot 1938), 43–5.

10 Ibid., 44.

11 Pierre Margry, "Une famille dans la marine au XVIIIe siècle (1692–1789)," *Revue maritime et coloniale* 68 (1881): 102, gives the same figure for 1744 as in Duchêne; they are also reprinted in A.M. Wilson, *French Foreign Policy during the Administration of Cardinal Fleury, 1726–1743* (Cambridge, Mass.: Harvard University Press 1936), 73n88.

12 D. Neuville, *Etat sommaire des archives de la marine antérieurs à la revolution* (Paris, 1898; Krause Reprint 1977), 664–6. The collection of reports, "Faits et décisions de l'administration de le marine 1723–1774," is in Marine G, nos. 47 to 50.

13 Marine E, 208, no. 111; printed in Neuville, *Etat sommaire*, 616–17.

14 Marine G, 47, ff. 274, 300, and 327–31 for the situation to 1749; g, 48, ff. 11, 16, 19, 24, 26, 28, and 32 cover the years 1750 to 1756; and G, 49, ff. 35, 49, 54, 62, 68, and 77 from 1757 to 1762.

15 Legohérel, *Les Trésoriers-généraux*, 179–80.

16 BN, Mss. frs., no. 11,145, "Traité concernant les Recettes et depenses du Roi

des années 1712, 1722, 1734, 1739, 1740, fait et arresté à Paris le 1er fevrier 1741."

17 M. Marion, *Machault d'Arnouville, étude sue l'histoire du contrôle-général des finances de 1749 à 1754* (Paris: Hachette 1891), 17.

18 Ibid., 388s; and Marine E, 208, no. 110.

19 AN, F^4, 1076, "Estat des dépenses du trésor Royal assignés et payées pendant l'année 1755."

20 Ibid., 1077, "Fonds Employés aux Depenses du Mois de … 1758."

21 Marine E, 209, no. 9. Other attempts to establish general statements of revenues and expenditures are in the Bibliothèque de l'Arsenal, MS 4066A and the Bibliothèque Mazarine, MS 2825; both cited in L. Kennett, *The French Armies in the Seven Years' War: A Study in Military Organization and Administration* (Durham, NC: Duke University Press 1967), 89–90. Also printed in detail in C.-J. Mathon de la Cour [Fortuné Ricard, pseud.], *Collection de comptes-rendus, pieces authentiques, états et tableaux concernant les finances de la France depuis 1758 jusqu'en 1787* (Lausanne and Paris: Cuchet et Gattey 1788), 3–26.

22 M. Marion, *Histoire financière de la France depuis 1715*, 5 vols. (Paris: Rousseau 1914–19), 1:191; Marine E, 208, no. 10. and Colonies F^{1}A, 58, f. 33.

23 AN, F^4, 1077, "Fonds employés au dépenses … 1759."

Manuscript Sources

I have provided full bibliographic entries for all printed primary and secondary sources used in this study in the endnotes. This note identifies the manuscript sources found in France, Great Britain, and the United States.

FRANCE

Archives Nationales

Fonds de la Marine

The chief guide to this collection is the excellent outline found in Didier Neuville, *Etat sommaire des archives de la Marine antérieur à la Révolution* (Paris, 1898; Kraus Reprint, 1977).

Series A^1 General Collection of ordinances, édits, arrêts, etc. concerning the navy. Vols. 83–96

Series B^1 "Travail du roi, travail du ministre." Vols. 65–7

Series B^2 Correspondence from the ministry. Vols. 334–71

Series B^3 Correspondence to the ministry. Vols. 466–556

Series B^4 "Campagnes." Vols. 62–105

Series B^5 "Armements" (an artificial series containing statistics). Cartons 3, 5, and 11

Series B^6 Galleys. Vols. 134–5

Series C^1 "Officiers militaires." Vols. 2, 37–41, 65–71, 162, 165–8, and 178

Series C^2 "Officiers civiles." Vols. 40, 41, 57, 58, 60, 116, and 117

Series C^4 "Classes." Vols. 5–16, 36, 60, 76, 78, 133, 136, and 137

Series C^7 "Dossiers personnels." The hundreds of dossiers are listed in the finding aids in the *Salle des inventaires* of the National Archives.

Series D^1 Naval Construction. Vols. 1–3

Series D^2 Hydraulic Works and Civil Buildings. Vols. 3 and 34

Series D^3 Matériel. Vols. 1–3, 6, 7, 24, 26, 31–4, 38, and 43

Series D⁴   Ordnance. Cartons 1 and 8
Series E   "Comptabilité" (Accounting). Cartons 204, 207, and 208. This series is
             remarkable for the absence of any records beyond a few miscellaneous
             papers for the years 1747–62.
Series F¹   "Invalides." Vols. 46–9
Series F²   "Prises." Vol. 67
Series G   "Mémoires et documents divers"
             No. 33 "Etat abrégé de la Marine" (1763)
             No. 38 "Liste générale des officiers de la marine suivant leur rang et
             ancienneté, le nombre des campagnes qu'ils ont faites depuis leur entrée
             dans le service jusqu'en 1754 inclusivement, à la quelle on a joint un
             extrait des differentes actions ou ils se sont trouvées pendant la guerre"
             (1755; bound with the arms of Machault d'Arnouville)
             No. 38 *bis* "Liste générale des gardes du pavillon et de la marine
             suivant leur rang et anciennété" (1748–55; also bound with Machault's
             arms)
             No. 47–50 "Faits et décisions de l'administration de la Marine"
             (attributed to Trousset d'Héricourt and his successor)
             No. 121–2 "Mémoires généraux sur l'organisation de la marine"
             No. 127 Collection of reports, including Maurepas' "Réflexions sur le
             commerce et sur la marine" (1745) and "Mémoire de M. le duc de
             Choiseul sur l'organization de la marine, 1763"
             No. 128 "Mémoires de MM Rodier et Truguet, premiers commis, sur
             divers parties de la marine (1761–62)"
             No. 132 "Documents relatifs à divers expédients financiers préposés
             pour le rétablissement de la marine (1757–78)"
             No. 224 "Etat abregé de la Marine, 1751"

Section Ancienne
Series F⁴   Comptabilité générale
             No. 1008 Affaires financiers concernant la marine et colonies
             (1756–82)
             No. 1076–7 Budgets divers: état et mouvement des fonds du
             Trésor public (1714–63)
Series F¹²   Commerce et industrie
             No. 555 Bretagne
             No. 564 Manufactures, rapports d'inspecteurs, Touraine-Provence
             No. 622 Commerce de Russie
             No. 1302 Forges fonderies de fer et d'acier Cosne (1764–75)
             No. 1316 Quincaillerie, Babaud de la Chaussade
Series K   "Monuments" historiques
             No. 909, no. 48 *Extrait de divers mémoires imprimé sur les nouvelles
             forges établies en Angoumois par le Marquis de Montalembert et sur*

les fabrications d'artillerie qu'il y a fait executer pour la marine depuis l'année 1750 (Paris 1768)

Series V⁷   Commissions extraordinaires du Conseil

No. 342–65 Archives of the Fontanieu Commission established to validate and liquidate the debts of the navy and colonies (1758–68)

Bibliothèque Historique de la Marine, Château de Vincennes

Ms. 29 "Mémoire sur les Classes"

Ms. 195 "Mémoire du Roy pour servir d'Instruction au S. Le Normant de Mezzy [sic], Intendant de la Marine" (April 1750)

Ms. 222 "Essay D'Administration de la Marine ce 26ᵉ avril 1758"

Ms. 268 "Lettres Ecrites par M. Lambert, commissaire-général de la Marine, ordonnateur au Cap" (3 vols., 7 January 1756–21 December 1757)

Bibliothèque nationale

Manuscrits françaises

No. 11,314 "Mémoires concernant la marine" (n.d.; red morocco cover stamped with the arms of Fontanieu)

No. 11,334–36 "Registres des deliberations de MM les commissaires nommées par arrêt du Conseil du 18 octobre 1758 pour procéder à l'examen et vérification des dettes de la marine"

No. 11,337–39 "Correspondance de la Commission" (17 December 1758–11 October 1761)

No. 11,340–42 "Mémoires sur la Marine" (1758–60)

No. 14,097–98 "Projets de Finances Presentées dans les Années 1757 et 1758 et Observations par M D[e] F[ontanieu]"

No. 14,278 "Table générale des édits et ordonnances concernant la marine" (1740–56)

No. 14,286 "Liste générale des officiers de la Marine survaint leur rang et ancienneté" (1759)

No. 14,287 "Liste générale des officiers de la Marine" (1757)

No. 14289–90 "Idée générale de la fourniture des vivres pour la marine française" (n.d.)

Nouvelles acquisitions français

No. 126 "Mémoire sur le service et l'administration du Port, et arcenal de la marine à Rochefort" (by Sébastien Le Normant de Mézy, written originally for Machault, then for Moras; incorrectly attributed to Joseph Pellerin)

No. 1217 "Journal de la première campagne que j'ai faite sur le vaisseau du Roy Le Formidable, commandé par M. de Macnémara, lieut. gnᵃˡ des armées navales en suite par M. Le Comte Du Guay Chef d'escadre" (3 May–3 September 1755)

No. 3530 "Description méthodique, historique et chronologique des papiers contenus dans le Dépôt de la Marine et des campagnes sur mer, depuis 1610 jusqu'en 1750" (by Horque de Hamecourt, bound with arms of Choiseul-Stanville)

No. 5399 "Recueil sur la marine"

No. 20,556 "Travaux de la commission de l'Examen des Dettes de la Marine" (1766)

Collection Clairambault

No. 872 "Meslanges pour servir à l'histoire et aux généalogies"

Archives de la Marine, Brest

Series 1A   Correspondence to and from the Port Commandant. Vols. 150–3 (1756–63): copies of letters from the court and the commandant's replies

Series 1E   Replies to letters from the court. Vols. 503–4 (Nov. 1747–Nov. 1749); 505 (Dec. 1750–Dec. 1751); 506–10 (June 1753–July 1757); 508 (Chiourmes) (July 1755–March 1765); 511 (April–Dec. 1758); and 512 (July 1761–June 1762)

Series 1L   Contrôle de l'administration. Vols. 44–6: registers of ordinances and regulations (1725–71); vols. 75–6: registers of officers' commissions and warrants at Brest (1747–73)

Archives de la Marine, Rochefort

Series 1A   Commandants' correspondence with the court. Vols. 111 (1748) and 112 (1752)

Series 1E   Intendants' correspondence with the court. Vols. 378–82: minutes of Lenormant de Mézy's correspondence (1750–4; many pieces missing); vols. 405–10: ordonnateur's correspondence (November 1752–December 1756); vols. 412–21: copies of Ruis-Embito's correspondence (1753–62; incomplete)

Series 5E³   Contracts, minutes of inspections, and miscellaneous. Vols. 18–20 (1739–71)

Series 2F¹   Hospitals. Vol. 539: mortuary register (1748–62)

Series 2G²   "Dévis d'armement et de campagne." Vols. 1–10

Series 1L¹   Controllers' Records. Vols. 7–8 (1753–60): Registers of regulations and ordinances; vol. 48: minister's letters to the controller (1759–61)

Series 1L²   Vols. 94–5, Miscellaneous letters to the controller

Series 1L³   Business and miscellaneous. Vols. 24–7: minutes (*procès verbaux*) of Councils of Construction; vol. 46: personnel and misc. (1744–86)

Archives de la Marine, Toulon

Series 1A¹   Correspondence général. Vols. 116–21 (1747–62): Port Commandants; vols. 196–214 (1748–62): Intendants and *commissaires-
généraux*; vols. 245–7 (1759–61): Commissaires de la marine chargés
de détails
Series 1L   Contrôle de l'Administration. Vols. 356, 357, 360, 364–5, 370–1, 374

GREAT BRITAIN

Public Records Office, Richmond

Adm 97/Admiralty, Medical Department, In-Letters. Vols. 105–7 (1758–68):
letters from French commissioners abroad concerning prisoner exchanges
Adm 98/Admiralty, Medical Department, Out-Letters. Vols. 5–9 (1748–64):
letters to the Admiralty from the Commissioners for Sick and Wounded Seamen
and Prisoner Exchanges
Adm 103/Admiralty, Medical Department, Registers of Prisoners of War. Vols.
502 and 508

UNITED STATES

*Cornell University, Olin Library,
Ithaca, NY*

Maurepas Papers: Miscellaneous memoranda (1742–9)

Index

Ships' names are listed alphabetically in one location under Ships